INTERNATIONAL RELATIONS
AND THE LABOUR PARTY

To Elizabeth, Julia and Sophia

INTERNATIONAL RELATIONS AND THE LABOUR PARTY

Intellectuals and Policy Making from 1918–1945

LUCIAN M. ASHWORTH

Tauris Academic Studies
LONDON • NEW YORK

Published in 2007 by Tauris Academic Studies,
an imprint of I.B.Tauris & Co Ltd
6 Salem Road, London W2 4BU
175 Fifth Avenue, New York NY 10010
www.ibtauris.com

In the United States of America and Canada distributed by
Palgrave Macmillan, a division of St. Martin's Press
175 Fifth Avenue, New York NY 10010

ISBN: 978 1 84511 558 6

A full CIP record for this book is available from the British Library
A full CIP record for this book is available from the Library of Congress

Library of Congress catalog card: available

Printed and bound in India by Thomson Press India Limited
camera-ready copy supplied by katherine@projectpublish.com

CONTENTS

PREFACE

There is something about the inter-war period that fascinates. For one reason or another a series of recent films have been set during the period: sometimes like *King Kong* because they are remakes of films of the time; sometimes because the era offers a clean-lined alternative form of steam punk as in *Sky Captain and the World of Tomorrow*, and sometimes like *The Aviator* because it was the era that saw the beginnings of many of the technologies that created the modern world. Television series like *Poirot*, especially in the opening credits, often share this interest in the era's unpretentious technological developments. The *Indiana Jones* series of films used the unstable politics of the time as a not-so-distant background, with the middle film even managing to capture some of the flavour of the decadence and poverty of Nanjing-decade Shanghai in the opening scenes. Perhaps that is the major reason that the period has such a fascination for us. The promise and freewheeling 1920s is seen to give way to the dark foreboding of the 1930s. The rise of fascism in an era of troubles and decadence is a central theme of *Cabaret*. There is an anachronistic element in much of the coverage of the period, however, most of our common popular perceptions are dominated by the rise of fascism, and particularly the threat posed by Nazi Germany. Given that the period covers over twenty years – and the main fascist threats to collective security did not come until the Mukden incident of 1931 almost thirteen years after the Armistice – it is a frightful anachronism to see the whole period as being solely a prelude to the Second World War. Most of the so-called twenty years' crisis involved frantic attempts to evolve new international machinery that would guarantee that another Great War would not occur. The fact that, by 1931, this machinery was not in place was the result of many complex and interlocking factors.

It is against this backdrop that the discipline of International Relations (IR) evolved. It has long fascinated me how little IR scholars know about the history of their own discipline. Most scholars seem happy to accept a mythic history of the discipline that makes the Medieval Arthurian romances look like good historical source material. In the last twelve years the history of international thought has received much more attention, and the last few years have seen some far more detailed studies that have acknowledged the complexities of inter-war IR thought. In all, IR has finally moved out from under the myth of an inter-war realist-idealist debate. Many of the scholars involved in this reassessment are given honourable mentions in this book. Yet, myths still persist, and most (but now, thankfully, not all) introductory textbooks still cling to a simplistic realist-idealist dichotomy when looking at the inter-war period – and sometimes even when evaluating the discipline as a whole.

The realist-idealist myth has served three roles in IR: first, it has provided a simple set of headings for teachers of introductory IR classes; second, it has acted as a justification for realism's intellectual hegemony in the four decades following the Second World War; and third, the category of idealism has provided a dumping ground for ideas that have been proved 'wrong'. As a result the concepts of realism and idealism have actually hindered our understanding of inter-war IR history, and especially the history of the emergence of the discipline of IR. This book is part of a wider, yet still relatively small, movement within IR to illuminate the history of international thought through detailed and specific studies. Here I have been influenced by Herbert Butterfield's attack on the Whig interpretation of history. The realist-idealist myth is a classic form of Whig history: it is a simplifying device that interprets the past through the cares and categories of the present. Butterfield contrasts this with detailed histories that attempt to understand the past on its own terms. Of course, we can never escape a certain Whiggish element to our history. After all, the one thing we can say about the past is that it is dead beyond full retrieval, and even the most scholarly analysis cannot escape the culture and concerns of the age in which the writer lives. C.V. Wedgewood, for example, admitted that her seminal study on the Thirty Years' War was heavily influenced by the then on-going Second World War. Having said this, though, there is still a difference between a history written solely as a political device for the present, and one that tries to put the fragmentary evidence together in order to learn about a different world. To fully understand the history of the discipline of IR it is necessary for us to engage in the construction of specific histories, sacrificing a wider analysis for a deeper one. This book is a modest attempt to do just that.

My interest in the Labour Party's role in the history of the discipline of IR began when I first started to look at the work of inter-war IR scholars.

I was amazed at how many big name writers worked for the Party, especially on the Advisory Committee on International Questions. The list of international experts that worked with the Party (Angell, Woolf, Mitrany, Hobson, Noel Baker, Brailsford, Toynbee, Laski, and Zimmern amongst others) almost reads like a who's who of IR in the UK. Since the UK was the major great power of the era, and the Labour Party a party of government on three occasions between 1918 and 1945, the link between IR and the Labour Party was also an important conduit between intellectual analysis and foreign policy. This book shows how this relationship affected both the quality of Labour foreign policy and the development of IR in the inter-war period. This book is also an attempt to demonstrate some of the complexities in inter-war IR, and especially the way that the use of the catch-all term idealist has masked the major fissures and debates within the IR of the period. Parts of my argument on the uselessness of the term idealist in inter-war IR have already been published in my 'Where are the Idealists in Interwar IR?' (2006).

Many people have helped me during the research and writing of this project. I owe a long-term debt to two people. David Long and Craig Murphy did much to help foster my interest in the history of IR, and specifically the inter-war period. More recently I have benefited from conversations with Peter Wilson, mostly by email. Without Peter's advice and suggestions this book would have been a poorer piece of scholarship. Much of the research was carried out during my sabbatical year, which was spent at the Institute for Commonwealth Studies in London. I would like to thank Tim Shaw for his help and support during this period. This book could not have been written without the help and sheer professionalism of various librarians. I would like to particularly acknowledge the help of Carmel Ryan and Anne Butler in the interlibrary loans office at the University of Limerick library. They managed to hunt down a myriad of now obscure inter-war pamphlets and books for me, and never flinched when they saw me coming with yet another request for some little-read text with no ISBN. The staff at the Labour History Archive and Study Centre in Manchester and in the archive section of the British Library of Political and Economic Science also deserve special mention. Tracey Butler prepared the book for publication, and I would like to thank her for the hard work she put into the formatting of the manuscript. The balance of the book was written over a six month period in the town of Afitos in Halkidiki. My thanks to the town's residents for their welcome. Finally, I would like to thank my wife Elizabeth and my daughter Julia for their support during the writing of this book, and a special mention to Sophia, the newest member of our family.

1

INTER-WAR INTERNATIONAL RELATIONS AND THE RISE OF THE LABOUR PARTY

From 1918 the British Labour Party worked closely with some of the best and most well-known names in International Relations. No other political party before, during or since has had such an intimate relationship with the cutting edge of International Relations (IR). Some, like the two main parties in the United States, have put IR academics in key positions, but the Labour Party established a committee structure through which these thinkers and writers were able to influence the foreign policy of the Labour Party. Through the Labour Party Committee on International Questions, and to a lesser extent the Committee on Imperial Questions too, writers such as J.A. Hobson, Philip Noel Baker, David Mitrany, Norman Angell, G. Lowes Dickinson, H.N. Brailsford and Leonard Woolf produced a constant stream of memoranda, recommendations, draft pamphlets and leaflets that were sent directly to the Party Executive and made available to Labour MPs. Because the membership of the Committees were open to all interested Labour MPs as well, they provided a locus of debate between experts and political practitioners, and the meetings of the committees were sometimes attended by James Ramsay Macdonald, Labour Prime Minister in 1924 and 1929–31; Hugh Dalton, a writer on foreign affairs in his own right and future Chancellor of the Exchequer; Sidney Webb, the pioneering member of the Fabian Society and co-founder of the Fabian Research Bureau; Ernest Bevin, Labour's post-war Foreign Secretary; Arthur Ponsonby, MacDonald's Under-Secretary during the first Labour Government and Labour Leader in the House of Lords until 1935; E.D. Morel, leading figure in the Union of Democratic Control who defeated Winston Churchill to become MP for Dundee; and even Oswald Moseley, who broke from Labour in 1931 and eventually founded the British Union of Fascists. The committees frequently asked guests to come to their meetings, amongst whom were the American Political Scientist James T. Shotwell and Mahatma Gandhi.

Of course, the Advisory Committees were not the only avenue through which these writers influenced foreign policy. Both Harold Laski and Philip Noel Baker were on the International Sub-Committee of the Party Executive, as well as being on the Executive itself. Two key writers on international affairs in the 1920s and 1930s, Norman Angell and Philip Noel Baker, where Labour MPs. Noel Baker was even a member of Arthur Henderson's team at the Foreign Office during the second Labour Government, and a minister in Winston Churchill's 1940–5 coalition government. Yet, as we shall see later in this chapter, the Advisory Committee remained an important forum for the discussion of foreign policy ideas within the Labour Party.

During the inter-war period Labour was only in power in 1924 and between 1929 and 1931, but arguably its greatest successes were in foreign affairs. The negotiations that led to the French evacuation of the Ruhr; the Ponsonby Rule; the Geneva Protocol, which provided the template for the Treaty of Locarno; the normalisation of relations with the USSR; and the signing of the Optional Clause and the General Act were legacies of international cooperation that were bequeathed to the Conservative-led National Government that followed Labour in government from 1931. Labour also formed the official opposition for the rest of the inter-war period from the 1922 general election, providing a vocal and sustained criticism of Conservative foreign policy that was later channelled into a broader cross-party anti-appeasement bloc in the House of Commons, as well as the country at large. Thus the involvement of major IR experts in the Labour Party – the second political party in the most important power in the international politics of the time – was no minor vignette.

From an IR point of view this story is an important, yet almost entirely forgotten, part of the early history of the discipline. Never before or since have so many IR scholars had such a large influence on a governing political party. This interaction between writers and Party politicians not only added an intellectual edge to the practical politicians; it also gave the various writers on IR an appreciation of the practical possibilities of their ideas. Many of the thinkers associated with the Advisory Committee on International Questions, especially Norman Angell, Leonard Woolf and Philip Noel Baker, have been derided by later generations of IR scholars and students as woolly-headed idealists. They are compared unfavourably with the later generation of so-called realists, most notably E.H. Carr, Georg Schwartzenberger, Nicholas Spykman and Hans J. Morgenthau. Much has already been written on why this is a partial and misleading interpretation. This study also provides a corrective to this myth of the realist-idealist debate. Although the story of how a large group of British academics worked with the Labour Party is only one part of the inter-war IR story, it reveals the richness and the attention to detail of the work of these thinkers. The myth presents the idealists as people who push an ideal, while ignoring the realities of the world around them. What this story demonstrates is that writers like Woolf, Angell, Brailsford, Mitrany and Noel Baker were in fact very conscious of the practicalities of foreign affairs, and demonstrated a remarkable attention to detail in the memoranda they wrote for the Party. Advisory Committee memoranda, many of them written by people now branded as idealists, show a clear awareness of the constraints on their proposals, and give clear facts and statistics about such diverse issues as the problem of the Saarland, reform of the British Foreign Services, the military balance between the European great powers, labour issues in Nyasaland and the pros and cons of the Locarno Pact. These people clearly accepted the realities of the world around them as constraints, but they were also very well aware of the failings of the world as it was. They were, in this sense, all normative thinkers, and the Labour Party seemed to provide the best vehicle for developing and realising these normative goals.

While there is now a growing body of literature on inter-war IR that has successfully demolished the myth of a realist-idealist debate, almost all of this work has taken a theoretical point of view. The intention has been to demonstrate the complexity of the thought of so-called idealist writers, and the extent to which they have been caricatured by the mainstream of the discipline. The starting point for this new appreciation was David Long and Peter Wilson's seminal collection *Thinkers of the Twenty Years' Crisis*, which demonstrated the complexities in the thought of many of the so-called idealists. There have also been book-length reassessments of J.A. Hobson (by David Long), Norman Angell and David Mitrany (Lucian Ashworth), David Mitrany (Ashworth and Long) Leonard Woolf (Peter Wilson) and Harold Laski (Peter Lamb). Later works have cast doubt on the idea that a realist-idealist debate ever took place at all. Articles by Peter Wilson in 1998 and Lucian Ashworth in 2002 largely debunked the idea of a realist-idealist debate. Brian Schmitt's *The Political Discourse of Anarchy* looked at the debates in the US before and during this period.[1] Despite the concentration on international theory and particular theorists there have been some more thematic studies. Craig Murphy's 1994 book on the origins and development of international organisations stands out here.[2] More recently articles by Ian Hall, on appeasement and British IR, and Casper Sylvest, on British international liberalism before and after the Great War, have placed the ideas of the many writers of the period into the context of particular debates and issues.[3] This study adds to this literature by examining inter-war IR theorists within the context of the work they did at the time for an increasingly important political party. It explores the context of their ideas, and also demonstrates how their ideas adapted and changed as the inter-war context changed.

From the point of view of historians of the Labour Party and its foreign policy this study also adds an untold chapter to an important story. There are many books on the Labour Party before 1945, and many books on British foreign policy, but only a few on Labour foreign policy. Many of the key works on Labour's inter-war foreign policy are fairly old, although they still stand the test of time. David Carlton's 1970 study *MacDonald Versus Henderson* gives an excellent account of the second Labour government from 1929 to 1931. John F. Naylor's 1969 *Labour's International Policy* continues the story from 1931 to 1939. Michael R. Gordon's 1969, *Conflict and Consensus in Labour's Foreign Policy 1914 to 1965*, puts Labour foreign policy within the context of socialist foreign policy, and has a good chapter on the inter-war period. More recently Henry Winkler's 1994 *Paths not Taken* explores the way that Labour's international policy developed from 1918 to 1929, while John Swift's 2001 study of Clement Attlee's leadership of Labour in opposition between 1931 and 1940 spends much of his time on foreign and imperial policy. Two further books came out in 2004. In the first Henry Winkler extended his study of the changes in Labour foreign policy that he had explored in 1994 to cover the period between 1900 and 1940. In the second R.M. Douglas concentrated on the changes that took place in the Party's foreign policy after the outbreak of war in 1939. Rhiannon Vickers' first volume of *The Labour Party and the World*, published in 2003, looks at the evolution of Labour foreign policy from 1900 to 1951 from an IR perspective.[4] While both Vickers and I come from an IR background, and are attempting to shed fresh light on this story through our IR training, our works are complimentary, rather than competing. Vickers' intent is to place the evolution of Labour foreign policy within the context and categories of academic IR, as a result she dwells more on the position of key leaders than on the Advisory Committee on International Questions and its membership. I wish to show how the Labour Party interacted, affected, and was affected by, contemporary writers and thinkers in IR. In sum, I intend to place the IR scholarship of the inter-war period into the context of the development of Labour's foreign policy, while at the same time putting the Labour Party, and its foreign policy, within the context of the twenty years' crisis and its thinkers. During the writing of this book I was pleased to note that I was not alone in my views on IR scholarship and the Labour Party. The publication in 2004 of Casper Sylvest's article on inter-war internationalism and the Labour Party has reaffirmed my view of the importance of the Advisory Committee to the study of inter-war IR.[5]

The structure of this book is very different from all of the works cited above. It is neither wholly a narrative history of Labour foreign policy, nor wholly an analysis of the ideas of inter-war thinkers. Rather, it demonstrates the crucial inter-linkages between the two. A book that deals exclusively with Labour's foreign policy would focus on the debates and decision of the Annual Party Conference, the statements of leaders, and the actions of the Party in government. Since I am interested in the links between the Party and experts in international affairs my focus is the fora in which these experts and Party policy intersect. The most important of these fora was the Advisory Committee on International Questions, so that while I do emphasise other forms of interaction, such as journalism or membership of other Labour bodies such as the Parliamentary Labour Party (PLP), much of my analysis covers the work of this committee. There is a narrative of sorts. Chapters two to five examine different periods in Labour's foreign policy, and show how the opinions expressed through the Party were influenced by the IR theory of the time. Each chapter begins with a section that analyses one of five theorists that played an important role in the shaping of Labour foreign policy. While each one of these theorists wrote throughout the period covered by this book, I use them as a means of introducing the theoretical concepts that are most relevant to the time covered by each of the chapters. Chapter two, which looks at Labour's criticism of the peace treaties, begins with an analysis of the writings of H.N. Brailsford. Brailsford's sustained criticisms of the unfairness of the treaties, and his unhappiness with the undemocratic structure of the League of Nations, highlight many of the problems that the Labour Party had with the peace settlement. Central here is the theoretical analysis of the international anarchy that had preceded the First World War, and the way that this anarchy was being perpetuated in the Peace and the League. Chapter three deals with the period of normalised relations from 1922 to 1931, which represents the high watermark of the League of Nations. The work of Philip Noel Baker, one of Labour's strongest supporters of the League, is used to highlight the issues that dominated this period. Particularly relevant here is the development of two inter-related theoretical constructs: first, an early version of what we would call interdependence theory; and second, the development of a working theory for the new League pooled security system. The period from 1931 to 1939, in which questions of peaceful change and the rise of fascism dominated the concerns of the main figures in IR, forms the subject matter of chapter four. I use Norman Angell's work to introduce this section, since his criticism of the notion of have and have-not states was a sustained attack on the notion of peaceful change as advocated by the most celebrated of inter-war theorists E.H. Carr, and because of his strong condemnation of fascism from 1931 onwards. Here notions of collective defence and the breakdown of power politics in the face of ideological conflict feature prominently. Chapter five looks at the war years and the lead up to the first majority Labour Government in 1945. I have chosen to introduce this section with David Mitrany's work, despite the fact that he was no longer working on the Advisory Committee for International Questions after 1931, since his focus on functional organisations reflects the institutional internationalism that dominated Labour plans for the post-war world. Mitrany's links with Labour, though informal after 1931, continued through his contributions to venues such as the Fabian summer schools. The question of whether the new post-war order should be more federal or functional underpinned much of the debates about the Party's war aims, and Mitrany was a participant in these debates.

I complete the list of five IR thinkers with a discussion of Leonard Woolf's international theory at the beginning of chapter six. Woolf is the only thinker that I do not tie to a period, and is the one that I have chosen to introduce the conclusion. Woolf was not a particularly original thinker. While I admire his work and output, as a theorist Woolf could be sloppy. As Peter Wilson points out, Woolf's books were rarely subjected to the careful redrafting required of academic books today.[6] Yet, Woolf's influence on the imperial policy of the Labour Party, and after 1945 on British government policy more generally, was profound and lasting. Woolf is key to our story in another way. He was the Fabian expert on international affairs in 1918, after the success of his *International Government*, and worked closely with the Labour Party throughout the period. Although his Parliamentary career never took off, he was chosen to be the secretary for both the Advisory Committee on International Questions and the Advisory Committee on Imperial Questions. His work for the two committees was tireless, and included quite a number of the memoranda prepared by both committees. He was also instrumental in the arguments within the Advisory Committee on International Questions that helped to change Labour Policy to one of confrontation with fascism after 1931. Woolf was the prime mover in the reformation of the Advisory Committee on Inter-

national Questions after its temporary suspension in 1939 with the outbreak of war. Because of the key role that he played, both as theorist and
as facilitator, it is appropriate that Woolf's inter-national theory should
round off our story of the Labour Party and its international experts.
My choice of Woolf, Brailsford, Noel Baker, Angell and Mitrany necessarily leaves out some key thinkers associated with the Labour Party. G.
Lowes Dickinson, Arnold Toynbee, Bertrand Russell, G.D.H. Cole, J.A.
Hobson, William Arnold-Forster and E.D. Morel were also members of
the Advisory Committee; Harold Laski was a member of the National
Executive and its International Sub-Committee; Alfred Zimmern joined
the Party in the 1920s; Konni Zilliacus was a member of the Party from
1919, and an MP from 1945; while politicians like Hugh Dalton, James
Ramsay MacDonald and Arthur Henderson did write on international
affairs as well. I had three criteria for my choice. First, the writer must be
primarily an international thinker; second, he must be heavily involved in
the Labour Party between 1918 and 1945, including the production of
memoranda and/or pamphlets for the Party; and third, the group as a
whole must be representative of the thought current in Labour Party
circles at the time. Dalton, MacDonald, Henderson and Cole were ruled
out on the first criteria; Lowes Dickinson, Russell, Zimmern, Toynbee and
Morel (who died in 1924) on the second. This leaves Laski, Arnold-
Forster, Zilliacus and Hobson. Although Laski was heavily involved in
Labour politics, including a stint as Party Chairman, I ruled him out because his contribution to the Advisory Committee was extremely limited,
although he was heavily involved in developing Labour's war aims after
1939. Arnold-Forster – who was an MP, a writer and advocate of the
League – would have been a good alternative to choosing Noel Baker, but
his written output was not great, and Noel Baker was more heavily involved than Arnold-Forster in the construction and execution of Labour's
foreign policy. Zilliacus' worked for the League Secretariat for the whole
inter-war period, and his direct involvement with the Party did not occur
until the very end of our period. Hobson was a more difficult choice. In
the end I had to choose between Brailsford, a follower of Hobson, and
Hobson. I chose Brailsford because he was heavily involved in the Labour
Party, was more active in the Advisory Committee, and edited the influential New Leader. Clearly Hobson was the more original thinker, but Brailsford was the more politically active. I satisfied my guilt about leaving out
Laski and Hobson by recalling that their international thought has already
been the subject of two recent books.[7] Zilliacus has been little read or
referred to in IR literature, but remained popular in British left-wing cir-

cles. He was the subject of a biography in 2002 that dealt extensively with his views on peace.[8] The work of Arnold-Forster is virtually forgotten. Turning to the third criteria, the five I have chosen represent a fair cross section of Labour intellectual opinion at the time. Woolf, heavily involved in Labour politics, was concerned with decolonisation, the possibilities of international government and international economic relations. Like many Fabians, he saw education and factual information as a major part of the solution to the stupidities of the world around him. Brailsford, a journalist as well as an activist, was more critical of the League, saw capitalism as a major cause of war and the development of socialism at home as more important to peace than international organisations. Brailsford's approach to international affairs was heavily indebted to J.A. Hobson's political economy. Noel Baker, the only one of the five to serve in government, was a powerful advocate of the League of Nations and chronicler of the new international institutions. Angell advocated international organisation and education as the solution to war, and saw the cause of war firmly in the atavistic passions of what he called the public mind. Like Brailsford, Angell was also heavily involved in a number of Labour and pro-Labour periodicals. David Mitrany was probably the most original thinker of the group, and the least active in the Labour Party, although he worked tirelessly for the Party's Advisory Committee on International Questions between 1918 and 1931. His work on minorities, mandates, and peasant economics pre-dated his turn towards the advocacy of a functional order as an alternative to the more institutional security organisations supported by Woolf, Angell and Noel Baker. While all opposed Hitler and the rise of fascism, Woolf and Angell were particularly vocal, and early, in their condemnation of fascism.

All, obviously, are men. This does not mean there were no women involved in the Advisory Committee, and the Labour Party more generally. In fact, the Advisory Committee boasted at least[9] five women members: Susan Lawrence of the London County Council and MP for East Ham from 1923 to 1931, Dr Ethel Bentham MP, Helena Swanwick the journalist and pre-war suffragist, a Miss Winter[10] and Dorothy Frances Buxton. The last named penned a pamphlet for the Party that had originated as a memorandum from the Advisory Committee.[11] Helena Swanwick and another Labour woman, Mary Agnes Hamilton, were both active writers and Party members during the inter-war period. Indeed, Swanwick and Hamilton were amongst the government delegation to the League of Nations during the second Labour Government. Hamilton was also MP for Blackburn between 1929 and 1931, while Swanwick was editor of *Foreign Affairs*, the Union of Democratic Control (UDC) periodical, after the death of its founding editor E.D. Morel. Swanwick was succeeded as editor of *Foreign Affairs* by Norman Angell.[12] I have not included any of these able women in my final list of five because they do not satisfy my three criteria. Hamilton and Swanwick come close, but Hamilton did not produce enough relevant written material on international relations to fulfil the first criteria. Indeed, Hamilton's genius lay in her biographies and narratives of the time, many of which are still key texts for historians of the period. I finally excluded Swanwick because I could not find any Advisory Committee memoranda written by her, and because I decided that she was so little known today that she deserved to be treated separately at another time and in another context. There is certainly room to write a book on the women of the twenty years crisis, which might also include the three American writers Mary Parker Follett, Emily Greene Balch and Jane Addams, but this is beyond the scope of the current work.

The rest of this chapter puts the discussion of the next five chapters into theoretical and historical context. The next section looks at the way that the inter-war period has tended to be presented in IR. Central to it is a criticism of the use of the term idealism, and the false realist-idealist dichotomy that still poisons our understanding of the IR of the inter-war period. The second section adumbrates the history and structure of the Labour Party, with particular reference to the situation that Labour found itself in 1918. During and immediately after the war many Liberals, and even some radical Tories, became Labour Party members. The views on foreign policy taken by these recruits mixed with that of the major Trades Union figures and those in the affiliated organisations like the Independent Labour Party (ILP) and the Co-operative Movement. While there were common strands uniting all these people, the interesting thing about the formation of Labour foreign policy, then as now, was the diversity of opinions that went into the discussions. The third section looks specifically at the form and role of the Advisory Committee on International Questions.

The Problem with Idealism

One of E.H. Carr's most quoted comments from *The Twenty Years' Crisis* is the distinction between the utopian and realist phases in the development of a science. The utopian phase is marked by the dominance of aspirations over a hard-nosed understanding of the world, and is a sign of immaturity. A gloss on Carr's interpretation of science might argue that the mark of a mature science is when it stops thinking in absolutes and regards each issue as complex. This is certainly true of Carr's own subject of history, where simplistic Whig-style interpretations have given way to complex

multi-layered readings of the past. Unfortunately, in IR the historical analysis of our own disciplinary history is riddled with over-simplifications
and a Whiggish history that interprets the past only in terms of the present.[13] This encourages the drawing of analogies with the past to justify
certain policies. A good example of this is the frequent use of references
to the League of Nations in order to justify unilateral acts in foreign
policy. IR fails in its duty when it is unable to criticise these misuses of its
own history.

What I intend to do here is to concentrate on one oversimplification in
IR's auto-history, that is the idea that we can talk about an idealist school
in IR prior to the Second World War. This is particularly germane to this
study, since it is this oversimplification that has crippled attempts to understand the place of IR scholarship in the policy debates of the inter-war
period. I have already dealt elsewhere with the issue of the non-existence
of a realist-idealist debate.[14] The purpose of this section is to demonstrate
that the concept of idealist not only does not accurately reflect IR's past, it
also does an extreme disservice to those who are written off as idealists.[15]
The list of idealist traits that often appear in introductory IR textbooks,
more often than not, bear no relationship to the actual ideas professed by
those who have been labelled as idealist. While this is also, to a certain
extent, true of those who have been labelled as realists (E.H. Carr and
Martin Wight, for example, often fit rather poorly with the list of realist
attributes found in introductory texts), the problem with the label idealist
is worse. Idealism as a concept in IR is inaccurate, confusing and is often
used to describe such a diverse group of people as to be intellectually wor-
thless. The fact that it is still employed by so many writers in IR reveals an
intellectual laziness of staggering proportions.

I have two major problems with the term idealism in IR. The first is
that the presentation of the concept of idealism does not accurately describe the writers who have been called idealist. The second is that the term
obscures major theoretical and policy debates between the vast number of
writers written off as idealist, while also overplaying the differences between the supposed realists and idealists. There is also a minor problem
that idealism, as used in IR, gets confused with the more specific use of
the term in political theory. The problem here is that the vast majority of
writers that have been written off as idealist in IR are, from a political
theory point of view, materialists rather than idealists. The other confusion here is that a number of those called realists, such as E.H. Carr, have
philosophical idealist moments. The Hans Morgenthau of *Scientific Man v.
Power Politics* is also strongly philosophically idealist, at least in the first
two-thirds of the book. The term idealism would, in fact, be better em-

ployed in describing those writers, many of them realists, who have criticised materialism and scientism in IR. In this sense, the 'second great
debate' of the 1960s between behaviouralists and traditionalists might be
better described as a materialist-idealist debate.

Any attempt to refute the charge of idealism in IR is immediately hampered by a lack of consensus about what idealism means. This is not helped by the frequent substitution of the term utopianism – Carr's preferred
term – for idealism. Generally, the terms are used interchangeably both
then and now, even though the two terms carry subtly different meanings.
Peter Wilson, in his masterful analysis of the international theory of
Leonard Woolf dedicated a whole chapter to the question of 'what is
idealism?' before he was able to refute the use of the label to describe
Woolf's work.[16] A further layer of confusion is added by the loose use of
the terms idealism and realism in the inter-war literature itself, although it
has to be pointed out that until the later 1930s realism and idealism were
not very common labels to apply to IR scholars and their work. Interestingly, Ramsay MacDonald, in his review of the socialist movement in
1911, uses 'idealist' and 'utopian' to describe political views that are positive and progressive.[17] A similar interpretation of idealism was later to be
taken up by Woodrow Wilson, when he frequently praised United States
foreign policy in the world as idealist. These positive connotations, however, were largely overshadowed by their use as terms of disparagement.
In this sense idealism and utopianism became useful rhetorical devices for
opponents of change in international affairs. In 1917 Leonard Woolf complained that the charge of Utopian was used by the opponents of any reform in order to discredit change: 'Everything is Utopian until it is tried'
was his response to these charges.[18]

The terms idealism and realism in the inter-war period were often used
in contradictory and inconsistent ways. Sometimes they would be used to
describe specific modes of thought, and at other times to describe particular groups. For example, in 1923 Brailsford used realist and liberal idealist to describe two groups of supporters of the First World War. Brailsford's intent was to refute both the supporters of the old diplomacy
(realists) and the liberals who saw the war as an opportunity to establish a
new order (idealists), and subsequently to argue his own socialist criticism
of the post-war order. By contrast, in 1924 Brailsford used the terms
realist and idealist to describe two methods of thought that were necessary
for good policy-making: 'To see the world as realists, and yet to keep the
driving force of our own ideal – that is the test for Labour come to
power.'[19] He returned to this theme of compatible modes of thought in
1928.[20] eight years earlier, in his condemnation of the Treaty of Versailles

Brailsford complained that it 'is not the unbending logic of the idealist which has made this sweeping settlement. Fear and ambition... have wrought these catastrophic changes.'[21] Here idealists are interpreted as a specific group that had no influence on the construction of the 1919 peace. In 1924 Alfred Zimmern, returning to MacDonald's positive definition of 1911, wrote approvingly of the 'fundamental idealism' of the British people,[22] while a month earlier J.A. Hobson saw hope for international cooperation in the revival of idealism in the United States.[23] A similar use of idealism to denote progressive ideals was applied to Russian policy in the Balkans by C. Delisle Burns,[24] while Helena Swanwick wrote of the failure of those who clung to the old pre-Great War fallacies of the militaristic international anarchy, and called themselves realists.[25] Idealism is given a more neutral, and descriptive definition by David Mitrany in 1925, when he refers to German supporters of a Pan-Europa plan as a 'more idealistic group'.[26]

Generally the 1920s saw little use of the term idealist and realist, and when they were used it was primarily as adjectives to describe particular policies, and certainly not as paradigms. There is no discussion of either a realist or idealist/utopian paradigm in the standard British IR textbook of the 1920s, C. Delisle Burns' *International Politics* published in 1920.[27] In Hugh Dalton's influential 1928 book *Towards the Peace of Nations*, which had a strong influence on the policy of the Second Labour Government, the terms realist and idealist are not used, mainly because they had little to add to the many debates over the form and structure of the contemporary international security architecture.[28] For the most part, those who were later derided as idealists spent too much of their time writing nuts and bolts studies on specific questions to dwell on abstract labelling. David Mitrany wrote on international sanctions,[29] Philip Noel Baker on disarmament and the Geneva Protocol,[30] William Arnold-Forster on arbitration[31] and, in the United States, James T. Shotwell studied the Kellogg-Briand Pact.[32] The major exception to this comes from the right of the political spectrum, where realism and idealism were used as labels for separate modes of thought. The most famous example of this from the 1920s is F.E. Smith's often-quoted rectorial address given at Glasgow University in November 1923. Smith was a major figure in the Conservative Party, and he used this opportunity to denounce what he saw as a flawed intellectual attitude in British foreign policy circles. Smith defined idealism in three ways: it was 'the spirit which impels an individual or group of individuals to a loftier standard of conduct'; the philosophical view that 'in external conceptions the objects immediately known are ideas'; and the antithesis of the 'school of self interest'.[33] The first two are specific and generally neutral descriptions, but the third is a dangerous creed that is undermining British foreign policy. This idealist school – no members are specified – is contrasted with a realist school that accepts the primacy of self-interest as the driving force of human relations. Realism, for Smith, was firmly based on an understanding of a fixed and knowable human nature.[34] Interestingly, though, Smith sees the period *before* the First World War, when British public figures were too willing to accept German assurances of peaceful intent, as the period in which 'Idealism became rampant with those in power.'[35] Smith brings his analysis to a conclusion with a defence of what he sees as the ultimate British realist policy: 'the road of our Imperial destiny.'[36]

After 1931, in response to the rise of fascism, idealism and realism began to reappear, mainly as terms of abuse. In 1933, in the light of the weakening of the League and the rise of fascism, the socialist H.N. Brailsford associated the dichotomy between idealism and realism with the question of the value of League collective security: 'To spend further time in elaborating the League's charter of paper safeguards against war would be to show a lack of realism', and later in the same piece: 'We have tasks more urgent than the mapping of Utopia.'[37] A year later Gilbert Murray, in his presidential address to the 1934 International Studies Conference in Paris went out of his way to condemn what he called realist ideas of a static power-hungry human nature and primacy of national interest. Interestingly, these ideas that Murray attacked were being advocated at the conference by a representative from Fascist Italy.[38] In the late 1930's realist came to mean those who advocated a return to pre-1914 norms of diplomacy (despite F.E. Smith's 1923 opinion on that period's idealist credentials), and idealist came to be used as a pejorative for those who supported the League collective security system. An exception is E.H. Carr's analysis of the Treaty of Versailles, originally written in 1937, which refers, despite Brailsford's 1920 claim to the contrary, to 'a substructure of genuine idealism' to the League system, that created institutions that were 'a regular and essential part of the new world order.' Idealism, for Carr, was seen as unhappily blended with 'the exigencies of the victorious Powers' in the other parts of the Treaty.[39] Here, the implication is that idealism was a positive influence, even if its mix with the realpolitik of the Allies was an unhappy one. By contrast, in 1938 Salvador de Madariaga saw realism as an atavistic and non-intellectual attempt to return to the pre-1914 diplomacy, and a failure to realise that international relations had changed since the war.[40] During the 1930s and early 1940s Woolf made occasional references to idealism and realism. In 1939 he talked about the 'ends justifying the means' realism of the Soviet Union, and their contempt for the 'idealism' or 'utopianism' of socialists and liberals. Woolf uses realism here to refer to the means employed by Stalin, and contrasts it with the idealism of the ends of Soviet policy.[41] When Woolf does refer to utopian it is usually as an adjective, as when he refers in 1944 to 'the utopias of militarists'.[42] When he talks about realists it is usually with reference to pro-appeasement right-wingers, who call themselves realists but have little grasp of international realities.[43] Looking back to the Munich agreement of 1938, A.L. Rowse in 1940 criticised the Chamberlain government for claiming that its disastrous appeasement policy was 'realism', and collective security against Hitler was 'midsummer madness'.[44] These later 1930's attitudes are summed up by Michael Foot in 1944, where realism is the intellectual tool of the right. The intent of the right, in which group Foot includes Carr, is to refute the supporters of collective security on the left, while advocating a return to the discredited pre-1914 diplomacy. This, for Foot, is a strategy that can only lead to fresh conflicts and future slaughters.[45] What is interesting about the 1930s is that the term realism is more frequently used than idealism, and when idealism is used it is almost always a term of abuse levelled either by conservatives at the liberals and socialists, or by some socialists at pacifists and (increasingly) supporters of the League.

Thus, the inter-war usages involve three not completely unrelated conceptions of idealism. It is the intellectual yoke-mate to realism that allows us to progress; it is a refutation of the belief in a static aggressive human nature and the primacy of the national interest; and it is a description, by their enemies, of the supporters of collective security through the League, who oppose a return to pre-1914 diplomatic practices. E.H. Carr's use of the term utopianism takes aspects of these three interpretations of idealism, although he reverses the association of realism with the right/reactionary and idealism/utopianism with the left/progressive.[46] What is important to note, however, is that the terms realist and idealist are used infrequently prior to 1939, and when they are they are employed as loose descriptions, rather than hard and fast scientific terms. Certainly in Britain it was far more common to use the more familiar terms conservative, liberal and socialist.[47] To inter-war writers these were clear and distinct paradigms that were applicable to the domestic and the international realms equally. Conservatism tended to be linked, especially by its enemies, to the old pre-war diplomacy that had caused the war; liberalism was linked to both free trade and the development of international institutions; while socialism supported liberal aspirations of transcending the old diplomacy, but believed that questions of economic imperialism and control had to be dealt with before an equitable order was possible. These tended to exist independently of the pacifist tradition, and the presence of pacifists in all three political paradigms created a second, paradigm-crossing, cleavage within IR. When used to describe modes of thought realism and idealism became separate attributes of all three, although idealism as a positive progressive attitude was frequently seen as a defining characteristic of liberalism and socialism, albeit tempered by an equal, and necessary, dose of realism. When describing particular groups, realism was most frequently used to describe the conservatives; idealism was often attached to the liberal; while socialist writers, like Brailsford and Carr, liked to see themselves as a balanced mixture of both realism and idealism. Just to confuse things, idealism and utopianism as insults were also used to describe the disparate pacifist traditions. In his 1937 evaluation of the Labour Party, for example, the historian A.L. Rowse refers to the pacifist wing of the Party as 'unrealists'.[48]

Part of the reason why Carr's work created so much debate at the time of its publication was the novelty of his labels. Dropping the tripartite conservative-liberal-socialist classifications, his notions of realism and utopianism consciously crossed ideological divides. His definitions of realism and utopianism, however, were based on previous uses of the terms. Carr, following the earlier definition of realism and idealism as modes of thought, presents realism and utopianism as two necessary elements in IR. Utopianism provides the positive side to the dialectic, while realism provides the negative. In *The Twenty Years' Crisis* Carr sees the need for both modes of thought, but is deeply critical of the current manifestation of utopianism. Carr's criticism of the utopians in inter-war IR follows much of the same pattern as the criticism that the 'realist' right directed towards the supporters of the League. In this part of his argument he reverts to using the terms as descriptions of actual writers. Despite his Marxist credentials, Carr's criticism of the Utopians follows the same ground as the conservative supporters of the old diplomacy, although many socialists are included in the realist camp, while virtually no liberal is. Not surprisingly, *The Twenty Years' Crisis* favours the Chamberlain Government's policy of appeasement, especially the recent Munich Agreement.[49] In later works, in which Carr does provide visions of the way the world should work, he clearly favours the mode of thought interpretation of realism and utopianism. In *Nationalism and After*, for example, he proposes a functional system of international government that he sees as a good combination of the recognition of realist power realities and utopian goals.[50] In short, the inter-war writers, including E.H. Carr, do not really give us a clear idea of whether idealism is a mode of thought – a tool open to any thinker or group of thinkers – or a way of defining a particular group of thinkers.

Prior to Carr most writers on international affairs in Britain preferred to define themselves using the more common ideological epithets.

Despite these confusions, the terms realist and idealist came to define the inter-war period for future IR scholars. This led to a series of definitions of realism and idealism by the authors of textbooks and reviews of the discipline. Summaries of these various definitions of idealism can be found in a number of recent publications.[51] The major difference is between those writers, particularly in 1950's America, who saw realism and idealism as two parts of the predominant realist paradigm; and those, particularly textbooks, that saw idealism as a separate paradigm with its own specific writers. The first group includes John Herz's 1951 book, Herbert Butterfield's 1951 article, Arnold Wolfers' short 1969 piece and, more recently, Martin Griffith's 1992 book.[52] All four stress idealism and realism as natural tensions within a broader realist dominated paradigm. For Herz idealism is linked to the use of rationalist solutions to solve problems, while Butterfield contrasts the scientific and moralistic approaches to international affairs. Arnold Wolfers' concern was to create a synthesis between realism, which concentrates on the quest for power, and an idealism that seeks to eliminate power relations through the promotion of universal principles. Martin Griffiths, by contrast, interprets the approaches of Morgenthau and Waltz as idealist, and compares them to the realism of the English school. A different take on this approach can be found within the British Labour Party after the Second World War. The influential Socialist Union pamphlet of 1953, *Socialism and Foreign Policy*, which includes a foreword by Philip Noel Baker, uses realism and idealism as two elements in the evolution of Labour attitudes to the world. The idealism is the essential socialist underpinnings, which where made workable by Labour's acceptance of the realism of power relations from 1914 onwards. Rather than competing poles, realism and idealism are necessary parts of a successful progressive foreign policy.[53]

By contrast, the other set of modern writers regard idealism as a fully fledged, albeit largely defunct, paradigm with recognisably non-realist proponents. Despite coming late to IR, Hedley Bull's analysis is the one that is closest to an accurate definition of inter-war IR. For him idealism was marked by 'progressivist doctrines'. The plural here is important. Bull recognised that there was not necessarily any agreement on what that progress was. This said, he does list a number of points that he sees as characteristic of idealism, which include democratisation, a more international mindset, the creation of the League, a stronger international law and the work of 'men of peace'. The role of International Relations, in Bull's definition of idealism, was to assist these changes.[54] Although Bull's define-tion brings together a number of disparate points (and authors, since not all of Bull's list of points were agreed to by all those classed as idealists), the central characteristic of a progressive outlook does unite the authors often classed as idealist. Although it should be pointed out that it would also unite them with much of Carr's writing too. In the bulk of the rest of the literature idealism becomes a parody, in which its central tenets seem to be defined by whatever the author sees realism as not being. In Kenneth Thompson's 1977 survey, for example, idealism (i) is the belief that institutions can change people's behaviour; (ii) distinguishes between good and evil; and (iii) sees justice as 'a pre-eminent concern'.[55] While (i) is true of some writers like Mitrany, (ii) and (iii) are not characteristics of the vast majority of the writers of the period, and certainly not of those most often classed as idealists like Angell, Zimmern or Woolf. Both John Vasquez and Trevor Taylor define idealism (or, in Taylor's case, utopianism) as having a faith in reason to create a peaceful global polity. For Taylor reason leads to a belief in a single moral code and a common concept of justice, while Vasquez repeats Carr's charge of the harmony of interests against idealism.[56] While this faith in reason is true for some (Woolf and Angell, for example), it was not true for all (Mitrany and Brailsford).[57] For Anne Tickner idealism is described as a 'legalistic-moralistic... approach', which is implicitly linked in her analysis to 'the misguided morality of appeasement'.[58] As we shall see later in our analysis, this link between appeasement and writers written off as idealists is deeply flawed.

There is also confusion in the modern literature about what happened and when. Groom and Olson, who single out Alfred Zimmern as an idealist,[59] argue that in the 1920s idealism was largely an attribute of non-professional IR writers, rather than of the 'mainstream literature'. Talking of the pre-1931 textbooks in IR, Groom and Olson ask the question 'to what extent was this literature "idealist internationalist?" The short answer is "not much."'[60] They see, like Carr, a major change after 1931, but then make the surprising claim, that certainly does not seem true of British IR, that there was a 'relative dearth of mainstream literature in the depression decade'.[61] This seems to suggest that they did not regard Brailsford, Angell, Mitrany or Woolf as mainstream thinkers.[62] Others, in contrast to Groom and Olson, assume that idealism was the dominant paradigm in IR prior to the 1930s, and that after that it was challenged by realism. Michael Banks talks of realism as a victor in a Great Debate with idealism in the 1930s; Dougherty and Pfaltzgraff see the 1930s as characterised by 'a growing recognition among international relations of the gap between the "utopians" and the "realists", which was best summarised by Carr'; Steve Smith states that the 'response to the failure of idealism to explain the dominant events of the 1930s was the emergence, in good Kuhnian fashion, of an alternative paradigm, realism'; while James Der Derian sees realism as cast 'from idealism's failure to stop Hitlerism'.[63] In a later publication Steve Smith relocates the debate between realism and idealism to the later 1930s and early 1940s,[64] which does correspond to the publication of *The Twenty Years' Crisis* and its many critics, as well as a flurry of more realist texts in the United States.

What comes out of this summary is a general air of confusion amongst those who refer to idealism and utopianism. There is no agreement about what idealism is (is it an attribute of realism, a mode of thought along with realism, or a separate paradigm?), what it stood for (is it a belief in institutions, or a common morality, or justice, or reason, or science?) where it lay on the political spectrum (conservative, liberal, socialist, or moralistic pacifist?) or when it existed (pre-1914, 1920s, 1930s or 1940s?). Even Carr's definitions of utopianism are not always consistent. Wilson manages to distil three common charges against idealism, largely taken from Carr's definition of utopianism. These are:

1. Utopians 'pay little attention to facts and analysis of cause and effect, devoting their energies instead to the "elaboration of visionary projects for the attainment of ends which they have in view"...'

2. Utopians 'grossly underestimate the role of power in international politics, and overestimate the role, actual and potential, of morality, law, public opinion, and other "non-material" sanctions...'

3. Utopians 'fail to recognise that their espousal of universal interests amount to nothing more than the promotion and defence of a particular *status quo*... utopians fail to appreciate the self-interested character of their thought'[65]

Let us now take a look at each of these three charges in turn in relation to the five thinkers we will be exploring, each one of whom has been called a realist or utopian at one time or another.

The first charge does not seem to have any applicability to the writers that we are dealing with in this study. The attention to factual details that are a common attribute of the Advisory Committee memoranda, for example, are a clear refutation of this charge. The inter-war writings of all five are often deeply concerned with cause and effect. In the 1920s worries about the effect that the peace treaties would have on future relations is an example of this, while in the 1930s the common concern amongst these writers about the effects of the National Government's policies towards the League is another. Despite the common normative thread that links writers such as Angell, Woolf, Brailsford, Noel Baker and Mitrany, there are precious few 'visionary projects' amongst them. In all five cases their concerns were with gradual reform, rather than imaginary utopias. There is no grand final vision in Angell's thought. His concern is far more with people's failure to recognise the facts of the changing nature of our new globalised economy.[66] Brailsford does have a vision of a more peaceful world populated with democratic socialist governments, and certainly David Mitrany criticised him for his over-optimism on this score,[67] but he did try and back this up with arguments, borrowed from Hobson, for why he thought capitalist states were more war-prone.[68] Mitrany has a vision of a world made up of inter-connected functional organisations, but he presents clear reasons why he thinks that this can, and is, happening, and he also argues why he thinks it conforms to the 'spirit of the age'.[69] Woolf, as befits his Fabian background, frequently backs up his arguments with facts, and his most visionary pronouncements about decolonisation actually became British colonial policy from the 1940s onwards.[70] Noel Baker's concern with making the League of Nations work hardly seems visionary. Rather, it was a recognition that the League existed, and despite its flaws was the only serious means for establishing an alternative to an international system based on war.[71] His knowledge of the realities of League politics, along with his attention to detail on such questions as the Geneva Protocol and British war aims during the Second World War, do not seem to make him an idealist in terms of the first charge.[72] Perhaps, though, it could be argued that Noel Baker's continued faith in the League after 1936, when Woolf, Brailsford and others had regarded it as severely wounded, is an example of utopianism in his thinking

The charge of underestimating the question of power all depends on how you define power. Certainly, one of the major differences between the pessimism of conservatives and the optimism of progressives is the assumption amongst the latter that power has a positive social side, in addition to a negative exploitative side. All the writers that I deal with had this progressive view of power. The import of the charge, however, is that the utopian writer is one that wilfully ignores the problem of the power relations in the world around them, and assumes that other, weaker, forces will suffice to cancel out the 'pole of power', to use Wolfers' phrase. This charge could certainly be levelled at George Lansbury, the leader of the Parliamentary Labour Party from 1931 to 1935, whose strong faith in leading by example convinced him that the way to answer the rise of fascism was to disarm as an example of our own peaceful intent. It is interesting to point out that Lansbury had little to do with the Advisory Committee, unlike the other Party leaders. For Angell the very existence of irresponsible power, coupled with his low opinion of the public mind, made some kind of international authority like the League a necessary precondition of a more peaceful world.[73] Morality, for Angell, was a transitory thing that was a reflection of legal norms, while the law required some form of powerful authority to make it work, and public opinion was too easily led by jingoism towards irrationality[74]. Brailsford's concerns about power reflected Carr's. His international thought was influenced by a deep mistrust of the powerful capitalist classes, which he saw as having a vested interest in the system of modern war.[75] Rather than 'grossly underestimating power', Brailsford was extremely worried about the role played by the powerful both domestically and internationally. It was the very existence of powerful state interests that led Mitrany to reject federalism as utopian, and to present his functional approach as an alternative that was compatible with the power relations as they currently existed.[76] Hans Morgenthau certainly seems to have thought that Mitrany's ideas were realistic, since he endorsed Mitrany's functional approach in 1966.[77] Mitrany's approach was also intensely materialist, basing his arguments on the concept of human needs, and firmly rejecting reason as a unifying force. Mitrany's approach here was a direct response to Graham Wallas' criticism of the use of rationality in politics.[78] Noel Baker saw the League as necessary in a world where, left to their own devises, states would revert to power politics. A League with teeth, therefore, was a necessary alternative to the violent world of independent states.[79] Noel Baker was not entirely convinced that the League, as it was currently constructed, was up to the job, and regarded a series of reforms as necessary if the League was to succeed in creating a less violent world.[80] Woolf's analysis of inter-state relations reveals that he certainly did understand the role played by power politics, although he did not see it as permanent or even desirable.[81] For example, in his 1940 response to Carr he recognised that the world was going through a time when 'the use of power, force, or violence is playing a predominant part in human society.'[82]

The final charge, the failure 'to appreciate the self-interested character of their thought', is on the face of it more problematic. One part of the charge, however, is easily dismissed: that their ideas were used to promote and defend the status quo. All were normative thinkers, who were deeply critical of the status quo. In each case their ideas were used to promote radical changes to the way that international affairs were conducted. In this sense the writers we deal with here fit better into the earlier definition of idealism and utopianism as progressive, rather than conservative modes of thought. What can be sustained in many cases is the charge of failing to recognise that the espousal of universal principles masks the sectional interests behind those principles. Certainly, both Angell and Woolf saw concepts like security, peace and justice as universal in the modern world. Angell's work on the optical illusion of war, as we shall see, was premised on a belief in a common human reason that often seemed to serve the interests of developed western states.[83] Yet, Angell and Woolf were certainly not uncritical about their own thought. Angell's writings after 1918, which were never used by Carr in his *Twenty Years' Crisis*, take a much more critical line on the possibilities of a universal reason,[84] while Woolf's 1940 attack on the concept of the harmony of interests gives a good defence of his support for the development of rules to govern security at the international level.[85] In David Mitrany's case, his use of the concept of human needs, and his gravitation to the functional approach as a response to the failings of security policy in the inter-war period, was a product of his deep distrust of universal principles such as human reason or an abstract justice.[86] H.N. Brailsford's ideas were rooted in the socialism he shared with Carr, and consequently he was also suspicious of claims to universal truth made by what he saw as a capitalist elite. Rather, his analysis is rooted in discussions of questions of naked self-interest, especially the clash between the interests of capitalists and the rest of the world's population.[87] For Noel Baker, on the other hand, his faith in the League of Nations resided in his mistrust of the idea that some kind of universal concept of justice or ethics was enough to bring about a working security system.[88] Lorna Lloyd, in her analysis of Noel Baker's work, does point out, though, that he had a strong faith that progress and the 'twin power of reason and of public opinion' would eventually lead us to more peaceful alternatives based on law.[89] So, while this charge is somewhat substantiated, it is not in any comprehensive way that might lead us to say that these thinkers formed a coherent idealist paradigm. Flipping this argument around, it could be argued that Carr's views in 1939 were themselves an unconscious defence of the status quo, represented by the conservative foreign policy of the National Government of Neville Chamberlain.

Thus, Carr's criticisms of utopianism are hard to use against the small cadre of writers that I shall be examining in detail. The problem with Carr's analysis is not that his methodology was wrong per se, although his immediate grasp of the international situation proved horribly wrong, it is more that he was pushing at an open door. His vision of a science of IR that combined a realistic grasp of the world as it was, as well as a commitment to a sensible and progressive utopianism, already existed in the inter-war period. The problem for Carr, and it is a big one, is that they had not agreed with his support for Chamberlain's foreign policy. Perhaps the biggest failing of *The Twenty Years' Crisis* is that it works backwards from a support for appeasement. Because of this it also tends to lump the large group of anti-appeasers it discusses into one amorphous mass: 'Again and again he seizes the opportunity to trounce the opponents of Mr Chamberlain's policy as utopians'.[90] Carr's insistence on linking his argument to the ongoing debates about appeasement successfully poisoned the wells of inter-war IR by presenting a picture of a realist-idealist conflict where none existed. By glossing over the differences between many of the people classed as utopians, as well as down-playing their similarities with his own thought, Carr's analysis did not present a rounded picture of the debates of the inter-war period. But, of course, it was never Carr's intention to do that. The failure to see beyond Carr's argument lies with those later writers who took *The Twenty Years' Crisis* at face value without examining the issue more deeply.

So what were the big splits in English-speaking IR in the inter-war period? The first point to make is that the state of the debate was different in Britain than it was in the United States, although there was a certain intellectual overlap. The second is that the common parody of the inter-war period seems to assume that the same issues were relevant throughout. That, in a curiously anachronistic way, the problem was always how to deal with Hitler, or someone like him. This is a gross distortion. To support pooled or collective security under the League had very different connotations in 1920, 1929 and 1938. The context of international relations changed so rapidly over the two decades of the inter-war period that the various debates over foreign affairs, especially in British circles, tended to shift dramatically. In all, there were four distinct phases. The first, from 1918 to 1924, is dominated by the hopes and failures of the peace treaties. During this period the major points of discussion within IR focused on the shape of the new order; the prospects for, and disappointment with, the new League of Nations; and, for many on the left, the possibilities for renegotiating the peace treaties to make them less punitive. The period ends with the French occupation of the Ruhr. The second period, between 1924 and 1931, saw a marked drop in calls from the left for the revision of the League and the peace treaties, and a growing commitment to work within the realities of the League. The major issues were German reparations and inter-Allied debts, copper-fastening the pooled security system by outlawing war, and sorting out the relationship between arbitration, League sanctions (including League-approved military intervention) and disarmament. The period began with the normalisation of Franco-

German relations, and the abortive Geneva Protocol, continued with the Kellog-Briand Pact and the Locarno Pact (seen as a weaker form of the Geneva Protocol by many on the left), and ended with an abortive disarmament conference, the Japanese invasion of Manchuria and the economic crisis sparked by the Wall Street Crash. The third period between 1931 and 1936 marks the overlap between the period when the League offered a viable alternative world order and the confrontation with fascism. The League still remained a realistic option around which to organise resistance to fascism, but the reluctance of the British and French governments to use the League, the growing independence of the British Dominions, and America's continued semi-isolation led to the League being increasingly sidelined in relations between the democracies and the dictatorships. The electoral disaster of 1931 hamstrung the British Labour Party, which had been a major supporter of the League system since 1924, and left British policy in the hands of a National Government that tended to be suspicious of League collective security, and was increasingly committed to a policy of appeasement towards Nazi Germany and Fascist Italy. Finally, 1936 to 1939 saw many of the pro-League commentators on international affairs switch to advocating rearmament and collective defence arrangements to isolate Germany. The original opponents of League collective security, as well as many pacifists who had been suspicious of the League from the beginning, supported policies of peaceful change and the appeasement of Germany. The inter-war debates, especially in Britain, cannot be understood without first grasping the way that the changing international environment altered and informed the debates.[91]

The major split on the left in Britain, and therefore one of great relevance to this story, was the debate over whether capitalism was the cause of war. It reached its zenith in Britain with an exchange of articles in the New Statesman and Nation from February to April 1935, which, amongst others, pitted Brailsford and Laski against Woolf and Angell. The debate was published in book form in the same year. We shall return to this debate in chapter four, but the major difference centred on whether, as Brailsford claimed, capitalism created the conditions that made war likely, or whether the causes of modern war lay more in intangible problems like xenophobic nationalism. In this sense the debate could be called a materialist-idealist debate, although a least one side of this debate saw it as pitting socialism against non-socialists.[92] A second debate within the left centred on the value of the League of Nations. The League had started off deeply unpopular with the left in Britain, but many had reconciled themselves to making the best of a bad job. Others, especially the communists, continued to see the League as a bourgeois institution serving imperialist interests.

In Britain the main split between the left and the right did go some way towards resembling a realist-idealist debate. The major figures in the Conservative Party, many of whom would go on to develop the policy of appeasement, wanted a return to the pre-1914 diplomatic system, and resented Britain being tied into any kind of pooled security system. An exception to this was Robert Cecil, who remained the strongest voice for League collective security amongst the Tories, and to a lesser extent Anthony Eden. Interestingly, Cecil was retained by the Labour Government in 1929 as an advisor to the Foreign Secretary. Amongst supporters of League collective security the major debate remained the question of League sanctions. Did an international body need, or even have the right, to use force against a sovereign state? Underlying this was the question of the viability of the concept of sovereignty in the modern world, and the role of the nation state in a viable alternative to power politics. This debate became less pronounced after 1936 with the failure to sustain League sanctions against Italy after the invasion of Abyssinia. It was superseded by the debate over the question of how to deal with the dictators, and the issue of rebuilding a more limited collective security system to confront Germany and Italy. A major distinction has to be drawn between those, like George Lansbury or Stafford Cripps, whose positions remained unchanged even as the international context fluctuated wildly, and those such as Brailsford, Woolf, Angell, Noel Baker and Mitrany, who altered their positions as events unfolded. If there can be said to be a group of idealists or utopians, in Carr's sense, then perhaps it should be used to describe those who failed to modify their positions to fit the new realities. What is remarkable about the writers associated with the Advisory Committee was the extent to which they did react to changing realities. Angell's switch to supporting the League in the 1920s, despite his reservations expressed in 1919, or Woolf's sidelining of the League in his memoranda from 1936 onwards, are good examples of this realistic appreciation of the changes occurring around them.

What is interesting about this split between the conservative supporters of the old diplomacy and the liberal and socialist supporters of the new is that between 1924 and 1936 there was largely a consensus on the importance of the League of Nations. The question was more of how the League should be used. Some writers in IR that have looked at the inter-war period, myself included, have sometimes made the mistake of assuming that the conservatives were deeply suspicious of the League, while the liberals and all but the extreme socialists supported it in one way or another.[93] This is only partially true. In fact the majority of the leadership of the British Conservative Party supported the continued use of the League. Where they differed from the major liberals and socialists in the Labour Party leadership was in how they saw the League being used. For them it was a tool for the continuation of the old diplomacy of inter-state balance of power.[94] This should not surprise us considering that it was Conservative Politicians who helped forge the League, as a League of cabinets, in the first place. Initially it was the disappointed liberals and socialists who attacked the League, and interestingly many liberals and socialists abandoned the League system in the 1930s, while many conservative commentators continued to see it as a weak, yet functioning, institution within the broader context of power politics.

The situation in the United States was quite different, and I shall only gloss over it since it is not central to our story. Although clearly a great power in terms of its economic and military strength, Americans assumed that they had a choice over whether or not to engage in global politics. Thus, much of the American debates focused on an issue that hardly cropped up in Britain: the extent to which it was possible to remain aloof from international affairs. Another source of difference was the ideological climate. Britain had clear parties of the left and the right, a strong socialist tradition, as well as a robust (albeit declining) patrician class. This contrast is reflected in foreign policy debates. The United States debates did not give the same prominence to questions of the effects of capitalism, for example, and the divisions over the role and usefulness of the League were dominated by questions of United States involvement. The closeness of British and American intellectual and political circles, however, did mean that there were strong similarities, especially in much of the theoretical and methodological background. Also, like the British debates, the ones in the US changed as the international situation developed. Hans Morgenthau, in his retrospective review of the American foreign policy debates, interpreted the 1920's as a debate between advocates of international co-operation and isolation, while in the 1930s this changed into the intervention versus abstention debate. In both cases the immediate debate was underpinned by a perennial and largely implicit idealist and realist split within American foreign policy, although Morgenthau was not suggesting that these debates were self-consciously a realist-idealist debate, merely that they reflected an underlying division.[95]

In all, though, the concept of idealism does not help us understand our subject in the least bit. The various disparate and contradictory concepts associated with the term idealism do not describe the writers of the interwar period in any meaningful way. Nor does idealism help us understand the varieties of thought that existed at the time. The concept of idealism also underpins a Whiggish version of history that ignores the complexities and changes that have occurred over the twenty years of the inter-war period in order to construct a simplified history that serves modern concerns. In fact, there seems to be no reason for keeping the term idealism in the IR lexicon at all. It is, to use Hayek's phrase, a weasel word with so many contradictory meanings that its single useful purpose seems to be to obscure rather than reveal. In the case of idealism it acts as a convenient way to write off a whole generation of progressive writers.[96] Worryingly, recent progressives seem to have colluded in this process.

Ironically, one of the causes of the poor understanding of the inter-war period amongst IR scholars is a book written by one of the greatest and most popular left-wing historians of the twentieth century. One of the most useful texts for the IR scholar wishing to present a summary of the inter-war period has been A.J.P. Taylor's *The Troublemakers*.[97] Not only was Taylor a rare British example of a public academic, but his writing is smooth and convincing. Add to this Taylor's own radicalism and membership of the Campaign for Nuclear Disarmament (CND), and his comments about the dissenting tradition in British foreign policy, especially when they are not complimentary, are bound to carry weight.

The Troublemakers sets out to debunk myths about attitudes to British foreign policy, especially the idea that foreign policy was free of the controversies found in discussions of British domestic policy. Most relevant to our period, he set about demolishing the myth that the inter-war Labour Party travelled a slow road from foggy idealism to hard-edged pragmatism in its treatment of foreign policy. Taylor was not wrong in debunking these myths, but in so doing he unfortunately was guilty of creating fresh ones. He makes the claim that there was continuity in dissenting thinking on foreign policy within the Labour Party, which privileged capitalism as a cause of war, and that dissenting ideas remained largely the same from 1919 to 1939. As we shall see in this study, this was certainly not the case, although it was certainly true of some people like George Lansbury, who even Taylor says was not a typical Labour man.[98] His over-use of Brailsford's 1920s works, and his brief mention of others like Angell or Woolf without mentioning their ideas, gives the impression that the dissenting tradition was a single homogenous group. He overplays the continuity in thinking within Labour circles, and in order to underscore the uniqueness of Ernest Bevin's position states that no 'issue of principle divided Attlee [Labour leader from 1935] from Cripps [the anti-League radical] as far as foreign policy was concerned.'[99] Since Attlee and Cripps had been close associates of Lansbury there is certainly truth to this, but this is a rhetorical trick. The divergence of views in the Labour Party was very real, and there certainly were issues of principle that divided Cripps from Henderson, Dalton, and Citrine. These differences are discussed below. By underplaying the divisions between writers like Brailsford, Hobson, Angell, Woolf, Noel Baker and Morel, especially their public splits on the question of whether capitalism caused war or the role of the League, Taylor creates the idea in the mind of his readers that we are talking about a single tradition that failed to alter its ideas. He then makes the surprising assertion that 'Most of all, the Dissenters relied on appeasement'.[100] Given the strong criticisms of fascism and appeasement that issued from the published and unpublished work of Woolf and Angell from 1931, of Brailsford from 1936, and from Noel Baker after 1937 this claim appears to be completely unfounded. The problem is that Taylor's book has been a convenient crib sheet for IR scholars, who do not have the time to read the primary sources for the period themselves. The fact that the source is such a popular historian adds legitimacy to his statements. The problem is that, while Taylor's overall thesis is sound, his details and use of sources are sometimes misleading, and he often lets his desire to shock get in the way of his duty to inform. Much of this may be due to the nature of the text, which was a reworking of a set of lectures and a radio broadcast.

So, having demolished the main tool by which academic IR has understood the inter-war period, namely the realist-idealist debate, we need a new ordering principle around which to organise our thinking. The best replacement for a Whig history, which orders its narrative around modern concerns and oversimplifications, is a history that tries to recreate the complexities of the past through detailed studies of particular parts of the story. The story in this book is just such a history. It is a story of the intellectual development of international thought amongst key thinkers within the Labour Party, all of whom were, in one way or another, connected to the Labour Party Advisory Committee on International Questions. Before jumping in to an analysis of the Advisory Committee, however, it is necessary to give some background to the Labour Party and its foreign policy on the eve of the inter-war period.

Labour's Great Transformation. The Party in 1918

The rise of the Labour Party in the first half of the twentieth century was meteoric. A product of industrialisation, the rise of the Trades Union movement and the widening of the franchise, it was initially a coalition of affiliated trades unions, the Fabian society, the Marxist Social Democratic Federation (SDF, which left again a year later in 1901) and the largely non-

Marxist socialist Independent Labour Party (ILP). Formed out of a series of Trade Union Congress meetings in 1899 and 1900, the Labour Representation Committee, which was originally designed merely to promote candidates from the labouring classes, became the Labour Party after the 1906 election, when its thirty new MPs formed the first Parliamentary Labour Party (PLP). In addition to its affiliates, the Party structure now consisted of a Party Executive, the PLP and the annual Party Conference, the latter made up of the block votes of the affiliates and later on included the delegates of the Party constituency branches.

Despite its important role, along with the Irish Party, in supporting the Liberal Governments of 1906 to 1915 (in exchange for concessions to Labour such as the repeal of the punitive Taff Vale judgement), it was still only the fourth largest party in Parliament behind the Irish Party. It also remained an ideologically and structurally ambiguous grouping. In sharp contrast to the social democratic and socialist parties now making major inroads into the centres of power in Germany and France, there was no unifying ideology for Labour, except a common commitment to the use of political action and a criticism of the existing society.[101] Although a member of the Second International, the Labour Party, in comparison with its larger sisters on the continent, appeared small and liberal, rather than socialist. In 1911 the leader of the PLP, James Ramsay MacDonald, specifically stated that the Labour Party was not socialist, but rather "a union of socialist and trade-union bodies for immediate political work" particularly suited to "British conditions".[102]

The turning point in Labour's fortunes was the First World War, although in the short term it led to a sharp split in the movement. Labour initially opposed the declaration of war, but reluctantly supported the war-effort. The leader of the PLP, Ramsay MacDonald, resigned in protest, going on to help form the largely liberal Union of Democratic Control with E.D. Morel, Norman Angell, Helena Swanwick, Arthur Ponsonby, J.A. Hobson and others. After a year of supporting the Liberal war effort, Labour entered the wartime coalition government of 1915–1918. This gave Labour its first taste of government, although Labour's single Cabinet Minister, the future Foreign Secretary Arthur Henderson, held the relatively unimportant post of President of the Board of Education; a position for which he felt particularly ill-suited given his lack of formal education.[103] Close links between Labour's leadership and the UDC helped facilitate the recruitment of a number of ex-Liberals to Labour, while the split between the supporters of the Prime Minister, Lloyd George, and Liberal leader, Herbert Asquith, left the Liberals in disarray and led to a flood of defections from the Liberals to Labour. In addition, a small group of radical Conservatives defected to Labour.[104] By the 1922 election, when Labour became the second largest party in Parliament and hence the official opposition, Labour had broadened into a coalition that included many middle and upper class radicals. Amongst these was a cadre of intellecttuals, including much of the membership of the UDC. Of the three major parties in Britain, it was Labour that could boast a membership that was the most representative of all the social classes in the country.

One of Labour's great weaknesses was its lack of access to the national press. The vast majority of the daily newspapers, the Times, the Daily Mail and the Express, were hostile to Labour. The Manchester Guardian was sympathetic, but still fundamentally liberal. Labour's own periodicals, of which the *Daily Worker* and the TUC-owned *Daily Herald* were the only daily national newspapers, had a good reputation, and the quality of the journalism available to Labour was, for the period, impressive. In terms of foreign affairs Labour was well served by the ILPs *New Leader*, edited initially by Brailsford, although Angell was acting editor for a number of editions, and the UDCs *Foreign Affairs*, edited by E. D. Morel until his death in 1924, and by Helena Swanwick and Norman Angell after that. The weekly *New Statesman and Nation* provided a soft left line, which was broadly supportive of Labour, as well as a forum for the various factions within the Party to publicise their ideas. Yet, this dynamism did not make up for the Tory bias of the vast bulk of the popular press. By comparison with its ideological allies in France, Germany, the Netherlands and Sweden, Labour had to overcome high press hostility. Perhaps the worst example of this was the fake Zinoviev letter, which was published in the *Daily Mail* five days before the 1924 election, and caused a mini-red scare that helped return a Conservative majority.

Where the Labour Party found itself suddenly thrust into greatness was at the international level. Although the Party was quite viciously slighted during the Peace negotiations by not having any official representation on the British Empire delegation, it played an active and crucial part in the international socialist meetings that took place before and during the Paris peace talks. Part of this greater role was a result of the vacuum caused by the relative quiet of the German Socialists, who before 1914 were only rivalled by the French Socialists in terms of size and influence. Part of it, though, was the result of the quite deliberate lead role that Labour played in trying to develop a socialist response to the new conditions created after the war. Tellingly, four major inter-Allied Labour and Socialist conferences were held in London. The Advisory Committee played an active role in preparing Labour for the international socialist conferences after the Armistice in November 1918. Labour's representatives to the Berne conference, which opened on 3 February 1919, came equipped with a list of recommendations prepared by the Advisory Committee, including a criticism of representation at the League of Nations written by H.N. Brailsford.[105] The Labour representatives managed to push through their recommendations on international organisations, which were adopted by the conference as a whole.[106] There was also heavy Labour involvement in the preceding 26 April Amsterdam meeting of the Second International's Permanent Commission, which was a vehicle for socialist dissatisfaction with the peace treaties.[107]

Labour's involvement in the reconstitution of the second international, as well as the TUC's continued links to other Trades Union movements around the world, was mirrored by Labour's growing awareness of the importance of foreign affairs to its domestic agenda. This was very much a legacy of the war, although Trades Union figures in the Party like J.R. Clynes and Arthur Henderson were already turning their attention to the international arena, and many of the ex-Liberal converts to Labour were critics of the old diplomacy. This interest was a major sea-change. Before 1914 there was still a strong resistance in Labour circles to pursuing an active Party foreign policy. In 1907 the then leader of the PLP, Keir Hardie, reported to the Annual Conference that while foreign policy had been dealt with by members of the Party, it, like certain other issues, has 'been merely incidental to the *real* work of the Party.'[108] Famously, Labour's 1906 manifesto only contained one line, making up half of a sentence, on foreign policy ('Wars are fought to make the rich richer…');[109] while Ramsay MacDonald's 1911 book on socialism does not mention foreign affairs at all.[110] The War provided the main stimulus to Labour's interest in foreign policy, however, and a series of books and pamphlets written by Labour members supplemented an increasingly internationalist TUC and Labour conference circuit. At the same time the UDC and its membership had become increasingly involved in Labour Party politics. By 1918 the view of the Labour Party as a movement exclusively concerned with domestic issues was difficult to sustain, although the myth persisted amongst opponents of Labour.[111] The War, in particular, had helped to foster a widespread belief in Labour ranks that domestic and foreign issues were inextricably linked; a theme that Labour memoranda, conference resolutions and pamphlets returned to again and again.[112] Alongside this interest in foreign affairs came Labour calls for the democratisation of foreign policy, which for the vast majority of Labour's leadership and opinion formers meant greater Parliamentary control of foreign policy, although it also manifested itself in calls for the reformulation of the foreign services.[113] On its foundation, a member of the Advisory Committee (probably Leonard Woolf) saw the Committee itself as a step in the direction of the democratisation of foreign policy 'and a break with the evil tradition of the foreign office.'[114] This support for the democratisation of international affairs was one of the main causes of early Labour (and Advisory Committee) dissatisfaction with the League of Nations Covenant, not to mention opposition to the peace treaties themselves.

Despite the diversity of opinion over foreign policy within the Labour Party, Rhiannon Vickers argues that 'internationalism has been the underlying basis of Labour's world-view and foreign policy.'[115] She goes on to identify five principles of Labour's international thought. These are that reform of the international state system is possible because states share common interests and values; that all states belong to an international community in which they have a responsibility to work towards a common good; that international politics should be based on democratic and moral norms; that collective security is superior to the self-defeating balance of power; and finally a commitment to an anti-militarist stance.[116] Certainly, all five of these were at play during the inter-war period, although there were varying levels of dissent to some of these principles from some groups and individuals in the Party over time. Collective security – or pooled security as it was more frequently called before the mid-1930s – was sometimes attacked or dismissed by pacifist and radical socialist elements. Many of these anti-pooled security elements in the Party are discussed in more detail in chapters two and four. The anti-militarist element came under strain from the mainstream leadership and Labour's international experts after 1936, although in many respects this was less of an attack on the principle, as a suspension of it for the duration of the crisis with fascism. Underlying these principles Vickers identifies two meta-principles: 'a belief in progress and an optimistic view of human nature, which reflect an internationalist perspective.'[117] While the belief in progress towards a better world is a constant in Labour's international policy – it could hardly be a progressive and reformist Party without it – optimism in human nature was not so common amongst Labour's international writers. Indeed, many like Norman Angell regarded human nature as destructive and basically violent, especially when people were in large groups.[118] For many it was probably more true to say that they did not see human nature as the sole determinant of human action. Rather, the ability to learn meant that, while human nature did not change, human behaviour could. Thus, if by optimistic about human nature we mean the idea that human nature is controllable, or is not a sole determinant of human action, then Vicker's statement does accurately describe many of Labour's international experts. If we mean the view that human nature is good, which is frequently represented as an attribute of idealism, then it most certainly is not true. This question aside, Vicker's depiction of Labour's internationalism accurately summarises the position of its international experts on the Advisory Committee on International Questions from 1918.

The growing importance of internationalism, as defined by Vickers, to the Party was also reflected in its new 1918 Constitution. Changes to the membership of the Party, its growing standing with the electorate and new voting laws in Britain had forced the Party to review its constitution. Under the chairmanship of Sidney Webb and Arthur Henderson the new Labour constitution allowed individuals to join the Party via their constituency branches. Before then individuals who were not Union members had to join an affiliate organisation, usually the ILP. This reform made it easier for defectors from other political parties to join Labour, amongst them many of the internationalists from the Liberal Party. It also weakened the power of the ILP, making the Labour leadership less dependent on its support and contributing to the more independent, and League-friendly, line of the leadership from 1922. The new constitution also provided a wider space for foreign affairs within the Party. The constitution itself stressed the importance of foreign affairs, committing Labour to co-operation with other labour and socialist organisations around the world in the establishment of a 'Federation of Nations for the maintenance of freedom and peace, for the establishment of suitable machinery for the adjustment and settlement of international disputes...'[119] It also established the system of advisory committees, of which the Advisory Committee on International Questions proved the most active over the next two decades.

Thus, by 1918 Labour had a strong party machine despite the weaknesses and the mere paper existence of many constituency parties; access to high quality expert advice through the advisory committees; a membership beefed up by defections from the other major parties, which included a good cross section of British society; the experience of being part of the wartime coalition government; and had developed a new appreciation for the importance of foreign affairs to the concerns of the labouring classes. It was also four years away form gaining official opposition status with a full shadow cabinet in 1922, and could present itself as a potential party of government, although it would have to wait another six years before it had experience of government. This said, the 1918 election result was not a triumph for the Party. The Coalition of Conservatives and Coalition Liberals was returned with a massive majority, and the non-Coalition Liberals under Herbert Asquith were still a major force in Parliament. While increasingly important in British public life, to the extent that the Coalition Liberal Winston Churchill had advocated the merger of the Coalition parties in an anti-socialist centre party, Labour 'was still in an uncertain and transitional phase... it lacked clear leadership [after the electoral defeat of many of its leading politicians] or a strategy for obtaining power.'[120] Increasingly, though, its political platform was that of a government in waiting. Much of the maturity in the development of its foreign policy was the result of the work done by the Advisory Committee on International Questions.

The Labour Party Advisory Committee on International Questions
Although there is very little written on the Advisory Committee on International Questions, its influence on the Labour Party in the inter-war period was profound. Since Labour formed two minority governments during this period, and was the official opposition for almost all of the time, the Advisory Committee was amongst the most influential non-governmental committees on international relations in the country. David Mitrany saw his membership as a piece of good fortune, despite his own intention not to get involved in any political party or ideological group, and the Committee itself as a centre of 'considerable influence while the post-War arrangements were in the making'.[121] Crucially, the Advisory Committee acted as an important point of contact between some of the most respected minds in International Relations writing on the one hand, and practical politicians engaged in foreign policy on the other. Many of its members, such as Philip Noel Baker and Hugh Dalton, crossed the divide between intellectual International Relations and practical foreign policy. As well as Noel Baker and Dalton, the members of the Committee included some of the most influential writers on international affairs of their generation. J.A. Hobson, David Mitrany, Leonard Woolf, Norman Angell, G. Lowes Dickinson and H.N. Brailsford all wrote memoranda for the Committee. Some of these memoranda, after alterations in the Committee and passage through the Party Executive, became official Labour Party pamphlets. Other occasional members of the committee included Arnold Toynbee, Bertrand Russell, G.D.H. Cole and its first chair Sidney Webb.

The Committee on International Questions was set up, along with a series of other advisory committees on other policy topics, in early 1918, and met for the first time in May. The idea of the advisory committees, which were probably suggested by Leonard Woolf, were a product of the broader changes to the constitution of the Labour Party, and conformed to Fabian notions of the importance of expert advice and detailed studies of political subjects. The terms of reference for the Committee, initially communicated by Arthur Henderson to the prospective members, were typically open-ended. The Committee was to 'consider, report and advise upon international policy and all questions of an international character, and to watch and advise upon current international developments.'[122]

As well as being sent on to the Executive of the Party, the memoranda were also made available to members of the Parliamentary Labour Party in order to keep them informed on debates on foreign policy in the House of Commons or on relevant Common's committees.[123] In fact, this role as a source of information for Labour MPs, and for Party activists as a whole was always seen by the Committee as a central part of its task. In an un-dated memorandum, obviously written shortly after the Committee had been constituted, it is stated that:

> In addition then to watching and advising current international questions on behalf of the Executive of the Labour Party, it will be one of the principle duties of this committee to provide Labour speakers and publicists with information and "ammunition" on the subject of foreign affairs.[124]

This was all tied up with the then hot topic of the democratisation of foreign policy. The establishment of the Committee was seen as 'a step in the direction of that much to be desired Democratisation of Foreign Policy and a break with the evil tradition of the Foreign Office.'[125]

Although the Executive of the Party rarely interfered with the working of the Committee, not wanting to upset a formula that worked very effectively, the Committee members jealously guarded their independence, especially when it came to their terms of reference. In their meeting of 19 November 1920, following a review of the work of all the advisory committees, and the appointment of Arthur Greenwood as Secretary to the Advisory Committees, the Committee complained about the narrowing of its terms of reference. They resolved to communicate this to Greenwood, while detailing Woolf to draw up a new programme of work for the Committee.[126]

The Committee on International Questions shared much of its membership with the smaller Committee on Imperial Questions, and both were ably served by Leonard Woolf, who acted as secretary for both committees throughout the inter-war period. Indeed, the Imperial Questions Committee began life as a sub-committee of the International Questions Committee, and was only formally constituted as a separate committee in 1920. The membership of the Committee on International Questions, like that of the other advisory committees, was made up of both invited non-Parliamentarian experts and any interested Labour MPs. The membership varied over time, and the attendance at meetings fluctuated,[127] but the nature of the Committee allowed the various experts on international affairs free reign to express their views. There were frequent disagreements between the members, but the output of the Committee was nothing short of impressive. 'We simply bombarded the leaders of the Party and the active politicians' Leonard Woolf recalled in 1967, 'with reports, briefs, recommendations, covering every aspect, question or problem of international and imperial politics.'[128] Indeed, the volume of reports being sent up to the Executive was so large that as early as 22 June 1921 a meeting of the Committee discussed a point raised by the chair, C.R. Buxton, that the force of the Committee's advice was being compromised by the sending up of "too large a number of detailed recommendations to the executive".[129] As well as providing memoranda on specific issues, the Committee would often make the Executive aware of certain issues, invite outside experts or visitors to address the committee, and even drafted leaflets that were used by the Labour Party during electioneering.[130] By the time the Committee was temporarily suspended in 1939 it had produced, not including redrafts and pamphlets, over 500 memoranda to the Party Executive.

The nature of the Committee, and the tenor of its advice, varied over time, but there were some constants. Generally, the Committee was more pro-League and, later, more anti-Hitler than the average for the rest of the Party.[131] It was also the main forum for the various ex-Liberal recruits to Labour, and as a result often displayed an intellectual radicalism in international affairs that was less common in the Party as a whole, although Henry Winkler saw them as a force, over time, for moderation.[132] At the same time the Committee commanded a lot of respect amongst the Party leadership. Arthur Henderson, the Party Secretary and Foreign Minister in the second Labour Government, 'made frequent use of the policy papers produced by members of ... [the] Advisory Committee on International Questions.'[133] In the Annual Report to the 1920 Labour Party Conference the International Questions Committee was singled out, amongst the nine then in existence, as the 'most active of the Committees on general questions.'[134] In a letter to Leonard Woolf dated 29th April 1937 Hugh Dalton stated:

I have always thought that the large amount of valuable material provided by [the Imperial Questions] Committee should be of great use to M.P.s desiring to follow colonial questions in detail... I have always thought, on the other hand, that the International Advisory Committee is doubly valuable, even more for the National Executive than for the Parliamentary Party.[135]

In 1943, just prior to the Executive's decision to revive the Advisory Committee, J.S. Middleton, now Secretary of the Party, said of the Committee that it had 'done such valuable work for the Party since Webb instituted it nearly 25 years ago.'[136] When in 1933 the Secretary of the International Department, William Gillies, briefed the then leader of the Parliamentary Party, George Lansbury, on the state of the Locarno Pact he forwarded a copy of the November 1925 Advisory Committee memo on Locarno without amendments. Although Lansbury's own pacifism was at odds with the general tenor of the Committee, there were a number of the Committee's memoranda in his private papers.

The relationship between the Committee and members of the Parliamentary Party were not always cordial, however. On at least two occasions, for example, the Committee found itself on the wrong side of James Ramsay MacDonald. MacDonald was an occasional member of the Committee in the 1920s, but his style in government tended to be more secretive. Both Leonard Woolf and Norman Angell found MacDonald's temperament troubling, despite Angell's close friendship with MacDonald before 1918.[137] In 1925 MacDonald wrote to Arthur Henderson criticising the Committee's memo on reform of the Foreign Office, with particular reference to the memos suggestion that when the Party returned to government they should replace civil servants in the foreign office with pro-Party appointees. This criticism was reiterated in a letter from MacDonald's secretary to William Gillies, the Assistant Secretary of the Party, on 9 April 1925.[138] During MacDonald's second stint as Prime Minister he informed the Executive that he had read the Advisory Committee's memorandum submitted for that meeting, but 'is not very favourably impressed by it. It does not seem to be based on accurate information as to the facts.'[139]

In fact, during his time in government, MacDonald, who was also Foreign Secretary in 1924, made little use of the Advisory Committee. This was in sharp contrast to other Labour leaders, and was a worry to his Parliamentary Under-Secretary at the Foreign Office, Arthur Ponsonby, who wrote to Norman Angell about his concerns.[140] David Mitrany thought it a pity that such a 'commanding group' as the Advisory Committee should have been sidelined by MacDonald during the first Labour Government, and he welcomed Arthur Henderson's more open and welcoming approach during Labour's Second.[141] MacDonald's greater reliance on his civil servants during his stints in government, and the distance that he put between himself and the organs of the Party, including the Advisory Committee, have been seen as early symptoms of his break with the Party in 1931, although Catherine Cline argues that 'it would have been both unnecessary and improper for the government to rely for advice solely on an unofficial body of this sort.' Cline is certainly correct when she says that the Advisory Committee's influence was the greater when Labour was not in office, and it did not have to compete with official channels of information.[142]

The Advisory Committee was subject to intermittent reviews of both its remit and its non-Parliamentary membership. In general, these did not affect the basic terms of reference. In 1924 the Advisory Committee, which had been directly under the Executive with the other advisory committees, was placed within the Labour Party and TUC Joint International Department. The fact that the Party had a full International Department demonstrates the importance that Labour attached to international affairs, as well as its contacts with other labour and social democratic parties. Moving the Advisory Committee to the International Department did not change its role, but did reinforce its distinctiveness. The report on the Advisory Committee was always an important part of the report by the International Department to Conference, even after 1926 when the Committee officially reported directly to the Executive. The Committee continued to meet and produce memoranda for the Executive up until September 1939, when it was suspended due to problems caused by the blackout.[143] Some members of the Advisory Committee continued to serve on the Executive's International Sub-Committee, with Philip Noel Baker and Hugh Dalton being particularly active. Hugh Dalton also organised informal symposia on foreign affairs during this interim, in which Leonard Woolf was involved. The Advisory Committee was reconstituted in 1944, with Philip Noel Baker in the Chair and Leonard Woolf as Secretary. After Labour won its landslide victory on 5 July 1945 the Advisory Committee remained suspended, pending the re-appointment and re-constitution of its membership. On 18 September, however, the International Sub-Committee of the National Executive decided that the Advisory Committee should be dissolved, and its membership rolled into a panel of experts working under the Sub-Committee.[144] The Advisory Committee on Imperial Questions continued to meet, although Woolf finally resigned from the Committee in 1946. Poor attendance dogged the Committee after Woolf's departure, and on 10 November 1949 the Commonwealth Sub-Committee of the NEC decided to disband it.[145] The Advisory Committee experiment ended with a whimper, to be replaced by panels of experts answerable to sub-committees of the NEC, and called upon only when advice was needed on specific subjects.

Woolf's central role in the two Advisory Committees spans our period from 1918 to 1945. The form and operation of the Advisory Committee displays many of the characteristics of Woolf's own work. His belief in the value of expert opinion, the importance of detailed factual information as displayed in the memoranda, the ultimate goal of using knowledge as a tool of influence for the improvement of the world, and the value of a committee structure as a democratic and democratising tool. While the work of the Committee was the culmination of all the efforts of its members, it was Woolf who was most closely associated with it. Yet, because it was also part of Woolf's intention that the Advisory Committee should be a forum for ideas, it also brought together many different opinions, and there were frequent dissenting voices to the memoranda that went up to the Executive. Splits over the form and role of League sanctions, the causes of fascist aggression, or the role of the League after 1936 were often wide and divisive. In 1918, however, there was a sizeable consensus on the need for a league of nations and a non-vindictive peace. As the details of the peace filtered out in 1919 the Advisory Committee, at least initially, became a prime source for denunciations of the peace and the flawed League Covenant. The next chapter deals with this period.

2

LOSING THE PEACE?
(1918–1921)

H.N. Brailsford

I often wrote in the *New Leader*, the ILP weekly, then brilliantly edited by Brailsford, from whom I learned much both as to style and
substance. *(Hugh Dalton)*[1]

A crucial difference between the major IR texts of today and those of the
inter-war period was the way that even quite theoretical books in the
1920s and 1930s were an often uneasy mix between intellectual rigor and
polemic pamphleteering. 'Such was the intensity and sense of urgency of
the time that the gap between advocacy and analysis was rarely wide.'[2] Of
all the five writers discussed in this book H.N. Brailsford is the most polemic. This is not to say that there was no intellectual rigor in his works, the
comparison is after all a matter of degree. Brailsford's theoretical framework came from an interpretation and adaptation of the economic theory
of J.A. Hobson, combined with a British socialist outlook that was more
millenarian than Marxist. While Brailsford was not the most original of
thinkers, he made up for this by the power of his journalism. His editorship of the ILP's journal *New Leader* made him an influential figure in the
Labour debates about the Peace Treaties and the newly formed League of
Nations. Brailsford's sustained criticism of both gave way to a guarded
optimism about the possibilities of the League, especially after the successes of the first Labour Government at Geneva. While Brailsford often
raised the ire of Ramsay MacDonald by occasional criticisms of the two
Labour governments, he reserved his strongest language for the Conservatives, especially the Conservative-led National Government of 1931 to
1940. During the 1930s Brailsford considered the League as rather tooth-

less, and his deep criticism of the dictators mixed with an almost as deep suspicion of British imperialist pretensions.

Brailsford's *magnum opus*, which remained his most well known work during the inter-war period, was his 1914 book *The War of Steel and Gold*. I will discuss the argument of this work in more detail below. While he published many more books afterwards, the influence of his synthesis of J.A. Hobson's economics with Norman Angell's assessment of the international anarchy remained strong amongst the British left, despite the fact that Brailsford's prediction about the prospects for a general war proved less accurate than Angell's earlier one in *The Great Illusion*. Interestingly, Norman Angell, despite major disagreements with Brailsford on other topics, always felt indebted to Brailsford for the latter's positive review of *The Great Illusion*, which single-handedly saved the book from an early oblivion. In addition to his journalism and his books on world order, Brailsford also wrote books and articles in support of the Macedonians, and later the Bulgarians too. Like many British intellectuals of the time, and not a few during the collapse of Yugoslavia in the 1990s, his deep interest in the Balkans led him to take sides in the many internecine conflicts that occurred in the region.

There is no recent book-length study of Brailsford's contribution to IR. The nearest approximation is F.M. Leventhal's biography,[3] which reminds us how much Brailsford was a product of the dissenting tradition in British journalism that goes back to the pamphleteers of the seventeenth century, the radicalism of Paine and Cobbett, or the Irish nationalism of Daniel O'Connell. Much of his lack of popularity today is probably based upon the time-specific nature of most of his work, which has meant that he rarely figures in the various footnotes that pass for a discussion of 'idealism' in the mainstream IR literature and textbooks. 'Almost as soon as his articles ceased to appear in print', laments Leventhal, 'his name was forgotten, and his books, generally written in response to particular events, retained only historic interest for the next generation.'[4] Despite this, Brailsford's death in 1958 provoked glowing tributes in the left-wing press. Michael Foot in *Tribune* called him 'the greatest Socialist journalist of the century', and in the *New Statesman* Kingsley Martin praised his scholarship and passion for freedom.[5] Yet, Brailsford was more than a mere pamphleteer and follower of Hobson. His synthesis of new liberal economics, socialist theory and current affairs makes him a key intellectual figure of his time, and a reminder that the kind of intellectual polemics on global affairs that we now associate with people like Noam Chomsky or John Pilger have been a part of the IR landscape from the beginning.

Many of the ideas that were to underpin Brailsford's analysis of the problem of international order were already present in his 1906 study of the peoples and politics of Macedonia. Like David Mitrany, Brailsford maintained a lively interest in Balkan politics, although he tended to fall into the outsider's trap of taking sides in ethnic conflicts. This said, his study of Turkish Macedonia – a region marked by its polyglot of ethnic groups and religions – helped hone Brailsford's dislike of nationalist xenophobia. He stubbornly refused to take sides in the various ethnic conflicts in the territory, even showing some sympathy for the Turks, although he was also deeply critical of past Ottoman despotism. 'There is little to choose in bloody-mindedness between any of the Balkan races' he wrote, 'they are all what centuries of Asiatic rule have made them.'[6] While guilty of what would then have been a common disparaging orientalism towards Asia and its political practices, Brailsford was very aware of the local mini-tyrannies that affected the lives of the Macedonian peasantry. As far as he was concerned, the major problems were not the issues of ethnic identities, but rather the kleptocratic structures that kept the region from fulfilling its potential:

It matters very little whether a village which was originally neither Greek nor Bulgarian nor Servian is bribed or persuaded or terrorised into joining one of these national parties. But it does matter profoundly that it should be freed from the oppression of its landlord, its tax-farmer, and the local brigand chief.[7]

These two themes, the opposition to nationalist thinking and a concentration on the underlying social and economic inequalities, were to be the main themes in his international writing throughout his life.

Brailsford's solution to the Macedonian question was to by-pass the competing nationalist claims by internationalising the territory under great power control ('the five protecting powers'), and establishing strong local government with a deliberately mixed police force.[8] Yet, in the final analysis Brailsford was pessimistic. While he saw his solution as practical and desirable, he also understood that 'the forces which make for it are feeble and those which oppose it deplorably powerful.'[9] Thus as a good normative thinker, he was at pains to point out both what was needed to be done to solve a particular problem, and the serious obstacles that lay in the way of the solution. While it was important for Brailsford that these major constraints were known, this did not mean that he condoned compromising or abandoning the ultimate goal. Rather, acknowledging the strength of the forces ranged against reform was a spur to try harder.[10] Since for

Brailsford there could be no peace and harmonious living without equality and fairness it stood to reason that compromise with the forces promoting inequality and unfairness could never end war and human suffering. He returned to this theme in 1914 with his next bestseller.

The War of Steel and Gold, like Angell's The Great Illusion and Lowes Dickinson's later book The International Anarchy, was an analysis of the workings of the pre-First World War diplomacy and state system. Where it differed from the other two works was in its use of J.A. Hobson's analysis of imperialism in order to pin the greatest blame for international disorder on the nature of capitalism.[11] Hobson, in his influential Imperialism, had argued that modern capitalist states, but particularly his case study of Britain, were creating international instability through their economic and political structures at home. By keeping wages low and profits high capitalists were simultaneously accumulating pools of capital in need of investment opportunities, and impoverishing the domestic market. As a result, the people in the metropole were incapable of purchasing a greater share of the goods produced so cheaply by the home factories. Rather than raise wages and stimulate demand at home, financial interests looked to investment opportunities abroad, and enlisted the help of their home governments in acquiring new colonies and other opportunities for investment. This new form of imperialism was detrimental to both the population of the metropole and to international stability. The world was made less secure by this new scramble for colonies and market access. The answer to this problem lay in greater democratic control of foreign policy and fairer wages at home.[12]

In The War of Steel and Gold Brailsford took Hobson's comparatively underdeveloped notion that booty capitalism caused instability, and produced the argument that great power competition was fundamentally over investment opportunities and access to economically useful resources, rather than the fear of conquest and annexations that had dominated the eighteenth and nineteenth century forms of the balance of power. The mistake of many contemporary analysts, he argued, was to assume that the current (1914) balance of power was the same as that a century before. The balance of power is not a 'self-sufficing ideal... Power is sought for certain ends.'[13] Now that wealth was predominantly in finance, rather than land, the balance of power focused on struggles over investment opportunities.[14] At the same time states were now based on specific nationalities, and there was little room for multi-national imperial states. As a consequence of these two changes the epoch of conquest in Europe was over. In its place was the competition in the extra-European world. The War of Steel and Gold wove an argument that put the blame for international instability on a lethal cocktail of the system of sovereign states and the exploitative economic system that encouraged economic imperialism.[15] Brailsford contrasted this new economic imperialism with the anti-imperialist free-trade 'Manchester School' of Richard Cobden and John Bright, arguing that the Manchester school ideals brought liberty and peace, but had been superseded by banking interests that stood to make greater profits under a more exploitative system.[16] While the Manchester School required free exchange between free peoples, the new investment-based capitalism required some form of control: 'John Stuart Mill roundly denied that one nation can ever govern another; a nation may, however, keep another people as a human cattle farm.'[17] Consequently, the purposes of modern armaments were not the preparation for a great power war, but rather intimidation so that 'one may bully profitably for a generation, keeping a risky peace.'[18] Conquest, after all, has no profit in it, as Norman Angell had already demonstrated in 1911.[19] Where Brailsford differed from Angell was that he believed that the great powers would do what they could to prevent a system-damaging war, while Angell thought that they were deluded enough by their own expansionist illusions to spark a great power war. In the end it was Angell's prediction that proved closer to the mark.

While *The War of Steel and Gold* had highlighted the problems with the international anarchy, the question that was to dominate Brailsford's writings during both the war and the inter-war years was what form should international relations take in order to eliminate the international anarchy and replace it with a more stable and peaceful system. Although he was to become disillusioned with the League as it was constructed in 1919, he was one of the early advocates of a League of Nations as the basis of an alternative order. In 1917 Brailsford laid out his view of the tasks that any future League would need to face. The two main problems that the League would have to confront if the world was to move away from armed conflict and instability were 1. the problem of the sovereign state, and 2. the lack of justice and equity in human relations. The sovereign state was the main obstacle to any just settlement of international disputes through its refusal 'to allow any interference with its internal questions'.[20] The jealous guarding of the right to be judge and jury in its own case meant that any serious territorial dispute could only be settled by war.[21] Yet, if the League was to work it would require more than just the substitution of peaceful coexistence between nations for the insanities of sovereignty. 'No League, however powerful, can in the long run enforce peace, unless it will enforce justice'.[22] Justice, broadly defined to include economic equality, would both remove causes of conflict and create a sense of gratitude towards the League, which in turn would translate into loyalty towards the new organisation. In the final analysis the League would have to deal with these twin horrors of national sovereignty and in-equality due to economic imperialism if it was to survive. 'No promise to arbitrate and no machinery to enforce arbitration will preserve the world from war, unless it has first removed by a bold treatment of the questions of nationality and economic expansion the chief causes of war.'[23]

Brailsford's vision of the new League was structurally different from the League that emerged from 1919 in one crucially important way. In both his work for the Labour Party and his journalism he advocated the establishment of a Parliament for the League. The experience of the war-time alliance structures demonstrated that cabinet and diplomatic repre-sentation alone entrenched the institution of the sovereign state. Creating a sovereign parliament for the League, chosen either by direct elections or via delegates appointed by national parliaments, would diminish the sense that delegates represented a particular state and encourage the develop-ment of aggregations of representatives along the lines of ideology and class.

> The result would be to diminish the importance of the states as Power, and to emphasise the sovereignty of opinion. The class line of cleavage would be seen to be international, and a great step would be gained in emancipating the workers from the obsessions of a narrow nationalism.[24]

Brailsford's arguments on parliamentary representation were largely adop-ted by the Labour Party, and were included in both the Advisory Comm-ittee's June 1918 'Short Statement of War Aims' memorandum, and the May 1919 British Labour dominated Committee of Action of the Berne International Labour and Socialist Conference.[25] Brailsford returned to the idea of international democratic representation in 1944, when he recomm-ended it for the new international authority that would emerge after the defeat of the Axis.[26] Yet, when the Covenant finally emerged represent-ation in the League lay firmly with the diplomats and the representatives of the state executive. On the one hand, this came as no surprise. Brails-ford had predicted in January 1919 that, because democratic represent-ation in the League would expose the international flavour of class domi-nation and remove the chimera of national aggregations that obscured economic exploitation, 'our opponents will resist' such moves.[27] On the other, the peace treaties in general, and the Covenant in particular, turned Brailsford's natural guarded optimism into rampant pessimism.

The bitter fruit of this pessimism was his 1920 book *After the Peace*, which Leventhal called 'too unrelievably gloomy to appeal to its readers.'[28]

In general terms he predicted the collapse of the capitalist old order, without any new set of ideas necessarily waiting to redeem civilisation by stepping in to create a new order.[29] As a clear example of this the immediate problem of the treaties of 1919 was that they were consistently organised around the old principles of the sovereign state that had failed so miserably in 1914. 'Fear and ambition, and not the dynamite of new doctrine, have wrought these catastrophic changes.'[30] Indeed, until 1924 it looked as though Brailsford had written off the League of Nations as a failure from the start. The incompatibility of capitalism with democracy and the grossly unfair provisions of the Treaty of Versailles based upon ideas of state sovereignty remained unchallenged by the toothless League institutions. Although he continued to believe that the League was inadequate in its present form because it ignored 'the economic factor' and accepted 'the myth of the sovereign national state',[31] he was heartened by the use that the first Labour Government made of the League's institutions in 1924. He welcomed the resulting Geneva protocol, with the proviso that it should be linked to a revision of the peace treaties, admission of Germany to the League, the reduction of armaments and the curtailing of economic imperialism.[32] In September 1924, after Ramsay MacDonald's success at Geneva, Brailsford wrote that the 'League which had been nothing became everything', although he warned that 'I doubt the efficacy alike of arbitration and disarmament to solve the problem of war until we grapple with economic imperialism.'[33] The mandate system, which he had written off in 1920 as serving 'only as a disguise to cover the fact of annexation',[34] was re-evaluated in 1928 as a possible template for the development of a non-exploitative alternative arrangement for European colonies in Africa and the Pacific.[35]

Brailsford's reconciliation with the League reached new heights with the rise of fascism, although as the League machinery was increasingly underutilised or ignored by its member governments, he steadily removed his support. By then he had been joined in his scepticism by Leonard Woolf and David Mitrany. He urged the imposition of strong League sanctions against Italy over Abyssinia in 1935,[36] was deeply critical of the lacklustre British implementation of those sanctions in 1936,[37] and in his reaction to the Sudetenland crisis of 1938 he criticised the Conservative-dominated National Government in Britain for abandoning League collective security in favour of the tired old principle of national self-preservation.[38] In fact his 'articles during 1938 show even greater support for collective security, but for him it meant a defence of human rights, not of imperial acquisitions.'[39]

Yet, despite its potential role in the immediate crisis – a role that in the end the major powers did not let it fulfil – Brailsford's analysis of the League in the longer term were always compromised by its failure to deal with the twin problems of economic injustice and state sovereignty that he had highlighted in his 1917 book on the forthcoming League. He returned to this theme in *Olives of Endless Age* (1928), where he praised the League as both an idea and as a practical alternative to many of the self-destructive tendencies such as imperialism, but criticised it both for still basing its membership on the sovereign state and for only very tentatively dealing with the problems of economic interdependence and imperialism.[40] In 1933, in a contribution on the possible policy directions of a future Labour Government, Brailsford laid out his final judgement on the League. The League's major flaw remained its constitution, which 'was based throughout on the absolute sovereignty of its member-States.' This meant that 'it could not impose the organic changes which alone can remove the causes of war.' This would require the League to impose its authority on 'the domestic jurisdiction of a member-State… it cannot cure the political or economic maladjustment that drives nations to war.'[41] The Manchurian crisis had exposed the weakness of the League machinery: that it could only function if there was the will amongst its great power members to act. 'It means that the League is a reality when its system of impartial justice happens to be in line with the self-regarding calculations' of Britain and France.[42] Yet, it was also wrong to write the League off entirely. It still embodied an international ideal. 'It is at least a clearing in the jungle, and a conspicuous one. Clearings may be enlarged.'[43] 'With all its limitations in conception and its failures in achievement, it represents an aspiration that is transforming the thinking of a great part of mankind.'[44] On a less passive note the League had done excellent non-political work through its specialised agencies, it had 'consolidate[d] the procedure for the pacific settlement of disputes, put a check on ultra-nationalist military intervenetions, and it provided a forum for statesmen to meet in the full view of international public opinion.'[45] In sum, while Brailsford was opposed to leaving the League, the emphasis for him was on necessary reforms. By 1936 those reforms centred around the idea of creating an inner federal League consisting of like-minded states that were committed to an international pooling of security and economic resources.[46] This proposal bore a strong resemblance to the proposals for a revived League made in the late thirties by other members of the Advisory Committee. Ironically, despite the virulence of many of his articles, Brailsford's later views on the League put him closer to the Labour leadership and the mainstream of the Advisory Committee than it would at first seem. The difference was more one of emphasis than principle. Indeed, Hugh Dalton, in his *Towards the Peace of Nations* that laid out the international position of the group around Arthur Henderson, praised Brailsford for his view of international affairs.[47] This contrasted strikingly with Dalton's less enthusiastic analysis of Norman Angell's work.

Underlying all of Brailsford's analysis of the inter-war imbroglio was a continuity of argument with his *The War of Steel and Gold*. Although he was later to argue that he and Hobson had over-estimated the economic basis of the crisis of the 1930's, and that the barbarism of the Nazis was more psychological than economic in its roots,[48] he still saw the rottenness of the international economic system as key to the continued international anarchy. A new capitalist-style imperialism, linked to the idea of state sovereignty, was responsible for the instability of international relations, and the answer to this threat could be at least partially addressed, he argued, by greater democracy both at the national and international level. Increasingly for Brailsford this democracy, at least at the national level, meant greater socialism. The collapse of the Labour Government in 1931 in what seemed like a deliberate banker's plot underscored for him the basic incompatibility between capitalism and democracy.[49] Greater socialism was a necessary precondition for the protection of democracy from capitalism and capitalist interests. This caused a certain amount of tension with his internationalist spirit. The socialist alternative to capitalism at the time centred on national planning, and national planning meant strengthening the sovereign state. When Brailsford's friend David Mitrany gave a talk at a Fabian Society meeting in the winter of 1942–3, in which he argued that national planning without international planning would lead to greater conflicts between states, Brailsford admitted to Mitrany the next day that he had been up all night worrying about it.[50] In a friendly exchange of letters in September 1945 Mitrany and Brailsford discussed their views on the dangers of national planning. Brailsford conceded Mitrany's point on the need for international planning, but felt that it could start at an imperial or national level: 'So, personally I don't plead guilty to nationalism, but I'll watch myself'.[51]

Indeed, during the Second World War Brailsford was, as he had been during the First War, a strong advocate of an effective international political organisation to deal with the problem of power. Not to have such an inclusive organisation would leave the world to fall back on the 'Big Three' great powers as arbiters of the post-1945 world.[52] He prophesized that a world based on the untrammelled power of the United States, Great Britain and the Soviet Union would revert to an international anarchy as soon as the Big Three 'cease to have a collective will.'[53] In 1944 Brailsford prophesied that the most likely outlook for Europe after the war was its division by the great powers into two spheres of influence, and that eventually the Big Three would lose their collective will and revert to the international anarchy: 'The present war has settled one of Europe's problems of power [Germany] only to raise another.'[54] Brailsford was to be as disappointed in the peace of 1945 as he had been in the one in 1919. Yet, the deep pessimism of 1919 never really returned. In 1928 he wrote an apparent explanation for this period in his intellectual development. 'Deep in the nerve centres even of the most civilised men,' he wrote, 'there lurks an expectation which makes fatalists of us. What once happened will happen again.'[55] What was true of Brailsford was true of so many of the other international experts in Labour's ranks. They feared that the peace and the apparently still-born League would continue to mire the world in the conditions that had made the Great War possible, even inevitable, in the first place.

Opposition to the Peace Treaties

Labour entered the immediate post-war period in an optimistic mood. Although Lloyd George had failed to appoint a Labour representative to the Empire delegation in Paris, the power of Woodrow Wilson's commitment to a non-vindictive peace and the complete collapse of the imperial governments in Germany and Austria-Hungary seemed to point towards a just peace that might yet make a repeat of the insanity of 1914 impossible. Deep suspicion of the direction being taken by the Bolsheviks in Russia was matched by tentative moves towards the re-establishment of the Second International of Socialist and Labour parties. Unlike many liberal commentators in the United States, Labour pundits were less optimistic about using national self-determination as a cure-all for Europe's problems, feeling that a just peace combined with reasonable reparations for actual damage should be the foundation of the post-war order. Even before the end of the war the Advisory Committee recognised that there were limits to the usefulness of self-determination.[56] Soon the Peace Conference itself realised these limits when it became clear that national self-determination, strictly applied, would leave Germany bigger than before by the inclusion of Austria, and in most of Europe failed to provide clear lines on a map, left significant and turbulent minorities behind, or failed to take into consideration major issues of state viability or security. The proliferation of nationalities and national delegations to Paris bewildered many supporters of national self-determination.[57] Above all, though, the main Labour activists and pundits were looking forward to the new League of

Nations that would help usher in an era of democratic accountability in foreign affairs, without the curse of the old secret diplomacy.

I shall deal with the Labour criticism of the League in the next section. Here I want to look in detail at the Labour reaction to the peace treaties, especially the Treaty of Versailles with Germany. Particularly relevant here is the Advisory Committee memorandum no. 61 of May 1919, written by Norman Angell and entitled 'Peace Terms', although a large number of the memoranda written in the first few years of the Committee were, in one way or the other, written as suggestions or reactions to the peace treaties or the new League Covenant. The main reason for Labour disquiet with the treaties was that the logic underpinning them was the same logic that had caused the war in the first place. The indemnities masked as reparations; the annexations based on security or raw material access without regard for the views of the population of the territory annexed; the mandate system that effectively gave the mandated state the power of any other colonial overlord; the one sided disarmament of Germany and her allies; and the war guilt clause all pointed to the continuation of the same pre-1914 international anarchy. Even where the treaties tried to be new, and gave a nod in the direction of liberal sentiment, it looked botched. Plebiscites, it seemed, were not held in regions where the Allies felt that they had a vested interest. The key region of South Tyrol, a predominantly German-speaking region who's ceding to Italy was one of the few Italian territorial demands that had been met by the treaties, not only had no plebiscite, but its German speakers never received the protection of the League like other minorities. Similarly Eupen and Malmedy went to Belgium, all of Transylvania, including the predominantly Hungarian speaking regions, went to Romania, the Tsingtao treaty port in China went to Japan, and Alsace-Lorraine went to France, all without a vote. Even where plebiscites were held there were complaints of partiality. The borders of the plebiscite regions in Upper Silesia, for example, were gerrymandered to guarantee the key coalfields for Poland. All of these added to Labour's sense of outrage, and made the bitterness of their exclusion from the negotiations even harder to bear.

Central to the Labour criticisms of the peace treaties was an analysis of the nature of the international anarchy that had preceded the war, how that anarchy had been responsible for the outbreak of hostilities, and the extent to which the treaties still conformed to the old diplomacy, and therefore did not prevent the outbreak of another war. What united the various factions within Labour was the opposition to the old international anarchy, even when the solutions to the problem of that anarchy split them apart. Norman Angell expressed the general feeling of the Party towards the pre-1914 states system when he argued that in any self-help system of states conflicts over power are inevitable, and generally lead to war.[58] Consistent with the general view amongst the Party opinion formers that there was an intimate connection between domestic and international politics, the international anarchy was seen as a problem for both political spheres. While the division of the world into squabbling states was an important factor in creating the problem, the failure of states to develop democratic control of foreign policy was seen as a crucial exacerbating factor: 'there can be no real diplomacy where there is no democracy.'[59] Secret treaties, binding a people without their knowledge, decisions made at an executive level without the input of the representatives in the world's legislators, and the lack of discussion of foreign issues in public fora were seen as an important distinguishing feature of the pre-1914 system. State sovereignty was, therefore, only part of the problem. The way that sovereignty was exercised, in a non-democratic and 'genteel' way, was an immediate question that could be addressed by an incoming Labour government.

Thus, the old international anarchy was a combination of a distorted political rendering of the old liberal laissez faire concept that was deeply suspicious of any overarching authority above the sovereign state, and the thoroughly conservative and anti-democratic idea that foreign affairs was the bailiwick of the 'best people' in society. The conservative supporters of the old diplomacy argued that any interference by democratic institutions was an inefficient clouding of a system that worked best when it was left to those who, through their class, education and upbringing, were best suited to engaging in diplomacy. Crucially, the old diplomacy assumed that state power and wealth were readily definable, and that consequently it was easy to calculate relative gains and losses in inter-state conflict. This led to what Labour opinion formers saw as the major fallacies of the international anarchy, that it was possible to extract wealth from one country to another (the indemnity fallacy), and that security was fundamentally relative and impossible to collectivise. The peace treaties seemed to entrench these fallacies, rather than to challenge them. In this sense the Paris treaties represented the last gasp of an old order, with all the connotations of senility that that implies, rather than any attempt to usher in a new era. What made the challenge to this old order an imperative was the destructive potential of modern war. The international anarchy was premised on the ultimate use of war as a means of inter-state competition. The Great War had shown that this was no longer sustainable:

> British Socialists are convinced that the ever-increasing range of destruction in warfare makes it impossible that the present system of

belligerent competition among states should continue. Science has so increased the power of men for good and evil, that only through co-operation and mutual restraint can our race now be saved from destroying itself.[60]

The very destructiveness of war now made the construction of an alternative to a system based on inter-state conflict an imperative. This sense of urgency, in the face of increased destructiveness, worked itself into the arguments of both the left and the right in Britain. One of the most unlikely converts to the idea of a new international order clustered around a League of Nations was the geographer and Conservative MP Halford Mackinder. In 1904 Mackinder had written an influential article, entitled 'The Geographical Pivot of History', which assumed that states were in perpetual conflict.[61] In 1919 Mackinder threw his support behind the League, arguing that the preservation of the British Empire rested in transcending the determinism of geopolitics that he had articulated fifteen years before.[62] Interestingly, Mackinder's optimism in 1919 contrasts with the overriding pessimism in Labour circles that centred on the failings of the 1919 peace. We can cluster the Labour criticisms of the peace treaties around four issues: the indemnity fallacy; the development of economic nationalism and protectionism; war guilt; and the entrenchment of national security concerns over the requirements of global security.

Indemnities and their futility had already been the subject of a devastating criticism by Norman Angell. Angell had given this issue a full chapter in his ground-breaking *The Great Illusion*, concluding that the experience of the German-imposed indemnity on France in 1870 had been the opposite of what had been intended. Forced to pay an indemnity to Germany, France had had to provide a spur to its industries by increasing production in exported goods, while the availability of French capital to Germany via the indemnity had provided easy capital that had acted as a disincentive to German industrial development and a source of higher inflation.[63] Angell had also laid out the case against reparations in terms of goods, an issue that was to be of particular relevance to the reparations imposed on Germany seven years later. The transfer of goods and raw materials from the defeated to the victorious state would provide such a cheap source of products for the winner that it would undercut and bankrupt the victor's domestic industries. In peacetime such a policy would be called dumping.[64] It is not difficult to see Angell's influence in the Advisory Committee memoranda that covered the question of German reparations.

The peculiar case of the German reparations made for specific economic problems for both Germany and the Allied states. The main worry of

the Advisory Committee members, and by extension the Labour Party itself, was the effect of the swamping of the French and Belgian market
with German reparations coal. Under the Spa agreement of July 1920 Germany was to hand over 2 million tons of coal a month, with 1.5 million of
the total to France. The availability of cheap German coal made the coal
from the French, Belgian and British coalmines unproductive, causing
mine closures and unemployment in coalmining regions. In March of 1921
there was a 50 percent drop in coal output in the Liege region of Belgium.
With the French market glutted, and the excess reparations coal being sold
to third countries such as the Netherlands, the market for British coal,
already reduced by British government export restrictions, fell dramatically. Britain exported 5.5 million tons of coal in February 1913, 2.6
million in February 1920, and 1.7 million in February 1921. Thus, unemployment and wage cuts in the British coal industry, along with the costs of
this to the whole British economy, were a direct result of the fallacy of
indemnities.[65] The problems of the British coal industry may not have
been completely a result of reparations coal, the over-valuing of sterling
had a longer term effect on coal exports,[66] but the example of coal and
reparations highlight the extent to which the reparations issue directly
effected the domestic issues of concern to Labour's rank and file.

While the German indemnity against France had actually acted as a
spur to French finance and industry after 1871, the fear in Labour circles
was that this was not the case in Germany after 1919. Rather, the need to
provide reparations was being used by the employers as an excuse to
lower workers' wages and increase working hours. Dorothy Frances Buxton's study of the effects of the coal reparations on Germany devoted a
large section of her pamphlet to the impoverishment caused to German
workers, and how this poverty was having a knock-on effect within the
rest of the international economy.[67] Despite the bitterness towards Germany caused by the war, there was a strong sympathy for the German
Trades Union movement and the German socialists amongst British Labour supporters and leaders. A major exception here was Hugh Dalton,
who remained suspicious of German intentions, and later would be one of
only a few voices supporting Poland's claims on the territories it took
from Germany.

Amidst the denunciations of reparations made in Advisory Committee
memoranda, the parallel concern with the creation of a functioning international machinery can also be heard. Particularly interesting here is a
memoranda written by David Mitrany in 1920, which while clearly opposed to the Allied policy of reparations, made a case for Labour's engagement with the Reparations Commission. This would be a continual theme

on the Advisory Committee, where criticisms where often mixed with discussions on how imperfect institutions could still be used to further the ends supported by the Party. Although having no representation from the enemy states or the smaller Allies – being largely appointed by the main Allied governments – and being strongly influenced by the French government ('official France'), Mitrany made a strong case for Labour engagement with the commission on three levels. First, in order to counter the influence of vested interests and those who are likely to favour conservative circles in Germany, Labour should press to have its own representatives on the Commission. Second, since the Commission does act as an independent body producing its own assessment of the reparations situation Labour should press for the publication of Commission documents. Finally, since the Commission, in the words of Keynes, 'will come into very close contact with the problems of Europe', the potential exists for it to become an 'economic council of Europe'. Mitrany endorsed Keynes' call for the Commission's transference to the League of Nations as a technical organisation.[68] Thus, an organisation set up in bad faith and for a bad reason could be used for broader internationalist goals. Mitrany's colleagues on the Advisory Committee would soon extend this attitude to the whole League system.

The Advisory Committee was not completely opposed to the idea of reparations per se. In 1918 Woolf's memo on the subject argued that Germany should be responsible for damage it had done in Belgium, although he favoured an international commission to settle the claim. Other reparations, he felt, should be settled out of an international fund.[69] The major objection to reparations was the sheer scale and vindictiveness of the sums involved, as well as the counter-productive nature of the indemnity. The whole reparations issue was dominated by a dangerous misconception of the old diplomacy that the wealth of a country could be appropriated by another state, and was oblivious to the inter-connectedness of global economic relations. This economic nationalism, that was damaging the prosperity of the post-war world, was another legacy of the treaties from the point of view of the Advisory Committee members and Labour's opinion-formers.

This economic nationalism, so clearly a hangover from the old diplomacy of the international anarchy, had its roots in the inter-Allied agreements developed during the war. Of particular concern was the agreement reached at the Inter-Allied Economic Conference held in Paris in 1916. The Allies effectively agreed to continue a policy of economic discrimination against the Central Powers after the conclusion of the war. 'These proposals mean economic war with the Central Powers after the military peace, a policy utterly subversive of any real League of Nations.'[70] For, the Labour argument went, how could you promote a new system of collective military security if your economic policy was designed to impoverish the former enemy? Beyond this, the main problem seemed to be the fallacy pervading the Peace Conference that in order to maintain its security a state should have control of the raw materials necessary for its industry. Because this was not possible for almost all of the world's states, this created a ready source of conflict as they struggled for control of border regions rich in coal, steel or zinc, oblivious to the wishes of the population of the contested region. The various decisions taken during and after the treaties on the Saar, Teschen and Upper Silesia were all based on the assumption that resources were national property.

While those who pushed for a punitive peace claimed to be working under the realities of power and the naturalness of conflicts over relative power, the answer from Labour's international experts was that the self-styled realists were the ones who had failed to understand the international realities. Part of the punitive nature of the treaties had been to punish the enemy states – as well as Soviet Russia outside of the formal treaty process – with impoverishment. This assumed that national economies were insulated from each other. A major part of Labour's position in the post-Conference period was dedicated to arguing that Europe, not to mention the wider world, was an interdependent economy. The impoverishment of any country, while it reduced the security risk to Britain from that state under the logic of the international anarchy, also impoverished Britain by removing the buying power of foreign markets.[71]   More deeply, and for this Labour writers drew freely from Norman Angell's pre-war analysis of the international economy, Europe's integrated economy and intensive industrial system was what allowed it to support such a large population on such a small amount of land. By smashing this cooperation post-war nationalism, as manifest in the treaties, threatened to undo the complex system that sustained this population.[72] The effects of this dislocation of normal economic links lay in abundance throughout Europe. The various famines in Central and Eastern Europe seemed to threaten the continent with mass depopulation. In what thankfully turned out to be an over-estimation, Dorothy Frances Buxton even quoted a claim that the starving city of Vienna would be wiped out in fifteen years under current trends.[73] Labour's view of the international economy as an interdependent whole was a major influence on its foreign policy during the rest of the inter-war period, and represents an early manifestation of what would later be called interdependence theory.

While for some of the supporters of the war within the Party the war guilt clause of the Versailles Treaty seemed unproblematic, the many others who saw the international anarchy as the cause of the war regarded blaming Germany alone as both untrue and unfair. Some like E.D. Morel even reversed the guilt, blaming the French and the Tsarist Russians for bringing about the war.[74] The war guilt clause alone did no material damage to Germany; in that respect it was less damaging than reparations. The concern was more with what it did to the psyche of the German population, especially the support it gave to the German militarist argument that the peace was punitive, and the way that it undermined support for the socialist dominated German Republic. The 1919 Party Conference singled out the war guilt clause as one of the main elements of the harsh treatment of Germany in the Versailles Treaty.[75] There certainly were many within Labour who did regard Germany, through its militarism, as a criminal state, but the general feeling was that the overthrow of the imperial government and just reparations for actual damage would be adequate retribution.[76] Generally, though, war guilt tended to be less of an issue for Labour's intellectuals and leadership than the bigger problems of the material damage done to Germany, and the failure to develop an alternative security system to replace the international anarchy.

The establishment of an effective and stable system of international security was a priority for many of the opponents of the international anarchy, whether on the left or the right. In their 25 June 1918 memo on war aims, drafted for the Westminster conference of Allied socialists, the Advisory Committee had made clear its view on the link between security and effective self-determination. The Mazzinian tradition of liberal nationalism during the nineteenth century had assumed that the granting of national self-determination would remove a major cause of war. By contrast, the Advisory Committee saw the settling of national security concerns through a system of pooled security and League government as the means by which national self-determination could be realised. By removing the need to control territory for security and military reasons, pooled security and world government would make the 'grouping of peoples within boundaries consonant with their racial and emotional affinities' possible.[77] Rather than self-determination being the golden road to security, it was the settling of security issues that would make self-determination possible. The Peace Conference understood this limit to self-determination, since early on national self-determination often took a back-seat to concerns over economic viability and military security. Delegations switched between advocating national self-determination, military security, or economic necessity depending on which argument gave them the advantage in claiming a region. Thus, Italy argued self-determination in its claims on Trieste and the Istra, economic and military concerns in its claims on the majority Slav Dalamatia, and military security when it claimed the predominantly German South Tyrol. In the absence of an over-arching authority guaranteeing an economic open door and military security, the Advisory Committee recognised, it would not be possible to fully implement national self-determination. Even the Advisory Committee may have been overly optimistic here. The mixed populations of Europe were to make a full implementation of self-determination impossible to implement, and the creation of national minorities inevitable in the absence of coercive population exchanges.

The more general problem with the way that the treaties dealt with security was that they still conformed to the logic of the international anarchy that had preceded the war. The one-sided disarmament of Germany and her Allies was based on the logic of relative power. The Allies had reserved for themselves the right of military intervention, which they exercised in Hungary and Russia. This was later to culminate in the 1923 French and Belgian invasion of the Ruhr following Germany's default on its reparations payments. While lip-service had been paid to a possible alternative system in the Covenant of the League, the lesson being taught to the former Central Powers and Soviet Russia was that without military power to protect them they would be subject to Allied intervention. This was not building a new world, this was entrenching the idea of the international anarchy. Rather than proving the German militarists wrong, the actions of the Allies were sending the signal that without military power Germany was vulnerable to her enemies. This also seemed to make a mockery of the reciprocal disarmament clause of the Versailles Treaty and the Covenant of the League, in which the Allies had pledged themselves to disarmament and the peaceful settlement of disputes.

Thus the inequality and vindictiveness of the treaties would, it was believed, hamper any effort to secure a new international order. Hopes that a reformed League system could eventually evolve were tempered by the view that the treaties themselves would make it impossible for a collective security system to work through the League. 'The fatal obstacle to the League is that if it were to attempt to function it would have to administer these impossible Treaties. Only force can impose them, and only a military alliance can exert sufficient force.'[78] Right from the start, it was argued, the treaties would poison any new order, although there was also deep disquiet over the form that the League was taking, and even without the vindictiveness of the treaties, Labour activists argued, the new system of pooled security was flawed from its inception.

Criticisms of the League of Nations

One of the major assumptions of the Whig interpretation of history that dominates IR auto-histories is that the so-called idealists were major advocates of the League of Nations. This is necessary in order to distinguish them from a modern realist suspicion about the role and independence of international organisations. Idealist support for the League, and the League's failure, is a necessary support for the criticisms of the United Nation System and the myriad IGOs and NGOs that pervade modern IR. It may come as a surprise, therefore, to realise how unpopular the resulting League was to so many of the writers who have been written off as idealists. Much of this unhappiness with the League was a result of the disappointment with the limited and conservative nature of the League that came out of the Paris conference. The left felt jilted by the new Covenant. It also has to be pointed out that, despite the vicious criticisms of the League after 1919, Labour was, by-and-large, reconciled to the League system by the mid-twenties. Despite the venom of the criticisms that they levelled at the League, Labour and Labour-leaning opinion-formers were ultimately committed to the League project. There were exceptions, and a major split that developed on the left was between those who were willing to work within the League system, such as Philip Noel Baker, Norman Angell, Arthur Henderson and Hugh Dalton, and those who saw the League and collective security in a less positive light, like Arthur Ponsonby, George Lansbury and Stafford Cripps. The main criticism of the League Covenant revolved around its system of representation, especially the domination of cabinet level control, the lack of legislative and popular representation. The second criticism focused on the weakness of the mandate system, while a third was the exclusion of Germany and Russia.

The major fear for many of the members of the Advisory Committee and the Labour leadership was that the League would become merely an embodiment of the old diplomacy, rather than the basis of a new order. It was for this reason that before the end of the war the Advisory Committee was arguing against the immediate establishment of the League amongst the Allied nations. The fear was that if the League began as a League of the Allies it would largely serve, and be seen to serve, Allied interests. Since the objective for Labour was a League that would prevent future wars, the tying of the League to one particular side in the war would defeat this object.[79] It was necessary for the League to be a completely new body, with the first objective being 'to substitute for war peaceable methods of settling disputes', and generally to establish 'the habit of cooperation'.[80] In order to make the League something new it was necessary to make it democratic, and to remove it from the control of the secret cabinet diplomacy that had started the War in the first place:

> So long as international action is confided only to Governments, it may be doubted whether we shall ever escape from the obsession of force. It is a fiction that any Premier or Foreign Secretary represents a nation. He represents the nations as power...The real basis of internationalism, the common thoughts and interests of populations, will not be reflected.[81]

The League Covenant went some way towards rectifying this by requiring the publication of treaties in order to make them legal. This system of registration was designed to prevent the reoccurrence of the secret agreements that tied states to particular actions without the knowledge or consent of their parliaments. The shock of many Parliamentarians at the revealing of the Anglo-French secret agreements in 1914, agreements that tied Britain to a course of war, was still fresh in the memory. This was, however, as far as the League went. The lack of Parliamentary representation left the League as an organisation of governments, rather than of nations and peoples. H.N. Brailsford had argued that Parliamentary representation in the League was essential both in order to facilitate popular control of League affairs and to break down the national divisions that were at the core of the conflicts under anarchy and the old diplomacy. Parliamentarians, he argued, would tend to group around their party affiliations, which cross national lines. With parties in the League Parliament, national concerns would be blurred and class issues internationalised.[82]

Thus, by making the League a league of sovereign governments the Allies had, in the words of E.D. Morel, 'perpetuated the *pre*-existent anarchy reigning in international relations and consecrated it. They gave it force of law.'[83] The League had emerged as yet another forum for interstate competition, rather than the cornerstone of a new global order. A golden opportunity for ending the threat of war had been passed by.

Some disappointment was also expressed over the new mandate system put in place to administer the former German colonies and non-Turkish Ottoman territories. In its discussion of Labour's war aims in 1918 the Advisory Committee had been wholeheartedly in favour of a League of Nations mandate system, but under the following conditions: 1. that while the 'backward' regions of the former German and Turkish Empire should not be returned to their former masters, they should instead be put under the international control of the new League in trust for their peoples alone;[84] 2. that this system should be extended to all other non-self governing colonies, including those of the victorious powers;[85] 3. since the fight for raw materials, under the logic of anarchy, had largely spurred the scramble for colonies, it would make sense to introduce an open door policy in which trade with these mandates was entirely free, thus removing the control of strategic resources as a cause of international conflict;[86] 4. that the local population's property should be protected from expropriation and foreign exploitation, their resources held in trust for the whole population;[87] and 5. that they should be demilitarised, especially in relation to sub-Saharan Africa, and no troops levied from the native population for use by European powers.[88] This differed slightly from the original position of the Party, which had seen League protection for colonial territories leaving the actual formal sovereignty of the colonial power in place.[89] Generally, though, the position of the Advisory Committee reflected, or became, the view of the Party as a whole.

Although the Mandate provisions in the Covenant were broadly welcomed by Labour, the Party had major reservations about its form. Largely reconciled to the failure of the other colonial powers to respond in kind and make their colonies mandates too, Labour's criticism concentrated on how the former Ottoman and German mandates were treated. Particularly worrying was that, despite League oversight of the mandate system and the ultimate sovereignty of the League, these possessions seemed to remain colonies in all but name for the mandated power. The most flagrant abuse was the unilateral ceding by France of mandated territory to Turkey in exchange for concessions. France had behaved as though the territory was hers to dispose of as she saw fit.[90] In addition, the mandates were not demilitarised, and under French pressure the final draft of the Covenant did not prevent the hiring of native troops.[91] Yet, despite the weaknesses of the mandate system that allowed the continuation of old-style colonial policy, it was cautiously welcomed by Labour writers for the precedent it set. The mandate system was a recognition of the illegality of simple colonial control. 'Like the treaties for the protection of minorities, it gives a legal basis for international criticism and control.' The goal now should be to give the Mandate Commission of the League greater powers of inspection, and action in the case of the infringement of the mandate by the mandated powers.[92]

While the Mandate system showed partiality to the victorious Allies, it was the partiality shown towards the Allies in other aspects of the League that were more worrying. In 1918 Leonard Woolf had counselled that if the League was to function as an effective organisation to prevent war and promote peace it would have to be seen as more than just an organisation of the victorious Allies. For this reason he opposed the establishment of a league amongst the Allies prior to the end of the war.[93] Certainly much of the establishment of the League conformed to Woolf's advice for the establishment of an effective and non-partisan organisation. The League was set up as part of the peace, and the neutrals were encouraged to join. Where the League fell down was in the exclusion of the former Central Powers and Soviet Russia. As a result, the League was perceived as a tool of the victorious Allies.[94] To compound this sense of partiality, the early form and actions of the League were distinctly pro-Allied. The League failed to intervene to stop the Russo-Polish war, there was no effective move towards general disarmament, and no establishment of judicial methods for settling international disputes. In fact, the League remained dominated by the cabinets of the main Allied nations.[95] The belief on the Advisory Committee was that the Allies had never intended the League to be anything more than a continuation of the pre-war order:

> The principal Allied powers, when they made peace in Paris, created a League of Nations, but their object was not to break with the old international system, nor was it reconciliation or co-operation or law and justice. The peace which they made was founded upon force and designed to establish their own military and economic hegemony in Europe and the East. It was an imperialistic peace. But such a peace could not succeed or exist side by side with a real and active League of Nations, and the Governments of the Principal Allied Powers have therefore consistently sabotaged the League created by them.[96]

For many, although not all, in the Advisory Committee and within the Labour Party the main culprit on the Allied side was the French government. It was French foreign policy in the immediate aftermath of the treaties that was most consistently attacked in the Labour press and in the Advisory Committee for returning to the logic of the international anarchy that could only cause another war in the future.

French Imperialism and the Renewal of the International Anarchy

In the immediate post-war period many in the Labour movement became deeply unhappy with the attitudes of the French government towards Germany. This reached a crescendo with the French invasion of the Ruhr in 1923. Looking back in 1924, as Labour formed its first government against the background of continued French occupation of the Ruhr, Norman Angell summed up this attitude to France: 'The very heart of the problem which confronts MacDonald as Foreign Minister, as it was of the problem which confronted Wilson, is the French Statecraft, which has now stood for five years, obstinately and implacably, in the way of European pacification."[97]

Angell was, by comparison, a moderate voice in the Party on the issue of French foreign policy in the early 1920s. E.D. Morel, the main force behind the UDC and editor of its journal *Foreign Affairs*, was quick to see in French diplomacy the main cause of post-war instability. Half-French himself, Morel used his editorship of *Foreign Affairs* to attack French foreign policy. From the first news of the contents of the Peace until his death in 1924 Morel saw little in French actions that was not imperialist, going so far as to view the French and their Tsarist Russian allies as primarily responsible for the war.[98] Perhaps the darkest moment in Morel's attack on France was the publication of his *The Horror on the Rhine*, in which Morel's journalism sunk to a low that seemed odd for a man who had campaigned for the rights of the Congolese before the War. Morel painted a picture of black French troops, removed from the 'unnatural restraints' of their homes, systematically raping German women.[99] Cline points out that Morel's account was largely unfounded, not only were the French troops North African Muslims, and therefore not 'black' or inclined to drunkenness, but there were no serious complaints, along the lines of Morel's argument at least, about their behaviour during the occupation.[100]

Nor could the French government find many friends on the ILP's *New Leader*, where its editor H.N. Brailsford was also frequently critical of French foreign policy. In a memo for the Advisory Committee dated April 1921 Brailsford wrote:

> The basis of the present continental system is the military hegemony of France... it depends on the one-sided reduction of the late enemies' forces, the maintenance of conscription by the victors, and the enlistment of the minor powers as satellites in the orbit of France.[101]

Brailsford saw this French armed hegemony as the military consequence of the peace treaties, and that revision of the peace treaties remained the best means of eliminating this problem.[102] While there were from Brailsford's point of view guilty Frenchmen, it was the context of the Peace and of capitalism itself that was at the root of the problem. This did not, however, stop him making cheap racial jibes, albeit without the hyperbole of Morel, when talking about French African troops.[103] Other voices were more conciliatory. For Helena Swanwick France's 'realist' policy was ultimately self-defeating, and it was necessary to save France from herself. France was bankrupting herself, as well as building up hatred that would eventually turn on her in revenge. The result was that France was now less secure. Swanwick's answer was to convince France that real security did not lie in a militaristic policy.[104] Mitrany made a distinction between the majority of the French and what he referred to as 'official France' that was out to use the Reparations Commission for its own narrow ends.[105]

In all, while the criticisms were rarely levelled directly at the French as a nation, and relations with the powerful French Socialist Party remained business-like, French foreign policy came to embody the threatening return of the principles of the international anarchy that most Labour members and opinion-formers feared would cause another war. This destabilising policy was seen by Dorothy Frances Buxton as a continuation of the war using economic tools. Drawing on an analysis already found in J.A. Hobson's earlier criticism of the economic policy of the Allies as a whole that did not single out France,[106] Buxton marshalled quotes from the French Press and politicians to show that France was deliberately trying to ruin German industry.[107] A dangerous combination of French capitalists after access to cheap coal and militarist patriots seeking security through the ruining of Germany, were following an economic version of the balance of power.[108] Ultimately, Buxton argued, the policy only benefited these cliques. This aggressive policy, by swamping the French and world market with cheap coal obtained as reparations from Germany, was causing unemployment in French and British coal fields. At the same time, as French labour journals were complaining, this same French leadership was blocking the rebuilding programmes in the devastated areas of France.[109] Apart from some of Morel's assaults, these attacks focused on France as the worse offender, but have to be seen within a larger context of the attack on the behaviour of the Allies as a whole. For people like Buxton France was the worst case of a common feature of Allied governments after the war: government dominated by an unholy alliance of militarists and sectional capitalist interests that were pushing an imperialist policy in tune with the international anarchy that started the war in the first place.

While the response to French foreign policy from people like Morel could be accused of grandstanding, hyperbole and serious overstatement, their descriptions of French policy were not far off what many in French political circles, especially but not exclusively on the French right, were thinking. Clemenceau's position at the Paris Peace Conference had been overwhelmingly that of narrow French security interests, and despite his socialist credentials and his hilarious bon mots at the expense of the pomposities of other delegates, Clemenceau's position was clearly that of a supporter of the international anarchy that had preceded the war. His main preoccupation was with the balance of power between France and Germany, and his stance at the Peace Conference was largely guided by the idea that either France had to be strengthened or Germany weakened. Outside of the negotiations, France established alliances with key states in east and central Europe such as Poland, Romania, Czechoslovakia and Yugoslavia. In the negotiations the French delegates insisted on the right to raise native troops in the mandates under French control, despite the objections of the American delegation. The French reasoning was that the serious imbalance between French and German manpower could be redressed by the use of more French colonial troops.[110] French attempts to weaken Germany included the abortive attempt to create a separate independent state in the Rhineland, supporting Polish claims in Upper Silesia and the Polish Corridor, the disarmament of Germany under the treaty, and pushing for higher reparations payments from Germany.[111] France's position was further underscored by anecdotal incidents, such as the strongly pro-Polish position of the French commissioner on the Upper Silesia Plebiscite Commission.[112] The logic that underpinned these policies was that another Franco-German conflict was inevitable. To many on the British left, and even many on the right, this was a dangerous self-fulfilling prophecy.

Yet, despite the tirade against French imperialism in the British left-wing press and parts of the Labour Party, Labour policy in government was more conciliatory. As we shall see in the next chapter, once in power in 1924 Labour tried to steer a middle course between French and German demands, with the ultimate goal of easing Franco-German tensions. The election in 1924 of a more conciliatory left-wing French Government also greatly helped here. Ultimately, while British Conservative Governments tended to be more open to French security concerns, Labour in Government never reflected the rhetoric of the anti-French diatribes of the early 1920s. At the same time, both Labour and Conservative Governments never really took seriously the French position that French security concerns should be settled prior to the establishment of any system of disarmament and arbitration. While the French position towards Germany in the 1920s may have been a self-fulfilling prophecy, French concerns about a rearmed Germany proved all too real a decade later. Whether that threat in the 1930s would have been lessened by a more conciliatory French attitude in the 1920s is one of those questions beloved of counter-factual history.

The Democratisation of Foreign Policy

Not all of Labour's intellectual activity in the immediate post-war period was taken up with criticisms of the flawed peace. On the constructive side Labour developed a clear programme for the democratisation of foreign policy. For many in the Party one of the major problems in the conduct of foreign policy was its secret and undemocratic nature. Indeed, the issue was the subject of a full chapter in Brailsford's *War of Steel and Gold* in 1914,[113] and the influence of Brailsford on the Advisory Committee's memoranda on this issue are evident in many of their proposals. Consistent with Labour's view of the intimate connection between the international and domestic political spheres was the contention that a cabinet-dominated secret diplomacy was a major contributing factor towards creating an anarchical international regime. The undemocratic consequences of the Peace and the League were, in their turn, a consequence of the undemocratic nature of the diplomacy that created them. The Advisory Committee worked on a number of policy documents that suggested democratic reforms in foreign policy, all of which had the intent of strengthening democratic control over the creation of foreign policy. A number of these suggestions were later implemented by Labour Governments, and to this day remain essential parts of the Parliamentary control of foreign policy in Britain. One Advisory Committee memo on this issue was even a source of friction with Ramsay MacDonald.

While there was a widespread feeling within the Advisory Committee, not to mention in society as a whole, that an undemocratic foreign policy structure was a major cause of the international anarchy, it was a former diplomat, George Young, who contributed the most detailed memos on the foreign services and diplomacy. The Advisory Committee also included one other former diplomat, Arthur Ponsonby, who also made vital contributions on this subject.[114] The importance that the Advisory Committee attached to the issue of the reform of diplomacy can be seen by the level of its output on the issue. As early as July 1918, only two months after the Committee first met, Young submitted an 11-page memo on the foreign services. Over the next three years there was a pamphlet on democratic control and a second 13-page memo on the reform of diplomacy.[115] A section on open diplomacy and Parliamentary control was also added to the 1921 Advisory Committee 'Draft Pamphlet on Foreign Policy.'[116] Throughout these memoranda the link is made between the lack of democratic control of foreign policy and the continuation of the international anarchy that makes the outbreak of another general war possible, a point already made by Ponsonby in 1915[117]. Secrecy, which was at the heart of the old diplomacy, was premised on the idea 'that foreign relations are really a struggle between two parties', and that this secrecy is needed to outwit your opponent.[118] This gave the talk of democratic reform a certain urgency, and led to detailed proposals for an incoming Labour Government. Generally speaking, there were two major areas for reform. First, there was the extension of Parliamentary oversight of foreign policy; and second, there was the overhaul of the foreign services.

With the Party's Parliamentary experience it is perhaps not surprising that the reforms aimed at extending Parliamentary control were the least contentious and easily enacted by the Labour Government in 1924. In addition to this, there was a ready template for Parliamentary oversight of foreign affairs in its regulation of home affairs. In fact, the memoranda used the generally accepted Labour notion that internal and external affairs were inseparable to argue that foreign affairs should necessarily be subject to the same constraints and processes as home affairs.[119] Initially, this would mean the removal of the right of the Foreign Secretary and Prime Minister to refuse to answer questions in the House on the grounds of national security. This did not mean that, during a negotiation at least, certain aspects could not be kept secret. It did mean, however, that the Foreign Secretary, and through him the Foreign Office itself, had a duty to inform the House of outcomes of negotiations.[120] A major part of the recommendations in the memoranda cover the establishment of a permanent Foreign Affairs Committee in Parliament, which would oversee the Foreign Office's execution of foreign policy, and would have access to relevant papers and documents.[121] Since similar procedures were now in place in France Germany and the USA there were ready templates already in existence for how this committee could function. Brailsford had suggested just such a committee back in 1914, while Ponsonby did the same in 1915.[122] This Committee might also play a major role in formulating the objectives for any international negotiations,[123] although the memoranda did not always question the government's right to set its own objectives providing that these were communicated to Parliament.[124] Interestingly, in a display of their realistic attitude towards legislative shortcomings, the pamphlet *Control of Foreign Policy* recognised that such a committee could be abused. A particular worry was that it could become a tool for the foreign minister, as it had in Germany, and turn into a weak institution that gave only the semblance of democratic control.[125] Despite this, the establishment of a permanent Foreign Affairs Committee remained at the centre of Labour's proposals for extending Parliamentary control. The memoranda also saw a crucial role for Parliament as a whole. In the new spirit of open diplomacy it was suggested that no treaty should enter into force until it had been ratified by Parliament, and that the consent of Parliament should be required for any declaration of war or military action.[126] One of the lasting legacies of the first Labour Government of 1924 was the establishment of the principle that Parliament should have the final word on international treaties through the exercise of the so-called Ponsonby Rule, named after Arthur Ponsonby, who by then was the Under-Secretary of State for Foreign Affairs. [127] The Ponsonby rule states that international treaties are made available to Parliament for a period of 21 days, giving Parliamentarians time to decide whether there would needs to be a debate on the treaty in Parliament. Despite exceptions and clarifications over the years, this rule is now a natural part of the power and role of Parliament in government.

The proposals for the reform of the foreign services owe much of their rigor and attention to detail to the work done by George Young on the Advisory Committee, although Brailsford's knowledge of the more meritocratic British consular service in Macedonia (part of the Levantine Consular Service) is also evident.[128] Without Young's insider knowledge Labour's recommendations for the democratisation and professionalisation of diplomacy would lack the force that they had. Yet, unlike the reforms to Parliamentary oversight, the proposed reforms of the diplomatic service represented a more root and branch overhaul of an institution that had little connection or sympathy with Labour and the labour movement. Young's starting point was that diplomacy as practiced under the international anarchy had made itself the opposite of democracy, and that this lack of democratic credentials and oversight had meant that diplomacy served itself rather than the interests of the nation. The net result was that British diplomacy was inefficient. Democratisation was, therefore, not merely an end in itself, but also a means by which the foreign services could be made efficient and productive: 'there can be no real diplomacy where there is no democracy.'[129] Young's criticisms and recommendations were accepted by the Executive, and formed a large part of Labour's *Control of Foreign Policy* pamphlet.

The major problem with the conduct of diplomacy was its obsolete structures and procedures. Despite the findings of a 1914 Royal Commission, which had recommended amalgamation, the British foreign services remained divided into a three tier system that still reflected the *ancient regime's* division of society into three estates. There were the senior diplomats, the consular service that dealt with trade and technical issues, and a third estate of clerks and minor functionaries. There was little mobility between these, and the lack of decent pay at the senior level meant that only those with access to other sources of income could afford it.[130] Stuck in an earlier age of gentility, the diplomatic service had little knowledge of the forces that were now dominant in international affairs, especially technical issues and the internationalising effects of both capital and labour.[131] This largely explained the atavistic policies followed by the old diplomacy, where an anti-democratic secret diplomacy was premised on the natural competition of discreet states. Young, following an analysis that drew freely from Angell's view of the interdependence of the global economy, argued that the failure of the old diplomacy to maintain the peace in 1914 was the result of its failure to apply the various economic and technical international forces and institutions that now existed. These new forces were non-national in character, and therefore outside of the competence of the old diplomacy.[132]

Labour's proposed reforms followed from these criticisms. The amalgamation of the three services was the least contentious, since the Royal Commission had already proposed the amalgamation of two of the three. The introduction of new recruits, so that the Foreign Service would more accurately reflect British society, was another easy proposal to make, although Young cautioned that this in itself was not enough, since without changes to the institutional culture of the foreign services bourgeois and proletarian recruits would merely be co-opted into the old gentility.[133] Real democratic control was necessary in order to develop a diplomacy that served real national interests. One of Labour's recommendations was to facilitate stronger political control by adopting the American system of making ambassadors political appointments, so that embassies abroad would mix political control at the top with administrative professionalism below.[134] The most far-reaching changes, however, were the proposals to reorganise the diplomatic services in order to reflect the realities of international affairs in the 1920s. This would mean simultaneously the introduction of technical and regional departments. The technical departments would liaise with the various functional organisations that now regulated so much of the international interactions and acted as 'machineries of internationalisation.'[135] The regional departments would continue the work of the diplomat, but would concentrate on interactions with specific regions. The result of this regionalisation would be to maximise local knowledge in the diplomatic corps, which was now seen as a necessity in a world that included so many more states with a myriad of new national problems and frictions.[136] In effect the diplomatic corps, which had been working inefficiently by applying pre-industrial social norms to an interdependent industrialised society, should be reshaped to conform to the new realities of industrialisation.

Thus democratisation of foreign policy was seen in two ways. First, it was direct political control or oversight of the machineries of foreign policy; and second, it was the reformulation of the machineries of foreign policy so that it would better reflect both British society as a whole, and the new internationalised realities of capitalism, labour and technical co-operation. This democratisation, however, was not merely a good in itself. It was a source of efficiency, both in the sense of a diplomatic corps that could better serve British interests and in the sense of a foreign policy that would reflect the changed realities of an industrialised and interdependent world. The undemocratic nature of foreign policy was a major cause, in the opinion of the Labour intellectuals, of the continuation of the principles of the international anarchy. Crucial to their analysis is the view that far from being more efficient, the old diplomacy and the international anarchy it served were inefficient leftovers from a more simple age. This was a central plank of the early interdependence theory that underpinned Labour's policy towards the League of Nations during the decade prior to the collapse of the second Labour Government in 1931. Earlier varieties of this interdependence theory had been propounded by Norman Angell and H.N. Brailsford in their pre-war classics *The Great Illusion* and *The War of Steel and Gold*, and were at this stage fully absorbed into the thinking of the Advisory Committee.

While there tended to be widespread agreement on the reforms suggested between 1918 and 1921, Labour's attitude to the Foreign Office bureaucracy was later a major source of friction between Ramsay Mac-Donald, the PLP leader and sometime Labour Prime Minister, and the Advisory Committee. In the wake of the collapse of the First Labour Government in 1924, for reasons that will be explained in the next chapter, Labour members were generally suspicious of the Foreign Office civil servants. In 1925 the Advisor Committee suggested that, in the event of a second Labour government, pro-Party appointees should be placed in key positions in the Foreign Office.[137] Having acted as his own Foreign Secretary in the outgoing Labour Government, Ramsay MacDonald felt that this suggestion was impractical and subversive.[138] From MacDonald's point of view a 'more prolonged tenure of office by us would have changed the spirit of the Office and that is the thing that we have to work for.'[139] While MacDonald's attitude to the Foreign Office was consistent with his habit as Prime Minister to trust his civil servants more than his Party colleagues (a character trait that was to exasperate friends like Norman Angell, and contributed to the disaster of 1931), his gradualist approach was the one adopted by Arthur Henderson when he became Foreign Secretary in 1929. Still, this vignette demonstrates that opinions within the Labour Party and the Advisory Committee were frequently divided. The divisions between the majority on the Advisory Committee and MacDonald were, however, minor compared to the divisions over foreign policy within the Party as a whole.

Pacifism and Radical Socialism:
The Splits in Labour over Foreign Policy

While the vast bulk of the Labour Party could agree on what they did not like in the immediate post-war period, the generally critical tone of Labour pronouncements at the time tended to hide the major disagreements in the Party over what a new international order should look like. These divisions would come out most clearly when the Party came to discuss the issue of League sanctions in support of pooled security during the mid and late twenties. As soon as support for the League became Labour policy disquiet about the militaristic consequences of pooled security began to concern the pacifist wing, while a belief that the League was a tool of capitalism worried many of the radical socialists. All could agree that the peace treaties had continued too much of the old international anarchy, and all were united in their condemnation of the old diplomacy. As long as Labour's position on foreign affairs concentrated on condemnation they could present a united front on the issues. Yet, because a large part of the leadership and the Advisory Committee were committed to working to reform the Peace through active participation in the League, confrontation within the Party over international policy was a foregone conclusion.

It is tempting to see the splits within Labour's foreign policy as a clear cut one between the old Liberals and the original Labour Representation Committee people. What is interesting, however, is that the divisions in Labour cut across these divides. While many former Liberals backed Arthur Henderson's position on the League, a not insignificant number of the new recruits to Labour were the most vocal in their opposition to League sanctions and to any use of the military. Some recruits, like Stafford Cripps, were the most openly socialist in their public pronouncements, and the most suspicious of any force employed by a capitalist state, even under League auspices. On the Advisory Committee Arthur Ponsonby and C.R. Buxton were vocal opponents of a stronger League with sanctioning powers. On the other hand, the major Trades Union leaders were often in the forefront of the campaign for rearmament and collective defence in the 1930s. Key ex-Liberal recruits, such as Hugh Dalton and Philip Noel Baker, worked closely with those who had come up through the Unions such as Arthur Henderson, and later Ernest Bevin. These splits in Labour can be overplayed, however. Only after 1931 did the splits over foreign policy lead to a sustained debate within the Party. This is not to say that differences did not surface before; E.D. Morel's vitriolic campaign against MacDonald's conciliatory policy to France in 1924, and the splits on the Advisory Committee over League sanctions in the mid-1920s show that they were never far below the surface. While chapter three will concentrate on the League foreign policy that was constructed by the majority on the Advisory Committee and the Party Executive, it is important to adumbrate the two alternative traditions that existed in the Party, which were particularly vocal during the period of the Peace Conference, and had a brief Indian summer after Labour's 1931 electoral debacle.

The main spokesman for the pacifist tradition in the PLP was George Lansbury, a dedicated Christian socialist from Bow in the East End of London. A working class man with a gift for writing passionate and articulate prose, Lansbury edited Labour's *Daily Herald* for much of the interwar period. He served as Labour MP for Bow and Bromley for most of his political life. Like Ramsay MacDonald, Lansbury had come to Labour via the SDF and the ILP, and like MacDonald he had opposed the First World War without reservation. Lansbury's condemnation of the Versailles Treaty, which he described as a 'peace of hate',[140] was based on the same rejection of the international anarchy that was found in the writings of Woolf, Brailsford or Angell, although Lansbury's stress was as much on the moral failings of the system as it was on the system's inefficiency:

'European diplomacy, with its secret arrangements, treaties, covenants, is proof that modern statesmen act up to a creed that what is morally evil must be politically right if it is to the interest of the nation it should be so. The result of this policy is seen in the world chaos amid which we live today.[141]

Where Lansbury parted company with the majority on the Advisory Committee and leaders like MacDonald and Henderson was over the issue of the use of coercion as a means of opposing aggression and upholding international law and stability. For Lansbury it did not matter whether a war was waged by a nation or 'a group of nations, called a League, against one or more offending members', it was impossible in his mind 'to establish peace by brute force'.[142] Rather, Lansbury supported the idea of disarmament by example. An illustration of the unilateral disarmament position that reappeared in Labour foreign policy debates in the early 1980's. His views on the League were, by and large, positive, but he saw it as a committee for discussing a new peaceful order, rather than one for imposing international order. The fact that he does not seem to have attended Advisory Committee meetings suggests that he felt that his faith and logic had already given him the answers he required to understand what was needed in foreign affairs.

While a major influence on the pacifist wing of the Party, Lansbury was certainly not its only leading figure. Arthur Ponsonby, a convert from the Liberals, shared his views about armaments and the League, although not necessarily Lansbury's strong Christian faith.[143] Ponsonby's influence amongst Labour pacifists led Catherine Cline to regard him as the leader of the pacifist section of the Party.[144] Like Lansbury, his attacks on the treaties were indistinguishable from the rest of the Party's opinion formers. Generally, he supported the idea of the League, but believed that the Covenant was ill-conceived, and the punitive peace based on the old diplomacy severely weakened the effectiveness of the League.[145] While other members of the Advisory Committee were moving towards support for League pooled security, Ponsonby attacked what he called the myth of the aggressor state. International conflict for Ponsonby was a complex mix of causes, and it was not possible to make a clear decision about who the aggressor was in any particular conflict. His resulting opposition to sanctions, and advocacy of disarmament by example brought him into alignment with George Lansbury.[146] Two other major pacifist figures in the Labour Party, C.R. Buxton and Helen Swanick, went as far as to accept the provision of League sanctions that were contained in the abortive League Protocol, but later reneged and returned to a more pacifist position. Buxton, whose pacifism was rooted in his Quaker faith, carried much weight in the Party through his chairmanship of the Advisory Committee. He finally resigned the chair of the Advisory Committee in 1937 in protest at the Party's decision not to oppose the National Government's defence estimates, complaining that his principles had often made him 'a minority of one on the Committee.'[147] Helen Swanwick, like many pacifists, continued to mix opposition to international sanctions with support for a League that led by moral example.[148]

While there was much overlap between the pacifist wing of the Party and the radical socialist group that opposed League collective security – after all pacifists like Lansbury were also strong socialists – there was also a sharp difference. Radical socialist opposition to sanctions, and later collective security under the League, did not draw its inspiration from a pacifist rejection of all war, but from a deep suspicion of the League's links to capitalism. To a certain extent Brailsford was linked to this way of thinking. Despite his conversion to the possibilities of the League in 1924, he still continued to feel that real change would only come about with the replacement of capitalism with socialism. This was the common view of many socialists: that without a proper socialist order that eliminated the forces in capitalism which created imperialism in the first place, there could be no permanent and stable peace. This led to some shared goals with the pacifist wing. For example, members of the ILP and SDF were frequently advocating blanket opposition to the Service Estimates that passed through Parliament.[149] While the pacifists opposed the estimates because of their opposition to armaments, the radical socialists did so out of opposition to the idea of arming a capitalist nation like Britain.

In the 1930s the main advocate of the radical socialist position in the PLP and the Party as a whole was Stafford Cripps, whose conflict with the Party leadership over rearmament and collective defence led to his temporary expulsion from the Party in 1939. For Cripps a functioning international order had to be preceded by the victory of socialism, and even as the storm clouds of fascism gathered, his opposition to rearmament remained a serious source of friction with Henderson, Dalton and Bevin. When Lansbury told Henderson that he hoped Cripps would follow him as Party leader, Henderson replied that 'if that happened, I would feel that all that I have worked for had gone for nothing'.[150] Since Henderson particularly prided himself on his international work we can assume that this was as much a comment on Cripps' view of foreign policy as anything else. Cripps' view of the League was famously negative. At the 1935 Party Conference he was quoted as having called the League, which included the Soviet Union at the time, an 'International Burglars Union.'[151] Throughout the late 1930s he denounced League collective security as a cloak for Anglo-French imperialism, likening it to the anti-Comintern pact between the main fascist powers.[152] This, combined with his obtuse oratory, led Dalton to write in his diary that 'Tory HQ regard him as their greatest electoral asset.'[153]

This aside, Cripps' undoubted talents as an advocate (he was a successful King's Counsel, earning as much as £30,000 a year from legal fees) and his heartfelt commitment to the creation of a just and egalitarian society made him many friends, especially in the United States. In 1936 John Gunther of the *Chicago Daily News* singled out Cripps as a potential leader of the Labour Party along with the more conservative Herbert Morrison. Gunther admired Cripps' 'passionate radical sincerity of his convictions'.[154] Cripps was also the subject of a hagiography by the American sociologist Eric Estorick, on the front cover of which the publisher's had written: 'Here is told for the first time fully the career of a man who sums up in himself what Americans think of as the best of England'.[155] What seemed to particularly endear him to his anti-fascist American audience was his strong advocacy of a popular front with the Communists against the National Government's policy of appeasement. The leadership of the Labour Party saw it differently, and Cripps' agitation through the Socialist League led to his expulsion from the Party in 1939 for reasons that will be explained in chapter four.

The pacifist and radical socialist oppositions to League sanctions and collective security would become particularly important after 1924, when their clashes with the supporters of sanctions formed part of a crucial debate within the British public in general, and within the Labour Party in particular. The success of the supporters of pooled security in influencing Party policy was to give the Party a clear and consistent foreign policy that, despite a low point after 1931, translated into support for collective defence in the lead up to war. In the short term, though, the often bruising public disagreements between the advocates of pooled security with sanctions under the League and the pacifist/socialist opposition frequently gave the electorate the impression that Labour was more confused over foreign policy than it really was. Attempts to placate the pacifist wing of the Party left Labour open to later criticisms by both Winston Churchill and Quentin Hogg that it was 'riddled with pacifism', and consequently partially to blame for Britain's lack of preparedness in 1939.[156] I will deal with this issue in more detail in chapter four.

The Peace Treaties as a Continuation of the International Anarchy
Labour's opposition to the 1919 peace settlement, especially the final form of the League, was no mere knee-jerk reaction to a peace from which it had been excluded – even though Mary Agnes Hamilton suggests that within her circle in the Party they would have denounced the Versailles Treaty 'whatever it had been.'[157] Rather, the opposition in the Advisory Committee was born of deep disappointment at the missed opportunities. Crucial to Labour's criticism was the failure of the treaties to create a new order that would eliminate what many saw as the major cause of the war: the international anarchy. Here Labour was drawing from a rich vein of theoretical work on the form and structure of the international system, and it was through such outlets as the memoranda of the Advisory Committee that the Party had access to analyses of the treaties and the League that grounded their findings in the theoretical literature of such IR scholars as Norman Angell, H.N. Brailsford, Leonard Woolf, G. Lowes Dickinson and J.A. Hobson. This literature had, even before the outbreak of war, viewed the international anarchy as a cause of destructive inter-state conflict. The criticisms of French policy were also rooted in this general analysis of the nature of the international anarchy, even if it reached extremes of xenophobic racism with the later writings of E.D. Morel.

Perhaps, though, the violence of the reaction to the peace treaties had as much to do with the hopeful signs that had punctuated the peace process before and during the Paris Conference. Wilson's Fourteen Points had raised hopes across Europe, but particularly in the Labour Party. The various labour and socialist conferences from 1917 onwards had offered serious alternatives to a vindictive peace, while the collapse of the Tsarist autocracy, the Habsburg Monarchy and the German Imperial Government seemed to suggest the broader triumph of democratic doctrines. In many ways the Peace had been loyal to many of these new principles. A League of Nations and the International Labour Organization were established as part of the Peace, Germany was not partitioned as many of the French Government and military wanted, plebiscites were held, self-determination was included as a criteria in deciding borders, and the mandate system for the ex-German and Ottoman colonial territories established the principle that colonial possessions were ultimately trusteeships for their populations, rather than the property of their colonial masters. Despite the ham-fisted nature of the reparations regime, Germany was able to recover economically, and abortive attempts were made to include Soviet Russia in the Peace process. Hamilton's view that Labour was bound to oppose the treaties may explain the over-reaction in the immediate aftermath of the Peace. After all, in many respects even those aspects of the 1919 Peace that Labour so viciously condemned proved to be more anodyne on closer inspection. Much of the anger in Germany at the Treaty of Versailles was based on the misconception that Germany had not been defeated in the war, when in fact from August to November 1918 the German Army on the western front had been soundly beaten: 'the collapse of Germany began... on the Western Front in consequence of defeat in the field'.[158] The terms of Versailles reflected that defeat. The so-called 'war guilt clause' of the Versailles Treaty with Germany, officially just Article 231 of the Treaty, was not a special clause added in order to deliberately target Germany, but was rather just used to establish Germany's liability to pay reparations. Similar articles appeared in the treaties of Trianon and Saint Germain with Hungary and Austria.[159] Reparations did not come as a shock to the German government. 'Reparation for damage done' had been part of Article XIX of the November 1918 Armistice.[160] Even the final reparations figures show that its damaging effect on Germany was more psychological.

The final figure was set in London in 1921 at 132 billion marks. In reality, through an ingenious system of bonds and complex clauses,

Germany was committed to pay less than half that amount…Germany also got generous credits for payments it had already made…

In the final reckoning Germany may have paid about 22 billion gold marks in the whole period between 1918 and 1932. This is probably slightly less than what France, with a much smaller economy, paid Germany after the Franco-Prussian War of 1870–1.[161]

The great failing of the Peace was not that it was a thoroughly flawed return to the old international anarchy that had caused the War to begin with. Its crime was that it adopted parts of the new approaches to foreign affairs, but ultimately adulterated them with an over-riding concern for the old power politics. If the Peace had been truly vindictive, like the peace without a treaty that followed the Second World War, Germany would not have been in a position to play the great power as it did after 1924, and certainly would not have been such a threat to world peace after 1936. The Labour critics were attacking a process and outcome that had promised so much, and yet had delivered so little. In this sense they shared with the German public a sense of outrage at the collapse of the high hopes that had been manifest in the Fourteen Points and all the talk of an effective league to replace the old international anarchy. In 1944 Mary Agnes Hamilton bemoaned the fact that she, and others like her, had been so successful in denouncing the Treaty of Versailles, and that their minority view in 1919 had, on the basis of shallow understandings of the peace, become the dominant view. 'We had gravely exaggerated the case against the Treaty', she admitted.[162]

Yet, the seeds of a more positive pro-League policy were here, even in the bitterest of the denunciations of the League and the Peace. While some strands of thought within the Labour Party continued to maintain an anti-pooled security position, others were convinced that in a largely interdependent world, were economic linkages meant that security itself had moved beyond the old diplomacy, the only serious alternative to international anarchy was an effective League-based system of common security. A few, like Philip Noel Baker, could certainly be described as pro-League, although for many the League was a rather imperfect means towards a far better end. Consequently, the support given to the League by Woolf, Angell and Mitrany tended to be conditional on the League being capable of delivering an effective system of security, and by the mid-1930s both Woolf and Mitrany, in different degrees, had ceased to give support to certain aspects of the League's work. The idea of the League continued in the concept of collective defence against fascism, and eventually evolved into support for the United Nations machinery after 1944.

Although it is anachronistic to use the term interdependence theory here, we can see in the 1918–22 discussions of the Peace and the League in the Advisory Committee clear parallels with the interdependence theory of the 1970s. The proposals for the democratisation of foreign policy on the Advisory Committee reflected both an attack on the old diplomacy, and an appreciation of the changed interdependent world that made a more democratic and technical diplomacy a necessity. Their views of the interdependence of the international economy, and their appreciation of the knock-on effects of international conflict, would blossom into a fully-fledged theoretical position that would support the development of a pro-League policy within the Labour Party. Much of the theoretical output of the Advisory Committee members fed directly into the policy debates in the Labour Party on the development of the League system. The discussions in the Advisory Committee about the use and reform of the League began to gather pace from 1922, but it was not until Labour's first experience of government in 1924 that the Party supported a fully-fledged League-based pooled security system. In the words of Catherine Cline, it was 'the sobering experience of the responsibilities of office in 1924 rather than the shock of Hitler's rise in the 1930s' which explains the change from a perfectionist and critical approach towards a policy that attempted to engage and use the machinery left to them by the Paris peace treaties.[163]

3

THE LEAGUE AND THE
NEW DIPLOMACY (1922–1931)

Philip Noel Baker

...it is undoubtedly the case that insofar as attitudes towards war
have been transformed, and machinery for preventing it devised,
much is owed to peace campaigners such as Philip Noel-Baker.[1]

Time has not been kind to the legacy of Philip Noel Baker. His eight
single-authored books remain largely unread and unreferenced by present
day IR scholars and students, even though his work on disarmament and
the international rule of law were highly regarded at the time, and he
received a Nobel prize for his writing on the arms race. He is rarely mentioned in histories of the Labour Party despite the positions he held in
both the Party and in government. Alone amongst Labour's international
writers he attended the Paris Peace Conference as part of Robert Cecil's
staff, and while there helped in the drafting of the League Covenant. Not
surprisingly he was not involved in the earlier denunciations of the
League, rather prior to 1922 he worked for the League in Geneva. On his
return he worked for Lord Cecil again when the latter, as Lord Privy Seal,
was given responsibility for League policy in the Conservative Government. In 1924 he became the first professor of International Relations at
LSE. Elected to Parliament in 1929, he was Arthur Henderson's Parliamentary Private Secretary at the Foreign Office from 1929 to 1931, and
then Henderson's assistant to the Disarmament Conference until 1933.
After holding a professorship at Yale in 1934, he returned to Parliament in
1936 He was a member of the wartime coalition, with responsibility for
transportation, and in the 1945–51 Labour governments held three
separate posts, the last of which held Cabinet rank. While Minister of State

at the Foreign Office he helped with the establishment of the new United Nations, and was a UN delegate during 1945–6. Following in the footsteps of Arthur Henderson and Norman Angell, he was awarded the Nobel Peace Prize in 1959. He continued to serve as a Labour MP until 1970, and was raised to the House of Lords in 1977, five years before his death. Within the Party, he served on the Executive, and was a regular member of the International Sub-Committee. Noel Baker co-wrote with Leonard Woolf the international section of the 1928 policy document *Labour and the Nation*, and was a major contributor to Labour's war aims statements discussed in more detail in chapter five. Noel Baker was a regular member of the Advisory Committee on International Questions, and wrote many of the Committee's memoranda. On top of all this he was captain of the 1912 British Olympic team. There remains a certain amount of confusion over his name. Born Philip Baker, he added his wife's name to his in 1922 to become Philip Noel Baker. Later he hyphenated the last two to become Noel-Baker. As a result of this his written work can be found under three different names. Indeed, this seemed to confuse the wartime German Gestapo. Noel Baker appears twice on their list – the Sonderfahndungsliste GB – of people marked for arrest in the wake of a possible German invasion of Britain: Once under Baker-Noel, and once under Noel-Baker.[2]

There is one recent book-length appraisal of Noel Baker's work, published in 1989, while Lorna Lloyd's sympathetic yet critical 1995 chapter in the Wilson and Long collection gives an excellent appraisal of his agitation for the establishment of international peace through law.[3] Lloyd admits that her chapter is only a partial study, and by concentrating on one aspect of Noel Baker's work she has not engaged with other features, such as his interest in the problems of disarmament. Noel Baker was a keen advocate of the connection between disarmament, arbitration and sanctions, and the need to develop international agreements that filled in the holes in the League's system of pooled security. During the 1930s he continued to promote the use of League collective security against fascism, even after other members of the Advisory Committee had lowered their sights and were advocating a smaller alliance built around France and Britain. He was the author of Labour's first comprehensive statement of war aims in 1940–1, and contributed substantially to Hugh Dalton's 1943–4 statement. Generally, his writing during our period can be divided into three parts. There was his work on the gaps in the Covenant up to 1931, especially his writings on the inter-relationship between disarmament, arbitration and sanctions; his appraisal of the role of the League; and his work on the post-war settlement.

If Philip Noel Baker is known for anything today it is for his work on disarmament. 'Five of his eight single-authored books dealt with disarmament, as did most of his other writings.'[4] While much of his international writings have been allowed to gather dust, his 1936 book *The Private Manufacture of Arms* was reprinted in New York by Dover in 1972. His work on disarmament, however, was embedded in a wider view of the functioning of the League system of pooled security. Specifically, a successful disarmament regime was dependent on the development and implementation of rules of arbitration and adequate sanctions at the League of Nations. Generally, the fulfilment and development of disarmament, arbitration and sanctions at the League of Nations was interpreted as closing gaps in the 1919 Covenant of the League. These issues will be discussed in more detail below. Here I want to concentrate on Noel Baker's contribution to the subject.

While many on the pacifist wing of the Labour Party advocated disarmament by example, Noel Baker insisted that a precondition for general disarmament was the removal of the main cause of the build-up of arms: the threat of private war between states. In fact, as far as he was concerned no progress could be made on the question of disarmament without an adequate resolution of the issue of security from war and aggression.[5] One part of this, he felt, was the giving up of the right to resort to war. The right to declare war under certain circumstances was still sanctioned under Article 15 of the Covenant. The French had already stipulated that they considered adequate security arrangements as a precondition for disarmament,[6] and Noel Baker knew that a mere paper denunciation of war and armaments would be valueless without adequate security arrangements in the event of aggression.[7] It was for this reason that Noel Baker did not advocate complete disarmament. Nor could disarmament follow to the letter the disarmament of Germany, which had limited the purpose of the German military to maintaining internal order. Member states of the League needed to have enough military might available in order for them to fulfil their obligations under Article 8 of the Covenant for 'the enforcement by common action of international obligations.' Any system that outlawed war would require 'the Members of the League to take a share by military action in the international policing of the world'.[8] This put him at odds with many of his colleagues in the Party, who opposed any form of military action even under the auspices of the League; but placed him firmly in with the group around Arthur Henderson and Hugh Dalton, who favoured a tougher sanctions regime.

The idea of 'League wars' sanctioned by the Covenant was a deeply controversial issue. While for Noel Baker it was a necessary part of the wider machinery of a more secure and peaceful world, for Labour colleagues like C.R. Buxton, Arthur Ponsonby and George Lansbury it was the continuation of war and the international anarchy under a new name. The major criticism levelled at the idea of sanctions in the event of an aggression was that it was not possible to adequately define aggressor in any conflict, and hence the whole concept of sanctions would be at best a muddle, and at worst open to abuse. Noel Baker heartily disagreed with this view. In 1925 he endorsed the Shotwell Committee's test of aggression as the unwillingness to submit a dispute to arbitration while resorting to war at the same time.[9] This test had already formed the basis of Leonard Woolf's conception of aggression in a draft report for the International Socialist Conference in 1922.[10] This definition of aggression had the added advantage of reinforcing the arbitration proposals contained in the various attempts to plug the gaps in the Covenant.

While Noel Baker was keen to point out that effective disarmament would only work alongside a system of arbitration and sanctions that could guarantee security, he also saw the current form and levels of national armaments as a cause of war in themselves. This was the main reason why he was so adamant that disarmament under the auspices of the League should go ahead. The existence of the huge arsenals associated with the modern state simultaneously led to instability via the fear of attack and to the temptation to launching an attack.[11] On top of this, the growth in the size of armed forces had created a military class that was unduly influential in international affairs:

> At moments of crisis this influence of the military staff, pressing for a decisive blow at a favourable moment, may become irresistible in circumstances where the statesmen, left to themselves, might aver to resort to war.[12]

Central to Noel Baker's analysis of disarmament was the view that the current level of armaments was of recent vintage. 'It is only from about 1860 onwards that the Governments began to build up their modern forces', and consequently disarmament was a response to a very recent and destabilising increase in weaponry.[13] While advocates of armaments build-ups claimed that the reasons for the acquisition of arms were rational ones of self-preservation, Noel Baker thought that it was often for far more complex and non-rational motives. The system of the private manufacture of arms – which made of armaments a business, and hence created a series of vested interests in the manufacture and sale of weapons – had developed a logic of its own that encouraged arms build-ups, and consequently added to global instability.[14] Alongside this, people had a sentimental attachment to arms that belied their dangerous destabilising aspect. 'General Smuts has told us of men who, at the end of the Boer War, were ready to give up the national independence for which they had been prepared to sacrifice their lives, but who refused to give up the rifles which had gone with them through the fight.'[15]

The final problem with disarmament was the nature of the technology itself. Military technology could not be easily disentangled from civilian technologies, and any disarmament treaty would have to cope with the problem that 'the transformation [of equipment like aircraft] from commercial to military use is the work of an hour or two.'[16] The linkage between civilian and military technology also meant that industrial strength, even when it was purely for civilian use, was now 'a factor of military force', while scientific research was regularly making new weapons available to governments.[17] For all of these reasons disarmament could never be a freestanding solution to the problems caused by armaments. Rather, it could only be realised within the broader problem of security. Disarmament without the establishment of a wider system of security would merely leave disarmed states open to invasion. It would only be possible after two conditions had been met: 1. the closing of the gap in the Covenant in Article 15 by removing the right of states to resort to war; and 2. the elaboration of arrangements in the event of aggression.[18]

Given his view that an effective security regime would require strong legal controls, it is no wonder that Noel Baker consistently supported the idea of a League of Nations with teeth. This did not mean that he was happy with the League as it had developed, but rather that he thought that the League and the Covenant had potential.

> The machinery and the principles of the League have not been uniformly successful, even when faithfully applied. But it may at least be confidently held that they have been sufficiently successful to justify the main contention... that they constitute a sound foundation upon which international cooperation can in the future be built up.[19]

Basically, the League would not live up to its potential as long as the world was 'distracted by competition in military preparation'.[20] Despite this faint praise for the League, Noel Baker saw it as the basis of a new international order built on law rather than on war and the threat of war: 'the true importance of the institutions of Geneva lies not in what they are today, but in what they will become'.[21] The unlocking of that potential was dependent on the success of disarmament and the establishment of a violence-free rule of law, which in turn was dependent on the establishment of an effective arbitration and sanctions regime under the League. Thus, there was a complex relationship between the establishment of a disarmed world on the one hand, and the development of the League on the other. Neither was necessarily prior to the other, and success in one was vital to success in the other. Noel Baker's hope was that a virtuous circle could be established whereby League cooperation would create the conditions under which a system of security could flourish, and that the resulting disarmament would make the evolution of the League into an effective law-based world government possible. There were some promising signs of this momentum in the late 1920s,[22] but by the 1930's he had come to realise that the main League governments, especially Britain and France, were blocking any progress on disarmament, thus stalling the whole process.[23] He was fully aware that there was a time limit on the construction of an effective League-based security system, and in 1927 he predicted that if nothing was done to firm up the League then a new world war 'would sweep away the fabric of the League.'[24]

Yet, his fears about the future of the League and its system of pooled security merely hardened his resolve to support the League and its efforts. As late as 1937 he reacted sharply to Leonard Woolf's criticism of the League's handling of the 1935–6 Abyssinian crisis, saying that he would even consider leaving the Labour Party if the Party ceased to follow a League policy.[25] Not for nothing was he jokingly called, during his stint as a Parliamentarian, the honourable member for the League of Nations. In a less jocular fashion A.L. Rowse in 1937 labelled Noel Baker a hopeless League fanatic.[26] Yet, in many ways the distance between Woolf and Noel Baker was one of degree. Woolf regarded the League as fatally wounded but, still holding on to the League idea, advocated the rebuilding of the League under the changed conditions of international anarchy that had returned with the foreign policy of the dictatorships and appeasement. Noel Baker also saw the League as damaged, but believe that the machinery already in place could still be used to restore international security. This, along with his past role in shaping the League, may have influenced his softer appraisal of the League in the mid-1930s.

There is, however, the possibility that there was a deeper difference here. Lorna Lloyd has claimed that Noel Baker's analysis was hampered by an implicit lack of a theory of international politics. 'He seemed to assume... that what went on at the international level was no more than the sum of what happened within individual states'. This led him to assume that 'every human conflict could be resolved by the right form of words...

laws role in resolving international differences... was an exemplification of
the power of reason in international affairs.'[27] Lloyd knew Noel Baker in
his later years, and therefore her criticism is based on both research and
personal knowledge. As a result it is not easily dismissed. This might mark
a major difference with Woolf, who as we shall see saw the international
rule of law as something constructed over the international anarchy.
Woolf's view of the international anarchy as the system that exists when a
more legal system is absent led him to write extensively on realpolitik and
its patterns of behaviour. Yet, the crucial qualifier here is the word implicit. Noel Baker certainly knew how the pre-First World War system worked, so he was not ignorant of the mechanisms associated with realpolitik.
Rather, he never wrote about them in a comprehensive manner. This did
not stop him referring to many of the mechanisms, however. For example,
in his *Disarmament* he describes the problem of what would later in IR be
called the security dilemma:

> ...when nations begin to arm in rivalry against each other, that rival-
> ry leads to ever greater preparation, first on one side, then upon the
> other; that it leads thus to the formation of alliances and groups,
> each group suspecting always that the other is about to strike, fear-
> ing always that the other is outstripping it in power, and striving
> always by some new effort to redress the balance;... their rivalry
> leads them to the catastrophe of war itself, and thus destroys by
> their very preparation for defence against attack the security which
> each of them set out to seek.[28]

Lloyd's criticism goes further. Having argued that Noel Baker relied
heavily on reason to construct a legal framework for dispute settlement
she then argues that 'Noel-Baker did not appreciate that they were fair
weather results and not schemes for all seasons.'[29] Certainly, this seems to
explain his continued enthusiasm for the League and its pooled security
system after Abyssinia in the teeth of Woolf's criticism, and there is no
doubt that Noel Baker's clinging to the wreckage of the League system
does substantiate this charge to a degree. In March 1936, for example, he
was still putting his faith in the paper guarantees found in the Locarno
Pact and the agreements reached at the Disarmament Conference in 1933
as the basis for defusing Franco-German tensions.[30] Having said this, such
an accusation does not hold out so well against the Noel Baker of the
1920s. He certainly believed that war-threatening crises were a natural part
of the international order as it was currently constructed, and his 1927
view that the League system had to be tightened up urgently before the

next world war threatened to sweep it all away hardly seems to substantiate the argument that he failed to see that the League was currently living under fair weather.[31] Indeed, he realised that the original Covenant was a fair weather result, and – to continue Lloyd's analogy – if the system was not properly constructed in time it would collapse with the coming of the next storm. It certainly seems that as the League came under increasing attack in the 1930s Noel Baker grew less critical of the organisation and its prospects. The fact that he continued to try to hold up the roof of the League system after the walls had caved in may be more an error of judgement than a failure of theory.

Underpinning this was the view that the failure of the League was not the failure of the ideas behind it, but of the specific actions and inaction of key governments, particularly the British government during the periods of Conservative dominated rule. Noel Baker's experience at Geneva had convinced him that peace through the development of a system of law and law-like arrangements was possible, and had worked on numerous occasions. Looking back on the League years from December 1939, three months into the war, it seemed very clear to him what the problem had been:

> ...don't think I am saying that the League was perfect... I am only saying that we failed because at decisive moments the governments allowed fear to dictate their policy, and so went wrong; because while they were trying to make a new world order they kept open their lines of retreat to the old world of power politics; because they let so-called "experts" tell them that things were impossible, which were well within their grasp.[32]

Although Noel Baker remained loyal to the League far further into the 1930's than the other five authors discussed here, this did not blind him to the dangers posed by fascism. His hope in 1937 that the League might still act as a means of controlling Germany was dashed after the Anschluss with Austria and the Czechoslovak crisis of 1938. He threw himself enthusiastically into Labour's war-effort, and contributed through propaganda broadcasts, the drafting of war aims and, after 1940, through work in the coalition government. Noel Baker was responsible for the initial draft of Labour's war aims in 1939–40, an amended version of which was accepted by the Executive and went to Conference in May 1940. Following on from his analysis of the reason's for the League's failures, Noel Baker advocated measures that would reduce the importance of state sovereignty, while resuscitating a system of arbitration and disarmament. He realised that this was impossible while the Nazis were still in power, and his major precondition for the signing of a peace with Germany was the defeat and replacement of its current government.[33] As a member of the International Sub-Committee of the National Executive of the Labour Party he commented extensively on Hugh Dalton's 1943–4 peace settlement proposals. His major concern, other than toning down Dalton's comparatively anti-German prose, was the establishment of a League-like political organisation to compliment and coordinate the economic organisations that were also part of Labour's proposals. His main reason for championing a large-scale global political organisation, which in time would become the United Nations, was that, unlike David Mitrany, he felt that 'effective international economic co-operation will remain impossible until governments and peoples are convinced that there is a solid hope of a stable peace.'[34] Thus, despite the deep disappointments of the inter-war period he remained committed to the idea of the League, albeit under a different name.

While the most committed to the League of the five writers focused on in this book, Noel Baker's support was not uncritical. Realising that the League Covenant would need extensive work if it was to function as an alternative to the international anarchy, his greatest contribution to international scholarship and practice in the inter-war period was undoubtedly his analysis of the linkage between disarmament, arbitration and sanctions. As a writer, activist and politician he worked hard to turn an organisation of cabinets and governments into the embryo of a new order based upon legal norms and values – a goal that he interpreted as both practical and achievable in the short-term as long as certain lead governments had the will. Like most of Labour's international experts he regarded the Conservative-led National Government's foreign policy after 1931 as a cause, rather than as a product, of the failure of the League to live up to its potential. While Labour would be shut out of power after 1931, in 1924 and 1929–31 Labour would form its first two governments with Liberal support. For people like Noel Baker these two governments, while short-lived, were opportunities to influence British international policy at a time when there was still enough international good-will to make the prospect of a major great power war a distant possibility.

Labour as a Party of Government 1922–31

The decade from 1922 to 1931 was a memorable one for Labour, as much as it was a hopeful one for those working for the creation of a new peaceful international order. Labour was in power for less than three of the ten years, yet its work on foreign affairs was impressive, both in comparison to the Conservative and National Governments and in comparison to Labour's more lacklustre domestic policy record. There is an irony here. While the Conservatives prided themselves in being the foreign and defence policy party, and even many Labour supporters regarded Labour as primarily a domestic policy party, it was Labour's success in the area of foreign affairs that it is largely remembered for. There were, however, serious structural weaknesses in both Labour Governments. Both administrations were minority governments reliant on Liberal support, and in the case of its first Government Labour was not even the largest party in Parliament. This meant that the passing of Legislation was reliant on it being consistent with Liberal Party policy. Both governments were headed by James Ramsay MacDonald, a principled and effective politician, albeit mecurial and often dangerously secretive. MacDonald's legacy as an efficient Prime Minister has been overshadowed by the damage that he inflicted on his own Party. To this day MacDonald's presence as Prime Minister in the first two Labour administrations taints the legacies of these governments in Labour eyes. The nostalgia is reserved for the 1945–51 governments of Clement Attlee.

In 1922, however, MacDonald was nine years away from his perceived act of betrayal, and both he and the Party were on the rise. In the elections of that year Labour overtook the Liberals to become the second largest party in Parliament, and consequently the official opposition to the Conservative Government. Having lost his seat in 1918, MacDonald returned to Parliament in the 1922 election, becoming leader of the PLP since the previous leader, Arthur Henderson, had lost his seat. The rethink in Labour's position and rhetoric towards the League from 1922 was linked to Labour's electoral success, and the consequent realisation that the Party was now a government in waiting. In the election of 6 December 1923 the Conservatives, under Stanley Baldwin lost their majority, winning 258 seats to Labour's 191 and the Liberal's 159. Prior to 1922 the Liberals had been split between those under David Lloyd George who where part of the coalition National Government with the Conservatives, and those under Herbert Asquith who opposed the National Government. In 1924 the Liberals had united under Asquith, and they refused to support a minority Conservative administration. After much wrangling, Macdonald, as leader of the PLP, was called to form a minority government. The contenders for Foreign Secretary included Henderson and the UDC leader E.D. Morel. MacDonald gave Henderson, who was still waiting to enter Parliament at the next by-election, the Home Secretary portfolio, and snubbed Morel by making himself Foreign Secretary in addition to his Prime Ministerial responsibilities. Arthur Ponsonby became MacDonald's Parliamentary Secretary at the Foreign Office, which effectively made him MacDonald's number two at the Foreign Office.

It was in the area of foreign policy that MacDonald's government met its greatest success. Helped by MacDonald's own intervention, the Dawes Plan for the reorganisation of reparations payments was hammered out. This helped the French and Germans find a way out of the crisis caused by the French occupation of the Ruhr. The negotiation of the Geneva Protocol for the Pacific Settlement of International Disputes, while never coming into force, increased Labour's international reputation, and laid out precedents for the definition of aggression, for the form of international arbitration, and the relationship between arbitration and sanctions. Finally, Labour opened negotiations for the normalisation of relations with the Soviet Union, despite MacDonald and Henderson's deep antipathy towards communism and the Third International.

Labour's first government lasted less than a year. Interestingly, it was an issue of foreign policy impinging on the domestic sphere that brought the Government down. The Labour Government had staked much of its reputation on normalisation of relations with the Soviet Union. This carried the risk that the Government would be too closely associated with Bolshevism, and therefore with a hostile foreign government. The crunch came when the Government dropped the prosecution against a British communist editor for inciting mutiny amongst British troops. The Liberal leader Asquith proposed a motion in Parliament, which was passed with Conservative support, to establish an inquiry into the Government's decision. Having lost Liberal support, MacDonald resigned, and fresh elections were held on 29 October 1924. To compound Labour's problems with the Soviet connection, the pro-Tory *Daily Mail* published a letter leaked from the Foreign Office that had purportedly been written by Zinoviev, the Secretary of the Third International. The letter, which was certainly a forgery, urged the Communist Part of Great Britain to do anything in its power to assist the Government in ratifying the two Russian treaties. The mini-red scare helped eat in to Labour's vote. Despite this, however, Labour only lost forty seats, and increased its overall vote by a million. The silver lining for Labour was the collapse of the Liberal vote, with only forty Liberal MPs returned. From 1924 onwards Britain became a two-party system, and Labour the only serious alternative to the Conservatives. Writing from her post in Baghdad just before the 1924 election Gertrude Bell – the archaeologist, traveller and member of the British government team in the Iraq mandate – wrote:

Upon my soul, I think I should vote Labour if I were in England. The turning out of the Government at a time when the peace of Europe is still on such thin ice seems to me to be such a mean party trick. And the programmes of the Conservatives and Liberals are poor hackneyed stuff don't you think?[35]

Labour had come a long way from its status in 1914 as a minor party of radicals.

From 1924 to 1929 Labour played the role of official opposition to the Conservative Government of Stanley Baldwin. The British institution of the Loyal Opposition is deliberately confrontational, playing the part of a negative dialect to the Government's positive policy proposals. Yet, to be taken seriously as a party of government an opposition needs to balance this with positive policy proposals that clearly distinguish it from the current party in power. True to this role, Labour kept up a sustained opposetion to the Government's foreign policy, including the Government's defence estimates. On the positive side, the Party continued to engage with the League of Nations, sending representatives to Geneva on a number of occasions, and perhaps more importantly produced the policy document *Labour and the Nation* in 1928, which laid out what Labour had to offer the country. In the next general election on 30 May 1929 Labour, for the first time, became the largest party in Parliament, with 288 seats to the Conservative's 260. This still did not give them a majority, but with Liberal support they formed a minority government.

MacDonald's second cabinet proved more difficult to put together than the first. Particularly acrimonious was the choice of Foreign Secretary. Arthur Henderson was finally chosen, although MacDonald reserved the right to handle Anglo-American relations, and the Chancellor, Philip Snowden 'pursued an international financial policy independent of...the Foreign Office.'[36] Henderson chose Hugh Dalton, a key player in the Advisory Committee and author of a 1928 book on international affairs,[37] as his Parliamentary Secretary at the Foreign Office. Philip Noel Baker was part of the Foreign Office team, and Henderson, over MacDonald's objections, gave the pro-League pooled Security Conservative Robert Cecil an advisory role in the Foreign Office. William Arnold-Forster worked under Cecil at the League. Despite frequent problems with negotiating Liberal Party support, as well as splits between MacDonald and Henderson, the Government pursued an active and effective foreign policy that will be discussed below. The policy of the Second Labour Government was a product of the discussions and arguments that dominated the Party between 1922 and 1929, and the first step in this construction of a pro-

League foreign policy was the development of an alternative to the denunciations of the Peace that had dominated the debate in Labour circles prior to 1922.

Making the League Work:
From 'Reconstitution' to a 'League Foreign Policy'

Despite the deep reservations expressed about the League Covenant within Labour ranks, there was probably little doubt that a future Labour Government would try to make the League system work. Henry Winkler presents the change in Labour from deep disappointment to active support for the League as the work of a small group of moderates against the majority of the Party.[38] While there is undoubtedly a lot of truth to this, he does overplay the depth of the anti-League feeling in comparison to the advocates of international organisation and collective security.[39] A majority may have been opposed to, or more correctly disappointed with, the new League, but many of them were easily reconciled with a Party policy that was overtly pro-League. This does not mean that the pro-League minority did not have much work to do in convincing the Party, but it does mean that it was not necessarily an uphill struggle. Key Labour opinion formers that had been the most vocal in their opposition to the treaties and the Covenant, like H.N. Brailsford, were reconciled to the League by the time that the first Labour Government had made such a success of its negotiations at Geneva. Following the success of British and French diplomacy at the League in 1924 H.N. Brailsford, who up to that point had been deeply disillusioned with the League, wrote, 'For a few days this international Parliament focused in itself the political life of Europe. The League which had been nothing became everything.'[40]

Brailsford was, however, relatively late in his conversion to a League Foreign Policy. Between 1922 and 1924 James Ramsay MacDonald and Arthur Henderson, both future Labour Foreign Secretaries, worked alongside the Advisory Committee on International Questions in constructing a Labour Foreign policy that was committed to using, and even defending, the League's machinery. Although there remained major differences between Henderson and MacDonald, differences that would emerge most glaringly during the Second Labour Government, in the early 1920s their positions on the League did not seem so far apart. The major difference between the two was more one of emphasis at this stage. Henderson shared the view of Noel Baker and the Conservative Robert Cecil that the League should develop into a strong international institution capable of imposing sanctions, including military sanctions, on disturbers of the international peace. The League was, and should be, 'an embryonic super-state'.

By contrast, MacDonald believed that the League should remain a world forum that would foster international goodwill.[41] With one eye on the strong opposition within the Party to the form taken by the Peace, Mac-Donald and Henderson continued to stress the need for reform of the treaties and the League in the years immediately after the signing of the main treaties in 1919. It was not until 1922 that both men started publicly to endorse the League Covenant and what it ultimately stood for. This built upon the strong support for the establishment of a league of nations amongst Labour members before 1919, as well as the joint Labour-TUC endorsement of the Covenant, with reservations, in April of 1919.[42] Both men tested the Party waters in 1922. In October 1922 MacDonald wrote in his regular *Socialist Review* column that the League had the makings of a really powerful body if the great powers would use it. In December Henderson endorsed pooled security and the League at the World Peace Congress.[43] Over the next two years the position of MacDonald and Henderson prepared the wider Party for the compromises the government would make in 1924 in the search for a workable system for maintaining international peace.

Throughout the lead-up to the First Labour Government in 1924 the rhetoric of the Party, and even of Henderson and MacDonald, continued to stress the centrality of the revision of the treaties and the League Co-venant. The clearest sign that the Labour Party in government had shelv-ed ambitious plans for revision and renegotiation came with MacDon-ald's reaction to a speech given by Henderson on 23 February 1924. By then MacDonald was Prime Minister, and Henderson was standing in a by-election having lost his seat in the general election. Henderson called the revision of the Treaty of Versailles an absolute essential. Under press-ure from the Conservatives in Parliament, MacDonald's response to the speech was evasive, and therefore implicitly unsupportive. The Labour Government refused to back a major revision of the Treaty of Versailles. Interestingly, Henderson's speech had been written by an official Labour Party speech writer for the 1922 election, and had been consistent with Labour policy prior to 1924.[44] After this last electoral flourish, Hend-erson's public pronouncements also fell into line with his preferred posi-tion of engagement with the League, and reform of the treaties by piece-meal international agreements, although his new cabinet position as Home Secretary took him away from foreign affairs for the preceding months. While both leaders leaned heavily on the advice of the Advisory Comm-ittee, it was Henderson who relied the most on the Committee's output.[45] MacDonald tended to distance himself from the Committee once he was in office, although it was in the Advisory Committee that many of the major policies of engagement with the League were worked out.

Between 1922 and 1924 the tenor of the memoranda coming out of the Advisory Committee had shifted towards working within the present machinery of the League, even though suggestions for reform of the League remained thick on the ground. Winkler is certainly spot-on when he states that the Advisory Committee was a key player in changing Labour policy towards the League. While in the immediate aftermath of the treaties the Advisory Committee had been disappointed with the form that the League had taken, the bulk of the Committee were clearly reconciled with making the League work, and with making Labour the party most committed to pooled security and the construction of a new international order. In June 1920, at the height of the deep disappointment with the League in both the Party at large and the Advisory Committee in particular, C. Delisle Burns laid out how Labour could develop a positive policy towards the League, since it 'is more practical to improve the existing League than to destroy or weaken this in order to make it better.' While dismissive of the Council, which he referred to as a set of windbags, he was supportive of the structure of the new International Labour Office (ILO). The ILO's provision for the inclusion of non-governmental units, he felt, should be extended to the League proper, while the office of the Secretary General should be held by a trustworthy administrator, rather than a diplomat tainted by the old diplomacy. Interestingly, Delisle Burns foreshadowed the emphasis in the functional approach of David Mitrany on bringing people together by what unites them, rather than by what divides them. He suggested that the League needed to do something positive, and that rather than concentrating on a divisive issue 'involving national jealousies', like an Armenian mandate, it should do something like reorganise European transportation.[46]

Although some members of the Advisory Committee remained suspicious of aspects of the League, specifically C.R. Buxton, Arthur Ponsonby and E.D. Morel amongst others, a majority including Leonard Woolf, Norman Angell, Will Arnold-Forster and Philip Noel Baker were in favour of developing a pro-League policy that included, most controversially at the time, the provision of sanctions against aggressive states. The issue of League sanctions will be discussed in more detail in the next section. This majority on the Advisory Committee found ready support amongst key figures in the Party, particularly J.R. Clynes, Arthur Henderson and Ramsay MacDonald, even though it did not necessarily have the backing of the majority of the Party membership. By 1924, and the formation of Labour's first government, there was a recognition by the majority in the

Party that there were going to be no major changes to the peace treaties, and any alterations of the League would have to build on the existing Covenant and structural arrangements. It is important not to underestimate this change of policy, for only two years earlier, in 1922, constructive engagement with the Peace and League in Labour circles still meant advocating major root and branch alterations of the treaties and the Covenant.

Before looking in detail at the proposals for a League policy and their operation during the First Labour Government it is important to give some idea of the international environment between 1922 and 1931, and hence the context for the debates within the Labour Party over foreign policy. E.H. Carr referred to it as the period of pacification: 'these years [1924–31], with all their uncertainties and imperfections, were the golden years of post-war Europe.'[47] Many of the major problems from the era of the Peace Treaty – the French occupation of the Ruhr, German reparations, Franco-German hostility and German and Soviet exclusion from international intercourse – would all find solutions during this period. While there were hotspots of instability, of which the ongoing Chinese civil wars were particularly notable, there appeared to be no major threats to international stability. This was true even after the 1929 Wall Street Crash had sparked an economic crisis: 'Despite the severity of the world depression and its immediate effects upon the stability of Germany, the relations between the major European powers appeared on the surface to be improving.'[48]

On a number of occasions the League was able to prevent a crisis becoming a full-blown war. In the case of the 1925 border war between Greece and Bulgaria the League was even able to impose a penalty on a former Allied nation, while finding in favour of a former enemy state. With no major threats to world peace, and the machinery of the League gaining respect through regular use, the potential for the construction of an alternative international order around the League and its specialised agencies seemed eminently possible and practical. For Britain in particular there were no serious threats to the Empire. The issue of Mosul had been settled with Turkey via the League; a compromise peace had stabilised relations with a new Irish Free State Dominion; and the Washington Conference had stabilised both the borders in the Pacific and the naval balance between the major maritime powers. Britain had to share equality on the high seas with the United States, but America was not regarded as a threat to the security of the Empire. The only ongoing problems for the security of the Empire were internal, and had more to do with the open question of what Britain's relationship should be with the rest of the Commonwealth and Empire. In short, the stability and relative prosperity of the period, not to mention the successes of the League system, made the discussion of an alternative and pacific world order a practical and reasonable undertaking.

In one respect the Advisory Committee was much freer to discuss ways of creating a League-friendly foreign policy than were the major Party leaders, whose positions were open to immediate public scrutiny. In another, the diverse membership of the Committee also meant that memoranda supporting an engagement with the League mixed with continued denunciations of the Peace and the League. This said attacks on the League and the treaties were usually phrased in a constructive way that suggested that reform and some kind of compromise with the structures hammered out in Paris were possible. An example of this can be found in the Advisory Committee's draft reports for the International Socialist Conference in 1922, which since they were to be made public played to the general anti-treaty sentiments still strong in the rank and file.[49] While Woolf's proposals for the reform of the Covenant were far-ranging, he was careful to point out that the League was still the corner-stone of Labour's international policy, and that because it was necessary to approach the matter in a practical fashion that the British Section of the International was not proposing 'either complete disarmament or that the League should attempt absolutely to forbid or prevent war. The world is not so minded at present.'[50] Rather, the Advisory Committee was keen to keep its proposed reforms within manageable limits. The more general draft resolution for the 1922 Annual Party Conference, however, was not so careful, although its stress was still on reform of the League 'so as to include and provide security for all the peoples of the world.'[51]

This position of constructive criticism, with its emphasis on reform, abruptly changed in 1923 with the submission of a 23 page memorandum on the need for a League foreign policy in the Party. Here the Advisory Committee's position anticipated the 1924 Labour Government's policy towards the League in a number of key respects, although given the diverse membership of the Advisory Committee the meeting that considered the memorandum must have been a relatively stormy one. A central plank of the memorandum was that calls for the reform of the League, which were often based on very little knowledge of how the League now worked, could be counter-productive. The trend amongst the key members of the League in 1923 was to claw back much of the freedom of action that they had given away in 1919. As a result the 'general tendency has been to revise the Covenant downward, that is, to regain as much freedom as possible for all States to do as they please and to abjure any binding international obligation.'[52]

Thus, the result of any reform would be the opposite of what Labour critics of the League intended. Rather than a general process of reform, Labour should focus on specific à la carte reforms that would strengthen League institutions. One such suggestion in the memo was giving the International Court compulsory jurisdiction; the so-called optional clause that the Second Labour Government signed in 1929.

A central part of the memorandum's analysis of the League and its structures was the acceptance that for the foreseeable future the League would have to remain as a free association of states, rather than a federal organisation. Pre-dating David Mitrany's criticism of federalism, and perhaps showing his hand here, the memorandum pointed out that a fully-fledged federation would entail 'the mechanical and psychological difficulties of federating all nations, with their different traditions, their different systems of government, languages, levels of culture, ways of thought, and so forth'.[53] Rather, and again in a Mitranian fashion, the memo envisaged a slow aggregation of the principle of free association extending to co-operation between 'supreme economic organs' of government, to the development of inter-parliamentary co-operation and the extension of the role of non-voting technical experts in the League's organs.[54] Finally, the memorandum pointed out that the Conservatives and the Liberals already had League policies, and since the League was likely to remain a central part of foreign affairs in the foreseeable future, Labour needed to address the issue directly, rather than just sticking exclusively to the line that reform was necessary.[55] In a nutshell, the League is up and running, international work is already being done, and if Labour wants to influence the way that the League develops then the Party needs to have a policy of engagement with the League.

This analysis of the League was consistent with the 'shell-state' conception of the League mentioned at the end of the last chapter. The League exists as part of the environment of international politics, and as a piece of machinery its character and role depends on how it is used, rather than on some kind of intrinsic ethos embedded in the organisation. If it is run by conservatives along lines of the old diplomacy then the League will serve as an instrument of the old international anarchy. If run along new lines the League would be the foundation for a new cooperative order. This social democratic conception of the shell-state, transposed onto an international organisation, remained a central assumption of the League's supporters in the Labour Party, and dominated the views of both Labour governments. Labour's comprehensive pamphlet-size policy statement, *Labour and the Nation*, interpreted the League as the machinery through which a Labour government could cooperate with the rest of the world.[56]

The interpretation of the League as an institutional shell also unpinned Hugh Dalton's influential 1928 analysis of international politics. '...the League is only an unusually elaborate piece of international machinery. Its value will depend upon who handles it, and upon the spirit and motives and competence with which it is handled.'[57] The emphasis in Labour's policy, in the run up to the 1929 General Election, was firmly on closing the various loop holes in the League Covenant and working through the existing League institutions for a secure and peaceful international environment. This was generally regarded as a reasonable mix between pragmatic acceptance of the world as it is, including the existence of the League, and an idealistic (in one of the inter-war senses) programme of reform.

Behind the shift in Advisory Committee advice towards acceptance of the League as-is lay the further assumption that, despite the continued existence of state sovereignty, the states of the world had become dependent on each other. As a result the international anarchy associated with the old diplomacy was counter-productive, and the crucial question was what could be done with the world *as it is now* to build a security structure that could best serve the interdependent world that now existed.[58] There was general agreement amongst Labour advisors and leaders that as long as sovereign states were the political reality then the development of some kind of system of peaceful arbitration, coupled with reductions in the number of arms (referred to at the time as disarmament), was necessary. The main fault-line in the party was over the question of whether there needed to be any sanctions, including if necessary military sanctions, against aggressor states that refused to abide by League arbitration. This dispute would see the majority of the Advisory Committee – including Woolf, Noel Baker, Mitrany, Angell and Dalton – line up behind Henderson against the pacifists and radical socialists. MacDonald tended towards the former group, but deliberately played down the role of sanctions when discussing the League in public.

Disarmament, Arbitration and Sanctions

A common anachronism within IR is to read the whole inter-war period against the backdrop of the rise of fascism. All IR works of the period are understood against what they have to say about the period from the invasion of Manchuria onwards. Not surprisingly, works written before the Mukden incident of 1931, Hitler's remilitarisation of the Rhineland in 1936 and Mussolini's invasion of Abyssinia in 1935 are silent on the threat of fascism, and write about League institutions as though they could work to prevent aggression. To write them off as 'idealistic' for being silent on both fascist aggression and the 'failures' of the League is, quite frankly, absurd. Again, it is important to point out that the debates of the 1920s were significantly different, although they do necessarily feed in to the questions of the 1930s. What is more, rather than being apologetic for their writings on the League in the 1920s, pro-League advocates of pooled security and League arbitration frequently felt that the rise of fascism justified their warnings about the consequences of failing to develop an effective League system. One of the major debates between 1922 and 1931 was over the question of the relationship between disarmament, arbitration and League sanctions (economic and military). Ostensibly this was about closing a major loophole in the League Covenant, but it also marked a major split between two views of how the League should work A number of the Advisory Committee memoranda dealt with the issue of disarmament, arbitration and sanctions, whether separately or together, and one of the biggest disagreements on the Committee revolved around the issue of defining sanctions. Part of this has already been discussed in the section above on Noel Baker.

A related failing of the IR accounts of its own history during the inter-war period is the implicit assumption that the League existed fully-grown from the Covenant of 1919 onwards. In fact, while the Covenant had made it a requirement of membership that disputes 'likely to lead to rupture' be submitted to arbitration, judicial inquiry or inquiry by the League Council (Article 11), and had made the immediate severance of trade and financial links between League members and an aggressor state mandatory (Article 16), there were still major gaps in the legal machinery of the League.[59] First, there was no clear definition of aggressor in the Covenant; second, while arbitration and other peaceful methods of dispute settlement were mentioned, it was not clear what the correct procedure would be in different disputes; third, while disarmament 'to the lowest point consistent with national safety and the enforcement by common action of international obligations' was made a condition of membership in Article 8, there was no definition of the 'lowest point', and no discussion of the mechanisms to be employed to bring about disarmament; fourth, the Covenant had not fully removed the right of a state to go to war unilaterally; and finally, the nature of appropriate sanctions in the event of aggression was not spelt out. Linked to the second point was the question of the validity of the Permanent Court of International Justice, and especially the signing of the Optional Clause, by which the signatory state would recognise the decisions of that Court as binding. Many of these issues lay unresolved in 1931 when the full force of the economic depression hit the world economy. In this sense, the League, as the first serious attempt to create a truly global security organisation, was very much a work in progress during its first decade. Statesmen were still unsure how it should be used, and League officials were managing an organisation whose powers were as unclear as they were unprecedented. Thus, the League did not enter the 1930s fully equipped to deal with the problem of aggression. Rather, after eleven years of existence, it was still being developed. In 1927 Philip Noel Baker asked if the League's institutions would 'be given time to build up their strength before the catastrophe of a new war sweeps them all away?'[60] Six years before Hitler's coming to power even the strongest of the League's supporters knew that there was much work to be done before the League was up to the test of a serious war-threatening crisis. The United Nations would, after that deluge, benefit from the League's learning curve.

Of course, these five 'gaps' were all related. In fact, from the point of view of the majority on the Advisory Committee and the group around Arthur Henderson, disarmament, arbitration and sanctions formed an inter-related triangle in which one could not be realised without the other two.[61] Disarmament was not going to be a serious prospect until a system of arbitration and conciliation that removed the necessity for armed defence had been put in place.[62] The question of arbitration and conciliation carried with it the question of what to do if the methods of peaceful resolution failed. The issue of economic and military sanctions also affected the discussions of disarmament: what level of arms would be required by a sanctions regime, and in the absence of a sanctions regime would smaller states feel that disarmament was not an option? Sanctions also introduced the thorny issue of the definition of aggression. Prior to 1931 the sharpest split in Labour's ranks in the foreign policy field was over the question of whether the League needed the power of sanctions in order to make arbitration and disarmament a reality within the League system. This was to be the main source of disagreement over the Geneva Protocol developed at the League under Labour Government auspices, and was to split Party opinion in the debates about the Locarno Pact signed by the successor Conservative Government. While Labour remained very much a pro-League party, the question of sanctions left the pacifist wing deeply suspicious and worried about the prospect of a future 'League war', while the hard core of radical socialists continued to see the League, as it had done in the immediate post-Peace period, as a predominantly capitalist organisation unworthy of support.

In fact, what is remarkable given the depth of feeling amongst many pacifists and radical socialists in the Party, is how little acrimonious disagreements there were in the Party over the overtly pro-League and at least implicitly pro-military sanctions policies of the two Labour governments.

The open public rift in the Party had to wait until the mid-1930s, and even then the split was driven by events in international politics, rather than by any endogenous disagreement on foreign policy principles.[63] The major exception to this was the reaction of E.D. Morel to the first Labour Government's foreign policy. While initially supportive of MacDonald's new foreign policy, Morel's vitriolic attacks on MacDonald might have led to a direct challenge to the government from within the Party had not Morel died suddenly in 1924. As it was, disquiet in pacifist sections about the military implications of the Geneva Protocol were threatening to split Party opinion in 1924, and only the collapse of the Government forestalled this conflict. Yet, as long as the emphasis in Labour policy remained disarmament and arbitration under the League the pacifists at least were willing, albeit with deep reservations, to live with the Party's support for League sanctions.

Not surprisingly, given the importance of the issues involved, the relationship between arbitration, sanctions and disarmament in the building of an effective League-based alternative to the international anarchy were frequently discussed in the Advisory Committee. The memoranda produced were, in turn, used by Arthur Henderson and the circle around him in the construction of Labour's foreign policy. Some of the memoranda also became Labour Party pamphlets. Generally speaking, there was widespread agreement in the Party about the need for a system of international arbitration, and that arbitration was a precondition for successful worldwide disarmament. There were exceptions even here, however. George Lansbury and some of the pacifist wing of the Party clung to the belief that disarmament by example, what we would now call unilateral disarmament, should be an immediate priority. Arthur Ponsonby continued to stress the central importance of moral authority and leadership to the achievement of an effective disarmament regime.[64] Even in the 1930s Lansbury continued to believe that British disarmament would lead to disarmament by the dictators as well. The major disagreement within the Party and the Advisory Committee in the 1920s, however, was over the question of whether sanctions were necessary to a successful arbitration regime.

The basic idea behind international arbitration was the substitution of an effective system of peaceful change for the reliance on war as the primary arbitrator of disputes between states. A major distinction was made between conciliation, in which the parties would be brought together through a third party such as the League Council, and arbitration that was a legally-binding decision made by an appropriately competent body. Thus, at its core arbitration assumes that a state is willing, under international agreement, to waive its sovereign right to be judge and jury in its own case in order to maintain peace. By the 1920s there was already a history of successful cases of arbitration, although each case prior to the League had been guaranteed by nothing more than the good will of the parties involved. Article 12 of the Covenant mentioned arbitration as one of three possible peaceful dispute settlements open to its members, the other two being judicial settlement and inquiry by the League Council. Article 14 of the Covenant required the parties to establish the Permanent Court of International Justice, which could be the arbiter of all judicial disputes between states once the states involved signed up to the Optional Clause that obligated the state to accept the rulings of the Court. Discussions of the place of arbitration during the inter-war period divided conflicts be-tween states into judicial and non-judicial (or political) disputes. There was widespread agreement in the Advisory Committee that judicial disputes, which involved clear cut cases of international law, could and should be submitted to arbitration, and that accepting binding arbitration by the Permanent Court by signing the Optional Clause made eminent sense.[65]

This is not to say that there were not concerns about the success of arbitration, even for judicial disputes, amongst Advisory Committee mem-bers. In fact one of the most influential books written during the First World War on the reform of international relations, Leonard Woolf's *International Government*, advocated arbitration with reservations. Arbitration could only be used for cases that could be phrased in a legal form, and the conservative nature of the law made it unlikely, at least in the foreseeable future, that states without a vested interest in the status quo would accept a wholly legal arbitration regime. The answer for Woolf lay in the option of taking the case to an international conference instead, and in giving states more of a say in the shape of the tribunal.[66] With the advent of the Permanent Court the machinery for the settling of legal disputes via judicial means was established, although the option of adding reservations when signing the Optional Clause (which bound a state to acceptance of Permanent Court rulings) allowed states to reserve the right to submit certain grades of judicial dispute to another venue. In fact Germany, amongst others, submitted just such a reservation when it signed the op-tional clause, and when Labour signed for Britain in 1929 this reservation was the first of three attached to the signature.[67] Woolf's concerns about the conservative bias of the law naturally took a back seat in the environ-ment of the 1920s. As Arnold-Forster frequently pointed out, when the alternative to the Permanent Court was the League Council – the later being composed mainly of representatives of the victorious Allies – the Permanent Court looked far less wedded to the status quo of the 1919 peace, and certainly far more impartial in its judgements.[68] Added to this was the serious gap in the Covenant that when disputes were submitted to the Council the parties were still allowed to resort to war if the Council failed to reach a decision within three months.[69] Woolf's reservation would resurface, however, in the colder climate after 1936.

A more vexing question was the issue of non-legal disputes, where the Permanent Court would not have the jurisdiction or the competence to adjudicate. The Labour Party, largely through the work of Advisory Committee members, was committed to the creation of an all-inclusive arbitration regime that would include non-legal disputes. If the settling of legal disputes was possible but problematic, the settling of non-legal disputes in a world of selfish states appeared daunting. Despite his earlier reservations about the limits of arbitration, Woolf collaborated with Arnold-Forster in 1927 on a draft convention that would lay out the possible shape of a system of arbitration for non-legal disputes. The League of Nations, as it stood, had a system of resolving non-legal disputes through conciliation. Conciliation was not binding, and it did not involve a renunciation of the use of force by the parties involved. There was no 'open convention by means of which States can bind themselves to submit all non-legal disputes to pacific settlement.'[70] Woolf and Arnold-Forster's proposals involved a long process in which the dispute would go first to the Permanent Conciliation Commission of the League, to the League Council, and finally to a committee of arbitrators agreed to by the parties. Throughout the process 'the parties undertake that, under no circumstances will they attack or invade each other's territory or resort to war unless in the fulfilment of their obligations as members of the League of Nations.'[71] Obviously the whole proposal rested on the willingness of the parties to renounce war. In a limited way this had already been accomplished through the various bilateral arbitration treaties that had come in to force between a number of states during the late nineteenth and early twentieth centuries. These treaties, encouraged by the League, had bound various states to settle bilateral differences through arbitration. Britain had such a treaty with Uruguay, while the treaty between France and the United States was the subject of much discussion in Labour Party circles.[72] In the final analysis, though, arbitration seemed unlikely to work as a stand-alone system of pacific settlement. Later David Mitrany would offer a radically different solution to the problem with his functional approach to security, but in the 1920s the other alternative, as proposed in different forms by Arnold-Forster, Woolf and Mitrany, was to tie arbitration to a sanctions regime.

The position of those who supported League sanctions was summarised by Hugh Dalton in 1928: 'Some provision for sanctions and coercive action... is a logical requirement of any legal system, it takes human shape in police and judges.'[73] This was far from being a universally accepted position in the Party, and was deeply criticised by both pacifist and radical socialist wings of the Party. The former because sanctions still entrenched violence, the later because they gave teeth to what was still regarded as a capitalist-run organisation. Arthur Ponsonby supplemented his pacifist convictions with the view that the inability to define aggression accurately ruled out the value of sanctions for the League.[74] The Geneva Protocol, discussed below, did provide a clear definition of aggressor – as those who refused to submit their dispute to arbitration while also engaging in hostilities – and from the point of view of the supporters of sanctions this remained clear and definitive.[75] C.R. Buxton and Helena Swanwick took a different line, arguing that it was extremely unlikely that there was a will to use military sanctions in the Labour Party, the country as a whole and the Dominions. Buxton was willing to countenance economic sanctions, but felt that, on the whole, it was best to concentrate on the less contentious issues of arbitration and disarmament.[76] Swanwick, on the other hand, felt that sanctions of any kind were likely to fail in times of stress between great powers.[77] Even Ramsay MacDonald felt that, in the long term, the spirit of cooperation engendered by an arbitration regime would make sanctions unnecessary.[78] Thus, opposition to sanctions covered a wide spectrum, but we can distinguish between a blanket opposition to all sanctions, and an opposition exclusively to military sanctions. The advocates of sanctions addressed both questions.

At a minimum it was pointed out that the whole League system rested on sanctions, and would continue to do so as long as there was still the threat of the outbreak of private war by one state against another. Article 16 of the Covenant made economic sanctions mandatory in the event of aggression, and the threat of League sanctions had worked on minor belligerents in 1922 against Serbian troops and 1925 against the Greeks.[79] Noel Baker argued that at a bare minimum an effective sanctions regime would reduce the risk of war by deterring possible aggressors.[80] A more positive reason was the continued likelihood of war, and the consequent insecurity of many states, including many of the minor powers. The threat of sanctions was the only means the League had of guaranteeing that the Covenant would be respected. 'And if "moral suasion" is all that the Lea gue can oppose to the would-be Covenant-breaker's armed force, then sooner or later the League's bluff will be called'.[81] Because many smaller states, and even larger ones like France, felt deeply insecure a strong sanctions regime presented the only alternative to the build-up of arms. In other words, an effective sanctions regime would be the only way to wean many states off relying on their own force of arms for defence, and consequently without sanctions there could be no comprehensive international disarmament or arbitration regime.[82]

> We know by now that we have not the smallest chance of being successful in this unless we can offer the nations some assurance that in disarming they will not be left at the mercy of some international miscreant... Without some guarantee, arbitration, even if formally accepted, will lead a precarious existence.[83]

The use of military sanctions was a more vexing issue. For Dalton the use of the military should be 'our last line of defence... But it is not possible to wipe it off the map.'[84] For Mitrany military sanctions 'must remain an extreme measure, to be adopted only in exceptional circumstances.'[85] This necessity of some form of military threat in the background was given a slightly different twist by Arnold-Forster, who argued that economic sanctions itself might require the enforcement of a naval blockade, and thus extensive use of the military, if it was to be effective.[86] A final note of caution was voiced by Mitrany. While he supported sanctions, and saw them as indispensable to the League system, he was worried that obligatory sanctions might encourage states, unwilling to contribute to a sanctions regime, to 'hamper the peace machinery of the League.' Thus, while 'it is doubtful whether the League could keep the peace without sanctions', their success, and consequently the success of the system of arbitration, rested uncomfortably on the willingness of states to act.[87] Mitrany's assessment of the weakness of the sanctions regime was to be proved horribly right during the Manchurian crisis of 1931–33. Given this structural flaw in the League's security machinery it was not surprising that by 1933 Mitrany had begun work on an alternative function-based system of security.

All members of the Party could agree on the ultimate end of disarmament, where disarmament meant the reduction of arms, rather than their complete eradication. Arms were seen as a product of the wasteful system associated with the international anarchy, and created instability by their very existence.[88] Even before 1914 writers like Norman Angell had written that armaments, by bringing security to the holder but insecurity to everyone else, actually increase the levels of insecurity in the world. The security of armaments can only be relative to the armaments of your potential opponents.[89] For Philip Noel Baker the value of disarmament was two-fold. It would save national resources for more productive enterprises, and would ease international tensions by reducing states' abilities to wage aggressive war abroad.[90] The sharp split in the Party over disarmament was not over its ultimate desirability, all could agree to that, but rather on its relationship to security. While the pacifist wing advocated a disarmament by example that would convince all other states to disarm, the group around Henderson, which dominated the Advisory Committee, saw disarmament as an outcome of a successful security policy based around international organisation. Norman Angell, a member of the Advisory Committee who by the time he wrote his memoirs had become disillusioned with his spell in the Labour Party, recalled Henderson's view on the subject with fondness. 'When I asked Henderson what in his view lay at the root of the disarmament failure he replied instantly: "the failure to tackle security effectively before we started on disarmament." That was the right reply and Henderson saw it more clearly than MacDonald.'[91]

The two top experts on disarmament, Noel Baker and de Madariaga, concurred. For Noel Baker disarmament must be built on security, while de Madariaga thought that an international spirit of cooperation had to replace the predominant one of conflict before disarmament could become a reality.[92] Interestingly, it was on the question of the desirability of disarmament that all political parties in Britain could agree. Conservative governments tended to support the efforts of the disarmament conferences, and it was not uncommon for Labour figures to grudgingly praise Conservative efforts.[93] The major split, which could and did cross party lines, remained over whether disarmament was a first or a final step.

Ironically, the much-hated Versailles Treaty offered, throughout this period, a precedent and template for disarmament in the arms limitation provisions imposed on Germany. The caps on German armaments were justified by the Allies at the time as being consistent with Germany's defence and security, it therefore followed for many advocates of disarmament that the reduction of the rest of the world's arms to a level commensurate with Germany's was a reasonable proposition. As well as a reasonable step, it was also seen as a necessary one. By reducing all arms down to the level of the defeated powers it was believed that the sense of grievance felt by Germany and her former allies towards the Allies and the peace treaties would be sharply reduced.[94] This principle of equal disarmament to Germany's level also cropped up in the German position at the 1931 preparatory commission to the 1932 Disarmament Conference,[95] which suggests that this would have been an effective confidence building measure in Germany. Noel Baker, though, did voice disquiet over this proposal, pointing out that disarmament to Germany's level might make it difficult for League members to fulfil their pooled security commitments under the Covenant.[96] Unfortunately, such disarmament to Germany's level remained a pipe-dream as long as France felt that her armaments were necessary for her security. France continued to link disarmament to a guarantee of its security, whether that was adequate League sanctions or a system of military guarantees. 'The reef upon which every scheme of Disarmament so far has been shipwrecked is Defence, Security.'[97]

Thus, progress in disarmament was once again linked up to the question of inclusive arbitration and effective sanctions. Yet, the failure to establish an effective system of security was not the only problem facing disarmament. The very nature of modern arms guaranteed that disarmament in certain areas was problematic. Rapid technological development made arms difficult to classify and control, while the inter-linkage between civilian and military technologies ensured that some weapons would be complex to control.[98] A good example of this was aircraft, which Philip Noel Baker had singled out as problematic.[99] The problem of controlling military aircraft led to one of the most interesting, although ultimately abortive, disarmament proposals. The idea of internationalising air forces was held up as a solution to two related problems. On the one hand it would remove a potentially destabilising group of weapons from national arsenals, on the other it would provide the international community with a tool for imposing military sanctions on aggressor states. While it was an official French proposal at the 1932 Disarmament Conference, the idea had been mooted by Hugh Dalton in 1928 and, while not necessarily happy with the idea, the Advisory Committee in 1931 saw the plan as an acceptable concession.[100] It rested on the assumption that air forces, as a new wing of the armed forces, would not have accumulated the traditions and procedures associated with the Navy and Army, and would thus be easier to alter into an international force. It also assumed, in line with the strategic writings of the advocates of air power such as Alexander de Seversky, Giulio Douhet and William Mitchell, that air power was now decisive and largely unstoppable.[101] This common perception of the decisiveness of airpower even found its way into both the book and film version of H.G. Wells' *Shape of Things to Come*. Interestingly, Wells also includes a post-war internationalised aviation as part of the solution to the world's problems. Not surprisingly, the proposal for an international air force was bitterly opposed by pacifists.[102] It eventually died with the Disarmament Conference.

Ultimately, with the exception of the Washington Conference on naval limits and a few smaller agreements, the disarmament process that had spluttered on throughout the 1920s failed to deliver. French intransigence, borne out of the failure to satisfy French concerns about security, played a major role. Some have even speculated whether acceptance of the Geneva Protocol in 1924 would have given the push needed to carry disarmament through.[103] Certainly, disarmament in 1924 would have been easier to negotiate than disarmament in the wake of the instability caused by the 1931 economic crisis. The importance of this link between disarmament and security, specifically the guarantee to French security afforded by an effective arbitration and sanctions regime, was well known. 'Concurrently with our demand for reduction of armaments,' Angell wrote in 1924, the year of the Geneva Protocol, 'we must show that we have some means for accomplishing those ends which armaments are supposed, however mistakenly, to accomplish – political and economic security.'[104]

The Geneva Protocol was the First Labour Government's major contribution to the development of the League of Nation's system. The attempt to close the gaps in the Covenant was also designed to satisfy the security concerns of France and many of the minor European powers, and thereby pave the way for disarmament. Although it never came in to force, the Protocol remained the template for future agreements and the basis of Labour's policy during the Second Labour Government. In essence it was an attempt to close several of the gaps in the Covenant, and through that closure to reassure France that she would not be left to face any future German aggression alone. The Covenant left the process of the pacific settlement of disputes vague, and under Article 12 the right to go to war was merely suspended for three months while the dispute was submitted to arbitration or conciliation. Article 16 merely required the members to cease trade, finance and general intercourse between League members and an aggression. France wanted a caste iron guarantee of immediate military aid in the event of aggression. The Protocol was an attempt to make the League's system of pacific settlement of conflicts watertight and to reduce Franco-German tensions. In fact, the road to the Protocol began with the question of French security, and was overshadowed by the French occupation of the Ruhr from 1923–4 in retaliation for Germany's default on her reparations payments. From 1922 discussions of disarmament at the League were held up by France's insistence that she would only reduce her arms if her security was first enhanced.[105] The initial response at the League was the drafting of the Treaty of Mutual Assistance, which required League members to provide military aid to the victim of aggression. The aggressor in the conflict was to be defined by the Council within four days, but the Draft was weakened by a failure to define aggression. Although deeply popular in France and central Europe, it was decisively rejected by Britain, the British Dominions, the Scandinavian states and the Netherlands. For its right-wing opponents the Treaty of Mutual Assistance created open-ended and mandatory military obligations that the signatory state would have little control over. For the left it was a primarily military alliance that had included little provision for arbitration and other peaceful methods of dispute settlement. The disarmament provisions were also worryingly vague for pacifists, although they were an improvement on the earlier French refusal. Article II required the parties to submit an estimate to the Council, work with the Council in producing a plan, and to carry out the reduction of arms within two years. Given that the Council was stacked by former Allied states many on the British left worried that the Draft Treaty effectively made the League a forum for militarised conflict.[106]

British Prime Minister Ramsay MacDonald did not want to be seen as merely rejecting French proposals, after all the Draft Treaty of Mutual Assurance was a legitimate if flawed attempt to close gaps in the Covenant. With the new found partnership with the left-wing government in France, MacDonald and the French Prime Minister Herriot both attended the 1924 sitting of the League Assembly. MacDonald's personal diplomacy was widely regarded as a triumph, both in Britain and in the rest of Europe. With the exception of E.D. Morel, the left-wing press was often ecstatic over MacDonald's demonstration that Labour could handle foreign affairs so much better than the gentlemen of the Conservative Party. In the immediate aftermath of the League Assembly Brailsford gushed that the 'new version of the Covenant is the crown of [MacDonald's] work.'[107] Alfred Zimmern joined the Labour Party directly after MacDonald's diplomatic triumph, stating in *The New Leader* that:

> MacDonald is the greatest Foreign Secretary we have had for many a long day... he has succeeded in half a year in restoring the moral authority of Britain and reviving the confidence of foreign governments, and – what is even more important – of foreign peoples, in the aims of British policy and the fundamental idealism of our people.[108]

The focus of this praise was MacDonald's blunt and no-nonsense diplomacy, which seemed a breath of fresh air after the apparent doubletalk and obstructions of previous British delegates. For the French government, however, MacDonald's strength was in galvanising the British delegation to come up with a set of alternatives for the firming up of the security provisions of the Covenant. The resulting compromise that was hammered out between Britain and France was the Geneva Protocol for the Pacific Settlements of International Disputes.

The Protocol was simultaneously a compromise between the British and French positions, and an articulation of the view that disarmament, arbitration and League sanctions represented mutually supporting pillars of an alternative world order.[109] The Draft Treaty of Mutual Assistance had lacked two things that the Protocol put centre stage. The Protocol laid down a clear system for the arbitration of disputes, and added to this a clear definition of aggressor based on a state's failure to accept arbitration or conciliation in a dispute likely to lead to rupture.[110] Arbitration was seen as the means by which security and disarmament could be linked, since a system of arbitration would provide a means of defining aggressor states that should be the subject of sanctions, while both reducing tensions and the need for a state to possess a preponderance of military might in order to guarantee its security. The Protocol's definition of aggression, which was simultaneously simple and practical, went on to form the basis of definitions of aggression in later treaties of the 1920s. This definition would also be used against the pacifist wing of the Labour Party by supporters of League sanctions. A cornerstone of the pacifist opposition to sanctions was that it was impossible for aggression to be defined; in fact this was an important part of the pacifist case put forward by Arthur Ponsonby in his *Now is the Time*.[111] The Protocol proved that aggression could be defined within a regime of arbitration and conciliation.[112]

The most important thing in the Protocol from the French point of view, and a key element from the point of view of Henderson and his intellectual supporters, was the provision of League sanctions in the event of aggression, although it fell short of making full military sanctions obligatory. Sanctions by the League members would be obligatory against an aggressor. This was key not only to get France to agree to disarmament, but was seen as necessary if the members of the League were to be weaned off relying solely on their own military might for security, and thus be encouraged to reduce their armaments and armed forces to an acceptable international policing level. The provision for the use of military force was played up to the French and the smaller central European states, but such was the fear of military commitment in Britain that these provisions of the Protocol were downplayed by the Labour leadership back in Britain. MacDonald seemed to hope that the habit of arbitration would make the sanctions provisions obsolete.[113]

Such silence on the question of sanctions was not evident amongst the members of the Advisory Committee. Certainly those most supportive of pooled security were vocal in their support for the Protocol's linkage of disarmament, arbitration and sanctions. Noel Baker's book-length treatment of the Protocol, written before the agreement was finally shelved, is a good example of this.[114] Looking back to the events of 1924 in a letter to MacDonald, Arnold-Forster wrote that:

Some of our friends still think we can achieve radical disarmament without having to think about [compulsory] arbitration, and without having to accept the responsibilities of pooled security. But your way the Protocol's way, is the only one between Scylla and Charybdis.[115]

J.A. Hobson was willing to trumpet publicly that League sanctions were a necessary part of dispute settlement:

The organised opinion, and in the last resort (I hold) the organised force of the law-abiding nations should be directed against the outlaw... whatever be the nature of the "sanctions" upon which the [International] Court would rely, whether arms, economic boycott, or the pressure of informed public opinion, there must be some executive machinery for giving effect to the sanctions.[116]

While sanctions, in one form or another, were discussed in the Advisory Committee throughout the 1920s, the main discussion of the issue, which brought out the divisions between its Chair C.R. Buxton and the majority represented by Woolf, Noel Baker, Mitrany and Arnold-Forster, did not occur until 1927.

Although the incoming Conservative Government finally announced in March 1925 that it would not sign the Protocol, aspects of the latter were included in what many of its supporters saw as a half-way house to the Protocol, the Treaty of Locarno. Unlike the Draft Treaty of Mutual Assistance and the Geneva Protocol, the Locarno Pact was signed and ratified, and therefore fully operational. What perhaps took Locarno beyond the Protocol, however, was that it included Germany as an equal partner with Britain and France, and paved the way for German membership of the League with a permanent seat on the Council. Both of these were goals of Labour foreign policy. Yet, in so many ways it was still only a half measure, and the problem with half measures is that they may stand in the way of full implementation. In July 1925 the Advisory Committee worried that Locarno, while not an old-style alliance, might be 'a return to the system of partial alliances':

The Labour Party does not urge that the present negotiations between Germany, France and Great Britain should be broken off, but they insist that the military commitments which might result from these negotiations could not be accepted unless they were merged in a general scheme of arbitration, security and disarmament... unless,

in short, they became subsidiary factors in a general League system
of "pooled security".[117]

By the time a draft treaty was available the Advisory Committee recognised that it was an improvement, and that the treaty had a 'League of Nations element', and that 'the League of Nations is brought in at every
possible point.'[118] Locarno reiterated the Protocol's commitment to disarmament, and required the signatories to seek a general disarmament agreement. Although vague, it was more specific than the Covenant on disarmament, and did at least specify a forum and a distant obligation. It is interesting to note that, while Labour eventually voted for ratification of Locarno in Parliament, they expressed 'regret that the Treaties did not contain definite provisions concerning disarmament, being of the opinion that
the real test of the Treaty depended upon whether it was followed by disarmament.'[119] Especially important for Labour were the arbitration treaties
in the Pact, which 'extend and amplify the provisions of the Covenant',
even though it was restricted to French, Belgian and German relations.[120]
The pact did attempt to close the loop hole in the Covenant that preserved a state's right to war if the Council was unable to reach a decision within three months on a dispute before the Council (Article 15). Instead:

> there is an engagement by France, Belgium and Germany that...
> they will resort to war against the State which was the first to attack
> ... The Party which is the first to attack, if this fact can be esta-
> blished, loses the help of the guarantors. *This is an attempt at an
> improvement of the Covenant procedure.*[121]

At this point there was a severe disagreement between the report's original
author, C.R. Buxton, and the majority on the Committee. Buxton was unhappy with the way that the arbitration was 'associated with military sanctions to which serious objection may be taken'.[122] This reservation of Buxton's was cut out of the later final draft sent on to the Executive.

Where all could agree, however, was that Locarno must only be seen as
a step on a process, rather than an end in itself. While all parties, even the
British Conservative Foreign Secretary Austen Chamberlain, agreed with
this, Norman Angell was quick to point out that 'the present mood of
reconciliation and appeasement' may change quickly, and if Locarno was
to have a positive impact it had to be the first in a series of institutional
developments that would copper fasten the present positive mood. Specifically Locarno:

> Can only be relied upon provided that it has meantime been
> supplemented (1) by general and firm undertakings to settle differ-
> ences by arbitral or judicial means; (2) by attenuating those features
> of the Versailles settlement…which are most provocative of ill-will,
> and which could be amended without raising the question of
> Revision; (3) by definite steps towards agreements for progressive
> disarmament.[123]

The fear was that without a clear development of the principles of arbitration and disarmament, as well as confidence-building measures that ameliorated parts of the Versailles Treaty, the Locarno Pact could revert to a
partial military alliance between the signatories, which could only be directed against the Soviet Union.[124] As it stood, Locarno 'is undoubtedly "a
form of limited military alliance or guarantee".'[125]

Once again, for the majority on the Advisory Committee the test of an
international agreement was measured against the way that it helped develop the links between arbitration, League-sponsored sanctions and disarmament. That the mid-1920s was seen as a window of opportunity easily
squandered by inaction comes out clearly, but a slapdash arrangement that
could be manipulated by those in favour of the old system of the international anarchy would be a serious retrograde step. The value of Locarno
could only be judged by what would come after it. While there were positive repercussions such as German membership of the League, the intransigence of the Conservative Government in Britain acted as a break on
further developments.

The same measure for judgment was applied to the various American
proposals for the outlawry of war that eventually led to the Kellog-Briand
Pact of Paris signed on 27 August 1928. There were at least three separate
American proposals for the outlawry of war in addition to the Kellogg-
Briand negotiations, two of which formed draft resolutions in the US Se-
nate. The Morrison proposal and Senator Borah's resolution came under
particularly strong attack from Leonard Woolf, although Senator Capper's
resolution was endorsed as conforming to Labour Party policy. Morrison's
proposals involved the complete abolition of the League of Nations and
the Permanent Court, the continuation of the old system of armed alliances, and contained no sanctions provisions for when a state breached its
obligations. Senator Borah's resolution, although still provisional, gave
legal form to Morrison's proposals.[126] The main problem with the Morrison and Borah proposals was the failure to build upon the existing machinery for arbitration, and to provide this machinery with a clear and operational sanctions regime. As a result it merely replicated the old interna-

tional anarchy, adding to it a toothless system of condemnation. By contrast, the Capper proposals did not require the dismantling of the current League machinery, but rather supplemented it by advocating bilateral treaties renouncing war as an instrument of policy. Capper also used the Protocol's definition of aggression, thus providing another opportunity for introducing an aspect of the Protocol into international affairs.[127] Capper's approach was to form the basis of the Kellogg-Briand Pact, which outlawed war between the signatory governments, while keeping the League system intact. Although Kellogg-Briand was to be overtaken by events in the 1930s, its provisions for self-defence would continue as a principle of the system of collective defence under the United Nations Charter. Perhaps, though, its most important contribution was to bring the United States into the process of constructing a new system of international relations, without undoing what had been achieved though the League of Nations.

By the time Labour returned to power in 1929 the gaps in the League Covenant were still apparent, despite the attempts to tighten up the mechanisms and definitions in the Covenant. Much had been achieved. The Protocol's definition of aggression had found wide acceptance amongst the international community, while the principle of arbitration had largely been agreed to both by delegates in Geneva and amongst British politicians, even if the specific mechanisms of it were not. There was still much to be done, and the gaps in the League regime were all too apparent. One of the biggest was Britain's refusal to sign the Optional Clause, which would have committed Britain to recognise the decisions of the Permanent Court of International Justice on legal disputes between states. Another was the failure of the various attempts at general disarmament, despite the disarmament clauses of the peace treaties, which continued to limit the military power of the defeat states to a level consistent with defence and internal security. In effect, the Locarno Pact had not been built on. In 1929 it still seemed reasonable that a mood of good will could be exploited in the service of firming up the provisions of the Covenant.

The Second Labour Government and the 'Peace of Nations'

The Labour government that took office in 1929 had many advantages that the First Labour Government did not have. While still a minority administration reliant on Liberal support in the House of Commons, Labour was for the first time the largest party in Parliament. There was, therefore, no doubt about its right to form the next government. After five years of Conservative foreign policy many foreign governments and delegates at the League welcomed what was hoped would be a less intransigent government in Britain. Labour had a clear foreign policy, laid out with the rest of the Party's policy in the pamphlet *Labour and the Nation*, the production of which had been the brainchild of Arthur Henderson. Since the fall of the First Labour Government in 1924 Henderson had seen the need for a clear pamphlet-sized statement by the Party on all questions of policy, which could then be used as a measure of the Party's success in government. The result was *Labour and the Nation*, which was finally passed by the Labour Party Conference in 1928. The importance that Henderson and his number two Hugh Dalton attached to *Labour and the Nation* can be seen in their decision, once in the Foreign Office, to distribute two dozen copies of the pamphlet in the Foreign Office so that its civil servants would have a clear idea of Party policy.[128] Cheekily, Dalton recalled, he had the Foreign Office billed for the cost of the pamphlets.[129]

The author's of the international policy section of *Labour and the Nation*, Philip Noel Baker and Leonard Woolf, were careful not to create a rift in the Party over foreign policy, and consequently the wording on some issues was deliberately low key. Crucially, while it stood for disarmament and arbitration – numbers 2 and 3 in the Party's 'Six Pillars of Peace' – there was no mention of sanctions, whether economic or military.[130] Since the sanctions provisions would be a vital part of any comprehensive system of arbitration, and since it was the question of sanctions that so divided the Party, its omission was a screaming silence. The only hint that sanctions of some sort might be contemplated comes in the careful preamble to the discussion of the six pillars:

> The whole structure of peace and of a foreign policy of cooperation must be built firmly on the foundation of the League of Nations. Through the League's machinery the Labour Government will co-operate with all other governments to promote the world's common interests.[131]

As C.R. Buxton had noted in his memorandum on sanctions mentioned in the last section, support for the League machinery included, under Article 16, mandatory economic sanctions and the option of military sanctions if a League member was attacked. Yet, the tenor of the six pillars emphasises the peaceful. The first pillar reiterated the call for the renunciation of war contained in the Kellogg-Briand Pact, while the second pillar of disarmament is to be pursued in order to 'abolish the element of force from international relations.' Arbitration, the third pillar, would be enacted in two ways: first, by signing the Optional Clause, and second by pursuing bilateral arbitration treaties 'covering all disputes, with any other state prepared

to do the same.' Pillars four and six cover economic and political cooperation with other states and peoples respectfully, while pillar five was a
commitment to submit all international engagements to the House of
Commons for ratification, and to keep the public informed of 'the handling of foreign affairs.'[132] The international relations section of *Labour and
the Nation* was left unrevised in its second edition, and only had minor
amendments added in the Revised Edition and Supplement.

What *Labour and the Nation* left unsaid was filled in by Hugh Dalton in
his *Towards the Peace of Nations*. While Dalton wrote in a private capacity,
and not on behalf of the Party, his writing nevertheless reflected the feelings of the group around Henderson. While not rejecting out of hand the
radical socialist view that there was a link between capitalism and war,
Dalton was willing to concede that some groups did benefit from war and
that some capitalists pursue policies that make war more possible. But,
quoting Angell, he saw the idea that capitalists as a class gain from war as
wholly false.[133] Rather, as Lowes Dickinson had argued in the case of the
First World War, 'it was the lack of international organisation that brought
us down.'[134] A properly put together international structure of arbitration,
disarmament and sanctions could prevent the outbreak of wars. Dalton is
not squeamish about advocating military sanctions, and quotes Mitrany's
comment that all political organisations require some form of sanctions.
Military sanctions might be the last resort, but they were necessary to give
force to an international legal system.[135] Dalton envisioned a two-pronged
approach:

> The first step must… be to make national governments more paci-
> fic, more internationally minded and more willing to pool their priv-
> ileges and powers, and this means to make them more socialist …
> Another line of future advance is the encouragement of genuinely
> international bodies, at first advisory and consultative, and their gra-
> dual endowment with real powers.[136]

Thus, government attitude counted, and a Labour government in this
sense could and would make a difference. At another level, this mood
needed to be given an institutional form, and Dalton was coming around
to the view that that institutional form should be predominantly functional. Having quoted Mitrany on sanctions, Dalton had ended by antici-
pating Mitrany's functional approach, albeit in a very vague form.

Generally speaking, there is widespread agreement amongst many historians that the foreign policy of the Second Labour Government was a
success.[137] By contrast, there is a similar large body of opinion that its

policy on the economic crisis and unemployment was an abject failure. Indeed Ben Pimlott wrote that foreign policy was the one field where the Government 'could claim some temporary success.'[138] Despite Labour's commitment to international conciliation its first major foreign policy success was the alteration of the Young Plan on German reparations, which benefited narrow British interests and little else. Philip Snowden, the Chancellor, over-ruled an earlier British concession, made by the Conservatives, which had effectively given part of its share of reparations to France. Snowden's pugnacity may have seriously disturbed Anglo-French relations, but proved extremely popular in Britain, especially in jingoistic circles. Although open to debate, Snowden's actions may have given Labour an early reputation for toughness that gave it a little more leeway with the Conservative-dominated press at home. Although the groundwork had been laid earlier, and the waters had been temporarily muddied by Snowden, the Young Plan was an initial public relations success for Labour. The rescheduling of reparations and the accelerated timetable for Allied withdrawal from the Rhineland settled two of the major outstanding problems in Franco-German relations.

Labour's first major success consistent with the principles of *Labour and the Nation* was undoubtedly the signing of the Optional Clause that committed Britain to accepting Permanent Court arbitration in judicial disputes. Britain, through inter-Imperial negotiations, brought the Dominions with them, although Ireland signed without the Imperial reservations. Many other states followed Britain's lead, and the number of signatures of the Optional Clause rose from nineteen to forty-two.[139] Consistent with Labour's commitment to a democratic foreign policy, the House of Commons was entitled to ratify Britain's signature, which it duly did after a heated debate in January 1930. The Optional Clause covered arbitration in judicial disputes. A year after the signing of the Optional Clause the Foreign Secretary Arthur Henderson started the process that led to the signing of the General Act of Arbitration, Conciliation and Judicial Settlement. By signing the General Act the signatory committed themselves to arbitration in judicial disputes, conciliation in non-judicial disputes, and arbitration in the event of the failure of conciliation. Britain and the Dominions, minus South Africa, signed after the Imperial Conference of October 1930, and the House of Commons ratified the signature on 9 March 1931. Thus, by the end of the Government Labour had committed Britain to much the same system of all-inclusive arbitration as had been laid out in the Geneva Protocol.

Of course, the arbitration regime was only part of the problem. There was still the question of the role of sanctions in the event of arbitration being refused, the related issue of the guarantee of security within the League system, and the stalled disarmament process that had largely been held up by French fears that the League as it was could not guarantee French security if France chose to disarm. British policy chose to deal with these problems in two ways, both of which had mixed results. The first was to close the perceived gap in the Covenant that still allowed the resort to war by parties to a non-judicial dispute if the Council was unable to agree on a settlement after three months. While covered by the General Act, this provision of Article 12, and to a certain extent Article15, of the Covenant appeared to contradict the Kellogg-Briand Pact's renunciation of war as an instrument of policy. In 1929 it did look as though a British and French supported amendment to Article 16 to extend sanctions to all wars prohibited by the Kellogg-Briand Pact would pass, thus reviving the central plank of the Protocol, but the vote was postponed until 1930.[140] The attempt, in 1930, to amend the Covenant broke down over differences between Britain and France, with France feeling that the British position on the amendment did not contribute to French security, and therefore did little to encourage French participation in disarmament. The second way was the Government's attempt to link the development of clearer sanctions provisions with progress in disarmament. This was a compromise between Henderson's position, in which security should be achieved before disarmament, and the position of much of the pacifist wing of the Labour Party as well as the Conservative isolationist position of no fresh foreign entanglements. Specifically, Henderson supported the Convention for Financial Assistance to States in Danger of Aggression, a major plank of the emerging sanctions regime, but limited British engagement with it to states that were party to a comprehensive disarmament treaty.[141] Initially, this seemed reasonable given the progress, however acrimonious at times, in the Preparatory Commission of the upcoming disarmament conference. Initially the German delegation had been unhappy at the failure of the Preparatory Commission to set a date for the World Disarmament Conference, but by 25 January 1931 the League Council was able to set a date of February 1932 for the opening of the Conference.[142]

At the end of the day Henderson's team had signed up to both the Optional Clause and the General Act, finally committing Britain to an all-inclusive arbitration regime. They had worked tirelessly to make the Disarmament Conference happen, often finding themselves brokering between a French and a German position, while increasingly and often reluctantly taking the French side despite the initial Francophobia of the Party. Thus, the long expected disarmament conference was now a reality. The lessening of Franco-German tensions with the final adoption of the Young Plan was a step in the right direction for providing a more stable European security environment. The major failure was in the area of sanctions, and the firming up of the provisions of the Covenant on the matter of the legality of war. Here, Henderson, Dalton and the majority of the Advisory Committee were far ahead of the thinking in the wider Party and even the Cabinet. For the Covenant to work effectively, and for arbitration to replace war as a means of settling disputes, there had to be effective sanctions to guarantee the security of states. Only then could disarmament be comprehensive. The Draft Convention for the World Disarmament Conference that emerged out of the Preparatory Commission recognised this gap when it allowed states to suspend their obligations to disarm if their security was threatened. Thus, once again, comprehensive disarmament was undermined by insecurity created by the weakness of the sanctions provisions in the Covenant. French attempts to include sanctions provisions in Britain's proposals for closing the gap on the outlawry of private war in the Covenant – which were supported by Cecil, Britain's delegate to the committee – were vetoed by the British Cabinet. Despite this, however, the British Foreign Office team helped make the 1929 League Assembly one of the most productive on record. Dalton, in his memoirs, was able to declare that by March 1931 the Government had done every-thing in the area of foreign affairs that it said it would in *Labour and the Nation,* except general disarmament.[143]

The figure who often stood in the way of Henderson's attempts to provide a clearer statement on sanctions or a security guarantee to France was the Prime Minister Ramsay MacDonald. While Henderson – as a loyal committee man who had come up through the ranks of the Trades Union movement – stuck to the letter of *Labour and the Nation,* despite its failure to endorse sanctions and security before disarmament, he did try to advance sanctions provisions alongside the Party's commitment to general disarmament. MacDonald, trusting far more to a spirit of peace and less to concrete institutional commitments, often led Cabinet vetoes of Henderson's initiatives, including the offer of security guarantees to France. This conflict between Labour's two top leaders is covered effectively in David Carlton's seminal treatment of the Second Labour Government's foreign policy.[144] While sanctions and adequate security remained an important part of the approach taken by Labour's foreign policy team at Geneva, the combination of its near exclusion from *Labour and the Nation* and Mac-Donald's scepticism undermined what was a central part of the approach to foreign affairs taken by Henderson, Dalton, Arnold-Forster, Noel Baker and Norman Angell, amongst others. Yet, despite this, Labour's record on foreign affairs during its Second Government stands out between the two periods of right-wing government before and after it. The previous Conservative Government could claim the kudos for Locarno, but this pact stood alone amidst the debris of the Conservative Government's refusal to engage in a constructive way in so many of the international initiatives that were launched through the League between 1924 and 1929. Labour has been criticised, with hindsight, for being overly optimistic.[145] Yet, its kick-starting of so many initiatives within the League – projects that had for a decade been regarded as necessary in order to construct a working alternative to the international anarchy – were fully in line with the thinking of the time, and with the possibilities offered by the relative stability between the great powers in the 1920s. We now know that these initiatives were too little too late, but what undermined them were not vast subterranean forces of history, but specific events constructed by the acts of particular individuals. The slow reaction of the various national banks, the panic of creditors, the militarism of the semi-autonomous Japanese forces in Manchuria, the lack of resolve amongst the key League members to deal with Japan, the mishandling of the emergency decree powers in Germany and the actions of MacDonald and his Chancellor Philip Snowden were all implicated in the collapse of the League project that had been championed by the Second Labour Government.

1931 marks a turning point in the international relations of the interwar period. The Wall Street Crash may have occurred two years before, and Hitler's rise to the Chancellorship was still two years away, but 1931 marks the end of an era. Specifically for Labour it witnessed the worst setback in the Party's history as a direct result of the actions of a group of the Party's senior figures. 1931 was the year that the full force of the economic crisis hit. Severe problems with international finance came to a head in May when the Austrian Kredit-Anstalt Bank became insolvent. The panic spread to Germany and Central Europe, where foreign lenders began to call in their short term loans. On 13 July the first major German banks collapsed. The financial crisis led to a dramatic slump in world trade, which caused a severe balance of payments crisis in Britain. Falling tax receipts and rising unemployment caused a major fiscal crisis for the British Government. The Labour Chancellor of the Exchequer Philip Snowden, a fiscal conservative who had already caused a split in the Party by his policy of cutting expenditure including unemployment benefits, suggested further cuts and tax rises to cover the deficit. The proposed cuts in unemployment benefit were particularly unpopular in the Party and Cabinet – many of the Trades Unionists in the Party and Cabinet, including Arthur Henderson, had known unemployment in their youth – and the Treasury was sceptical about the tax rises. The Trade Union Congress refused to endorse Snowden's economic measures. Influenced by Ernest Bevin they advocated a Keynesian approach to the problem, which included suspending payments to the Sinking Fund for the National Debt, a position that was anathema to the fiscally conservative Snowden. The Cabinet was also unable to agree on Snowden's proposals, and on 23 August, after failing to reach agreement, they decided that the government should resign. During extensive talks with the two opposition leaders and the King MacDonald had discussed the idea of cross-party cooperation for the duration of the crisis. These meetings were conducted with the full knowledge of the Cabinet. On 24 August MacDonald formed a national government, comprising Labour, Liberal and Conservative members, for the sole purpose of dealing with the current crisis. There is still strong disagreement about the sequence of events, and how much the rest of MacDonald's Cabinet knew, but what is clear is that MacDonald formed the National Government without the support of the Party or key members of the Cabinet.[146] The vast majority of the PLP refused to join the new coalition, and MacDonald's 'temporary' National Government not only held an immediate election, despite his promises not to, but would last, under Conservative control, until 1940.

In the elections in October Labour's vote collapsed. Labour's share of the seats in the House of Commons went from 288 seats to just 52. Labour's collapse occurred just as the League of Nations faced its first major challenge since Italy's invasion of Corfu. In September Japan started its invasion of the Chinese province of Manchuria. Looking back from 1937 the historian A.L. Rowse would write:

> ...1931: that year of disaster, the real dividing-line in contemporary Europe, when the hopes of the post-war period came to a resounding end and everything from that moment went wrong. The crimes of 1933, 1934, 1935, 1936, 1937... only followed the defeat of our own working-class movement in 1931, the complete victory of our governing class, and the betrayal of all hopes of a new order of public control within the nation and without, of internal economic security and collective security in Europe and beyond. That is how the historian of the future will see these tragic years since 1931.[147]

For Henderson, perhaps, the thin consolation on top of his deep disappointments was his earlier appointment to the Chair of the upcoming 1932 Disarmament Conference, and his award of the Nobel Peace Prize in 1934 for his work on disarmament. He was only the second Briton to have received the award – after Norman Angell, who had collected the same prize in 1933. Interestingly, in 1956 a third Briton, Philip Noel Baker, would receive the same prize.

Making the League Work: Labour and the Last Chance for Peace
Henry Winkler's assessment, that the 1920s shift by Labour towards 'the gradual acceptance of the "League of Nations" outlook marked a signifycant change in Labour's approach in the international area and reflected its growing maturity as an international force', seems more than warranted. Certainly, the development of a coherent approach to foreign policy through existing institutions like the League was a sharp change from the angry denunciations of the Peace that had preceded it, even if those denunciations had contained within them the seeds of Labour's policy of collaboration with the structures of the League. This collaboration took the form of firming up the Covenant so that it could form the basis of an alternative world order. Behind this was a theoretical approach that was premised on the interdependence of states and the crucial inter-relationship of arbitration, sanctions and disarmament in the construction of a regime of peaceful change that would best serve the security concerns of an interdependent world. It was accepted that basing the international system on states, particularly nation-states, was a cause of friction. Without an over-arching sovereign authority states were free to settle disputes by violence and war. The idea that peace could be achieved by the construction of international institutions was simultaneously an acceptance that states left to their own devices would resort to unilateral violent solutions to security problems, and that moral example was far too weak a force to prevent violence on its own. Global institutions were a necessary link between the amorality of states in the international anarchy and the moral aspirations of the fair-minded. The first step was to create the mechanisms that would substitute peaceful change for inter-state conflict.

The concept of peaceful change was central to inter-war thinking on international relations, as much for the likes of Angell and Noel Baker as for Carr. In the 1920s many looked to the League of Nations as the basis for a peaceful change regime, while in 1938–9, E.H. Carr saw in the policy of appeasement, and especially the Munich agreement over the Sudetenland, the basis of a new non-League system of peaceful change. The efforts by the group around Henderson to create a functioning system of all-inclusive arbitration linked to disarmament was an attempt to create the institutional structures necessary to make peaceful change a realistic alternative to the old diplomacy. While by 1931 they had achieved much, especially the general acceptance of the jurisdiction of the Permanent Court and a firm date for the World Disarmament Conference, most of their achievements were premised on the continuation of the regime of relative goodwill that had existed since 1924. Norman Angell in 1925 had warned that there was a short window of goodwill in which the institutional framework for a more peaceful world could be constructed.[148] By 1931 that window was closing fast, and the institutional arrangements in place proved to be inadequate to the serious tasks at hand. A second window would not open up until 1944, and then western politicians were not slow in establishing as much of the international institutions as the wave of late war idealism would allow. In 1927 Noel Baker had asked whether the League's institutions 'would be given time to build up their strength'. He warned that unless something was done about disarmament and its related security requirements a new world war 'would sweep away the fabric of the League.'[149] In the end it was these forces of disintegration that triumphed, ushering in a conflict that was to exceed the wanton destructiveness of the Great War.

The major question mark that hangs over their endeavours, however, is whether the arbitration, sanctions and disarmament provisions being mooted would still have been enough. Here Mitrany's concern that there was a lack of will amongst states to use sanctions surfaces as a major criticism of the attempts to close the gaps in the Covenant. It was not only that governments might be reluctant; it was also the case that the population at large, especially in Britain, were suspicious of military actions that looked too much like foreign adventures. The famous story told by Harold Nicolson is relevant here, although it dates from 1935. A constituent sent him a letter asking him if he stood for the League and collective security, but opposed any entanglements in Europe. More worryingly for Nicolson was how few people recognised the contradiction in the letter when he read it out at meetings. 'Only in rare and isolated cases did my audience see that the above formula was self-contradictory nonsense.'[150] That there was not the will to use the machinery of the League for adequate sanctions in the 1920's is also clear from Labour's deliberate downplaying of the issue in its public pronouncements such as *Labour and the Nation*. While this does lend support to the argument – found in Mitrany, but also present in the work of Woolf, Dalton, Angell, Brailsford and others – that the problem of the sovereign state was still a key cause of the international anarchy, it also puts the dispute between Henderson and Ramsay MacDonald in a different light. My intellectual instinct, as an IR scholar, is to favour Henderson's approach. His support for concrete institutions and guarantees appears far more pragmatic at first glance. By contrast, Ramsay MacDonald's hope that the habit of cooperation might make the use of sanctions unnecessary seems deeply deluded in the light of what was to happen after 1931. Yet, was it Ramsay MacDonald who had the clearer vision? As a professional politician did he realise that in the climate of the 1920's it was very unlikely that British public opinion would lend its support to sanctions? In the absence of an alternative to the sovereign state was the habit of cooperation the best that could be hoped for? We will never have a definitive answer to this question because the League's arbitration-sanctions-disarmament regime was never fully developed. What is certain, though, is that the League of the early thirties – a League that was still built around the primacy of the sovereign state – did fail. The alternative to the League, the policy of appeasement advocated by self-styled realists, also failed.

In the eight years that followed the collapse of the second Labour government many who had worked hard to construct a League-based working peace system shifted gears and became supporters of collective defence against fascism. They found themselves at odds with the pacifists (who had been suspicious of League sanctions) the old-school Conservatives (who turned to a policy of peaceful change by appeasement of German demands) and a radical socialist suspicion of any policy that armed a capitalist state. In association with the major Trades Union leaders, particularly Ernest Bevin and J.R. Clynes, they managed to carry the Party with them, but only with great difficulty and much public washing of laundry. During the same period David Mitrany would develop a new system of peaceful change that was meant to by-pass much of the problems associated with the League system that had been emerging during the 1920s – but that is a story best told in chapter five. At this stage in our narrative it suffices to say that the world changed in 1931, and that the Labour Party's academics changed with it.

4

PEACEFUL CHANGE
AND THE RISE OF FASCISM
(1931–1939)

Norman Angell

...Mr Norman Angell. He is probably the ablest pamphleteer who
has used the English language since Thomas Paine, and he brings to
his task a knowledge of affairs and an insight into the detailed
working of the world's machinery which few of the early Radicals
possessed. (*H.N. Brailsford*)[1]

Although very little read within IR today, Norman Angell was certainly
one of the most important figures in IR before 1945, perhaps *the* most important in the English-speaking world. Unusually for the time Angell's
books were extremely popular on both sides of the Atlantic, and his classic *The Great Illusion* was translated into ten languages alone in the first two
years after its first publication. Measured by book sales, and the languages
that his books were translated into, Angell might be the biggest figure in
the history of IR. This makes his exclusion from the mainstream of IR
over the last five decades the more bizarre. Angell's publication record
was amazing. This includes over twenty books, hundreds of articles and
the editorship of a number of periodicals, including the UDC's *Foreign
Affairs*, which he took over after the resignation of H.M. Swanwick. Many
of the books were bestsellers. Amongst the people he influenced were
Woodrow Wilson and James Ramsay MacDonald. Despite this popularity,
Angell was little read after the 1950s, and references to him in the IR
literature now tend to be through Carr's misleading interpretation of him
in *The Twenty Years' Crisis*. He is often quoted as the archetypal idealist in
IR texts, and amazingly his works do not even warrant a reference in the

two inter-war chapters of Groom and Olson's review of the history of IR.[2] Despite this, Angell's ideas have been the subject of at least three books over the last thirty years,[3] and he is often singled out as a fore-runner of interdependence theory.[4] Outside of the academy Angell was honoured with the Nobel Peace Prize in 1933 for his writings on international affairs, and a knighthood in 1931. As late as 1963 Kenneth Younger, director of the Royal Institute of International Affairs and former Minister of State, praised Angell as a prophet in a special BBC radio tribute programme.[5]

Certainly there are weaknesses to Angell's thought, but his written work always followed a clear and logical argument, while remaining sensitive to changing international conditions. His writings before the First World War focused on the interdependent nature of modern civilisation, and the consequent atavism of war carried out for any purpose other than policing. During the war he worked closely with the UDC, an organisation that he helped to found, and his opposition to the destructive and anti-democratic nature of the war led him to join the Labour Party soon after. Between 1919 and 1921 Angell was particularly critical of the failings of the treaties and the League. His discussion of the peace terms for the Advisory Committee damned the whole process as a continuation of the international anarchy that had caused the war,[6] and during the 1921 Labour Party Conference Angell emphasised the importance of the revision of the peace treaties to the future prosperity and stability of the world.[7] Perhaps Angell's most influential book in this period was his *Fruits of Victory*, which – like Keynes' *Economic Consequences of the Peace* – attacked the futility of reparations.[8] By his own admission, Angell found himself travelling 'pretty rapidly to the Far Left' during the last years of the war, and the first years of the Peace. He worked closely with George Lansbury on the *Daily Herald*, at the time a major focus for socialist and pacifist opinion, and was deeply influenced by G.D.H. Cole's Guild Socialism.[9] After this initial blast of radicalism, Angell settled down as a supporter of Arthur Henderson's policy towards the League. Like Dalton and Mitrany he was not convinced that a socialist state would be intrinsically pacific, and as editor of *Foreign Affairs* he trumpeted internationalism through the League as the alternative to nationalist conflict. His main theoretical work of the period was his influential *The Public Mind*, which largely argued the case for a proper international machinery to cope with the innate irrationality of group (particularly national) psychologies.[10] From 1929 to 1931 he sat as a Labour MP, losing his seat in the election following MacDonald's defection to the National Government.

After 1931, despite disillusionment with the Party following the co-llapse of the Second Labour Government, Angell continued to be associated with the Party and the Advisory Committee. Except for the debate with Brailsford and others over the question of whether capitalism caused war,[11] his attention now turned to the question of what to do with the increasing aggression of the Dictators. He criticised the idea of Italy, Japan and Germany as have-not states, the argument that was used to justify fascist aggression,[12] and advocated strong League action, up to and including war, against Japan during the Manchurian crisis of 1931 and against Italy over Abyssinia.[13] His main criticisms, however, were levelled at the Nazi regime in Germany, and a side-swipe at the Conservative-dominated National Government in Britain for its passivity towards Germany.[14] Angell's implacable opposition to appeasement may have influenced E.H. Carr's decision to treat Angell as one of the utopians in *The Twenty Years' Crisis*, remembering that Carr's definition of utopian often worked back from his support for appeasement. Interestingly, Carr only quoted Angell's pre-First World war work, and none of Angell's inter-war publications get a mention, which is odd for a book that from its title downwards claims to be dealing with the inter-war period. Angell responded to Carr in 1940, and the central part of his rebuttal revolved around the dubious categories of realist and utopian.[15] During the Second World War Angell supported the war effort both through his writing and by campaigning for the Allied cause in the United States. Much of his war-time writing focused on the issue of freedom and the delusions of fascism.[16] His post-1945 works concentrated on what he saw as the continued delusions about conflict, although now he tended to be as critical of the left as of the right. While opposed to the policies of the USSR, he did not relish the prospect of East-West conflict.[17]

Before looking in more detail at the construction of Angell's argument against appeasement and the dictators I wish to summarise Angell's theories of international politics. The first issue to point out is that, while many of his assumptions remained unchanged throughout his life, his world view changed dramatically during the First World War. Elsewhere I have distinguished between two phases in Angell's thought, Angell (I) before the First World War and Angell (II) after the war, although – as I mentioned then – the distinction was sometimes blurred by Angell's frequent republishing of older works in new formats or editions.[18] Despite this, the distinction between the two periods is crucial to an understanding of Angell's thought, and it was Carr's failure to address this difference, manifest most clearly in his lack of references to Angell's work after 1914, that undermines his cursory criticism of Angell in *The Twenty Years' Crisis*.

The ideas of Angell (I) were fundamentally those of a late Victorian liberal, and were premised on the optimistic British Victorian faith in progress. Angell contrasted the steady progress in human technology and economic interdependence with the more awkward and slow progress in human ideas about their own social world. The growth of international interdependence changed the whole nature of human society, but the ideas that people used to make sense of their world continually had to play catch up, and were usually products of an earlier and simpler world. We have, as humans, a tendency to rely on our passions, which leads us to fall back on atavistic ideas that we were brought up with, but which belong to an earlier age. Consequently, we need to use our reason to work out new ideas that fit the current form of our world. In order to accomplish this task we need to carry out detailed research on how the world around us really works. Thus, human history is a unilinear evolutionary process, in which the violent passions give way to more rational and cooperative forms of society.[19]

In terms of his analysis of the pre-1914 international anarchy, Angell's focus was on the mismatch between the interconnectedness of trade and finance on the one hand, and the atavistic nationalist and militarist ideas that assumed that states were self-contained units in a natural state of violent conflict on the other. As interdependence deepened (a phrase that Angell would not have used, but a good description of his view) military conflict between states ceased to have any economic value at all, and in fact became a threat to prosperity through the disruption of world trade and global financial flows.[20] A major part of the flawed thinking of the militarists was that wealth was owned by nations, when in fact trade and financial links were controlled by individuals, not by states, and the raw materials and commodities, the access to which was always an important part of the militarist argument for imperial expansion, were owned by individuals and non-state companies.[21] The result of the development of a non-state interdependence was the separation of economic and military power. The possession of military might did not affect economic success:

> If the British manufacturer can make [goods]... cheaper or better than his rivals he will obtain the trade... and the possession of *Dreadnoughts* will not make a wit of difference...

> It is evident that the foreigner does not buy our products and refuse Germany's because we have a larger navy.[22]

Military power, while it cannot bring wealth, is capable of disrupting wealth, and the impoverishment caused by war affects the victor as much as the victim of aggression. Economic power, in short, cannot be captured, and its interdependent nature means that its destruction has wider global ramifications.[23] For Angell (I) the only acceptable use of military force is in a policing role that safeguards international interdependence.[24]

Angell (I) saw modern war is a futile exercise if its goal was national aggrandisement and economic power. Once people recognise this simple fact, and realise the fallacy of pursuing militarist goals, then the problem will disappear. It is here that the main difference between Angell (I) and Angell (II) – Angell's intellectual output after 1914 – is at its starkest. The central difference was that Angell (II) no longer had Angell (I)'s optimistic faith in reason, and as a result stressed the need to introduce new international institutions in order to control the dangerous and violent forces that threatened global prosperity. The First World War demonstrated for Angell how easy it was for large groups of people to become attached to a violent course of action that was, in the long run, against their own interests. The pugnacious element in human nature was stronger than Angell (I) had assumed, and was available for exploitation by jingoistic elements in society; thus, as our society develops a more interdependent and prosperous economic civilisation it becomes necessary to construct an institutional security framework to protect our peace and prosperity. Angell (II)'s analysis concentrated on two related areas: the form and construction of irrational pugnacity in international relations, what Angell called the public mind; and the institutional reforms necessary for the safeguarding of international economic progress. Angell's shift from reason to group psychology and institutions also marked his move from late Victorian liberalism to twentieth century socialism. 'Capitalist Trusts' were blamed for fomenting the instability that had helped bring the war on by their lobbying for overseas possessions,[25] while the war had shown Angell that the state could effectively manage an economy and efficiently deal with problems such as unemployment.[26] While Angell (I) saw political and economic power as separate, Angell (II) saw the two in the new post-war world as subtly mixed. The important question was what form that mix took.[27]

The first issue, and the one that for Angell shaped the debate about the necessary form of the new global institutions, was the nature of the mass psychology – the public mind – that had allowed the war to happen in the first place. Individually, Angell argued, people are potentially rational and able to coolly weigh up facts and details. In groups, however, people have a tendency to let collective passions carry them away, and to propound things that they would never do individually.[28] Other factors would exacerbate this tendency, and Angell as a journalist single out an irresponsible mass media as a major contributory factor,[29] alongside demagogue politicians who played to the public's worst tendencies.[30] Angell's template for the public mind was the mass jingoism that had seized the belligerents during the First World War, and it was the strength of these feelings that had swept away the complacent Edwardian world. From this he concluded that the violent irrational forces within human nature were stronger than he had first suspected, and it was the quality of a society's public mind that determined the quality of society as a whole.[31] There were two complimentary answers to the problem of the public mind. The first was to increase the power of rational argument and dissent in order to improve the quality of the public mind, and thus to make it less susceptible to knee-jerk violent passions. The answer here lay in a combination of education and widespread protection for freedom of thought within society.[32] The second answer was to deal with the symptoms. Since these violent public passions were so close to the surface their eruption could occur in any society at any time. There had to be institutional arrangements to control and contain them when they emerged. Internationally, therefore, there would need to be effective mechanisms in place to restrain potential aggression and lawlessness.

While many on the pacifist wing of the Party put their faith squarely on disarmament and good will, Angell saw arms as tangential to the problem. If it was the mind behind the gun, rather than the gun, that was the problem, then the disarmament of the mind must come first. Only then could the gun be put beyond use.[33] To make this psychological disarmament a reality, however, the unpredictability of the public mind need to be controlled by the development of an effective set of institutional arrangements.[34] It was for this reason that Angell after the First World War became a strong advocate of an effective League of Nations pooled security regime. Good will alone, he realised, would never be enough.

With the rise of the dictators Angell's conception of international organisations changed in response. Although the main theoretical arguments remained the same, he quickly came to realise that an inclusive international organisation that included the dictators was unlikely to create peace. Rather, the dictators were now the major threat to international stability. Angell's response to the aggression of the dictators was swift and unequivocal. He was an advocate of strong League action against Japan over Manchuria in 1931, believing that if the actions of the League risked war with Japan then it was a risk worth taking.[35] In 1936 he advocated the same strong action against Italy when it invaded Abyssinia.[36] At home he attacked what he saw as the self-defeating policy of appeasement advocated by the Tory-led National Government. The fascist dictatorships, he argued, would be a threat to Britain however much they were appeased.[37] This formed the basis of his criticism of Carr's argument for appeasement, published a year after *Twenty Years' Crisis* in *Headway* under the title 'Who are the Utopians? And who the Realists?' The major choice for Angell was not between a belief in a harmony of interests and a realisation of the conflicting interests inherent in international relations. Rather it was between allowing individual interests to sort themselves out on their own, as the appeasers advocated, and collective international action that used the power of the world community to channel these interests into less destructive forms of conflict.[38] Thus, while he remained committed to the longer term goal of organising a system of peaceful resolution of international conflicts, Angell recognised very early on that the threat, or even the use, of force was essential in order to counter the claims of the dictators. This use of force was necessary, from Angell's point of view, because unlike Carr he regarded the claims of the dictators to be have-not states as no more than smoke screens for their policies of conquest. After all, if the dictators really felt that the problem was their lack of raw materials surely the answer was an end to the autarky advocated by Hitler and Mussolini, and a return to the open system of trade that had preceded their rule?[39]

Angell's analysis of the dictators mirrored the majority view on the Advisory Committee, and was frequently at odds with the view, common on both the left and the right, that the dictators were merely a symptom of the poor treatment of their countries by the status quo powers. While Angell and Woolf both felt that the dictator's needed to be confronted, people like C.R. Buxton on the left and the appeasers and Carr on the right thought that a just settlement of the dictator's demands would remove the cause of the dictator's aggression. Angell's advocacy of confrontation, supported by Labour leaders such as Hugh Dalton, Ernest Bevin and Walter Citrine, meant a temporary abandonment of the concept of peaceful change, although Angell remained committed to the idea of the re-establishment of another League-like organisation. Peaceful change, via an accommodation with the dictators using the mechanisms of the old diplomacy, now became the policy of the Conservative-led National Government. People, like Angell, who had been proud to call themselves pacifists in the past,[40] were now in the uncomfortable position of being cast in the role of warmongers.

Does Capitalism Cause War?

Yet, the debate about how to deal with the dictators was not the only IR debate of the 1930s. Although frequently involving friends and political allies, and consequently carried on with a level of gentility often absent from the debate over appeasement, the debate over the question of whether capitalism causes war was nevertheless a major part of inter-war IR. The fact that it is virtually unknown to IR scholars today is another aspect of the general ignorance of the history of the discipline. The part of this debate that was carried out amongst the left in Britain reached its zenith with an influential exchange of letters in the *New Statesmen* that saw contributions from H.N. Brailsford, Leonard Woolf, Norman Angell and Harold Laski. These letters were quickly published as a book in the same year. Interestingly, the editors asked the Conservative Robert Cecil, a strong supporter of pooled security through the League, to provide the foreword. Rather than concentrate on the divisions between the various writers in the collection, Cecil chose to focus on the division in the current international situation between those who 'believe that international relations depend on force', and those who feel 'that all states are parts of one community governed by the same rules and principles as govern individuals, and that... all states must take collective action against any antisocial aggression.' Cecil felt that all the antagonists in the capitalism and war debate were in the latter camp, and he saw the purpose of the publication of the debate as a means by which their differences could be resolved. 'It would be tragic if those who stand for the community idea... were to be so divided on the causes of our danger as not to be willing to co-operate in repelling it.'[41] The implication was that this debate between political allies was increasingly taking place under the shadow of a much more immediate threat to world peace.

The roots of the inter-war debate over capitalism and war rested on a sharp division between two fundamentally left-liberal interpretations of the nature of capitalism before the First World War. On the one hand there was J.A. Hobson's economics that stressed the internationally destabilising nature of current capitalism, on the other was Norman Angell's view that the current level of economic interconnectedness meant that capitalism was not necessarily belligerent, and the problem lay more with outdated ideas of conquest. For Hobson the root problem of contemporary capitalism was that, because the wealthy were able to convert their economic strength into political power, they were able to keep domestic wages low in order to maximise profits. This resulted in an abundance of investment capital, but left the domestic market with little money with which to purchase any goods produced by increased investment. This led to the overproduction of goods and a lack of domestic investment opportunities as a direct result of chronic underconsumption. The response of the western capitalists was to export capital and goods, and in order to guarantee the security of their investment and markets they put pressure on their governments to carve out colonial territories and protectorates. Competition over the control of colonies and market shares brought instability to the international system, and made war more likely.[42] Hobson's answer to this problem was to increase the power and wages of the labouring classes, thus reducing under-consumption, and eradicating the need for colonial adventures. H.N. Brailsford used Hobson's economics for his 1914 book *The War of Steel and Gold*, discussed in more detail in chapter 2. Brailsford claimed that, while war did not serve the interests of civilisation as a whole, it did make sense for a capitalist elite, who used war to improve the prospects for investment abroad and social position at home.[43] By contrast, Angell saw this booty capitalism, to use Max Weber's phrase, as an aberration. This is not to say that there was no overlap between Angell and Hobson. Both accepted that peace was in the long-term interest of society as a whole, and even the capitalist class as a whole. The main difference was that Angell saw in the current state of economic life a hope for a more peaceful world, while Hobson did not. For Angell, the material interdependence both made it in the interests of all, including capitalists, to maintain peaceful relations in order to preserve the prosperity that made human civilisation possible, and made any belief that wealth could be gained by force outmoded and ultimately self-defeating. Basically, this boiled down to the question of whether the propensity for war was grounded in the self interest of one very powerful group, or whether the idea that anyone gained from war was nothing more than an optical illusion based on outmoded ideas.

Interestingly, although J.A. Hobson's economic analysis was the basis of the argument used by many, such as Brailsford, to push the capitalism as the cause of war argument, Hobson himself was deeply suspicious of such an argument by the 1930s. In an unpublished paper that has recently come to light – undated, but internal evidence seems to suggest a date in the mid 1930s – Hobson criticised the argument that capitalism, and rational capitalist interests, could be the cause of war: '… the war spirit cannot be explained in purely economic terms. Nations do not consciously range themselves behind their business men in a struggle for markets.'[44] Not only did Hobson dismiss what he saw as the 'Marxist' view of the cause of war, but he also fully endorsed Norman Angell's position. 'As individual animals, men are not particularly reasonable or moral, as herds or nations reason and moral are often clouded over or submerged in collective illusions and passions. Sir Norman Angell has done a great service in his masterly analysis of these follies.'[45] Hobson, like Angell, saw the solution to the problem of war in the abolition of 'sovereign nationality':

Until the Nations and their Governments are willing to surrender their sovereignty to a reconstructed League which shall possess an over-riding sovereignty over economic and political nationalism, with legal and in the last resort forcible powers to repress rebellions among its member states, the conditions of a stable peace are unattained and unattainable.[46]

The problem of economic imperialism, so central to Brailsford's 'Hobsonian' view of the cause of war becomes a symptom of psychological and national factors. Interestingly, Brailsford continued to present his ideas as coming from Hobson – which they did if we are looking exclusively at Hobson's pre-1914 writings – and even when he backtracked on his views of the economic causes of war in his 1948 tribute to Hobson, Brailsford presented the too heavy an emphasis on the economic causes of war as being common to 'Hobson and we who were of his school'.[47]

In the immediate aftermath of the 1919 peace the debate took a back seat to the almost universal Labour denunciations of the treaties and the Covenant. While those like H.N. Brailsford continued to regard capitalism as a cause of war through the tensions caused by the interests of the capitalist classes; Angell, amongst others, still saw war as a threat to the interests of all including the capitalists. Both could agree that the vindictive peace and government-run League were exacerbating international tensions. The switch to a League-centred foreign policy brought out the tensions in the two sides, although there was still space for broad agreement about the practical necessity of developing a League-based system of arbitration and disarmament. H.N. Brailsford reflected the extent of the consensus when, in a 1924 article praising the work of the League, he added that 'I doubt the efficacy alike of arbitration and disarmament to solve the problem of war until we grapple with economic imperialism.'[48] Interestingly, even a quite pro-League of Nations work, like Hugh Dalton's 1928 *Towards the Peace of Nations,* could side with Brailsford and Laski against Angell, Woolf and Philip Noel Baker. Dalton accepted that 'it is not true that all capitalists, nor even that capitalists as a whole, gain by war.' On this point, he said, he was in agreement with Angell. 'But... it is undoubtedly true, first, that certain important groups gain by war and, second, that certain much larger groups of capitalists gain through the pursuit of policies which greatly increase the likelihood of war. These truths are fundamental.'[49]

Dalton's attack on Angell, and his support for Brailsford's position on capitalism and war, might explain why Angell was not completely taken with Dalton. Writing in 1951, but looking back to the events of 1931,

Angell claimed that 'Dalton... could talk of it all with the best of the demagogues'.[50] What is interesting here, though, is that there could be wide disagreement over the role of capitalism and war, yet this had very little effect on the practical proposals for international affairs as long as the League was seen as a practical means for the organisation of international cooperation. Dalton's book may have criticised Angell, but it also advocated an engagement with the machinery of the League that was indistinguishable from Angell's.

This was to change after 1931, when the rise of the dictators and the ambivalence of the British and French governments to use the League to stem aggression undermined the consensus between the two groups. The National Government's increasing failure to use the machinery of the League, coupled with its policy of appeasing fascist regimes, was seen as serving capitalist interests. This was taken as proof by people like Brailsford that the economic imperialism of British capitalism could explain the British policy of selective capitulation to fascism. 'Class, indeed, talks audibly in any attempt to define [Tory] policy... Its ultimate principle of selection [of when to give in to fascist demands] is the maintenance, not merely of its own privileged standards, but of class-rule, abroad as at home.'[51] Brailsford was not the only one to see the connection between the policy of the National Government and the vested interests of capitalists and investors. Konni Zilliacus, while framing the argument differently, also saw the role of the Conservative-supporting plutocracy as key to a rounded understanding of foreign policy.[52] Increasingly Brailsford and his supporters saw the League as too weak to oppose fascism, although unlike the radical socialists he opposed leaving completely.[53] Brailsford placed his hope first in the establishment of a socialist league of peace, not unlike Kant's league of peace, except made up of states with democratic socialist governments.[54] Later he was to call for an 'inner-League', made up of democratic states with left-leaning governments and the Soviet Union, that would form an economic and security union.[55] For Laski the international planning necessary to create a peaceful and prosperous world would not be possible under the League because the nature of capitalist society would not let it work. The answer lay in establishing democratic socialism at home, which would make possible the establishment of a proper international organisation able to eliminate the other causes of war.[56] Woolf and Angell, even when they saw the League as seriously undermined by Tory inaction, saw the solution to the problem of fascist aggression in the creation of a League-like collective defence involving the major democratic governments, however capitalist they were.[57] If the major cause for war was the result of the international anarchy and the failure of

modern ideologies, particularly fascism, to understand the futility of a policy of aggression, as Angell and Woolf argued, then the sensible immediate response to fascist aggression was to unite the civilised states in a system of collective defence. If aspects of the capitalist class, and the capitalist system, was to blame, as Brailsford and Laski claimed, then this collective defence would be a utopian pipe-dream. The wolf would be locked
in the pen with the sheep. Thus, the debate took on a policy quality that it
did not have before, centring on whether or not capitalist-dominated
states could be trusted with the defence against fascism. This mirrored the
general loosening of the Labour consensus on foreign policy between
1931 and 1935.

The exchange of letters in the *New Statesman* in 1935 did not reveal anything new. The major collaborators did not say anything that they had not
already said, and despite Cecil's hopes the debate did not resolve itself. It
did, however, provide a forum for both sides to respond to each other's
respective positions. Brailsford reiterated his adaptation of Hobson's economics. He began by arguing that Angell's position only existed in an ideal
world. In the real world the existence of the coercive sovereign state
allows capitalists to keep an unequal division of wealth, which causes underconsumption. As a result, capitalists require an imperialist state that will
carve out markets and investment opportunities for them abroad. This
creates tensions and wars between states. Brailsford's remedy was the
victory of socialism domestically, leading to a federation of socialist states
trading on a more equal basis.[58] Woolf responded to Brailsford by arguing
that it was the delusions that 'Angell has given up his life to exposing' that
had caused the Great War, even while he conceded that Angell had not
given enough weight to the problems of mercantilist capitalism.[59] Angell's
response to Brailsford centred on the international anarchy as the cause of
war, and the creation of a collective system against aggression as its solution. He pointed out that this was also official Labour policy. 'We believe
that in such a task we must have, and can secure, the co-operation of large
sections of the capitalist world... in view of the financial and economic
results of the last war'.[60] Angell was dismissive of Brailsford's view of the
capitalist drive for imperial expansion. He doubted that investment capital
abroad could solve the glut problem, but would rather lead to further
overproduction, while he pointed out that most British investment was
outside the Empire.[61] The main problem still remained that people fought
wars against their own interests. 'We face here a phenomenon that should
be deeply interesting to Socialists: a tendency among men to disregard,
and act against, their interest and welfare without even knowing that they
are so doing.'[62] Brailsford still maintained that there were powerful groups

under capitalism that benefited from war, and that the nature of capitalism itself was never to reach equilibrium, and therefore it created the initial conditions for international instability. 'In a class State it is not the general good that is the criterion of policy, but rather the interest of the class that controls the State. For that reason, among others, Socialists hold that peace can be secure only within an international classless society.'[63] Laski underscored this point by arguing that the capitalist bargain with the state was a bad one, but one nonetheless. He criticised Angell for relying too much on reasoned argument, when this was not how capitalists thought.[64]

Generally though, the debate in the *New Statesman* revealed weaknesses in both positions. Angell underplayed the problem caused by the poor distribution of wealth under inter-war capitalism, and especially its failure to satisfy basic human needs while simultaneously creating a remarkably efficient system of production. Economic dislocation and maldistribution of wealth was a major factor in the rise of fascism. On the other hand, Brailsford's view that there were capitalists who benefited from war failed to explain both why war was so popular amongst non-capitalists, and why capitalists would support wars that did so much damage to so many influential capitalist enterprises. Indeed, it was a British Government dominated by capitalist interests and led by a capitalist, Neville Chamberlain, that proved most loath to go to war against Hitler. Brailsford and Laski's contention that capitalism, as it was practiced in 1935, was destabilising did seem to carry weight, but Angell and Woolf's concentration on the problem of the international anarchy and mass delusions seemed equally promising as explanations. David Mitrany's functional approach would return to the security problems inherent in the distributive failures of capitalism when it put the fulfilment of need at the centre of a working peace system. Perhaps, though, the greatest problem for the protagonists of this debate was that, no matter how much they honed their arguments, from 1931 to 1940 the reins of government remained firmly in the hands of their political enemies.

Labour in the Wilderness: Rearmament v. 'Pacifism' and 'Socialism'
The 1931 defeat was more than just the collapse of a government; it also stripped Labour of many of its leaders and diminished the power of others. MacDonald, Snowden and Thomas were formally expelled from the Party for forming the National Government without authorisation, while key members of the Cabinet lost their seats in the 1931 election, the most high profile of them being Arthur Henderson. As a result of the electoral cull – Labour was left with only 52 seats compared with 288 when Parliament had been dissolved – the only former member of the

Government still in the PLP was George Lansbury. Lansbury, who had been Minster of Works, was a major figure in the pacifist wing of the Party, and while universally liked (Angell called him '*le bon vieux papa* of the Party'[65]), his strict pacifist position put him at odds with the line that had been followed by Henderson, a line that continued to be Party policy. During his spell as PLP leader from 1931 to 1935 Lansbury relied heavily on the support of Stafford Cripps, the radical socialist opponent of the League, and Clement Attlee, who would succeed Lansbury as leader and later become the next Labour Prime Minister in 1945. In the House of Lords Labour was led by Arthur Ponsonby, who was perhaps the most articulate Labour pacifist in Parliament, and a strong supporter of Lansbury.

Thus from 1931 the position of the PLP tended to be at odds with general Party policy, and particularly the policy of the Trades Union leaders, who remained committed to Henderson's view of foreign affairs. With the rise of fascism in Europe, and the persecution of trades unionists by fascist governments, the TUC leadership became more adamant in their support of a security first policy, in opposition to Lansbury's preferred disarmament by example. Although Lansbury's position never became Party policy, friction was bound to occur between the National Executive and the leadership of the Party in Parliament. Lansbury and Cripps frequently aired their own views on foreign policy in the teeth of officially agreed Labour policy, helping to create the impression that Labour had no clear international policy. 'It is *wonderful* how good the Labour Party is at giving points away to its opponents', wrote A.L. Rowse in 1937, 'never was there such generosity in a political party; it insists upon washing *all* its dirty linen in public'.[66] Henderson continued to support the international policy laid down in *Labour and the Nation*, advocating loyalty to the League, and the strengthening of the system of compulsory arbitration, disarmament and pooled security against aggression.[67] Although amongst his supporters, especially on the Advisory Committee, there was a growing feeling that the increasing number of fascist states meant that a smaller 'inner-League' more willing to take strong action against aggression was needed in the short term.[68] This would also mean a greater willingness to use sanctions, including military sanctions.

The final showdown between the pacifist wing and the TUC leadership came at the 1935 Party Conference, shortly after Arthur Henderson's death, although the roots of the confrontation ran deeper. With growing unease at the rise of militant fascism, the TUC and the Party had endorsed the principle of military sanctions, albeit in a rather round about way, in its *For Socialism and Peace* document and the Executive report 'War and Peace'.[69] Indeed, 'War and Peace', which was published in February 1934, 'accepted for the first time that Labour must be prepared to support military action in support of the League.'[70] The outcry from pacifists – who believed that Labour was back-tracking on its commitment to peace by supporting a war 'under the auspices of the League of Nations' – even led to the publication of a popular pamphlet that was distributed at the 1934 Labour Conference in order to remind Labour of its commitment to peace.[71] Despite this agitation, *For Socialism and Peace* was approved at the 1934 Labour Party Conference at Southport; and at a special joint meeting at Margate the Party and TUC Executives met to discuss the implications of the decisions by the Southport Conference. Stafford Cripps sole contribution to the discussion, according to Bevin, was to say that 'We must be careful we do not use the League for imperialist ends.'[72] Lansbury, in line with Labour's policy, informed the meeting that he had gone to Samuel Hoare, the Foreign Secretary, to pledge Labour's support over sanctions in the current crisis between Italy and Abyssinia, while the Labour Leader at the Lords, Arthur Ponsonby, had failed to answer Bevin's questions about whether he would be willing to follow Labour Party policy if he was in the Foreign Office.[73] Just prior to the 1935 Conference Stafford Cripps resigned from the Party Executive and Arthur Ponsonby resigned as Labour Leader in the Lords. In his formal letter to Lansbury Ponsonby said that he felt unable to give voice to foreign policies that he did not agree with. 'I have... placed the subject of Peace first as one of outstanding importance on which all else depends [including socialism]... I have unceasingly maintained that peace can never be secured by force of arms'.[74] In his short personal note he told Lansbury that he believed it best to make the move before the 1935 Conference.[75] So Lansbury entered the Party Conference fully aware that two of his closest allies had resigned over the issue of the support for sanctions.

The confrontation between Lansbury and Bevin at the 1935 Conference has since reached mythic proportions, perhaps deservedly since its result was the resignation of the Party leader. Lansbury's speech was a direct challenge to the policy on sanctions agreed to by the Executive and the 1934 Conference, and contained in *For Socialism and Peace*. 'I have never been more convinced that I am right, and that the movement is making a terrible mistake', he told Conference. 'I personally cannot see the difference between mass murder organised by the League of Nations, or mass murder organised between individual nations'.[76] Bevin's angry response to what he saw as Lansbury's betrayal of democratically arrived at Party policy has entered legend. When 'Lansbury says what he has said today in the Conference, it is rather late to say it... It is placing the Executive and the Movement in an absolutely wrong position to be taking your conscience round from body to body asking to be told what you ought to do with it.' Bevin went on to remind Conference that it was Trades Unionists who were falling victim to fascist violence: 'The middle classes are not doing too badly as a whole under capitalism and Fascism... The thing that is being wiped out is the Trade Union Movement... It is we who are being wiped out and who will be wiped out if Fascism comes here.'[77] After the speech someone told Bevin that he had been rather rough on Lansbury. Bevin responded 'Lansbury has been going about dressed up in saint's clothes for years waiting for martyrdom. I set fire to the faggots.'[78] Lansbury resigned as PLP leader shortly afterwards, and was replaced by Clement Attlee.

The 14 November 1935 General Election, which followed closely on Lansbury's resignation, saw 154 Labour MPs returned to Parliament. While this still left the National Government with a healthy majority, Labour's position as the alternative party of government was affirmed. Labour's policy was now firmly in favour of collective security through the League of Nations, although this did not stop the disputes within the Party, nor did it ultimately help the League since Labour was shut out of power. The question of the form and effectiveness of collective security continued, and the pacifist and radical socialist wings of the Party used this dissent to continue a rear-guard attack on Party policy. While the leader of the PLP, Clement Attlee, had been associated with Lansbury and Cripps, the core of the Party's foreign policy was now substantially what had been pushed by the triumvirate of Hugh Dalton, Ernest Bevin and Walter Citrine. Yet, Attlee was not a silent partner here, and 'was at times prepared to give a strong lead in the foreign policy debate.'[79] Dalton, the Party's spokesman on foreign affairs, had pushed for a reversal of the Party's policy of voting against the National Government's defence spending (the Service Estimates). He failed in 1936, thanks in part to Attlee's refusal to support the measure, but in 1937 the PLP agreed to abstain when the vote for that year came up. The outbreak of the Spanish Civil War may have had a profound effect on this change of heart, and the call by Spanish socialists for arms now, not collective security later, certainly helped Dalton and Bevin push the case for rearmament against fascism.[80] Michael R. Gordon sees the decision to abstain, rather than support the Service Estimates, as an example of the tensions and lack of clarity in the Party's policy.[81] Here he underplays the significance of the PLP's decision. In the confrontational politics of the Westminster system an opposition's decision to abstain is a significant move, and represents an effective acquiescence to the government policy in question. Certainly the pro-Conservative press saw it that way, and the decision to abstain was welcomed by both *The Times* and the *Daily Telegraph*.[82]

Dalton's second great success of 1937 was to commit the Party publicly to the use of force against aggression, whether in self-defence or under the auspices of the League. The one page summary of Labour's international policy in *Labour's Immediate Programme*, a document produced by the Executive under a mandate from the October 1936 Party Conference, made this clear:

> A Labour Government...will take the lead in seeking to strengthen and reinvigorate the League of Nations as an instrument of international co-operation and Collective Security...

> A Labour Government will unhesitatingly maintain such armed forces as are necessary to defend our country and to fulfil our obligations as a member of the British Commonwealth and of the League of Nations.[83]

This position was confirmed at the 1937 Annual Conference. Here the National Council of Labour's generally pro-rearmament policy document *International Policy and Defence* was debated and accepted. *International Policy and Defence*, while still declaring support for disarmament and the reinvigoration of the League, declared that under the current international conditions the policy of re-armament could not be reversed if Britain was to live up to its collective security commitments. Yet, while Labour was firmly committed to the use of force in the event of fascist aggression, the policy was still hedged around with carefully chosen words and by the continued commitment to disarmament. Dalton, Bevin and Citrine interpreted this to mean that disarmament was an ultimate goal, and this was certainly the way it appeared in *International Policy and Defence*, although *Labour's Immediate Programme* made no such distinction. As a result it appeared as though Labour policy was more confused than it really was. Labour accepted the necessity for rearmament, and it accepted the need for military action under certain conditions as a deterrent to aggression. In order to avoid splits in the Party, and accusations from the Conservatives that Labour was the war party, the leadership did not feel that it could say these things in anything but an oblique fashion, and certainly not without a continued commitment to disarmament. A further confusion lay in the continued support for the League, and League collective security. While Abyssinia had weakened the authority of the League, the failure of the League to respond to the crisis in Spain, and especially the appeal by the

Spanish Republican Government, led many of its former supporters to suggest that until such time as the League could be rejuvenated Labour should look to a more limited alliance against aggression.[84] This, of course, was anathema to the still vocal pacifist and radical socialist sections of the Party, whose weariness of League commitments was matched by their wholehearted opposition to military alliances.

Opposition to Labour policy from within the Party continued from George Lansbury in a personal capacity, and from the radical socialists in the form of the Socialist League. While Lansbury's actions were regarded as constitutional and in line with Party rules, the Socialist League, and Cripps in particular, were criticised for being a party within a party. From 1937 the Socialist League advocated a distinct policy that was at odds with Labour's position that had been hammered out at the 1937 conference. The main features of the Socialist League's position was: 1. the use of a general strike in the event of a war; 2. unity with the communists and the disaffiliated ILP; 3. dismissal of the League as a tool of capitalism; and 4. opposition to British rearmament.[85] With the Spanish Civil War still raging, and the continued aggressive behaviour of the dictatorships, the position of the Socialist League was increasingly at odds with the majority view in the Party. In January 1937 The Executive struck. The Socialist League was banned, and when Stafford Cripps Aneurin Bevan, Charles Trevelyan and G.R. Straus continued their agitation they were expelled from the Party in 1939. Cripps was, however, gradually converted to the cause of collective defence against Hitler and readmitted to the Party. In a major change of heart during the House of Commons debate over the Munich Agreement he said: 'You won't forever satisfy rival imperialisms by handing over to them the smaller nations of the world. The time will come when the clash will be at your own door.'[86] Dalton, Bevin or Citrine could not have put it better.

Lansbury's personal campaign for an overtly pacifist Labour policy gradually lost support in the years between 1937 and 1939, but he remained committed to this position, and was the lone Labour voice in the PLP to give Chamberlain his support over the Munich agreement in 1938. Lansbury's personal mission to Hitler in April 1937 made a deep impression on him, convincing him that Hitler could be appeased and war prevented. Although he regarded Hitler as fanatical and ruthless,[87] he came away from his interview convinced that Hitler 'really wants peace'[88], and that he 'will not go to war unless pushed into it by others.'[89] Convinced that the problem with Germany was its status as a 'have-not' power, Lansbury's trip to Hitler reassured him that war could be averted if Germany was treated fairly, and if Britain disarmed as a gesture of good will. The

Party as a whole remained unconvinced, and while Lansbury remained highly regarded and even admired, his influence on policy after 1936 was negligible.[90]

Underlying the Party's policy were intellectual debates about the changing nature of the international order, and the decade of the 1930s saw the Advisory Committee's hottest debates to date. Its Chairman, C.R. Buxton, resigned in 1937. While the PLP's decision to abstain on the service estimates was the immediate cause of his resignation, Buxton cited his increasing differences with the other members of the Advisory Committee as a contributing factor. 'I have several times found myself in a minority of one on the Committee.'[91] With the exception of Buxton, the Advisory Committee was largely united in its support for collective security and military sanctions, although the question of the role of the League was to cause a split with Noel Baker. Just as the Advisory Committee had acted as an important source of policy for Henderson and his supporters in the 1920s, so the Committee in the 1930s provided an important forum for the anti-appeasers around Hugh Dalton, Ernest Bevin and Walter Citrine. As a result of this hard work in the Party it was possible for the otherwise jaundiced Adolf Sturmthal to write that in 1938 'England constituted the centre of leftist resistance to appeasement.'[92]

The Rise of the Dictators and the Weaknesses of League Security

The failure of the League of Nations has now become the stuff of legend and myth, and the breakdown of its system of collective security has been used in IR to discredit those who had been the most vocal in its support during the 1920s. This discrediting of the League's supporters is usually based on the simplistic rubric that the League failed therefore those who supported it were wrong. Thus, the League's failures are assumed to be intrinsic to the very ideas upon which it was based. In fact, the League's relationships with the different schools of international thought at the time were much more complex than this. Supporters of the old diplomacy, such as many of the British Conservatives, were happy to work with the League, seeing it as an extension of inter-state conflict (see chapter 1). Supporters of a new system of pooled security saw the League as the only existing institution upon which such as system could be constructed, but were often sceptical about its ability to deliver. The main problem with the League was that there had been so little time in which to develop its security arrangements. The Covenant was vague on so many details, and the attempts to construct a functioning pooled security regime, founded on arbitration, sanctions and disarmament down to an effective policing level, were still at an early stage in 1931 when the first major great power challenge to the League system struck. That the League's security system was not yet properly functioning allowed a certain amount of latitude amongst its members when dealing with aggression, and consequently it was not difficult for a major power like Britain to bend the League towards its policy of appeasement of the Dictators. In other words, as it stood in 1931 the Covenant and its ancillary agreements did not require any sustained or effective action from its membership in the face of a serious breech of the Covenant, with the possible exception of financial sanctions and support, while a clear definition of aggressor was yet to be agreed to by its full membership. So much was left vague that the pooled security arrangements of the Covenant would have to rely on the will of its most powerful members in order to be fulfilled.

In September 1931 Japanese soldiers, who were guarding the Japanese railway concession in the Chinese province of Manchuria, clashed with Chinese troops. The Japanese had claimed to have found the Chinese soldiers about to sabotage the railway. Independently of their government, the Japanese authorities in Manchuria took it upon themselves to launch an offensive against the Chinese, and by January 1932 the Japanese had conquered Manchuria. Initially, the Chinese government appealed to the League Council under Article 11 of the Covenant, which allowed for conciliation through the Council, but required unanimity in the Council. Since Japan was a permanent member of the Council this was problematic for China, but Article 11 had been used to settle the Bulgarian-Greek dispute in 1925, and in the absence of any firmer form of League arbitration it was widely regarded as the best means of League dispute settlement. The result was deadlock, and the Council could only agree to send out a League Commission to the Far East under Lord Lytton. In January 1932 China submitted the dispute to the League under Articles 10 and 15, which would mean that the matter could be decided in the Council without a Japanese veto, and the dispute could be referred to the Assembly, which would most likely decide against Japan. The Lytton Commission report was not submitted to the Council until November 1932, and while critical of Japan, it fell short of defining the Japanese action as a resort to war, thus avoiding the painful prospect of automatic sanctions against Japan. Despite this, the Japanese opposed acceptance of the Commission's report, and on 24 February 1933, when the League Assembly voted 42 to 1 to accept the Report the Japanese delegation walked out of the Assembly. Shortly afterwards Japan announced its intention to leave the League. No further action was taken by the League. The bottom line was that the League structure lacked clarity, and the League powers lacked the will to act.

Clearly the League had not prevented aggression, and this disappointment was felt amongst the League's supporters in the Labour Party. Soon after Japan's walk-out at the League Assembly the Advisory Committee assessed the damage done to the League by its failure to resolve the crisis, a failure that had been compounded by the lack of progress at the Disarmament Conference. The first memo in March 1933 did not offer any policy prescriptions, but was clear about the change that had occurred in the international situation to the detriment of the League. This had major implications for Party policy on foreign affairs that had largely been based on building a new peaceful order around the League. Further, the memo worried that 'among the rank and file of the Party during the last few years the feeling has been growing that the League has failed and that "it is not a reality", and that this was largely due to Manchuria. There was, not surprisingly, a growing isolationism in the Party that saw 'the best thing for this country to do is to stand out of any international embroilment'.[93] The second memo in April went into more detail. Central to it was the 'necessity for the Party to re-define its attitude towards the League.'[94] The failure of the League was seen as being inherent in its structure as a 'League of Governments and it cannot be effective as an instrument of international peace unless the Governments of which it is composed are determined to use it as an instrument of co-operation, justice, and peace'.[95] The memo singled out the British Government, which it argued had 'connived' with the Japanese by making it clear that Britain 'would not comply with her obligations to stand by China in resisting Japanese aggression.'[96] While the League had been badly shaken, the Advisory Committee was of the opinion that the League project was still worth advocating. 'The Labour Party remains… convinced that the only possible hope of maintaining peace in the world is through a system of pooled security and cooperation such as it was intended should be created by the League.'[97]

If the Advisory Committee regarded the Manchurian crisis as damaging the League, it was the 1935–6 Abyssinian crisis that undermined the League's authority as an effective vehicle for pooled security. It was this, rather than Manchuria that was, in the words of Leonard Woolf, 'the final test … of the League of Nations and of what is called a system of collective security' for both the Government and the British public.[98] The Abyssinian crisis was also the catalyst for the 1935 Conference showdown between Bevin and Lansbury, where Lansbury's pacifism clashed with the Party's endorsement of the Government's policy of supporting League action against Italy. Ironically, Italy had an arbitration treaty with Abyssinia signed in 1928, so that when Italian and Abyssinian troops clashed near the village of Walwal on the Abyssinian-Italian Somaliland border in

December 1934 the League Council postponed the Abyssinian appeal under Article 11 subject to arbitration under the 1928 treaty. Throughout the
summer of 1935 British and French diplomats attempted to meet Italy's
concerns through negotiations, even going so far as to suggest border revisions that would see Britain giving up territory in British Somaliland. In
September the arbitrators reported that neither government could be held
responsible for the clash, and with mounting evidence of Italy's preparation for war, the League began to consider Abyssinia's appeal. Britain,
in the form of the Foreign Secretary Samuel Hoare, committed itself to
fulfilling its obligations under the Covenant, but on 2 October Italy finally
launched its invasion. Showing what could be done when the will of the
great powers was behind it, the League reacted swiftly. By 19 October the
League had a clear plan of action that involved comprehensive economic
sanctions under Article 16 of the Covenant. 'On November 18, 1935, for
the first time in the history of the League, sanctions – though only of an
economic character, and these far from complete – came into operation.'[99]
Despite having the satisfaction of witnessing the defeat, via public anger in
Britain and France, of an attempt to appease Italy through territorial concessions in Abyssinia, the supporters of the League had little to cheer
about in the following months. Sanctions were not able to bring Italy's
invasion to a halt, and by May 1936 Italy annexed Abyssinia. Two months
earlier Germany had repudiated Locarno and remilitarised the Rhineland.

Labour's foreign policy proposals prior to 1936 rested on a fully functioning League. The finale of the Abyssinian crisis – in conjunction with
Germany's repudiation of the Locarno Pact – demonstrated the impotence of the sanctions provisions of the Covenant as it stood. The arbitration and sanctions regime, which had developed so painfully slowly
throughout the 1920s, now seemed defunct to many. As with the Manchuria crisis, the failure of the League was seen as residing both in a structure that made the League reliant on its members for effective action, and
in the poor policies of the League's key members, especially Britain. Speaking in Geneva in August 1936, Herbert Morrison argued that the assumptions that had underpinned League success in the 1920s no longer existed, and as a consequence the 'collective peace system' of the League now
only existed on paper.[100] For Leonard Woolf, writing for the Advisory
Committee the following July, the various League failures had undermined
both popular and state support for the League, leading to full rearmament
as the only effective means of defence:

> ...a collective security system cannot be effective unless it rests
> upon a belief in both governments and peoples that the obligations

of collective defence will be fulfilled. That belief no longer exists anywhere in the world, and that is why governments are everywhere feverishly rearming and why in this country there is a movement towards isolation and extreme pacifism.[101]

In fact, as far as Woolf was concerned, in the absence of an effective League system the international situation would fall back on the realpolitik associated with the old international anarchy. This reality had to be accepted and worked with in the absence of an effective League system, and under a system dominated by the balance of power Britain's main competitor in Europe would be the stronger peace-threatening power, in this case Hitler's Germany. 'The immediate danger of war comes solely from the Fascist powers.'[102] This meant that the Labour Party needed to formulate a foreign policy that was independent of the League structures, but took into account the ideals of the League in the event of a possible future revival of a collective security system. Thus, a short-term policy of thwarting the aggression of the dictators should be coupled with the longer-term objective of recreating a collective security system.[103] In other words, a full-blown League system required the existence of certain international conditions to function effectively. In the absence of those conditions new policies were required that would take into account the existence of this international anarchy, while holding out the possibility of a return to a more stable and cooperative world order. Woolf did not restrict his advice to Advisory Committee memoranda, however, and his articles throughout the late thirties dealt with the same issue.[104] As we will see below, not all of the Advisory Committee members shared this view of the impotence of the League after 1936.

One possible alternative that still remained loyal to the League ideal was to create, in the words of Susan Lawrence, 'a League of states with common aims – a League indeed open to all willing to co-operate, but a League facing from the first the temporary exclusion of groups of states.'[105] What this amounted to was an alliance, 'open or disguised as "The League", of those states which want peace against the fascist states'.[106] Woolf regarded this as the only serious alternative other than a dubious isolation, and by 1937 this was to be part of Labour's foreign policy, although it would not be accepted without serious disagreement both in the Advisory Committee and the wider Party.

In the Advisory Committee the main critic of a policy of organised collective defence against the dictators came from the increasingly beleaguered chairman C.R. Buxton. The crux of Buxton's criticism was that the cause of the aggressiveness of the dictators was 'Economic distress, the sense of injustice, and in Germany's case the Treaty of Versailles and the post-war policy of the Allies... the economic crisis came before the political crisis, and... the latter has arisen as a consequence of the former.'[107] Buxton felt that Woolf and others were too quick to ascribe evil intent to the dictators, which was contradicted by the peaceful statements of the dictators. Woolf and his co-writer were too ready to disbelieve 'every pacific statement on the part of the "dictatorships" and believing every statement made by their opponents.'[108] Buxton's answer was a policy of economic appeasement, in which the status quo powers admit that the Peace was unjust, and work towards a more equitable distribution of economic privileges.[109] Buxton's position was open to the same criticism, made by Angell and discussed above, of creating a false distinction between have and have-not states. A slightly different criticism, by an anonymous critic on the Advisory Committee felt that Woolf made too many concessions to the pseudo-realism of the Foreign Office in his return to the logic of the old diplomacy. The critic's answer was not far off from Woolf, however, when he or she advocated a British-French-Soviet alliance to deter the dictators from further aggression.[110] The proposed temporary abandonment of the League also had the effect of dividing the advocates of collective security. Philip Noel Baker was deeply unhappy with the memoranda on the current situation coming out of the Advisory Committee, likening them to the 'unrealistic theorising' of the anti-League pacifists of the 1920s.[111] As far as Noel Baker was concerned the League was still capable of working, even in relation to the Spanish Civil War. This led to A.L. Rowse's 1937 attack on Noel Baker as a hopeless League fanatic, who was incapable of understanding the extent to which Hitler had changed the nature of international affairs.[112]

It was here that the Spanish Civil War acted as both accent and catalyst. Accent in the sense that it underscored the failure of the League to preserve peace and deter aggression, and catalyst in that it helped to persuade many of the members of the Party that an effective collective defence, with or without the League, was necessary to halt the aggression of dictators, even if that threatened war. The Advisory Committee debates of 1936–7 may have laid the groundwork for the crucial foreign policy debate at the 1937 Party Conference, but it was events in Spain that smoothed the passage of the revised Labour foreign policy that emerged from Conference. In February 1936 a left-wing Popular Front coalition government was elected in Spain. An attempted coup by elements of the Army in July 1936 met stiffer resistance than they expected, and by November 1936 Spain was divided into two warring entities: a right-wing quasi-fascist vacant throne monarchy led by General Franco, and a Popular Front republic that also received support from the widespread anarchist movement and nationalists in Catalonia and the Basque country. Despite initial Italian assistance to the insurgents, Britain and France managed to persuade the other European states to support a policy of non-intervention in Spain. In a matter of weeks after the formation of an international non-intervention committee it was clear that Italy and Germany were supplying Franco, while The Soviets were providing the Popular Front Government with war materials. It has been estimated that the Italian's sent 40,000 troops in addition to arms, while the Germans sent up to 15,000 personnel.[113] With the left-wing government in France supporting non-intervention, Labour initially supported the National Government's position on Spain, but the open breeches of the non-intervention agreement by the dictators, and the inability of the League to act, even after the Spanish Government had formerly complained to the League about German and Italian intervention, added to the doubts about a League-based foreign policy. The defence of the Spanish Republic, and the brazen intervention by the dictators, did not necessarily change Labour opinion or policy, but it did strengthen the position of those within the Party that were calling for a policy of confrontation with the dictators. The arming of Franco by Hitler and Mussolini had the unintended effect of morally arming the wing of the Labour Party that was in favour of open British rearmament in the face of fascist aggression.

Going into its Conference in late 1937, Labour was now increasingly influenced by the Advisory Committee's hostility towards the dictators and suspicions of the League's ability to maintain global order. While the Advisory Committee, and more specifically its Secretary Leonard Woolf, feared that League impotence in Manchuria and Abyssinia might lead to isolationism within the Party, the galvanising effect of the Spanish Civil War and the continued strength of the internationalists in the leadership largely guaranteed that this would not happen. The Executive's report to Conference, *International Policy and Defence*, borrowed freely from the year's Advisory Committee reports by emphasising the current weakness of the League, the short-term need for Britain to be able to defend itself in alliance with other pro-League powers, and the longer term goal of a resuscitated League system. In introducing the report J.R. Clynes emphasised all three points.[114] The close links between the Advisory Committee and the Party Executive – especially via the personal link with Hugh Dalton, who doubled up as the Chairman of the Executive's International Sub-Committee – provided a direct conduit between advice and policy.

Between 1931 and 1937 Labour's intellectuals on the Advisory Committee had moved towards an analysis of the international situation that, while supportive of the League idea in the longer term, had accepted the League's weakness in the immediate circumstances. Working with Hugh Dalton, Walter Citrine and Ernest Bevin, the advice of the Committee had contributed to the development of Labour policy in 1935 and 1937. In what was the most divisive time for Labour and its international outlook, the intellectuals on the Advisory Committee had been quick to respond to changing international circumstances, and had based their analysis on detailed studies of the crises under review. Since 1931–7 makes up the larger proportion of the period by which later IR scholars have judged the effectiveness of those written off as idealists, the work of people like Woolf on the Advisory Committee stands as a clear refutation of the charge of ignoring the facts and relying exclusively on institutional arrangements and agreements that were increasingly ignored by the dictators. In the last two years of peace this charge of idealism becomes even more absurd.

The National Government and Appeasement

As the official opposition to the Conservative-led National Government between 1931 and 1940 Labour's constitutional role was to question the policy of the government and to provide a shadow government in waiting. An old adage in British Politics is that oppositions do not win elections; it is governments that lose it. It follows from this that an effective opposition should expose the weaknesses in government policy, rather than trying to construct a clear policy of its own. Underscoring this, Randolph Churchill is quoted as saying that the opposition's job was 'to oppose everything, propose nothing and turn out the Government. Judged by these standards,' writes John F. Naylor, 'the Labour Party proved a singular disappointment in… opposition during the 1930s.'[115] Labour supported the Government over sanctions against Italy over Abyssinia in 1935, on non-intervention in Spain in 1936, and ceased to oppose the service estimates in 1937. It proposed major foreign policy initiatives in both 1934, with *Socialism and Peace* and 'War and Peace', and 1937, with *International Policy and Defence*. While recovering much of its support in the 1935 elections, Labour failed to overturn the heavy National Government majorities in Parliament. The increasingly serious nature of the international situation seemed to make a traditional opposition inappropriate, while the lack of clarity in National Government foreign policy made it a moving target that was difficult to hit. It was often easier for Labour figures to attack the National Government for its lack of a clear policy, and in this climate it seemed responsible to present clear policy proposals.

This oddly reflective opposition is even evident in Labour's most 'oppose everything' stand on the service estimates. While Labour's policy of voting against the service estimates every year until 1937 seems on the face of it a deliberate nay-saying that had the added effect of satisfying the pacifist and radical socialist wings of the Party, it was also for many a direct response to the lack of clarity in the National Government's defence policy. In 1934 the Advisory Committee was recommending to the Executive that its position in the year's service estimate debates should concentrate on the Government's lack of a clear foreign policy. 'The armed forces and armaments which a country requires depends upon its foreign policy', and without a clear foreign policy it was not possible to decide what size, form and structure the armed forces should take.[116] Thus, until there was a clear agreement within the Government on what foreign and defence posture it wished to take, it was unwise for Labour to support defence spending that seemed to have no clear objective. Rather than opposing a policy, Labour should oppose the failure to develop a clear policy. This remained a central plank of the Advisory Committee's opposition to National Government foreign and defence policy well into 1939. The lack of a clear policy towards the aggression of Japan, Italy and Germany led to a reactive strategy that handed the initiative to the dictators. By contrast, the Advisory Committee spent much of its time locating the major threats to British security, and suggesting both long and short term strategies to deal with those threats.

While the secular trend of National Government policy tended towards a reactive appeasement of the dictators outside of the framework of the League and collective security, its content was often more complex than this. The National Government, after all, had been instrumental in the imposition of the League's only case of sanctions under Article 16 of the Covenant, even if they abandoned them once Italy had occupied all of Abyssinia. It also initiated a policy of rearmament, even if that rearmament was often accused of being haphazard and slow. Interestingly, the National Government's policy of appeasement towards the dictators was based upon a policy that it shared with Labour: a commitment to peaceful change as an alternative to the use of war. In the past, it was argued, changes in power and the distribution of important resources were settled through war. With the growing destructiveness of war it made sense to replace violence with diplomatic agreement as the final arbiter of international disputes. Underlying the concept of peaceful change used by the National Government was a belief that Japan, Italy and Germany were relatively resource poor 'have-not' states, and that in the interest of peace it made sense for the resource rich 'haves' such as Britain and France to make concessions. This 'have' and 'have-not' distinction, which had been attacked by Angell in his 1936 book, was also common on the left. C.R.

Buxton used it as part of his attack on Woolf's 1936 memo, and H.N. Brailsford referred to it in his 1938 analysis of Conservative foreign policy.[117]
The 'haves' – Britain, France, the United States and sometimes the Soviet
Union – were rich in resources and space for an expanding population.
The 'have-nots' – Germany, Japan and Italy – did not have enough natural
resources for their growing industry, and not enough land for their populations. As the have-nots expanded there would be a need to redress this
imbalance either by war or by negotiation. The National Government preferred peaceful change properly negotiated. As the 'have-nots' were given
concessions, the argument went, they would become more satisfied and
less aggressive. It was for this reason that E.H. Carr praised Chamberlain's
Government for its successful negotiation of the Munich agreement,
which for him represented a template on how to organise peaceful change
between 'haves' and 'have-nots'.[118]

A major criticism levelled by many in the Labour movement, including
Norman Angell and Leonard Woolf, was that this policy of appeasement
failed to accomplish what it intended. From the Advisory Committee's
point of view the self-defeating nature of the National Government's foreign policy was never clearer than in its attitudes to the League and collective security. As early as 1934 the majority on the Committee clearly believed that Germany was now the only 'possible belligerent against us in
the near future', and that pursuing 'a consistent policy of pooled security'
through the League would mean that Britain could count on the full support of France and the other League members.[119] While the National Government did use the League in 1936, much of its actions undermined the
authority of the League. In 1935 the Advisory Committee complained that
British inactivity in the face of the Polish unilateral abrogation of the League's Minorities Clauses had effectively led to the dismantling of one of
the major pillars of the League-based peace.[120] Similarly, after the abrupt
ending of sanctions against Italy Leonard Woolf accused the National
Government of turning the League into a sham by gutting its collective
security provisions, and substituting it with a British policy of vacillation
and muddle.[121] By March 1938, the month that Germany occupied and
annexed Austria, the Advisory Committee was accusing the National Government of diplomatically disarming Britain. Prime Minister Chamberlain's
public statements had in effect told the world that Britain would ignore its
obligations under Article 16 of the League, and that 'British power will
only be used for the defence of British interests.' This weakened the crucially important Anglo-French alliance, made it more likely that the Soviet
Union would cut its losses by making a separate peace with Germany, it
would entrench American isolation, and make a grand alliance against the

dictators unlikely. 'In short, the Chamberlain policy of liquidating the great alliance is not only morally indefensible but politically insane. It means murder to the wounded League and suicide for the menaced British Commonwealth.'[122] The underlying point to all this was that, rather than being an inconvenience likely to suck British troops into overseas adventures, the Covenant of the League had been an important tool in protecting British interests from potential aggressors. By pulling back from its collective security commitments the National Government was leaving Britain isolated and vulnerable.

These sentiments were mirrored in the writings of Norman Angell. For Angell, the old associations of the left with pacifism and the right with imperialism and overseas adventures had been reversed. It was the left and the liberals who were arguing for confrontation with the dictators, and the right that was refusing to protect their overseas capitalist interests through war and militarist expansion. Rather than following policies that helped their capitalists, Angell argued that the Conservatives running the National Government were psychologically blind to the interests of their nation, capitalism and their class.[123] A slightly different line was taken by H.N. Brailsford, who – unlike Angell, Woolf and the majority on the Advisory Committee – saw method in the National Government's madness. Rather than muddle, the Tory policy of peace was designed to protect the British Empire only, and to maintain capitalist class interests through the prevention of working class revolutions and the weakening of the Soviet Union. Within the confines of these aims it has been possible for the National Government to accept Italian conquests in Abyssinia and to leave the Spanish Republic to be over-run by the Fascist Nationalists. In short, the Government was pursuing mere self-preservation of Empire and Capitalism, rather than the protection of higher ideals such as freedom, humanity and integrity of thought.[124] While sharing some of the same elements as Angell and Woolf's analysis of National Government policy, Brailsford's view that there was a clear underlying ordering factor in Government policy was at odds with the wider Advisory Committee view that the Government was in a self-defeating muddle.

While the Labour Party spent the last three years of peace presenting a working alternative to the foreign policy of the National Government, there were significant overlaps in their policies. Both Labour and the National Government were primarily concerned with maintaining peace if possible, and both were willing to make a certain amount of concessions to the dictators.[125] The crucial differences were in the intellectual underpinnings of both policies and Labour's greater willingness to risk war in the various crises leading up to the war. This greater belligerence, in comparison with the National Government, led many in the Party to fear that Labour would be branded as the war party in Britain, and consequently that the Government would be able to use this to claim that Labour was irresponsible and reckless in foreign affairs.[126] While it must be conceded that we are not comparing like with like – the National Government's policy was the active policy of a government, and therefore subject to the whims and compromises of the diplomatic world, while Labour's policy remained a theoretical alternative – it is still possible to compare them as legitimate alternatives. By 1937 Labour's internal conflicts over foreign policy had largely been settled. Underlying Labour's policy was a two-track approach that was meant to remain loyal to long-term Labour Party goals, while recognising that the current state of international affairs made the realisation of those goals unlikely in the foreseeable future. In the short term it was recognised that re-armament and 'standing up to the Dictators' was a necessary part of the current international situation.[127] In the longer term Labour still stood for the goals that informed its policy up to the 1930s. These were a working system of pooled security through the League, or League-like institution, and the promotion of international justice, peaceful change and disarmament.[128] This longer term part of Labour policy easily slipped into the background as the urgency of the international crisis gathered pace towards the end of the 1930s, but it was frequently reiterated within and without the Advisory Committee throughout 1938 and 1939. The result of these restatements was a Labour policy of appeasement that was meant to supplement the more bellicose short term policy, while avoiding the mistakes of the reactive National Government's policy of appeasement.

The Labour criticisms of National Government appeasement had focused on its reactive nature. Britain waited for the dictators to threaten war in a time and place of the dictators' choosing, and reacted piecemeal to these individual aggressions. By contrast, the policies advocated within Labour circles were premised on taking the initiative out of the hands of the dictators by suggesting a comprehensive set of settlements. Like the National Government's policy these were premised on the idea that the dictators were 'have-not' states short on raw materials and outlets for their populations.[129] If their 'have-not' status was the cause of, or excuse for, their aggression then it followed that a comprehensive settlement directed at ameliorating the concerns of raw materials and population settlement should remove the main cause of aggression. Five Advisory Committee memoranda, written in 1938 and 1939 and one being the product of the merging of an earlier two, dealt directly with the creation of a Labour appeasement policy. Each slightly differed from the others, but the bottom line was the recreation of an embryonic League bloc that would be attractive to the states that had abandoned the League. The institution of free trade and free mobility of labour between its members would eliminate the problem of raw material shortages and overpopulation that had been a direct result of protectionism and state autarky.[130] The dismantling of Empire preference and the development of a general open door policy in colonial possessions was frequently mooted,[131] although the most ambitious scheme was the resuscitation of an earlier plan to put all colonial possessions under a system of League mandates. The gradual increase in the power of the Mandates Commission of the League, and the placement of all existing colonies under categories B and C of the Mandate system, would institutionalise the internationalisation of the colonies, make their raw materials open to trade, and would provide protection for the local population. It would also be a major step in the revitalisation of the pooled security system of the League.[132] The important point about Labour proposals for appeasement was that they should be a widespread reformlation of international economic policy, rather than ad hoc responses to military aggression. The assumption was that the removal of these underlying economic causes of fascist aggression would make it much more difficult for the fascist regimes to mobilise their populations for further aggressions. The short term policy of meeting fascist military aggression head-on would hopefully help steer the dictators towards the easier long-term strategy proposed by Labour. 'The starting point of such a policy should be international economic policy and the question of the standard of living for all peoples. It should be offered, not as a bribe to international blackmailers, but as part of a new international settlement.'[133]

While Labour attempted to overcome the reactive muddle that distinguished it from the National Government's appeasement policy, with hindsight we now know that even this form of appeasement was based on a faulty assumption about the motivation for the aggression of the dictators. The idea behind the categorisation of the dictators as 'have-nots' was that a policy of appeasement would eventually convert them into peaceful 'have' states. The flaw in this strategy was that the more the dictators were offered, the more they would demand in the future. Like Napoleon before them, the dictators knew no limits to their ambitions, and as a result a diplomatic settlement could never be more than a temporary ceasefire. The Labour proposals did, however, carry less risk than the National Government's for two reasons. First, the policy was not intended to be piecemeal, but was part of a longer-term international settlement that would try to lock the dictatorships into a peaceful system that they could not necessarily control. For this reason alone it is exceedingly unlikely that the

dictatorships would have accepted Labour's plan since it would have undermined their freedom of action. Yet, while not acceptable to the dictators, it would have also aimed at the creation of an 'inner-league' built
around the Anglo-French alliance. Second, although the National Government had backed up its appeasement with a policy of rearmament, Labour's short-term policy included confrontation with the dictators in the
event of military aggression. Thus it would not have allowed the ad hoc
concessions to the dictators that we now know emboldened the fascist
powers, although it did carry with it the very real danger of war. For the
majority on the Advisory Committee 'collective defence against aggression, and provision for preventative sanctions' remained key to any collective peace system, even if this form of brinkmanship made the outbreak
of hostilities a real possibility.[134] Labour's opposition to on the hoof concessions like the Munich agreement, and its condemnation of the lack of
will on the part of the National Government to develop a strong anti-
fascist alliance, were central parts of Labour's policy in the last years of
peace. In the end, though, it was the Labour intellectuals, like Norman
Angell, Leonard Woolf and Hugh Dalton, who were spot on about the nature of the dictators. Dalton was clear that only collective defence would
deter Hitler from aggression.[135] Woolf remained sceptical about plans for
'rebuilding the League or calling a World Conference', both central to the
appeasement proposals being discussed in Labour circles, and continued
to criticise doing deals with the dictators.[136] Norman Angell's early realisation that the 'have' and 'have-not' business was no more than a cover for
something a lot more sinister put him well ahead of most of his contem-
poraries[137] – including E.H. Carr, who remained wedded to the idea well
into 1939.

The events of 1938 proved to be both the culmination and final refutation of the National Government's policy of appeasement, despite what
Carr was to write about it in *The Twenty Years' Crisis*. On the one hand the
National Government fully applied its policy to the most serious threat to
world peace posed by Germany to date. On the other, the scale of the
threat saw a final reversal of National Government policy, which ended
with the British guarantee to Poland in March of the following year. On
12 March 1938 Germany invaded and formally annexed Austria. While
there was widespread support in Austria for union with Germany, the invasion was carried out against the wishes of the Austrian government and
without any attempt to provide international legitimacy for the action. It
was also yet another direct challenge to the Versailles treaty, which had
explicitly forbidden union between Germany and Austria. The annexation
of Austria represented a new twist in the German policy of the unilateral

revision of the Versailles Treaty in that Austria had never been part of the pre-war Second Reich. Rather, Germany's demands had shifted ground from treaty revision to the idea that the German state should rightly include all the lands inhabited by Germans, even those which had never been part of Bismarck's state. Since the list of countries that had German minorities included Czechoslovakia, Poland, Belgium, Denmark, the Baltic states and even Italy and Romania this was more than merely a challenge to Versailles. Soon after the Anschluss with Austria Germany began preparations to give force to its claim to the Sudentland. The Sudetenland, with its majority ethnic German population, lay within Czechoslovakia along its border with Germany. The region, as part of Bohemia, had been an integral part of the Habsburg Empire since the late Middle Ages. Czechoslavakia had treaties of guarantee with both France and the Soviet Union. The crisis came to a head on 12 September when Hitler urged the Sudeten Germans to press for inclusion in the Reich. Chamberlain had implicitly given Britain's support to the French guarantee, and on 15 September he made his first trip in his two week round of shuttle diplomacy. Despite outrageous German demands made by Hitler at his second meeting with Chamberlain at Godesberg, which resulted in partial mobilisation in both Britain and France, the situation was finally resolved in Germany's favour on 29 September at the Munich Conference. Italy was invited to attend, but despite the Soviet Union's treaty with Czechoslovakia, Stalin was not invited. The National Government had managed, simultaneously, to give Germany the whole Sudentenland, thus fatally weakening a key French ally in the region, and to alienate a potential great power ally, the Soviet Union, and thus killing off the May 1935 Pact of mutual guarantee between France and the Soviet Union. A year later the Soviet Union made a separate peace with Germany.

On 8 October the Policy Committee of the Labour Party reported on the political consequences of the Anschluss and the Munich agreement. It concluded that it had severely weakened the British and French position in Europe, had strengthened Germany's political, military and economic position in Central Europe, and had removed the Soviet Union as a potential ally for the western powers.[138] The political situation had tipped so firmly in Germany's favour that Labour's 1937 international policy was now obsolete. Convinced that Germany would continue its claims to territories with significant German minorities, a general war was likely to break out over any number of regions.[139] The document concluded that:

> It is deeply repugnant to the spirit of the Labour Movement to have to consider once again the question of rearmament and the pouring

out of wealth on weapons. But it must be remembered that it is most probably already a question of whether this country and France will defend the democratic faith which they have in common and endeavour to rebuild the collective peace system, or whether they will refuse to make that effort of defence, see themselves further and further outstripped in the building up of power, and finally be faced with a Nazi dominated Europe… [fascism] constitutes such a threat to all the ideals we profess that it is even more painful to contemplate than is the prospect of rearming to defend those ideals.[140]

While there were still those in the Party who were, in the words of Bob Fraser, 'prepared to eat a lot of mud to avoid war',[141] Labour now endeavoured to put clear blue water between themselves and the National Government's foreign policy. In two speeches in October Hugh Dalton accused Chamberlain of grievously misjudging 'both the personalities and intentions of foreign dictators… I have heard it suggested that, as a consequence of his policy, OHMS [On His Majesty's Service] now means "On Hitler's and Mussolini's Service."'[142] 'Mr Chamberlain, by his own admission, led us to the brink of war, having thrown away one opportunity after another to organise an effective system of collective defence against aggression in Europe… He may lead us to the brink of war again, and this time without a single friend or ally in the world.' The incompetence of the rearmament programme left the question of what exactly had been done with the money voted by Parliament.[143] Dalton's position was consistent with the earlier complaints of the Advisory Committee about the threat posed by Germany, the need for adequate collective defence, and the "diplomatic disarmament" practiced by the Chamberlain Government. These points were reiterated by Advisory Committee members at the informal foreign policy symposium organised by Dalton on 19 October. Woolf saw Chamberlain's policy as a threat to European democracy, and complained of the inefficiency of National Government rearmament. Both Woolf and Ivor Thomas thought that there was currently no point in talking about the League and its role. Arnold-Forster accused the government of 'recklessly disarming us by stripping us of friends and allies', and reiterated the Advisory Committee's position that Labour policy should aim at recreating the conditions necessary for collective security.[144] Collective defence centred around the Anglo-French alliance was to be the basis for the recreation of a system of collective security against aggression.

Within the Advisory Committee itself, even while a system of economic appeasement was being contemplated, any future Munich-style agreement was strenuously opposed. There was now 'a very strong case for opposing any boundary changes which [appeared] to be a surrender to threats.'[145] While the re-establishment of an inclusive system of pooled security was to be desired, it could never be anything more than a partial system as long as the Nazi regime still existed.[146] There were also major weaknesses in the arrangements upon which France and Britain were relying in order to check future fascist aggression in central Europe. Arnold-Forster, in a memorandum that was heartily endorsed by Norman Angell and the former Committee chair C.R. Buxton pointed out that the current system of bilateral pacts had failed to live up to the standards expected of a collective peace system. He singled out the problem of the reaction to sudden flagrant aggression. 'Some means must be devised whereby the right to hit back... is not paralysed by delay, but yet is not left wholly to the judgement of the belligerent.'[147] This was the problem that had dogged the League during the crises over Manchuria and Abyssinia, and the various bilateral pacts that were all that was left of the western power's alliance system did not offer an effective answer to this perennial problem. What was clear was that, while a reformulation of the League – or a system like it – remained a long term goal, the 'League as a system of collective security collapsed decisively in the summer of 1936. Nothing has replaced it.' Instead 'we have Europe definitely divided into two opposing systems of alliances... a balance of power with each trying to tip the balance to its own side.' Such a system 'cannot be a permanent condition.'[148]

The final effect of Munich was to open up a radical change in Labour's tactics. The events of 1938, and the immediate problem of German aggression, brought up the issue of coalition. The disaster of 1931 still haunted Labour, and the idea of a popular front of the left was still tainted in Labour eyes by its association with the Communists and the now discredited Socialist League. Yet, with growing opposition to Chamberlain's National Government within the Conservative Party, and a Liberal foreign policy almost identical to Labour's, Labour leaders began to think about the establishment of a common front against the government. Interestingly, this possibility was only seriously considered once a significant group of senior Conservatives began to oppose the Conservative-dominated National Government. The strong distrust of the Communists was such that their advocacy of a popular front had been strenuously rejected, and while Labour members were suspicious of Conservative intentions, the general feeling amongst Labour supporters of an anti-National Government front was that Conservative support lent an air of bi-partisan dignity to any Labour-led alternative. Of all the Conservative opponents of Chamberlain it was Robert Cecil, the League of Nations enthusiast who had worked for the Second Labour Government, who was the most respected within Labour's leadership. In a letter to his former colleague at the 1929–31 Foreign Office, Hugh Dalton, Cecil wrote that it was 'literally true that a few more mistakes like Munich, and Peace (not to speak of the Empire) may be a lost cause.' The only effective answer was a Labour Government.[149] Yet, Cecil was doubtful this could be realised without help from sympathetic quarters outside of the Party, and he suggested that Labour should at a minimum, given the state of the international emergency, consider electoral pacts with sympathetic non-Labour people.[150] Unbeknown to Cecil, Labour had already discussed such a possibility during a meeting of the Policy Committee at the beginning of November. The crux of the paper presented to the Committee was that the seriousness of the situation and the growing level of disquiet amongst the Tories made a coalition to defeat Chamberlain's government possible. At the present moment the electorate was being forced to choose between the National Government and Labour's full socialist programme. A broad coalition would allow those unsure about Labour's programme the opportunity of opposing the National Government, while the war measures that would be necessarily undertaken by a Labour-led coalition would include socialist elements, such as the public control of key industries, that would be strenuously opposed by large sections of the country if undertaken unilaterally by Labour.[151] While receiving much warm support from the leadership, especially given the perception that European democracy was in danger, many members of the Policy Committee feared that such a proposal would split the movement. While no decision was taken, the fact that Labour was willing to contemplate a coalition so soon after the disaster of 1931, and risk a split in the movement, was testimony to how seriously the leadership took the international situation and the inadequacy of the National Government.[152]

While the Munich agreement helped to crystallise the opposition to the National Government, a large part of the National Government, publicly at least, believed that the storm had passed. Chamberlain's policy of appeasement had brought about peaceful change, and had succeeded where the League of Nations had failed. The 'have-nots' of Germany and Italy had been converted into 'haves' by a series of agreements and territorial readjustments. In the words of 'Cato', between Munich and the German invasion of rump-Czechoslovakia '…the great mass of the British politicians spent their time telling us that all was well, that Hitler was tamed, that the tiger had been transmogrified into a tabby by that old wizard of Number 10 Downing Street.'[153]

Those who criticised the optimism of the National Government were denounced by the government's supporters as jitterbugs, alarmists or warmongers.[154] British Pathé News, in a special tribute film to Chamberlain, referred to him as the man of the moment, who had come to the fore to save world peace when his talents were most needed. Even Lloyd's of London in December 1938 put the odds of Britain being in a war by December 1939 as 32 to 1 against. It was in this climate that E.H. Carr wrote *The Twenty Years' Crisis*. The National Government's optimism was based on the promise given by Hitler to Chamberlain that the Sudetenland was the last German territorial claim. In March 1939 Hitler went back on his word and invaded Czechoslovakia. Britain had guaranteed the security of the truncated Czechoslovakia, but in March the National Government chose not to intervene. Instead it extended a security guarantee to Poland. Writing just before the outbreak of War, Woolf was optimistic that this time the National Government would stand by its international commitments, and that the seriousness of the situation had put a stop to Chamberlain's 'wobbles' and '*volte-faces*'. There would be no new Hoare-Laval pact this time.[155]

In the last few months of peace Labour, while supporting the National government's tougher stance against Germany, played the role of an official opposition. Labour, ironically given its stand against Munich, became the peace party again in the debate over conscription. Attlee later admitted that Labour's opposition to conscription was a mistake, [156] and there were those in the Party who had already realised this in the run-up to war.[157] Here, at this late hour, the National Government was able to play the bellicose role, and conscription was introduced on 26 May 1939. Labour's hopes of a British-French-Soviet anti-fascist alliance finally collapsed on 23 August when the Soviets sought their separate peace with Hitler. By the time that Hitler finally invaded Poland on 1 September the anti-fascist alliance had been reduced to Britain, France and the British dominions (minus Eire). Labour offered its full support if the Government chose to fulfil its commitment to Poland. In the House of Commons debate Labour's deputy leader Arthur Greenwood – speaking for the Party, but being urged by the anti-appeasement Conservative Leo Amery to 'Speak for England, Arthur' – called for an end to vacillation and the honouring of the Polish guarantee.[158] At 9am on the following day, the 3 September, the British ambassador handed to the German government an ultimatum demanding the withdrawal of troops from Poland. The ultimatum expired at 11am, and Britain duly declared war on Germany. France, Canada, Australia, New Zealand, South Africa and India soon followed.

Defending Capitalism? The Road to War

The period between 1931 and 1939 is the block of years most frequently referred to by IR scholars when they mention the inter-war period. It is here that the so-called idealists were meant to have failed to stop Hitler, and kept up a utopian faith in institutions like the League when it had failed to keep the peace. A cursory glance at the period is all that is needed to refute these charges. The failures of the League were due to a number of factors, but two stand head and shoulders above the other causes. The immediate cause was that the British and French governments chose not to use the League, or used it half-heartedly as they did over Manchuria and Abyssinia. In the longer term the failure to construct a clear system of rules and regulations for pooled security allowed half-hearted governments, like Britain's National Government, to wriggle out of their treaty commitments under the Covenant. The failure of the League was a failure of will amongst its members and the failure to develop adequate machinery under the League in order to make the high ideals of the Covenant a reality. Once the esteem of the League had been seriously dented many of those dismissed as idealists, such as Woolf or Angell, advocated a system of collective defence outside of the League. The occasional throwaway claims, mentioned in chapter one, which link idealism to appeasement are just absurd. Rather, appeasement was the policy linked to those who often referred to themselves as realists, and were associated with, or supported, the foreign policy of Chamberlain's Conservative-led National Government. Appeasement, after all, as a policy that recognises the realities of power relations *as they are now*, rather than how they should be, is the ultimate realist policy. Thus, we can easily dismiss the myth that the 1930s was a decade that refuted the ideas of the writers frequently associated with the mythical idealist paradigm.

A more sophisticated question to ask would be to what extent did these writers, and the Party they were involved with, offer an effective alternative to the appeasement policy of the National Government? Here we do run into the problem that we are not comparing like with like. The National Government's policy of appeasement was a real existing policy, while Labour's only existed as an abstract idea. When comparing existing systems with an abstract alternative the abstract alternative has the advantage of not being tested. This said the policy supported by Labour's international experts did have much to recommend it. Angell and Woolf had by 1936 realised that it was going to be necessary to confront the dictators, rather than acquiescing to their territorial demands. While Labour did have its own idea of how to appease the dictators, their policy of offering the dictators a place in a wider international structure, which would not have been acceptable to Hitler, Mussolini or the Japanese, did not entail dangerous concessions and the rewarding of aggression by territorial adjustment. More importantly, perhaps, Labour and its international experts were willing to adjust their policy in light of the changing international system, while keeping faith with the same long-term goal. This compares well against the muddling through and mixed signals of the National Government. Interestingly, the writings of Angell, Woolf and Noel Baker conform well to the Machiavellian ideal that decisions and policy should adjust to the times (necessity), while remaining true to fundamental goals (constancy). Chamberlain's policy, by contrast, corresponds to the Machiavellian vices of half-measures and a misreading of the times. Where the genius of the National Government shone through was in its ability to read and use British public opinion, helped along by their close links to the media. This was particularly clear in the 1935 General election, where the National Government used the Abyssinian crisis in order to present itself as pro-League and the best choice for a peaceful but secure foreign policy. Labour's failure was in presentation; a product of its attempt to reconcile its opposition to the dictators with the concerns of the pacifist and radical socialist sections of the Party. The resulting muddle made Labour look ill prepared and contradictory. This tendency continued well into 1939, with Labour's poorly timed opposition to conscription.

That the Labour leadership and its allies in the Advisory Committee where fully aware of the seriousness of the international situation is clear from the development of their analysis of the problem. Prior to 1934 Labour was deeply split between supporters of League action against aggression and the pacifist and radical socialist wing that rejected all use of League sanctions. With the resignations of Lansbury, Ponsonby and Cripps support for League sanctions was largely unchallenged at the top of the Party, although the language was often toned down in order not to completely alienate pacifist opinion. Despite this, many pacifists did feel that the Party had betrayed their ideals.[159] Between 1935 and 1938 Labour developed its own proposals on how to confront the dictators that largely by-passed the League, but held out the possibility of re-establishing the League as the paramount security organisation in the future. The Abyssinia crisis and the Spanish Civil War were instrumental in changing Labour Party attitudes towards a war of collective security against the dictators, and increasingly the Party as a whole moved closer to the position that predominated on the Advisory Committee. After the Czechoslovak crisis and the Munich Agreement of 1938 the Party and the Advisory Committee were a part of the body of pessimists, denounced as jitterbugs by the Government, who saw the agreement as a retrograde step that made war more, not less, likely. With the exception of the embarrassment over the conscription vote, the Party and its intellectuals supported preparations for a possible war.

In terms of IR theory, Labour Party foreign policy and the advice of the Advisory Committee fits within what today we would call interdependence theory. Support for the League flowed from the idea that its institutions were the most consistent with the reality of the economic, social and political interdependence of states. This approach, while at odds with the realist idea of the primacy of the sovereign state, also accepts that in the absence of proper institutions for the maintenance of this interdependence, then the international system will fall back on principles associated with reason of state and the balance of power. This can be seen most clearly in the works of Leonard Woolf and Norman Angell, where the principles of the international anarchy and realpolitik are seen as relevant to international affairs once more structured and socially superior arrangements have broken down. In the end, the system associated with the international anarchy is unsustainable, both because it is out of step with the interdependent nature of modern society and because it relies on a relative security that is fundamentally unstable. This does mean that in the short term it is necessary for statesmen to work under the principles of the international anarchy once they find themselves in it. So Norman Angell in 1938–9 found himself urging Britain to take account of the balance of power when dealing with the dictators,[160] while loyal in the longer term to the construction of a better system that would ultimately rely on something less unstable.

With the outbreak of war in September 1939 Labour's short-term goals changed to winning the war by support for the war effort. The long-term goal remained the building of an alternative world order consistent with the realities of global interdependence. This preparation for a new world built upon an analysis of the failures of the inter-war period. More specifically, the functional approach to world order championed by David Mitrany competed with plans for a more visible political-security organisation.

5

A WORKING PEACE SYSTEM?
(1939–1945)

David Mitrany

According to Professor Mitrany, an international community must grow from the satisfaction of common needs shared by members of different nations…For nationalism as a principle of political organization is not only obsolete; but in the nuclear age it is also self-destructive. Thus the future of the civilized world is intimately tied to the future of the functional approach to international organization. (Hans J. Morgenthau)[1]

Although he had effectively ceased to work for the Labour Party after 1931, when Party membership became a requirement of membership of the Advisory Committee, Mitrany continued to influence Labour thinking through his writings, and Mitrany's feelings for the Party, and his past connections with it, continued to be positive. I have included Mitrany in this section on the development of Labour foreign policy largely because of the influence of his functional approach, but it is important not to forget that prior to the 1930s Mitrany's major work in foreign policy had been on sanctions and South-East Europe. In addition to this, Mitrany's work on peasant economics, and his consequent attempts to bring the social democrats and agrarian parties of Europe together, was influential. Incidentally, his work on peasant economics, which first appeared in an edited collection co-edited by Hugh Dalton and T.E. Gregory, was the research project that Mitrany was personally the most proud of.[2] Within Labour's international policy circles prior to 1939, however, the most often quoted of Mitrany's works was his short monograph on international sanctions.[3] When we talk about Mitrany's contribution to Labour, therefore, it is not just his

work on functional government that we must look at, but also his contributions on the myriad problems of central and Eastern Europe and the
issue of international sanctions.

Mitrany stands out from the other writers in this collection for a number of reasons. Perhaps the most important is the originality of his thought
and that, amongst all of the writers discussed in this book, Mitrany is the
only one that is still considered as a mainstream IR writer. His writings
were the basis of many scholarly studies in the 1960s and 1970s, his *Working Peace System* has been an essential part of the many anthologies on
European Integration, and there have been three monographs in the last
six years that have been wholly or partially concerned with assessing Mitrany's contribution to IR.[4] While Mitrany has not been forgotten, he has
been frequently misread. The major misrepresentation has been the myth
that Mitrany's functional approach is fundamentally an economic approach that tries to by-pass politics. In fact, as we shall see below, Mitrany's
functional approach is a theory of government that makes economic concerns subservient to political goals. This myth seems to have originated in
the neo-functionalist misreading of Mitrany's work. He also stands out as
being the only member of the five writers discussed in detail in this book
that became a British citizen, rather than being born one. His experience
of being brought up Jewish in Romania, at the time one of the most anti-
Semitic countries in Europe, along with his experience of hunger at a
young age, gave him a very different set of formative experiences to the
largely middle class British writers. Part of this influence was a deep distrust of dogmatic political positions that almost certainly influenced his
decision not to join any political party.[5] This makes his membership of the
Advisory Committee all the more interesting, and in his memoir he saw
his work for the committee as a very rewarding exception.[6] This positive
attitude was reciprocated by the Labour Party. In a letter to Ramsay Mac-
Donald in 1925 the then head of Labour's International Department, William Gillies, refers to Mitrany in glowing terms.[7] Despite Mitrany's deliberate attempt to distance himself from political parties and ideological
groups, he always stressed the influence of British left-liberals on his thought. He particularly singled out the philosopher Graham Wallas and the
political scientist L.T. Hobhouse as the primary influences on his political
theory. From Wallas Mitrany took his scepticism about the value of reason
as an organising principle of society, as well as his view of the aggregation
of our social heritage that had constructed a 'Great Society' that was larger
than the sum of its parts. From Hobhouse Mitrany took the notion of
organising society upon the basis of function, as well as a distrust of the
Hegelian metaphysical theory of the state. In fact, Hobhouse's 1911 book

Liberalism, the companion to Ramsay MacDonald's *The Socialist Movement* in the Home University Library series on the three prevailing ideologies of the time, was the basis for the functional theory of government that underpinned both Mitrany's approach to world peace and G.D.H. Cole and R.H. Tawney's guild socialism.[8]

Mitrany's work, both inside and outside the Advisory Committee, revolved around four related issues. The first was the problem of national minorities, which became a primary concern with the establishment of national states in central and eastern Europe that contained substantial national and religious minorities. The second was the problem of peasant agriculture, and the related problem of government in southeast Europe. Thirdly, Mitrany worked on the question of international sanctions that had been part of the debate about the closing of the gaps in the League Covenant. Finally, there was the development of his functional approach in the early 1930s, which Mitrany saw as both a development of government in keeping with the times, and as a practical peaceful alternative to the state-based system associated with the international anarchy. The functional approach, therefore, was Mitrany's answer to the problem that had dominated the discussions of foreign policy within the Labour Party during the 1920s: how to create a working collective peace system that would provide security while eliminating war as an instrument of state policy. While the vast majority of Labour's international experts, especially on the Advisory Committee, had concentrated on developing a system of inclusive arbitration, sanctions and disarmament through the League, Mitrany eventually took a more indirect approach that focused on the gradual spread of international government function by function. While Mitrany's work on the functional approach came to fruition during the Second World War, and remained a central part of his thinking until his death in 1975, aspects of his functional approach appear in his earlier works. His first attempt to give his new approach to international government form occurred in his 1933 book *The Progress of International Government,* while functional processes of government were explored in his 1936 study *The Effects of the War in South Eastern Europe.*[9] The functional approach, therefore, was part of the wider debates of the inter-war period over the construction of a new more peaceful international order, and was as much a response to the failings of the international anarchy, as it was a friendly criticism of the failed attempts to create a League-based alternative international order.

While the functional approach still remains the most lasting aspect of Mitrany's intellectual legacy, much of his work initially focused on the more immediate problem of national minorities. Certainly, his earliest contributions for the Labour Party were on conditions in Germany,[10] on the one hand, and the problem of minorities in relation to security and the League on the other. While his mission to Germany was a fact finding one to ascertain attitudes in the country, his work on minorities explored ways in which the League could improve its role as a security organisation. His 1928 memoranda for the Advisory Committee pointed out that national self-determination, far from solving the major irritant of national minorities, had left 30 million people in central and eastern Europe in states that did not represent their national or religious identities. Although, under League auspices, 'sixteen treaties were concluded for the purpose of securing them the right to live according to their customs and beliefs' persecutions of minorities continued, and 'the danger of conflict on this score has not disappeared.'[11] Disputes over minorities remained the primary cause of conflict in central and eastern Europe, according to Mitrany, so a solution to the problem would obviously be a major contribution to international security. He immediately ruled out changes of frontiers as a solution, since the attempt to do just that in 1919 have not solved the problem.[12] In the immediate term the solution lay in stronger League oversight of minority rights, akin to the system already in place for the Mandates.[13] The memo makes clear that Mitrany considers national sovereignty and the sharp division of state boundaries as the primary obstacle to a solution to the minorities problem. In this sense the minorities problem, which threatened to undermine the security of so many states, was itself a clear product of the sovereign national state. By the 1930s Mitrany would turn to a more root and branch solution to the problem of the sovereign state, which would also aim to solve the thorny issue of minorities.

Mitrany always tried to see the minorities problem as a common one shared by all European peoples. The problem with much British liberal and socialist interest in the minorities problem was that it could often get carried away in supporting one group over another. A sense of moral outrage could easily attach itself to a single cause, or group of people, to the detriment of other concerns. Nowhere was this more true than in the British liberal and social democratic attitudes to South East Europe. The Balkan Peninsular, from the 1820s onwards, tugged on the romantic heartstrings of the British liberal and radical tradition. 'For a number of reasons, political and sentimental,' David Mitrany recalled 'devotion to the cause of the Balkan peoples came naturally into play with English opinion… it intruded deep into English politics and policy.'[14] By the beginning of the twentieth century the interest in South East Europe had become something of a publishing phenomenon. Liberal journalists and opinion-formers travelled over the Peninsular, returning to write detailed accounts of what they had seen. Between the 1880s and the 1930s, with national conflicts on the rise, these writers tended to take sides in the various Balkan conflicts, favouring one group over others. Edith Durham supported the Albanians; H.N. Brailsford the Macedonians; James Bouchier, C.R. Buxton and Noel Buxton, the Bulgarians, Wickham Steed and Rebecca West, the Serbs; and Dr Seton-Watson, the Romanians. Whenever tensions arose in the Peninsular these British liberals would fight a proxy Balkan war in the newspapers and lecture halls of Britain. With the waning of the British Liberal Party the Labour Party and its press took up the mantle.[15] While many of his fellow internationalists tended to see the Balkans as a problem,[16] a kind of half-world between the old and the new where the ideas of the West were often aped in the service of something older and more violent, Mitrany saw it as a region in transition that contained within it the seeds of new approaches and ideas that might have relevance to the rest of the world. In fact, Mitrany argued strenuously against the view of the Balkans as the powder-keg of Europe, and did much to counteract the negative views of the Balkans without falling into the trap that so many British liberals did of adopting and promoting one or other of the national groupings. Rather, Mitrany's view of the Balkans was as a region that was linked in and influenced by the wider European stage. 'The Balkans only broke out in a rash when Europe was in a state of fever' he famously told an American audience in 1937.[17] Since the Balkans were intimately connected to the wider European political world the influence could also flow the other way. The Balkan experience could have valuable lessons for Europe and the wider world. In fact, Mitrany's Balkan experience is a frequently overlooked influence on what would become his most famous accomplishment: the functional approach to international politics.

Central to Mitrany's analysis of the Balkans after the Great War was his view that the land reforms that followed the end of hostilities were a social revolution on the same scale as that of the liberal revolutions in nineteenth century Western Europe. The power of the landed aristocracy in South East Europe had been maintained through the power of the state. With the weakening of the state, and the aristocracy's role in it, the peasant class, and its political organisation had been able to push through expropriation, completely changing the economy of the region from one based on large latifundia to a decentralised peasant-owned agriculture.[18] The new power of the peasants brought the countryside into conflict with the cities in a way that had never happened in western Europe. There was no major migration of destitute peasants to the towns to provide cheap labour for industrial concerns, and the peasant parties emerged as a serious political force for advancing peasant interests.[19] This conflict between urban and rural was exacerbated by the divergent economic systems at play. Peasant agriculture was based on small-scale labour intensive enterprises, while the cities worked under the industrial capitalist logic of large enterprises employing economies of scale. This capitalist idea that larger is always more efficient had also become an article of faith amongst the socialist and Marxist left. The urban industrial abstract economics of liberalism and Marxism assumed, using industry as a model, that larger capital intensive farming was more productive, and therefore a more efficient system for providing those two necessities for industrial development: an agricultural surplus and cheap food for the urban population.[20] In fact, the First World War and other political developments had shown that peasant-owned agriculture, with its low capital overheads and intensive techniques, produced food more cheaply than did the capital intensive larger factory farms. It turned out that the link to the land, rather than being merely the stuff of mystic poets, was a central part of a highly productive and cost-effective agriculture.[21] The productive efficiency of peasant agriculture could be undermined, however, by the problems of distribution. Peasants lack a serious distribution system. The answer lay in distributive cooperatives, controlled by the peasants but working on a larger scale than they could individually.[22] 'It is an undoubted fact... that small-scale cultivation, assisted by co-operative arrangements, is much more effective for the production of high-quality products than extensive large-scale farming.'[23]

Mitrany's discussion of peasant agriculture contained two elements vital to the working out of the logic of his functional approach to international security. The first was that the different functions of the modern human social life did not necessarily follow similar logics. This was the reason that Mitrany spent much of his time attacking what he saw as social dogmatism. The major obstacle, from his point of view, to seeing things as they were – the 'relation of things', as he phrased it – was the assumption that one abstract principle could be applied to all aspects of life. Thus, an economics that had been developed in order to explain and enhance industrial productivity could not necessarily be applied blithely to the very different conditions of agricultural production. A centralising and totalising system of government or thought was liable to be counter-productive. Second, the solutions to modern social problems, such as the distribution of peasant produce, required inherently cooperative and function-specific solutions based upon the localised knowledge of those who actually worked within a function. While he clearly opposed the dogmatism that he found in certain aspects of socialism, Mitrany's solution to the peasant problem was itself a form of socialism that rested on the fundamentally anti-statist anarcho-communism of writers like Proudhon (whom Mitrany admired), and fitted well with the guild socialism of such Labour stalwarts as R.H. Tawney, G.D.H. Cole and Harold Laski. The answer was collective and cooperative structures, but ones that were developed on a voluntary basis and as a response to specific technical problems facing people in specific functions.

While Mitrany's experience of Eastern European peasant agriculture had convinced him of the need for a more case-by-case pragmatic approach to social problems, his categories and modes of thought were a product of British radical liberal and socialist analysis. This reflects the importance that his studies at the LSE, under the two eminent liberal socialists Graham Wallas and L.T. Hobhouse, had in focusing and ordering his concept of society. Wallas' rejection of the old Victorian liberal reliance on a dominant reason greatly influenced Mitrany. It was Wallas' contention, following David Hume, that in social analysis emotive forces created needs, and the use of reason only came in afterwards as a means by which we can calculate how to satisfy those needs.[24] Similarly, emotions are at play in the creation of the social entities that make up the political life around us. As a consequence in politics, unlike the physical sciences where the entities are fixed, the first task is to decide what entities exist and are relevant before being able to apply reasoned judgement to political questions. Since these social entities are constantly in flux this is no easy task.[25] One implication of Wallas' approach is that the emotive choices we make in highlighting certain entities over others can change our view of reality. Mitrany's functional approach has to be seen as at least partially a product of Wallas' notion of politics. By downplaying the role of the state, and playing up transnational forces Mitrany was engaged in the first emotive stage of political analysis, and was using this to change our view of the international reality. Mitrany's choice of function as the basic unit of modern society was not a new idea. It is almost certain that he got the idea from Hobhouse, who used the concept as the basis of his vision of a liberal socialist society in 1911. The concept of function also appears in the works of G.D.H. Cole (in 1920), R.H. Tawney (in 1921), H.G. Wells (in 1922) and Harold Laski (in 1925), so it was very much part of the British Zeitgeist.[26] While in Cole, Laski and Wells function is used to mean a social association, in Hobhouse, Tawney and Mitrany function is equated with social purpose. A function for Mitrany is, therefore, not an organisation itself, but rather something that needs to be fulfilled in order for society to replicate itself. Social organisations are, therefore, built up in order to perform functions. While Laski was using function in a somewhat different way from Mitrany there is still an important connection between the two. Laski, in 1925 was the first to apply the concept of function, and functional organisation, to the international sphere.[27] Mitrany's first use of the term in an international context is in 1933. Here his turn to functional government is very much a reaction to the failure of the League to live up to its promise as an alternative to the international anarchy.

Like his colleagues on the Advisory Committee, Mitrany was deeply opposed to the international anarchy associated with the old diplomacy and with state sovereignty. His major contribution to the debates over disarmament, arbitration and sanctions was his book on the problem of international sanctions, published in 1925. Like Angell, Woolf and Noel Baker he was convinced that sanctions were necessary if the system around the League was to have any chance of successfully introducing a new security system while making a start on disarmament:

> Whether the new organisation will ultimately rest on Covenant or protocol or regional pact, always they will have to contain some means for dealing with those who might be tempted to sin against the new peace creed, and for succouring their possible victims.[28]

That sanctions were an unfortunate necessity in a world in which not all could be trusted can be seen from the handwritten note that Mitrany scribbled on what is now the British Library's copy of *The Problem of International Sanctions:* 'If all people, my dear Ena,[29] had something of your kind nature… then sanctions would be superfluous; and instead of spending so many hours on this barbarous subject, I could have passed them much more wisely in enjoying your presence.'

For Mitrany there was no doubt that the vagueness in the Covenant over sanctions was a major flaw that stood in the way of the establishment of an effective pooled security regime, and while he felt that sanctions, especially military sanctions, should be a last resort, he applauded the Geneva Protocol's linking of sanctions with an effective arbitration regime.[30] Yet, he was fully aware that a major drawback with sanctions, and therefore of the whole League system, was the general reluctance of major League members to tie themselves to the use of sanctions in general and military sanctions in particular. He also agreed with Woolf that a drawback with a system based on the rule of law was that it would have a tendency towards supporting the status quo. While later his functional approach would attempt to address this problem of inflexibility, in 1925 he contented himself with the idea that a system that recognised the interdependence of sanctions and arbitration 'should cure the new system of any tendency towards ossifying the existing state of things.'[31]

While sympathetic to the work done by Woolf and Noel Baker on a League-based system of pooled security, combining arbitration, sanctions and disarmament, Mitrany came to see a series of flaws in the means towards their otherwise noble end. The problem with the attempt to develop a regime based on arbitration, sanctions and disarmament was that it required the agreement of all or most state representatives. As a result, the negotiations were unwieldy, and often ran into problems of national security and honour that proved to be difficult to reconcile. It also accepted and entrenched the idea of state sovereignty. It was states that signed up to the international agreements and – as the defections of Japan, Italy, Germany and even the Soviet Union over Finland showed – as long as states remained in control of their own security they were free to defect from the system. With a complicated and often unwieldy inter-governmental system of security it was also easy for other states to acquiesce in this aggression by refusing to act on the behalf of the system of pooled security. What was required was some form of internationalisation of those functions in the state that allowed a state to mobilise for war. It was for this reason that Mitrany applauded the European Coal and Steel Community for transferring coal and steel, the sinews of war, to a transnational organisation.[32] At another level Mitrany argued that since it was the sovereign state system that helped to create the irritants that led to war through the problems of minorities, access to raw materials and state-base loyalties, it made sense to argue that the diminution of the causes of possible wars via the blurring of national boundaries would reduce the likelihood of war by cuting off these irritants.[33] Obviously, the closing off of war-causing structures and the building of new peace enhancing ones were part of the same process that flowed from the realities of global interdependence.

Mitrany, while agreeing with his colleagues on the importance of the new interdependence, took this argument a step further by suggesting that functional interdependence could be the basis of a new system of security. This was possible because it fit two developments in human government. First, what Mitrany called the social life – the cluster of economic social relationships that made up a self-sufficient society – had burst the bounds of its security system, the state, and was now global. As a result, the state and its system of security was now parasitic on the social life, and a new security system based on a global social life was required.[34] Second, while the state had achieved its nineteenth century goal of providing legal justice – the nightwatchman state – the goal of government in the twentieth century was to fulfil social need – the welfare state.[35] Like H.G. Wells Mitrany thought that material forces, under laissez faire capitalism, had been allowed to get out of control, and in order to guarantee that the forces of production satisfied social needs some form of government planning was necessary.[36] Distribution, rather than efficiency, was now the major social problem.[37] The development of a welfare-based government through national planning alone, however, was rejected by Mitrany, since the state was no longer self-sufficient, and with a deepening of state sovereignty associated with state-based planning conflicts between states over resources would be accentuated, rather than ameliorated.[38] This point was a source of disagreement with H.N. Brailsford, as discussed in chapter 2. Mitrany also rejected federalism as a solution since trying to integrate societies at all levels of state activity all at once was not a practical alternative, and regional federalisation would just create a series of larger competitive states.[39] The existence of federated states would not solve the problems associated with the international anarchy. The only solution to the twin issues of a new globalised social life and the new needs-based approach of government was the development of international planning at the level of individual functions. In other words, a world government would be established function by function as people felt willing and able to integrate in a particular area.

There were already functional organisations at work when Mitrany constructed his functional approach. The public international unions, such as the International Telegraphs Union and the Universal Postal Union, established in the late nineteenth century already conformed to Mitrany's notion of functional organisations, while the International Labour Office operated under the auspices of the League. Mitrany envisaged the gradual expansion of the international functions covered by functional organisations, and the gradual shift of responsibilities and loyalties away from the monolithic sovereign state. While these functional organisations had not prevented war in 1914 and 1939, Mitrany believed that the shear volume of functional organisations that would develop in the future, and the new areas that they would deal with, would make it harder for states to go to war.[40] These new organisations would not compete, or confront, the sovereign state since they would be accomplishing tasks that the state did not feel competent to do on its own. This slow diffusion of authority for certain key functions would create a cobweb of interrelations at a global level, and while not much on their own, on aggregate they would amount to an internationalised tier of government.[41] Mitrany's work on war government in First World War South Eastern Europe had led him to the conclusion that in modern total war military preparedness was increasingly secondary to the ability to wage a sustained conflict, and for a sustained conflict it was the ability to marshal economic and social resources that was ultimately crucial.[42] The removal of the state's ability to create a centralised war economy by internationalising key aspects of planning and government was, therefore, an important part of preventing the return of total war.[43] A final hope was that the shift in government from a sovereign state-based system to a largely functional one that would be better at fulfilling human needs would also cause a shift in loyalties from the state towards a new functional order.[44]

Thus, Mitrany's answer to the problem of interdependence and the threat of a state-based anarchy was not to confront the state head-on, but to create an alternative functional and global reality parallel to the state. In other words, the institutions associated with interdependence should supersede the failed security system of the state. This led to the myth that Mitrany's functional approach was an economic, rather than a political, theory of integration that had no theory of government. It has been assumed by a number of casual analysts of integration theory that, because he concentrated on the role played by the functional integration of infrastructure and other relationships often associated with the economic sphere such as labour, Mitrany was ignoring the whole question of political relations.[45] This misses the point about Mitrany's approach. The functional approach *is* a theory of government. The concern of the functional approach is how government structures emerge at the international level. Rather than putting 'economics' first Mitrany makes economic concerns subservient to the political. The functional organisations are, after all, international planning bodies that control and direct their functions, and are consequently government institutions engaged in governing. The goal of the functional approach is not an economic one, but the political one of a global system of security. His analysis of the failures of the old international anarchy and the growth of interdependence were not dissimilar to those of Woolf, Angell and Noel Baker. Where he differed from them was in his lack of faith in the ability of international state-based organisations and federalism to deal with the problems of security. His functional approach was an attempt to find a workable alternative. Between 1939 and 1945 Labour policymakers would discuss the relative merits of functional and inter-governmental systems of international government.

Labour and the War Years:
Chamberlain's Fall and the Churchill Coalition

One of the first sacrifices to the war effort was the suspension of the Advisory Committee on International Questions from September 1939 until November 1944. The decision to suspend the Committee was taken by the International Department, within which the Advisory Committee was housed, on the grounds that the blackout conditions in London would make evening meetings largely impossible. William Gillies, the head of the International Department, was eager to stress that the Advisory Committee should not be closed down.[46] Members of the Advisory Committee continued to work through the other organs of the Party. Noel Baker worked with Hugh Dalton and Harold Laski on the International Sub-Committee of the National Executive. Woolf and Noel Baker were appointed Secretary and Chairman respectfully of the new International Relationships Sub-Committee of the Socialist Reconstruction Committee that met between 1941 and 1943, and included many of the old Advisory Committee stalwarts such as Arnold-Forster, Hugh Dalton and James Walker.[47] Hugh Dalton also continued his pre-war practice of organising seminars on Foreign Affairs that brought together Labour's international experts. In November 1943 Leonard Woolf wrote to James Middleton, Secretary of the Party, suggesting that the Advisory Committee be reformed. With the winding up of the International Relations Sub-Committee, Woolf argued, the Party was without an independent committee of experts on international affairs for the first time in twenty-five years.[48] Noel Baker was immediately supportive of the proposal, and reported back to Woolf in February that the International Sub-Committee of the National Executive had unanimously approved the re-establishment of the Advisory Committee, with Leonard Woolf as secretary once more and Noel Baker as chair.[49] While the Advisory Committee, as before, was free to discuss any issue it liked, the suggestions for topics for the Committee concentrated on functional questions and post-war reconstruction.[50] The issue of war aims remained the bailiwick of the International Sub-Committee of the Executive. The reformed Advisory Committee produced its first memorandum for the Executive in November 1944. Thus, through their positions on the International Sub-Committee and the reformed Advisory Committee, Labour's international experts contributed to both the immediate question of war aims and the longer-term questions of the form and functions of the new post-war international order.

While these policies and debates on foreign affairs remained largely academic during the 1930s when Labour was shut out of power, the Second World War gave Labour its fourth taste of government and access once again to the levers of power. Initially the National Executive and the PLP refused to join a coalition with the Conservatives as long as Chamberlain remained in office. Labour's lack of confidence in the Prime Minister's abilities led it to turn down several offers of a place in a coalition government.[51] Labour's gambit paid off. After the abortive British and French expedition to stem the German invasion of Norway between February and May 1940 the Labour, Liberal and Conservative opponents of the

National Government turned the debate on the Norwegian Campaign into a discussion on the effectiveness of the Government. Labour's leadership did not bother to hide from public view its feeling that Chamberlain and his Foreign Secretary Lord Halifax should resign. Calls for Chamberlain's resignation remained a mainstay of speeches by Labour leaders.[52] In the subsequent House of Commons vote on the Government's handling of the war on 8 May forty-two Conservatives voted with the Labour and Liberal opposition. Although the Government still won the debate by 281 votes to 200, the split in Parliament convinced Chamberlain that he could no longer command the full support of Parliament. His final attempt to form a coalition with Labour on 9 May was rebuffed, and the Labour leadership left the Prime Minister in no doubt that they could not serve under him. Chamberlain's subsequent resignation 'was to be the only occasion in the twentieth century when a majority government was forced out of office by a vote in the House of Commons.'[53] After much negotiation Winston Churchill became Prime Minister of an all-Party coalition, and the new status of the Labour Party was reflected in the number of government posts allotted to it. Two of the five seats on the War Cabinet went to Labour, and were filled by the Party Leader Clement Attlee and the Deputy Leader Arthur Greenwood. One of the three defence ministries, in this case the Admiralty, went to Labour, Herbert Morrison became Home Secretary, Hugh Dalton Minister of Economic Warfare and Ernest Bevin Minister of Labour and National Service. Philip Noel Baker was also eventually included, as Parliamentary Secretary of the Ministry of War Transport. The major implication of Labour's new role in government was that it was going to carry far more weight in both the conduct of this war and in the negotiations that would establish the new post-war order.

On the face of it Churchill was a strange choice as Prime Minister of a broad left-right coalition. Although he had had his brief radical stage during his time as a Liberal cabinet minister in the Liberal Governments between 1905 and 1915, his record since was that of a strongly reactionary Tory. He had become a hate figure for the labour movement through his role in the 1926 General Strike. Adolf Sturmthal singled Churchill out as one of the Tory diehards who saw the General Strike in class terms as a threat to middle class democracy.[54] In 1927 Churchill had praised Italian Fascism as a legitimate response to Bolshevism – right for Italy, but inappropriate for Britain. He had supported Franco in the Spanish Civil War, and had as late as 1938 paid tribute to Hitler for bringing Germany back to its rightful position in the world.[55] His implacable opposition to trades unionism and the left, coupled with his lack of sympathy for the victims of fascism, seemed to make him a peculiar choice for the Prime

Minister of an all-Party coalition. Yet, a combination of the seriousness of the situation and the undoubted abilities of many of the members of the wartime coalition government helped smooth over what would otherwise be strong ideological antipathies. Churchill and many of the other anti-appeasement Tories may have been fighting for narrow British power interests, rather than against fascism and for a new international order, but the common interest in unconditional victory over Hitler's Germany was a strong binding agent. In the final few years of peace Churchill and the Labour leaders often found themselves on the same side in Parliament, and Churchill himself wrote that in 'the eleven years before the outbreak of war, I had... come far more often into collision with the Conservative and National Governments than with the Labour and Liberal opposetions.'[56] Rumours that the Labour leadership was deeply unhappy about serving under Churchill seem unfounded, and may have originated from Chamberlain's appraisal of the situation in May 1940.[57] Indeed, A.L. Rowse claimed that it was the Labour leadership that insisted on Churchill as Prime Minister in their discussions with Chamberlain because Churchill was one of only a few Conservatives untainted by service to the National Government before 1939, and by 'a curious irony of fate it was the Labour Party that gave Mr Churchill his historic chance'.[58] There is no hard evidence of this either, but it seems just as likely as any other interpretation of the discussions during those three days in May. Interestingly, while he said he would be happy with Churchill, Hugh Dalton preferred Halifax. He also felt that Attlee agreed with him.[59] What was certain was Churchill's willingness to work with anyone who proved effective in the fight against the Axis – 'Eleven years in the political wilderness had freed me from ordinary party antagonisms' he later wrote[60] – and he forged stranger alliances than his coalition with Labour. Churchill's sincere support for the Soviet Union; his tolerance of General de Gaulle in the face of the American preference for the Vichy French regime and his instructions to Fitzroy Maclean on the eve of the British mission to Tito's Partisans that led to his eventual switch of British aid from the relatively ineffectual Chetniks to the Communist-led Partisans[61] – all reveal the man's willingness to win no matter what the cost. This goes some way to explain both his good working relationship with Labour, and the loyalty that he was able to command from Attlee and the other senior Labour leaders. It is telling that even now Labour still has a sneaking regard for Churchill. When the BBC recently launched its televised hunt for the greatest ever Briton, it was a former Labour cabinet minister Mo Mowlam who presented the case for Churchill.

Labour's experience in the coalition cabinet was not entirely a happy one, although most of its problems came from outside the Cabinet room. After Germany invaded the Soviet Union on 22 June 1941 left-wingers in the Party, such as Aneurin Bevan, kept up a campaign with the Communists to open up a second front to take pressure off the Soviets. This found a ready audience within American circles once the United States entered the war in December.[62] The Labour members of the Government remained loyal to the British strategic view that a second front on the European mainland in 1942 was premature at the current levels of British and American forces in Europe. They also opposed calls for more material aid to the Soviet Union, pointing out that they were in favour of aid as long as it did not detract from Britain's own ability to wage war.[63] Worker unrest caused by the strictures of the war economy found Labour ministers, particularly the Trade Unionist Ernest Bevin who was responsible for labour, at odds with many of their Trade Unionist constituents. The fear of losing wartime by-elections to left-wing pacifists and pro-Soviet socialists remained an ever-present danger. Underlying this was the fear of a substantial challenge from the Communists at home, and the worry amongst many like Bevin that Nazi tyranny would be replaced by a Soviet version.

Within the Government Labour ministers played an active role in the planning of both the war and the post-war settlement. Attlee chaired all the Cabinet sub-committees on post-war British foreign policy, while Bevin was on the committee for post-war settlement.[64] Hugh Dalton, as Minister of Economic Warfare, was initially responsible for the Special Operations Executive, the organisation that coordinated Britain's wartime espionage efforts and liased with the resistance in occupied countries. Stafford Cripps, still sitting as an independent between 1939 and 1945 after his expulsion from the Party, was Britain's Ambassador to Moscow during the key years of 1940 To 1942, and in March 1942 he headed up an abortive mission to secure Indian nationalist support for the war through constitutional reform. Labour's deep involvement in the war effort, and its close cooperation with the Conservatives, led Herbert Morrison to admit to King George VI in November 1945 that 'During the Coalition the Labour members had learnt a great deal from the Conservatives in how to govern.'[65]

Despite the hiatus in Advisory Committee activity, Labour's international experts were as busy during the war as they had been before it. The Executive, and its International Sub-Committee, included three of the top international specialists in the Party – Philip Noel Baker, Hugh Dalton and Harold Laski. David Mitrany continued to work with the Fabians, and appeared at Fabian organised events with Laski, and H.N. Brailsford. With the reformation of the Advisory Committee in 1944 Woolf and Noel Baker had another avenue for their views on international affairs. Generally speaking, we can divide the proposals formulated within the Party by its intellectuals into three areas. First, there were the immediate war aims that were necessary to end the war and to make a wider international settlement possible. Second, there was the longer term construction of a sustainable alternative world order. Third, there was the question of the future of the three power consensus between Britain, the Soviet Union and the United States. The Advisory Committee concentrated almost exclusively on the second strand, while the International Sub-Committee concentrated on the first, but also discussed the second. The third strand appears in the International Sub-Committee documents, but is rarely touched upon in the Advisory Committee. It was, however, increasingly reflected in the policy of the leadership.

Peace without Recriminations?
Immediate War Aims and the Party Intellectuals

During the war the International Sub-Committee of the Executive made two comprehensive attempts at formalising Labour's war aims, in both cases Philip Noel Baker and Harold Laski played central roles, although in the second case the main body of the text was the work of Hugh Dalton. While both sets gave large amounts of space to the longer-term issues of constructing a new order to replace the old one that had failed in 1939, they also gave pride of place to the immediate problem of constructing a peace with Germany and her allies. The first set of war aims was initially drafted by Noel Baker during September and October 1939, and after amendments the ideas found in Noel Baker's memo formed the core of the Executive's Declaration of policy issued in February 1940, which was in turn submitted to Conference in the following May. Written while Labour was still in opposition, it was directed towards the German people, and was written as a direct response to Hitler's peace feelers after the fall of Poland. The second set of war aims was initiated by the 1943 Party Conference, which called for a specific statement on the proposed postwar settlement. This followed an NEC interim report issued in 1942. In response to this call from the Conference the NEC mandated Hugh Dalton to write a draft for submission to the International Sub-Committee. Dalton submitted his preliminary sketch on the post-war settlement, which met with general approval, to the Sub-Committee in November 1943. After several drafts, and what appears to have been a stormy meeting of the NEC in April 1944, Harold Laski and Philip Noel Baker submitted substantial revisions and additions. Dalton redrafted the document to include large sections written by Laski and Noel Baker, and it was finally passed unanimously by the Sub-Committee on 18 April. The text was eventually presented as a policy document in the Annual Report of the NEC to the December 1944 Party Conference. The Advisory Committee, which had been reformed in 1944, largely stuck to longer-term questions of international order, and consequently had little to say on the shorter-term prospects.

Philip Noel Baker's original September and October 1939 drafts of Labour's war aims followed Harold Laski's own tentative proposals to the International Sub-Committee in September 1939. The outbreak of war had marked a clean break with the idea, still prevalent in Labour's discussions of economic appeasement in 1938–9, that a deal could be done with the Nazis. Both Laski and Noel Baker, in line with general feeling in the Party and the Country, made the overthrow of the Hitler government a precondition of peace discussions. Hitler's continued use of 'final' agreements as breathers between acts of coercive diplomacy that threatened the peace were seen as the major immediate cause of instability. Consequently, a permanent peace could only be secured with a German government that was willing to keep its word and could be trusted to keep the peace in the future.[66] For Laski it was 'impossible to maintain ordinary international relations with men to whom bad faith is a permanent principle of behaviour.'[67] The main precondition for peace, therefore, was the setting up of a German government that was representative of the German people, and willing to restore all the Nazi conquests so far. Once this precondition was met Labour would support an immediate interim peace with Germany.[68] Hugh Dalton also endorsed this position in his March 1940 monograph Hitler's War.[69] The removal of the Nazi government would only be a first step towards a new peace agreement that would remove the longer-term causes of war by reinstituting the system of collective security and peaceful settlement of disputes.[70] For both Laski and Noel Baker an added aspect, in harmony with Mitrany's views on functional government, was the establishment of a series of agreements that would make national sovereignty, and hence national boundaries, less important, although a more detailed discussion of these proposals will be saved until the next section.

The immediate aims proposed by Noel Baker, after the initial precondition of the overthrow of the Nazi government, focused primarily on the undoing of German conquests since 1938. Without mentioning the vexed question of the German-Polish border, the freedom of the Polish people 'with their own free government and State' took pride of place as the first condition. Second, Czechoslovakia should be restored, and Germany must accept that the Munich agreement was now dead. Although the Munich agreement had been freely entered into by both Britain and France Noel Baker felt that the German government had broken the agreement first by its invasion of the rest of Czechoslovakia in March 1939. Again, Hugh Dalton publicly backed this position in 1940.[71] Third, while not ruling out the possibility that Austrians of their own free will might wish to join Germany, the Austrians should be allowed to decide their own future without interference from Germany or the Allies. 'When the German Armies have been withdrawn from these invaded lands, questions of disputed frontiers can be honourably and amicably discussed.'[72]

The 9 February 1940 declaration of policy by the National Executive reiterated these proposals in an abbreviated form. 'Victory for democracy must be achieved' it stated, and the best way for this to happen was for the German people to overthrow the Hitler regime. The other option was for democracy to triumph through force of arms or economic pressure. 'Restitution must include freedom for the Polish and Czechoslovak peoples' and the 'Austrian people... must be left free to decide... whether or not they wish to remain within the German Reich.'[73] While these short-term aims were required of Germany, and therefore carried the force of a diktat, the longer-term issues of borders and the shape of the future order were to be sorted out with Germany as an equal partner. After all, history 'teaches that any attempt to keep Germany an outcast after this war, or to deprive her of such security as her neighbours rightly claim for themselves, will fail.'[74] Noel Baker had earlier highlighted Labour's intention to treat Germany as an equal after the overthrow of its Nazi government in his two radio broadcasts to the German workers in October and December 1939.[75] As with Noel Baker's memoranda, the National Executive also devoted much of its discussion of Labour's war aims to the question of the longer term development of a new post-war order. In general, there was little of substance that was different between Noel-Baker's and the NEC's position. The main exception was that, in line with the position that Laski took in September 1939, the NEC stated that both socialism and democracy were preconditions for the longer term plans adumbrated in its report.[76] Noel Baker, assuming that a major part of the audience for Labour's peace proposals would not necessarily be socialist, deliberately dropped socialism as a precondition.[77]

Obviously, the Noel Baker and NEC war aims assumed that the immediate, let alone the longer term, proposals would not be acceptable to the Nazis – this was another reason why the end of the Hitler regime had to be a precondition. They assumed that in the event that the Germans were not able to replace their government then the Allies themselves would have to depose Hitler. They did, however, leave open the possibility of a negotiated peace in which Germany would not be required to surrender. Rather, Germany could return, with honour, to the position it held in the world prior to 1938. While unlikely to be acceptable to the German Government, it did lay down what Labour's minimum requirement for Peace in 1939–40 would be. Harold Laski saw this as particularly important, both internationally and domestically, if the Labour Party was not to be presented as a party of bellicose 'bitter-enders'.[78] The alternative to Germany's acquiescence would be Labour's full support for the war effort against Germany. Labour was even choosy about the form of government that was required to replace the Nazis, and in this they parted company with other, more right-wing advocates of a compromise peace with Germany.[79] In a letter to Hugh Dalton, Noel Baker discussed a circulating memo from Rauschning claiming that the German General Staff was against Hitler, and that they would soon offer to depose Hitler. Noel Baker agreed with the German Social Democrats and several French Parliamentarians that, since the real enemy was German militarism that a German military government could not be seen as an acceptable replacement for the Nazi regime. 'The essence of the whole proposals [sic] would, of course, be the maintenance of Army control in Germany.'[80]

Three years later the situation had changed dramatically, and as a result so did Labour's immediate war aims, although there was more continuity in the longer term proposals. In 1939–40 Germany's conquests were still at an early stage, Labour was in opposition and Britain was the senior partner in an alliance with France. By 1943 German arms had disgraced themselves from the Volga to the Atlantic, Labour was a major part of a war time coalition and Britain was only one of three superpowers in the anti-Axis United Nations. As a consequence of this last point Labour's war aims had to take account of the positions taken by the Soviet Union and the United States. On top of this, there was now a war against Japan in the Pacific, and the level of Japanese atrocities in China was well known. Despite major revisions that were suggested by Harold Laski and Philip Noel Baker, Hugh Dalton maintained the right to draft the 1943-4 post-war settlement proposals, and his long-standing lack of sympathy with German complaints about the Versailles Treaty certainly influenced the tone, if not the substance, of the various drafts. His clash with Laski and Noel Baker in the NEC was mainly over the issue of the treatment of Germany and Japan after the war. While Dalton, in his letters, remained on cordial terms with both Laski and Noel Baker, his autobiography shows that his respect for Noel Baker, whom he considered an important expert on the League of Nations, was far higher than it was for Laski. Laski, from Dalton's point of view as an ex-Chairman of the Labour Party, was a poor Party Chairman and generally not to be trusted.[81]

The behaviour of the Germans and Japanese in occupied territories had a profound effect on the drafting of Labour's war aims, by comparison with the milder and more conciliatory tone taken by Noel Baker in 1939. In a passage that survived the various amendments proposed during March and April 1944, Dalton clearly believed that the Axis would not be able to escape the post-war Nemesis:

> The plain facts regarding all this should be frankly and fearlessly stated. It is wrong to try to hush them up. It is very easy for us in this uninvaded, unenslaved, relatively unscorched, island to preach to others, less fortunate than ourselves, that they should entertain no feelings of revenge or hatred towards their torturers. It is less easy for these pitiful victims to forgive and to forget.[82]

This was particularly true of Germany that, for Dalton, bore the brunt of the responsibility for the war and its prosecution. While Labour, ever since its denunciations of the 1919 Peace, had been deeply critical of the idea of blaming a whole population for the crimes of its government, the sheer numbers of Germans involved in the instruments of fascism – the Gestapo, SS, SA and the Wehrmacht are singled out in the document – along with the way that so many acquiesced in the establishment and continued existence of the Nazi regime, meant that the war guilt was seen as running deep within the German population. 'The trouble is, not that good Germans don't exist, but that they are singularly ineffective in restraining the bad Germans.'[83] Harold Laski had not been so happy with the idea of German guilt, and was responsible for the replacement of the word 'Nazi' for 'German' in several parts of the text.[84]

German and Japanese culpability underscored and justified the harsh measures proposed for the immediate post-war settlement. Given that Axis aggression had its roots in the various Axis societies, a preliminary measure would be the removal of the means of aggression. Germany and Japan must be completely disarmed 'without limit or date', and 'Germany and Japan should be occupied for some time after the war. Italy and the smaller Axis satellites are much less dangerous, and could be controlled less strictly, and for a shorter time.'[85] This open-ended disarmament and occupation was less controversial than the proposed reparations and restitution to be imposed on Germany. There was broad agreement that war criminals 'so far as they can be identified, must be handed over', and that 'the rank and file of the Gestapo, S.S., etc, should be required to perform for a period, 'reparation labour' in Russia or elsewhere'.[86] Noel Baker, amongst others, worried that the reparations proposals would be misinterpreted. Dalton's initial draft, while stating the need for substantial restitution, made a point of distancing Labour's demands from the reparations contained in the 1919 peace treaties. In 1919 the Allies had 'claimed too much, collected too little, distributed most unjustly what they collected, and incurred grave indirect damage from the process.'[87] This time it should be better organised and properly directed towards repairing damaged done by the Axis in occupied territories. Goods, labour and the costs of occupation were to make up the sum of the reparations. Ironically, it was the systematic expropriation by the Germans of goods, labour and capital in the occupied territories that demonstrated how reparations could be extracted without incurring the negative repercussions experienced after Versailles.[88] Noel Baker suggested that this section needed toning down if the war aims were not to be seen as a vindictive peace – imposing on Germany all that they imposed on their victims. The peace must not be seen as an attempt to institute a systematic impoverishment of Germany. Noel Baker argued against an economically vindictive peace. Such a peace, he felt, would be against the economic self-interest of Britain and the rest of Europe.[89] The section was duly toned down, but the specific recommendations, bar the suggestion that Germany and Japan pay for the armed forces necessary to patrol a future peace, remained.

On the question of the future frontiers in Europe, which was seen as a major immediate cause of the war, Germany could also expect little quarter. While leaving the final decision to a future peace treaty, Dalton laid down three aims:

> First, the frontiers should be so drawn as to reduce to a minimum any inconvenience, geographical or economic, in the transit of persons and goods. Second, the frontiers, once drawn, should be regarded as definitely settled, and all agitation for frontier revision should be discouraged. Third, we should seek such international arrangements as will make frontiers less and less important as economic or cultural barriers…[90]

Thus, the final arrangement of frontiers must not, as it did in the inter-war period, interfere with economic viability, foster political tensions, or be seen as sharp lines of division. Earlier, in his *Hitler's War* Dalton had addressed this problem of the poor fit of national borders and economic viability by encouraging the integration of national minorities into larger, presumably federal, political units.[91] The third requirement fed into the Labour concern with the creation of a new interdependent and transnational international order, which will be discussed in the next section. The major controversial aspect to this section was the support given to the transfer of populations, especially the uprooting of German minorities in formally occupied countries:

> ...all Germans left outside the post-war German frontiers, unless they are willing to become loyal subjects of the State in which they find themselves... should go back to Germany. Indeed, they will be well advised to do so in their own interests, for... there will be a depth of hatred against Germans in the occupied countries, which it is impossible either for us or for Americans to realise.[92]

Dalton thought that this process would occur anyway, since 'Germans in many areas may face the choice between migration and massacre.' Yet, he also advocated population transfer. 'The organised transfer of population... may indeed be one of the foundations of better international relations in a later phase.' Further, he pointed out the 'undoubted success' of the Greek and Turkish population transfer in the early 1920s. [93] Although largely kept in the final draft, and therefore unanimously agreed to in the International Sub-Committee, Noel Baker remained unhappy with the idea of population exchanges. While conceding that 'some transfers of population may be desirable', he pointed out that 'the frontiers of Europe will never be ethnologically perfect', and that there would be a need for 'a system of international Minority Protection' in Europe. The protection of post-war Jewish minorities was of particular concern.[94] Noel Baker singled out the use of the Greek-Turkish population exchange case as particularly problematic, pointing out that it only worked because it was a real exchange, rather than a one-sided expulsion, that it was geographically limited, and there was 'large scale financial help... by means of a foreign loan.'[95] Outside of the International Sub-Committee opinion was divided on the issue of population transfer. Brailsford thought that it would happen anyway, with German minorities voluntarily leaving 'countries which the Nazis have oppressed.' He called for an international commission to deal with the problem.[96] Stronger voices against such transfers could be found in *The Political Quarterly*, where Allan G.B. Fisher and David Mitrany opposed it on practical, economic and political grounds. Like Noel Baker, Fisher and Mitrany were at pains to point out that the Turko-Greek transfers had been abnormal, and even then they had caused major problems and distress. Amongst many concerns about the viability and desirability of population transfers, they were worried that such forced migrations accepted the Nazi conception that citizenship of the state had an ethnic and racial component. Rather than serving the cause of peace, population transfers would merely deal with a symptom of interstate conflict; achieving little and being both costly and cruel.[97] Leonard Woolf, the editor of *The Political Quarterly*, also spoke out against the stress on retribution within Dalton's document soon after it was released as an Executive Committee publication. He interpreted it, not as a recognition of realities, but as a simple vindictive desire for revenge.[98] Like Fisher and Mitrany, Woolf saw the transfer idea as a distraction from the more effective and permanent solution of an international authority. He was also at pains to point out what transfer really meant: 'It is the forcible expropriation of immense numbers of unfortunate individuals of the kind which Europe had not known for ages until the Nazis reintroduced this barbarism.'[99]

Despite the rather brutal language used by Dalton, no doubt both a product of the times and of his known sympathy for Poland over its post-Versailles border dispute with Germany, it did reflect the situation on the ground in occupied Europe, as Brailsford had also suggested. German minorities, if they did not flee on their own accord or endure deportation by the Soviet authorities, were frequently hounded out by the non-German populations that had suffered under Nazi occupation. Ethnic German populations in the Baltics, Poland, the Sudetenland – and even in the territories of East Prussia, Pomerania and Silesia that had remained German after Versailles – were almost completely deported. Even before the war ended the Soviets were using captured German soldiers and civilians as forced labour for reparations. Many would not return home until the 1950s. Japanese atrocities in China and elsewhere, while lacking some of the systematic qualities of much Nazi terror, were as brutal and sometimes more horrific. The need to introduce procedures to prevent any reoccurrence of these atrocities made any conciliatory peace that left Germany and Japan armed, militarily or psychologically, impossible. This, as far as Dalton was concerned, was necessary until the populations of Germany and Japan could be weaned off the ideas of fascism. In the April 1944 meeting of the NEC Laski and Noel Baker had objected to the harshness of the war aims. James Walker, a member of the NEC, complained to Dalton that people like Laski and Noel Baker would leave Labour with a 'nebulous' document that would be at odds, embarrassingly for the Labour members of the War Cabinet, with the British Government's war aims.[100] Dalton's insistence that the war aims be hard edged remained unbowed. In reply to a supportive letter from Mary E. Sutherland, Labour's Chief Woman Officer, Dalton wrote that 'I have kept a series of the successive versions of this Statement [on the post-war peace settlement]. Each is more genteel than the last, but I am obstinately retaining a residue of rude realism.'[101] In a reply to Harold Laski he followed a similar theme, underscoring the need for Labour to 'face hard and cruel realities.'[102]

Transfer of populations was only one of the retributive measures being proposed at the time. While partition of Germany found no place in Dalton's peace aims, it was discussed and Labour's international experts did give their opinions of it. In 1940 Dalton had rejected the partition of Germany as shortsighted. Such punishment, he argued, would only encourage the emergence of the attitudes that brought Hitler to power to begin with.[103] Brailsford argued that plans to dismember Germany were part of 'the old ruinous game of the balance of power.' The answer lay in a more integrated Europe that harnessed German strength to common goals, rather than Balkanisation that would weaken Germany's ability to contribute to world prosperity. Brailsford turned the argument around, suggesting that it was not German strength that was the problem, but the weakness of the rest of Europe in dealing with the problem of German militarism. A more cohesive and cooperative Europe, where borders were more fluid, would help solve the German problem.[104] Brailsford, along with the rest of Labour's international experts, saw the answer to the immediate problem of Germany ultimately in the longer-term goal of creating a new cooperative international system that would blur the borders that had been such a major contributor to the 1914–45 crisis. In the words of David Mitrany, 'the real problem of security and the task of statesmanship is not to keep the nations peacefully apart, but to bring them actively together.'[105]

While the drift in Labour's immediate war aims was towards harsher treatment of Germany – and later Japan – these were always set within a system of longer-term goals, and the harshness was often presented as a means towards a more durable and fair peace. As the tales of Axis aggressions and abuses had grown, so had the belief that the fascist societies were sick, and would threaten any nascent peaceful international system unless they were disarmed in the short term, and re-educated in the longer term. In the background was a vision of a peaceful world that would make the very boundary disputes that were the excuses for fascist aggression less important, and an eventual rehabilitation of the enemy. In the December 1944 Annual Conference, which overwhelmingly approved the war aims proposed by Dalton, a representative from the Brixton branch added a resolution, which was also carried with Hugh Dalton's blessing, calling for an education programme in the post-war Axis countries 'to counteract the poisonous propaganda and training which have instilled in their youth the glorification of war and racial hatred.'[106] Yet, this was only a small part of a much larger discussion about the form of the post-war international order. The major discussions of the shape of the post-war order would revolve around not necessarily incompatible notions of federal and functional organisation.

The Shape of the New Order: Federal and Functional Proposals

While the aggressive mentalities of the fascist societies, coupled with the minorities problem, were seen as immediate causes of the war, the longer term solutions proposed by Labour's international experts tended to focus on the threat to peace posed by the exclusive role of national sovereignty. While there was a clear difference in what they saw as the cause of the power of national sovereignty, both Harold Laski and David Mitrany agreed that it was the role of national sovereignty that was at the root of the war-prone nature of the international anarchy. This did not necessarily translate into an opposition to national governments per se. Rather, a distinction was made between national governments, that were an existing and powerful level of human administration, and national sovereignty, which was the idea that these national governments should be the primary form of human government without any restraint on their international behaviour bar their own power. National sovereignty, in short, denied the existence of any other form of government without the prior assent, and ultimate control, of nation-state governments. For Mitrany this dogma of national sovereignty was a deliberate policy, and had little to do with the culturally rooted nineteenth century nationalism. The modern twentieth century nationalism that supported the absolute claims of national sovereignty is a 'political directive', originating amongst those with an interest in the concentration of power in the hands of state organs, which aims to suppress other forms of expression.[107] This concentration of power created the system of tensions found in the international anarchy. Laski largely concurred with this position, and in his contribution to Labour's war aims in 1939 he singled out the principle of national sovereignty as the root cause of the problem of war:

> It is that principle which makes possible the evil technique of "power-politics". While it continues to hold sway, there can be no real League of Nations. Unless it goes, no disarmament is real disarmament. Unless it goes, no Collective Security can be built which is real Collective Security. Unless it goes, no solution of the problems of economic nationalism... becomes possible.[108]

While Mitrany saw the cause of the problem of sovereignty rooted in dogmatic thinking, Laski saw it as a natural outgrowth of the inequalities intrinsic to capitalism. Echoing Hobson, he saw the power of production as outstripping the power to distribute and make a profit. Sovereignty served the interests of a capitalist elite that needed colonies and protectorates as markets, while providing a convenient ideological cover for these interests.[109] The wars caused by the international anarchy were a direct result of capitalism. In the 1944 Labour peace aims, submitted to Conference in that year, Laski appended a paragraph to Hugh Dalton's text that affirmed that 'War is inherent in the nature of capitalist society.'[110] Despite this addition, Leonard Woolf still regarded the 1943–4 proposals as far too inconsistent and apologetic. The war had been a direct result of 'Tory capitalism', and 'the only way in which we can prevent history repeating itself is to rebuild the economic system and international society on Socialist principles.'[111]

Whatever the cause of national sovereignty, and there was no agreement on this point in Labour circles, there was an overwhelming consensus that it was the primary problem standing in the way of a peaceful order. Dalton's call for the minimising of the effects of national borders as a crucial part of a long-term peace settlement was fairly typical of the attitude amongst the Party's intellectuals.[112] The doctrine of national sovereignty provided an ideological argument for the international anarchy, and it was the re-emergence of the international anarchy, with its competitive armaments and secret diplomacy, that had undermined the League Covenant and led the world to war.[113] The international anarchy and its doctrine of national sovereignty had, in this sense, been a permissive cause of the war. In its synthesis of Noel Baker's peace aims document the National Executive report to the 1940 conference reaffirmed the Party's position that 'to have Peace we must subordinate national sovereignty to world institutions and obligations.' Labour committed itself to an association of states 'the collective authority of which must transcend, over a proper sphere, the sovereign rights of separate States.'[114] This was further elaborated by Hugh Dalton in his book-length treatment of the issue.[115] This was reaffirmed at the 1944 conference, in Clement Attlee's presentation of the peace aims drafted by Hugh Dalton. Attlee declared that 'if peace is to be preserved there must be some cession of sovereignty and that membership of a larger organisation does not conflict with the reasonable claims of nations to live their own lives.'[116] The state as an institution was not to be challenged, but the claims of those who saw it as a supreme authority were.

While Labour and Labour's international experts were to give increasing space to the prospects for functional cooperation, the idea of resuscitating the League – what was often referred to as the international political organisation – remained a major part of Labour's policy. This culminated in the warm reception given to the Dumbarton Oaks proposals, although for many the proposed United Nations needed to be supplemented by other less state based forms of cooperation. The major problem with the Dumbarton Oaks proposals was that 'there is no serious limitation on national sovereignty', and there was a need for an 'international political machinery' outside of the sovereign state with the 'ability to dissolve disputes before they involved the prestige of a Great Power.'[117] While there was a broad consensus in the Party and amongst the Party's experts that this machinery should be heavily functional in character,[118] there was also much agreement 'that functional co-operation by itself can never be an adequate foundation for permanent peace and security.'[119] In the words of Leonard Woolf:

> There is a place too for functional organs of international government... But the necessity for a central world authority is absolute: it is required both to coordinate the activities of regional or functional international organs and to deal promptly and authoritatively with any action or situation which may threaten the world's peace or prosperity.[120]

Labour proposals for a state-based formal security organisation consequently went hand-in-glove with new proposals for separate non-state functional organisations designed to meet specific problems of global government. Overlaying this discussion between state-based and functional machinery, and frequently confused with it unfortunately, was the division between the establishment of an international political and an international economic organisation. The failure of the League's system of political security was seen as a product of the failure of will amongst its member states. On the economic side, the international community's failure to deal with the serious consequences of the economic crisis of 1929–31 was interpreted as springing from the lack of an international economic infrastructure to provide the appropriate forum for concerted action. This economic organisation tended to get confused with a more functional approach both because it was intended to deal with economic and infrastructural issues that were frequently seen as good candidates for functional organisations, and also because many of the proposals suggested that the disparate functional organisations should come under the umbrella of a larger international economic organisation.[121] The crucial difference between functional organisations and more confederal intergovernmental organisations is that the former bring together representatives from those involved in a single function in order to coordinate the running of that function. By and large the proposals for an international political organisation were, for Labour's international experts, a resuscitation of the machinery of the League. The corresponding international economic machinery was plugging a gap in the previous League system, rather than building a more functional system of government as envisioned by Mitrany.

While there was much discussion of the weaknesses of the previous League structure, the consensus was that any new organisation should be a resuscitated League that learnt the lessons of the inter-war period. For the author of one document, included in the discussions about war aims in 1939, the main lesson to be learnt had little to do with the League itself, but rather with the way that it was used by its members. 'The League of Nations... all too rapidly became the battle-ground for power politics, instead of the great constructive effort that will and vision might have made of it.'[122] Both the 1940 and 1944 conferences reaffirmed this view of the League. The 1940 statement by the National Executive argued that the 'ineffectiveness of the League, often quoted to discredit international cooperation, was partly due to the lack of conviction and sincerity of its leading member States, and partly to its comparative neglect of economic questions.'[123] In 1944 Clement Attlee declared that the 'League fell not because its principles were wrong but because they were not practiced.'[124] The more public writings of Labour's international experts confirmed this view. For Dalton in 1940 the League had failed because its founders had not been brave enough, and so many of its members had proved unfaithful.[125] For Woolf in 1944 it was 'not the lack of force, but the lack of the will to use it to resist aggression, which made the collective security system of the League ineffective.'[126] Behind these statements lay the wealth of studies carried out by the Advisory Committee on the failures of will by the main League powers during the international crises in 1931, 1935–6 and 1938 discussed in the last chapter. This failure was also partially due to the early stage in the development of the League's security architecture. Noel Baker in 1939 had no hesitation in reaffirming the need for the development of the arbitration, disarmament and (economic) sanctions that he had championed for the League in the 1920s.[127] The Advisory Committee, which Noel Baker Chaired after its reformation in 1944, came out in support of the introduction of military sanctions as a last resort.[128] Certainly at an early stage of the war Harold Laski and Philip

Noel Baker could agree that a reconstituted League should form an important part of the next peace settlement, and this position was reflected in the Executive's report to conference in 1940.[129] While Laski and Noel Baker had still referred directly to the League, the Executive left the link with the previous League vague by referring to the establishment of a 'new Association or Commonwealth of States'. Dalton echoed this subtle distancing from the League in his 1940 book.[130] By 1943 references to a resuscitated League were dropped in favour of a discussion of the powers of the new 'political organisation'.

Noel Baker's position on the political organisation and peace, strongly supported by Ivor Thomas on the Advisory Committee, was in sharp contrast to Mitrany's. While Mitrany was critical of the failures and prospects of a largely confederal and state-based political organisation, Noel Baker and Thomas regarded peace as a political problem outside of the competence of a system of functional government. The solution for Noel Baker rested on a binding and comprehensive legal order, the very system that Mitrany felt that it was naive to hope for in the short or medium term. While not hostile to either's goals, Mitrany and Noel Baker clearly felt that the other had got the order wrong in the progression of international government. In his first comment on Hugh Dalton's peace settlement proposals Noel Baker wrote that:

> I am, of course, in full agreement that we must develop much more effective international economic organisation than we had before the war. The more we drive home this lesson, the better, but it remains true that the first and indispensable condition of either peace or economic prosperity, is the creation of a strong international political organisation. Indeed, effective international economic co-operation will remain impossible until governments and peoples are convinced that there is a solid hope of stable peace.[131]

Noel Baker went on to suggest that the economic organisations should be set up at the same time as the political organisation, and that it was important that the political organisation serve a coordinating role so that the economic organisations did not suffer from overlapping authorities.[132] Both Ivor Thomas and Dalton concurred with this view.[133] Despite this seeming subservience of the economic and technical to the political, Noel Baker subtly softened his view in his final additions to Hugh Dalton's 1944 Report of the National Executive Committee. While maintaining the division between a coordinating political organisation and smaller functional organisations, he admitted that 'any division between politics and "diplomacy" on the one hand, and social, economic and cultured welfare, on the other, is now unreal and out-of-date.'[134] Since all the major problems of international policy were world-wide in scope Noel Baker emphasised that the international political organisation needed to be global as well.[135] Despite this, he recognised that some matters, such as surface transport, would be better handled at a continental or regional level.[136] The Advisory Committee largely concurred on this issue, arguing that regional organisations might achieve a greater level of integration not open to a wider international organisation, although it was important that they should remain linked to the wider international purpose, and not become old fashioned great power spheres of influence.[137] Noel Baker's primary concern, however, was that the international political organisation must 'establish the binding force of international law' and outlaw international aggression.[138] 'All through history, civilized society has everywhere been built up on the foundation of law... Unless the acceptance of law becomes the rule of international life, we shall relapse into the lawless violence of total war.'[139] While their ultimate goals were the same, Noel Baker's insistence on the primacy of law put clear blue water between his own proposals for international order and those of Mitrany.

Labour's commitment to the international rule of law remained central to its vision of the post-war settlement throughout the war, and found expression not just in the contribution of Noel Baker, but also in that of Harold Laski, Leonard Woolf and the Advisory Committee. Here there was widespread agreement that an interdependent world of states required a shared law, 'made by them in common' to protect the collective interests of the international community.[140] Peace could not be established 'until lawless force has ceased to dominate the relations of Governments and States',[141] and the best way to ensure this was for all states to 'be willing to submit the points at issue to third-party judgement and to abide by the result.'[142] Thus, the major challenge 'is to invest international law with the same prestige and authority as is now enjoyed by municipal law.'[143] The new international machinery also needed to be capable of making and altering international law in order for it to be a dynamic and evolving body.[144] The influence of Leonard Woolf was evident in the Advisory Committee's discussion of the issue, where his classic distinction between 'justiciable disputes', solvable through a properly constituted international court, and 'non-justiciable disputes', requiring some form of third party arbitration predominated. Justiciable disputes were defined as those where 'the law has to be stated', and fit well with an impartial court. Political or non-justiciable disputes were those in which the law had 'to be made or changed.'[145] This making or changing of laws, rather than judicial interpretation, was to be left to the states themselves. Yet, despite the limits proposed for it by the Advisory Committee, there was a general consensus that an international court was indispensable to the workings of the post-war world. An international court with the power to settle judicial disputes was a central part of Philip Noel Baker's 1944 suggestions for the future international political organisation, and after minor amendments formed part of Hugh Dalton's final draft to the Executive and Conference.[146] Thus, despite their bow in the direction of functional organisations, the international political organisation envisaged by the majority of Labour's international experts remained a standard inter-governmental organisation with judicial authority, and hence what Mitrany would regard as a largely nineteenth century nightwatchman organisation. Labour proposals were, however, two track, and Mitrany's concept of a functional road to security formed a second pillar of the proposed post-war institutional framework.

Despite its criticism of the idea that peace could be achieved through functional organisations alone, Ivor Thomas' Advisory Committee memo-randum of September 1944 still regarded functional organisations as vital to the post-war order. In a section that suggests that he had some know-ledge of the content of Mitrany's 1943 pamphlet *A Working Peace System*, Thomas wrote:

> The Advisory Committee considers that functional cooperation should be encouraged in every possible way... such functional co-operation... cannot fail to increase an international sense among those who take part in it and to perfect the technique of coopera-tion; it will moreover lay the basis for an International Civil Service of wide scope.[147]

The concentration within Labour circles on the reformed League was, crucially, not at the expense of any functional alternative. Rather, the deve-lopment of international functional government was advocated alongside the more traditional inter-governmental structures. For Noel Baker they were an indispensable part of the 'large-scale international economic co-operation' necessary to prevent both the immediate collapse likely to occur after the war through the provision of emergency relief and coop-eration,[148] and a relapse into war in the future by internationalising certain crucial sectors.[149] Echoing Mitrany's view of the importance of concen-trating on what unites people, rather than what divides them, Hugh Dal-ton underlined how the 'common pursuit of world-wide economic im-provement will do far more to unite Governments and peoples than any pure political arrangements.'[150] Mitrany was also paraphrased by the Moseley Divisional Labour Party in its memo to the Advisory Committee, where it was stated that 'our policy should be to advocate, within the framework of the World Organisation, as much functional co-operation as it lies in our power to achieve', while 'we must also make it clear that our ultimate goal is world federation, however distant that goal may be.'[151] Strangely enough, despite his advocacy of international functional cooperation between the wars, Harold Laski made very little reference to it in his additions to the proposals, preferring to concentrate on other issues such as the negative aspects of state sovereignty and capitalism. This does not mean he had abandoned the concept of international functional cooperation. At a Fabian International Bureau conference in January 1944 Laski advocated federation by function, and interpreted functions as the basis of any future international government, although in opposition to Mitrany he favoured federation at the continental level.[152]

Functional proposals within Labour's war aims were of two sorts. The first was support for existing functional organisations and links, and the second was suggestions for future areas. In the first category, the most frequently occurring organisation was the International Labour Organisation. The ILO got special mention in both the 1940 and 1944 war aims proposals – in 1940 largely in response to Ernest Bevin's proposals for an enlarged ILO that would internationalise regulations on working hours, wages and industrial conditions.[153] Dalton's 1943–4 war aims singled out the ILO as 'one of the best creations of the Peace Treaties' and an exception to the failure of international organisations to regulate the international economy.[154] Dalton proposed that the ILO should be joined by a series of technical organisations designed specifically to manage the complex transition from the war economy to peace-time economic conditions. He suggested 'new international institutions and agreements to plan Relief and Rehabilitation, to organise abundant world-wide food supplies, to regulate international trading and transport and monetary relationships.' These post-war institutions, he hoped, would continue their work after the transition, becoming the nucleus of an international civil service.[155] Noel Baker added to Dalton's list regional organisations responsible for ground surface transportation and an international agreement on civil aviation to ensure that it 'shall be used to promote peace, instead of serving, as it did before 1939, to promote competitive preparation for war'.[156] This concern for the control of civil aviation flowed from his work on disarmament in the 1920's, which had pointed out the dangerous inter-connection between civil aviation and the military use of aircraft. In this case Noel Baker fully realised, as Mitrany had in his *Road to Security*, that internationalising a function could go some way to reducing its military use.[157] Explicit in these proposals for functional organisation was the concept, central to Mitrany, that economic stability and the fulfilment of need was not merely a good in itself, but was important in maintaining security and preventing war. Consequently the proposals concentrated on two areas: the improvement of economic and infrastructure management in order to increase and distribute prosperity in such a way as to remove economic-based grievances; and the removal of certain functions from national control, and their internationalisation so that they cannot be used for the preparation or execution of aggressive war. This latter concern lay not only behind the proposals for a civil aviation authority, but also the much more ambitious proposal to internationalise public broadcasting.

Writing in 1941, and looking back to before the war, A.L. Rowse complained that 'Social Democracy again had no conception of the cardinal function of propaganda in the modern State... it idiotically left the devil all the best tunes. Is it any wonder that it was defeated?'[158] Responding to similar criticisms that the left had not understood the role of propaganda and the broadcast media the NEC in 1943 'agreed to insert... things about the international use of Broadcasting for promoting peace and international understanding' into Labour's 1944 statement of war aims.[159] Its eventual mention in the NEC's report on the post-war settlement amounted to only one sentence, written by Noel Baker:

> The great service of Broadcasting should be internationally controlled and should be used to keep the peoples truthfully informed, to promote their sense of international solidarity, and to enable them to understand the policies that will lead to stable Peace.[160]

A similarly tantalising mention of the internationalisation of broadcasting, albeit a full page rather than a short paragraph, appears in a 1943 chapter by Will Arnold-Forster. Arnold-Forster advocated the establishment of an international radio service modelled on the independence of the BBC, but provided few details beyond suggesting that it would need an ample budget.[161] It was left to the Advisory Committee to fill in the details, which they duly did through Leonard Woolf's November 1944 memorandum on the issue, and the attached comments by an anonymous official with expertise in the area. Broadcasting already had an international body responsible for the management of technical problems, such as the allotment of wavelengths. The pre-war International Broadcasting Union (IBU) had, via the Montreux plan of 1939, largely settled the issue of wavelength allocation, and despite the war this agreement still largely functioned.[162] On the technical question of wavelength allocation Woolf suggested the revival of the IBU, but with 'pretty wide powers of decision... and of enforcing decisions'.[163] Far more complex was the political problem. 'Broadcasting has become the main instrument of propaganda and its influence upon international relations is therefore of immense importance.' Woolf saw two parts to the problem: how to prevent 'abuse of broadcasting by national authorities', and how to establish 'an international broadcasting service.'[164] In the first instance Woolf proposed a United Nations agreement banning the use of broadcasting to spread false news in the service of aggression, and the establishment of an organisation to monitor broadcasts. In the second he suggested that the United Nations establish its own radio station and broadcasting service with full-time staff, an independent mandate and Board of Governors modelled on the BBC, and an annual conference like the ILO.[165] The anonymous official expert took issue with much of this, as well as pointing out that aspects of the first suggestion had been agreed to by the IBU in 1933.[166] Woolf proposed the establishment of an International Broadcasting Organisation, which would incorporate the IBU. In this instance the official proved to be more functionalist than Woolf, when he objected to the stronger government representation that a UN organisation would imply. Echoing Mitrany, the expert felt that restricting the management of international broadcasting to non-state experts and practitioners would prevent the operation of the organisation from becoming politicised.

> There were very few technical difficulties which it was found impossible to settle amicably within the scope of the IBU because its proceedings were informal and did not involve acute questions of prestige and national standing. This would all be lost in the creation of a formal body.[167]

While Woolf's proposals were never completely enacted, the discussions about the development of an international broadcasting regime amply demonstrate the extent of functional thinking in Labour circles. Mitrany's link between the internationalisation of certain functions and the development of a more peaceful world was generally accepted, and while there was the feeling amongst many, such as Noel Baker and Ivor Thomas, that functional organisations by themselves were not enough to ensure peace, there was an equally strong conviction that they were a crucial component in any new alternative to the international anarchy. The basic idea within Mitrany's functional approach, that the nature of the function should dictate the form of the institutions to govern it, was replicated in the mix of formal inter-governmental, regional and technical organisations that made up the Labour proposals for the post-war order.

An interesting omission in the Labour peace proposals is a detailed plan for international democratic accountability. Democratic accountability, and the dangers of executive control in an international organisation of governments had played a powerful part in the Labour criticism of the League between 1919 and 1922, and the idea of functional democracy had been a central pillar of Mitrany's functional approach prior to 1945. Part of this silence may be because from 1940 Labour was part of a very powerful executive – the British wartime coalition government – and the Party as a whole felt more comfortable with the democratic credentials of national governments. Yet, this seems out of keeping with the explicit and implicit criticisms of national sovereignty and state borders found in both sets of war aims. Noel Baker did briefly address the question of democratic accountability in his contribution to the 1944 war aims, but even here the discussion was limited to making the proceedings of the new political organisation public, and the importance of public debate as 'an indispensable instrument of liberty and justice.'[168] There was not the same discussion of active democratic control of the international organisations as had occurred during the establishment of the League. The major exception to this was H.N. Brailsford, who unabashedly returned to the same proposal that he had made for the League of Nations. Brailsford advocated the establishment of an elected parliament to run any proposed international authority, which would make decisions, much as national parliaments do, through majority voting. Having advocated it, however, Brailsford was not optimistic about its chances of becoming a reality. 'This is the hopeful road, though all the traditions of the past will barricade it against our advance.'[169] He swiftly moved on to other issues more in keeping with the temper of the times.

One of the main unsubstantiated accusations levelled by modern realists against the various liberal and social democratic international thinkers, now labelled as idealists, is that they constructed plans for international institutions without any regard for the means by which they could be implemented in the world as it was. While Labour's international writers had developed quite a few plans for the post-war world, they had been mindful of the practicalities of establishing their new order. In a war in which raw state power was deciding the future of human civilisation it is probably not surprising that discussions on the implementation of the post-war international infrastructure rested on the active support of the members of the three power pact: Britain, the United States and the Soviet Union.

The Prospects of Allied Unity

There was complete agreement amongst Labour's international experts that there should be no return to power politics and the international anarchy if a system of peace and security compatible with modern conditions was to be developed. Consequently, there was also complete agreement that the Anglo-Soviet-American Alliance that formed the core of the United Nations war effort against the Axis should, in the post-war years, develop into something other than the old exclusive alliances of the past. Rather, the Three Power Pact would better serve world peace if it was used as the nucleus of a new and inclusive world organisation. This view of the potential of the Three Power Pact was an important part of the 1943–4 Labour war aims written and organised by Hugh Dalton. In a section cut out of the final version Dalton recognised that when discussing the form of the post-war international political organisation, no 'paper schemes are any use, unless there is sufficient and continuing power and will to enforce them. The practical question is, what can Britain, the USA and the USSR agree on?'[170] The final draft still recognised the importance of the wartime alliance. 'The Post-War Settlement must grow out of the immediate Post-War Situation. When the War ends... Britain, the United States and the Soviet Union will be the three outstanding Great Powers'. Close political cooperation must continue. 'If we three hold together, all will be well; if we fall apart, all will be dark and uncertain.'[171] This position was underscored at Conference, where the resolution in support of the NEC report stated that the 'Conference is convinced that no enduring Peace is possible unless there is continuing co-operation between the British Commonwealth of Nations, The USSR, and the USA.'[172] Clement Attlee's speech in support of the resolution elaborated on this relation between the raw power of the three main Allied governments and the potential for a new international order:

> A new world organisation must be created. Rather it is already being created. Its nucleus is the close and intimate co-operation of the British Commonwealth of Nations, the United States of America and the USSR... We want an organisation embracing small as well as great nations, but on the three, on account of their strength, the greatest responsibility for preserving the peace of the world must fall.[173]

Again, it has to be emphasised that the whole tenor of the discussions of the role of the Three Power Pact was that the Pact was a means towards the creation of an international political organisation like the League – a recognition of the raw power of the Pact, and the need to channel that power into something different. Thus, Vickers contention that the 1944 war aims (submitted to Conference under the title *The International Post-War Settlement*) 'moved away from traditional Labour Party policy in that it saw the basis of a future world organisation as being a continuation of the relationship between these three Great Powers, rather than some form of League of Nations' is erroneous.[174] Rather, the goal remained solidly the same. It was only on the issue of the means towards that end that Labour contemplated the uses and role of the Big Three. The hope was clearly that the Three Power Pact would fade into a larger organisation in the future.

Accepting the practical importance of the power of the Big Three did not mean that Labour's international experts were not aware of the dangers posed by the reliance on what was to all intents and purposes a military alliance between great powers. Philip Noel Baker was concerned that the use of language associated with power politics, especially the use of alliance to describe the Three Power Pact, gave a false impression of an acceptance of the old nineteenth century international system. It also misrepresented the relationship between the Big Three.[175] Disquiet was stronger on the Advisory Committee. Its commentary on the Dumbarton Oaks proposals saw something ominous in the Soviet proposals for a great power veto on the Security Council. There was a very real danger, they argued, that the great powers would construct an international machinery that they did not really mean to make use of in the future.[176] In other words, great power politics would be continued behind the façade of an international authority that lacked the power to prevent the great powers from doing what they liked. Leonard Woolf later repeated these remarks in his analysis of the proposals for the new United Nations.[177] In a comment that foreshadowed the breakdown of the Security Council's role during the Cold War the Moseley DLP memorandum to the Advisory Committee cautioned that the security arrangements envisioned in the Dumbarton Oaks proposals, by failing to deal with the problem of state sovereignty, were incapable of dealing with a dispute between any of the Big Three. 'Once a dispute between the Big Three reaches [a serious] level, no machinery is likely to prove any more effective than straight diplomatic negotiation. The value of any international political machinery is its ability to dissolve disputes before they involve the prestige of a Great Power.'[178] H.N. Brailsford remained deeply suspicious of what could be accomplished by the Three Power Pact, arguing that the best that could be hoped for from the Big Three was 'the bare maintenance of peace… They may be strong enough and harmonious enough to crush by sheer military force any possible law-breaker', but this was hardly the ordered international structure that they were hoping for. Brailsford foresaw that the reliance on the Big Three would probably end in spheres of great power influence. 'In particular you may get Europe caught [sic] in half between the Anglo-American sphere in the west and perhaps in the south, and a Russian sphere in the east.'[179] Thus, there was a distinct danger that the 'present war has settled one of Europe's problems of power only to raise another.'[180] This danger was closer to home than Brailsford thought. We now know that the division of Europe into spheres of influence was already a central part of the British Foreign Office's plans for post-war Europe in 1944.[181]

Leonard Woolf was equally concerned about too much faith being put into the peacetime continuation of the wartime alliance. In 1941 Woolf had accepted that the Big Three would have to play leading roles in any international authority, if that authority was to have any chance of success.[182] In 1944, however, he warned that the breakdown of the Three Power Pact after the war was inevitable unless it was replaced by some other common purpose through the establishment of an international machinery for solving common global problems. It is in the nature of states, Woolf argued, to follow their own self-interest. When that self-interest combines with the interests of other states there is the potential for great common effort, as the wartime alliance has proved. Yet, the defeat of the Axis will remove that impetus to work together. If a return to a great-power dominated international anarchy was to be avoided then the wartime alliance would need to be embedded in a new international order based around a different logic.[183] Here Woolf was returning to a theme he had explored in the 1930's as the League system collapsed. Rather than rejecting the logic of the international anarchy, as self-styled realists often accuse so-called idealists of doing, Woolf accepted that in the absence of a better organising principle international politics would fall back on the balance of power. What he argued, however, was that this logic of anarchy was neither desirable nor necessary, and that it was possible, as domestic politics had proved, to construct an order based on different principles. If the Three Power Pact remained just an alliance of states then it would of necessity break up, and the system of spheres of influence advocated by E.H. Carr and The Times – or feared by Brailsford – would come to pass. The problem with the realist solution is that they dreamed of a great power concert that would rule a partitioned Europe in peace. Woolf, like Brailsford, warned that this was actually a war-prone and unstable arrangement that could lead to international antagonisms.[184] In the event, the ensuing Cold War conformed much more closely with the fears expressed by Brailsford and Woolf on the collapse of Big Three unity than it did to the cosy concert of great powers advocated by those calling themselves realists. In the final analysis it was the self-declared realists, who clung to the hope of a returning Concert of Europe, that failed to understand the realities of international life, and consequently failed to predict the beginning of the Cold War.

Between 1942 and 1945 the prospects of the continuation of the Three Power Pact into the post-war period seemed like a real possibility. There is a tendency today, seen through the fog of Cold War relationships, to assume that American-Soviet relations were destined to deteriorate, but the experience of the war years pointed in an altogether different direction. If the three powers disagreed it was more likely that it was the United States and the Soviet Union against Britain.[185] Positive views of America within the British left and the Churchillian wing of the Conservative Party were not necessarily reciprocated, and a traditional American Anglophobia frequently surfaced in the actions and attitudes of United States officials. The best example of this was the debate over the second front. The Soviets, under extreme pressure from the Axis, lobbied for a second front in Western Europe from 1941. Communist organisations, such as the Soviet Today Society in Britain, held meetings to pressurise the British Government. Within Labour Aneurin Bevin led a second front campaign, while another Labour member Konni Zilliacus saw in Britain's foot-dragging a nefarious plot by right-wingers.[186] When the United States entered the war the American government also pushed for an immediate second front in accord with the Soviet requests. It was the British government, including its Labour ministers, that stood out against an immediate invasion of France. To its enemies within the United States administration the British Government was seen as deliberately leaving all the to fighting the Soviets, but the British position was that the western Allies were just not ready in terms of men and materials for a full-scale invasion of the European mainland. Instead they advocated operations in North Africa and the Mediterranean. Despite this, and other points of friction between Britain the United States, the two powers were still able to forge an unprecedented integrated military alliance. The experience of Anglo-American military cooperation became another example of the resilience of the Three Power Pact, and the Advisory Committee hoped that this military cooperation would continue under the auspices of the UN's military provisions.[187]

Concerns about Soviet attitudes towards the coming post war settlement surfaced only very slowly, despite the natural anti-communism amongst many of the trade union leaders like Ernest Bevin. Hugh Dalton told Conference in 1944 that Stalin saw the Three Power Pact as founded on vital and long-term interests, and that the maintenance of peace rested on unanimity between the big three.[188] While Soviet rhetoric was encouraging, there were fears that Soviet policy was still stuck in the mentality of great power confrontation. The Soviet insistence that the permanent great power members of the proposed UN Security Council should have a veto was a cause of concern to the Advisory Committee. This would effectively mean that the great powers would not be subject to the provisions outlawing aggression, since they would be able to veto any Security Council resolution aimed at them. 'There is to be one law for the permanent members and another for the small Powers.'[189] Concerns about Soviet intentions, and the Soviet commitment to the old diplomacy of the international anarchy, grew as news of the conditions of the Soviet occupation of Eastern Europe filtered through. Many like Konni Zilliacus remained loyal to the Soviet Alliance, but the mood amongst Labour's other international writers and the Party leadership was one of deep disappointment, and a strong commitment to Britain's partnership with the United States. Tellingly, Ernest Bevin's comment that 'Left understands Left', so frequently assumed to be a reference to the Soviets, was actually a reference to the socialists in France.[190] Bevin, like so many within the Labour Party, desired cordial relations with the Soviet Union, but was suspicious of the deeply undemocratic and capricious nature of communism. If it came to a choice between the Soviet Union and the United States Labour in 1945 would not hesitate to choose real common democratic traditions over apparent common socialist ones.

In the final analysis both the leadership of the Party and its international experts trusted more in the alliance with the United States than with any relationship with either France or the Soviet Union. Once again, Labour policy found itself inadvertently in agreement with that old imperialist Winston Churchill. Once in government, after its landslide victory in 1945, the Labour Government proved deeply suspicious of the Soviet Union. As early as the Potsdam three power meeting of 1945 Britain's new Foreign Secretary Ernest Bevin shocked his American counterparts with his aggressive manner towards the Soviet claims to East Prussia.[191] As Soviet-American relations deteriorated after the war Labour's international experts tended to side with the United States. In the final analysis the Three Power Pact failed to provide the stability necessary for the establishment of a stable peaceful order. In this sense Dalton's contention was spot on: 'If we three hold together, all will be well; if we fall apart, all will be dark and uncertain.'[192]

Wartime Idealism and Post-War Realities:
The Fate of Labour Aspirations

Ultimately, though, it was the Cold War that undermined many of the plans of Labour's international experts. True, the League was resuscitated and renamed; functional organisations, within the UN system and outside of it, developed and proliferated; the International Court was given a clear mandate and zone of competence; and the question of European state boundaries was largely put on ice. With the collapse of Allied Unity, however, the prospects of any further developments in international cooperation collapsed. In this sense Labour's international experts and wartime leadership were correct in their assessment that the construction of a functioning pacific world order required the power of the wartime three power alliance to make it a reality. Labour's war aims might have been idealistic in the broadest definition of the term, but they were grounded in an understanding of the need to marshal sufficient power in order to make them a reality. Labour's war aims were based on the prospect of a proper system of peace treaties, and while the inter-Allied agreements reached at Dumbarton Oaks and Bretton Woods covered some of this ground, there was no general peace with the main Axis powers. There is a supreme irony here. Labour's landslide victory on 5 July 1945 erased so much of the pessimism in Labour circles that had been produced by the disaster of 1931, yet international conditions seemed to give the government less power to change the international order for the better than it had had in 1929. The prime reason for this was that Labour's spectacular victory came at a time when Britain's power in the world had been superseded by the other two superpowers of the United States and the Soviet Union. Labour's power to change British policy was at its greatest, but British power to change the world was much diminished. In this sense, for Labour a great opportunity had been missed.

Yet Britain, and Labour, still had influence, and much was achieved. Looking back in 1953 Philip Noel Baker was bullish about what had been accomplished:

> The United Nations Charter is world law, founded on the total renunciation of armed force as an instrument of national policy; on the absolute equality of all men, whatever their race, colour or religion; and on international economic co-operation for full employment and rising standards of living. The wide acceptance of the compulsory jurisdiction of the International Court of Justice confirms a principle of the Geneva Protocol, and a practical success of Arthur Henderson in 1929. NATO... is wholly founded on, and

subordinate to, the Charter's law... Trusteeship for undeveloped peoples is a socialist principle. The UN International Bank has made loans... for Government projects of public value at low rates of interest...[193]

A major criticism of Mitrany, levelled at him by other Labour intellectuals, was that his functional approach, by leaving the issue of a higher coordinating body aside, ignored the issue of power.[194] Peace, it was argued, was a political problem, and only by establishing an all-encompassing political organisation could peace be guaranteed. Functional organisations could only ever be one part of the solution. Yet, after the war ended political conflicts made the signing of a comprehensive peace treaty impossible, and the state-based security organs of the UN remained ineffectual in dealing with great power conflict. The major successes of the abortive post-war settlement, listed by Noel Baker in 1953, were the functional links created by the myriad functional organisations established despite the ideological divisions of the coming Cold War. Mitrany's pessimism about the establishment of formal nineteenth century government institutions for the international arena proved correct, even if his hopes for functional government were only partially fulfilled.

Of all the periods covered by this study, it is during the war years that the writings of Labour's international experts, with the major exception of Mitrany, were at their most nuts and bolts, and their least theoretically deep. To a certain extent there was always a tendency, particularly in the work of Woolf and Noel Baker, for their writings to deal with specific problems peculiar to the age in which they wrote, but between 1939 and 1945 this tendency was heightened. Only with Mitrany do we see a major part of his IR theory being published during the war. The major criticism of the so-called 'idealists' by realist writers in IR is that the idealists were irrelevant because they wrote timeless utopias unconnected with the problems of the world around them. By an ironic twist of fate the opposite may be true. That the writings of Brailsford, Noel Baker, Angell, Mitrany and Woolf may be of less interest to us today because they wrote too much about the problems of their own era, and not enough about timeless utopias. In other words it was their very practicality and topicality that could doom them back into the oblivion that modern realism first cast them. I will explore this issue in more detail in the next chapter, but first the international thought of Leonard Woolf – the man who was so key to the story of the Advisory Committee on International Questions – deserves a closer look.

6

LABOUR AND THE IDEALIST MUDDLE IN INTERNATIONAL RELATIONS

Leonard Woolf

My dear Leonard...I wish you could have heard all the laudatory things which the [International Sub-] Committee said about the splendid work you had done for the Party over the last thirty years. They could not have been more appreciative than they were, and there was no dissentient voice.

(*Letter from Philip Noel Baker to Leonard Woolf*)[1]

Leonard Woolf's international thought is now well served by an up to date and detailed study written by Peter Wilson.[2] While it is obviously not possible to analyse Woolf's international theory without reference to Wilson's account, and this section does cover some similar ground, my stress is on that part of Woolf's theory that was directly relevant to his work with the Labour Party and the problems of inter-war IR. Those interested in a more detailed account of Woolf's thought should go to Wilson's book. Of particular interest are his concept of civilisation, his conception of international government, his changing views during the 1930s, and his colonial policy. Of these four areas, two (international government and colonial policy) are covered in more depth in Wilson's study. Woolf's activities, both through the Advisory Committee and his other writings, were prodigious and influential. Before 1918 Woolf had been the main foreign affairs expert in the Fabian Research Bureau, an organisation set up by Sidney and Beatrice Webb that tended to favour discussions on domestic political topics.[3] It was the publication of his book *International Government* that made Woolf's reputation as an authority on international topics, and this made him a natural choice for Secretary of the Advisory Committee on International Questions, and later of the Advisory Committee on Imperial Questions as well. Woolf's role within the Party remained that of a facilitator and expert adviser, despite (or perhaps because of) his unsuccessful attempt to become an MP in 1922. This said, Woolf was a major influence on Labour's colonial policy, and his views on the future of the Empire became both Labour and British government policy after 1945.[4]

Like many of the other key members of the Bloomsbury set, Woolf's thought was influenced by the philosopher G.E. Moore. Moore was one of the most prominent philosophers in the inter-war period, and his stress on the utility of reason in politics, the importance of aesthetic issues, along with his rejection of the idealist conception of the state associated with T.H. Green and Bernard Bousenquet, left their mark on Woolf. Certainly Woolf's conception of what makes a society civilised, his own forays into literature and his rejection of the idealist fetishisation of the sovereign state may owe their origins, at least in part, to Moore. Certainly, the ease with which Woolf straddled the worlds of literature and current affairs is a silent endorsement of Moore. Woolf's literary side, that included the publication of two novels, support for his wife's literary ambitions, and establishment of the Hogarth Press, was only marred by the Hogarth Press' initial rejection of Joyce's *Ulysses* on legal grounds. While Woolf's socialism led him to cast doubt on any scheme for the future that did not address the iniquities of capitalism, he was never as happy as Brailsford with a predominantly economic and materialist explanation for the world's problems. His discussions of the nature of civilisation, and his occasional support for Norman Angell's arguments about the problems of the public mind, reveal an interest in the psychological and cultural causes of the world's problems. There may also be a Freudian influence here, as Woolf is also credited with helping to introduce Freud to the English-speaking world.[5] Perhaps one negative influence of the aesthetic on Woolf's international thought was his tendency towards intellectual sloppiness, which has already been noted by Peter Wilson. His non-fiction often has the spontaneity and light touch of a piece of fiction, and sometimes sacrifices logical consistency and intellectual rigor to literary impulsiveness. In some pieces of non-fiction, *Quack, Quack!*, for example, the intellectual intent is almost swamped in a literary prose, and the conventions of current affairs writing are loudly forgotten.[6] Cohabiting uneasily with this more literary outlook was Woolf's Fabian self, which stressed the importance of the gathering of facts and understanding the world as it is before trying to change it. Many of Woolf's most famous works, such as *Empire and Commerce in Africa*, contain a wealth of data.[7] Commenting on Woolf's analysis of international government Wilson noted that 'the importance of Woolf's work to a large degree resides in the mass of information he collected on official and unofficial international associations.'[8]

An important constant in Woolf's thought was an abiding faith in the new liberalism that had emerged as a progressive alternative to the older laissez faire liberalism in the late nineteenth century. Especially germane here was new liberalism's reinterpretation of the individual, and its relationship with the idea of the state. Old liberals had stressed the fundamentally independent nature of individuals that, like billiard balls, are hard shelled perfectly formed and autonomous. The role of government in old liberalism, therefore, was to manage the relationship between the individual and society in such a way that the innate autonomy of the individual remained untouched. For the new liberals the individual was embedded in the social relations around them, and their identities were constituted by their interactions with others.[9] This meant that there was no clear split between individual and society. This concept of social embeddedness led directly to Woolf's socialism, although Woolf did not directly discuss the concept. The embedded individual was naturally dependent on the other individuals in society, and so social responsibility was a practical necessity, rather than an aspect of altruism. The problem with capitalism for Woolf was that it undermined the freedom of the embedded individual as well as sponsoring a capitalist class that could not be trusted to act in the interests of the society as a whole. The sacred rights of property undermined freedom and equality, and introduced an internal form of barbarism at the heart of civilisation.[10]

Woolf's new liberalism also imbued him with a strong faith in democracy, an opposition to imperialism and colonialism, and a belief in the importance of education in the attainment of progress. Woolf also seemed to believe that liberal ideals were historical constants that are always available if the political circumstances allow them to be, rather than a product of a particular period in time or a certain mode of production. This rational availability of liberal ideas of freedom seems to be a legacy of G.E. Moore's influence, and put Woolf at odds with Marxism and Marxist influenced writers such as Laski and Brailsford. Indeed Harold Laski saw this element in Woolf's world view as the source of the intellectual friction between them:

> I think the main difference between us, turns on whether there are unchanged absolutes in matters of social constitution (which I think is really your view) or whether, as I think, conceptions of good are in

relation to the general social environment, particularly in its economic content.[11]

While sharing Laski's antipathy for capitalism, Woolf did not share his
historicism or his materialism, and it was this that put clear blue water
between them in the does capitalism cause war debate of the 1930s. Yet,
this commitment to 'unchanged absolutes' did not mean that Woolf's
thought was rigidly dogmatic and unchanging. Rather, Woolf appreciated
that different circumstances over time mean that the achievement of his
constant goals required different means, and therefore different ways of
thinking about problems. As Peter Wilson has stressed, Woolf's opposition to power politics did not prevent him from analysing a situation in a
power political way when the international context was an anarchical
one.[12] This became particularly marked in Woolf's analysis of the international situation after 1936. Woolf, like Angell, did not argue that the
world of power politics did not exist, or that it could be wished away
through the force of moral example as George Lansbury believed. Rather,
the power arrangements associated with the international anarchy were a
lower order existence that should be superseded by a more complex and
less violent form of society.

     Central to Woolf's notion of the development of society was his con-
cept of civilisation. Certainly he shared with his colleague on the Advisory
Committee, Arnold Toynbee, the view of civilisation as a basic building
block of history.[13] Woolf thought of western civilisation as a single unit
like Toynbee, and that it had come into existence as a reaction to the
privileges of a more feudal, monarchical and aristocratic civilisation.[14]
There, though, the similarities stop. In Woolf's analysis civilisation was
packaged in a different way. It was fundamentally an attribute of both
social structures and the psychology of individuals 'in their social relations.'[15] At the same time, the creation of civilisation had also taken with it
elements of barbarism that, while not constitutive of the civilisation, were
a continual menace to the survival of the civilisation. At first glance this
seems to have a strong parallel with Toynbee's concept of the internal
proletariat, but in fact Woolf's notion of internal barbarism is different
both in terms of source and social status. First, Woolf's barbarism is not a
symptom of decline, but rather elements of past ways of thinking or of
ideas that once served freedom, but are now parasitic to it. Second, while
Toynbee's approach is elitist – seeing the motor of civilisation as the
preserve of 'creative minorities', and the decline of civilisation linked to
the development of an internal proletariat – Woolf saw the threat coming
largely from the elite. The barbaric and predatory nature of western civi-

lisation outside of Europe was, for Woolf, a product of technological successes of the industrial revolution and an elite-led capitalism that fuelled a
hunger for raw materials.[16] Without law to control it the force of Western
civilisation manifests itself as anarchy and barbarism.[17] Internally, the growing contradictions between property rights and freedom under capitalism
created a conflict whereby the formerly civilised old liberal ideas became
the bearers of a new class-dominated barbarism promoted by capitalism.[18]
Showing perhaps a nod to the British idealist tradition (in its philosophical
sense) and Hegel, Woolf saw the central value of this civilisation laying in
freedom.[19] Woolf's consequent criticism of capitalism was based on capitalism's failure to reconcile its concept of property with the core value of
freedom. The result was a Hegelian-style conflict brought on by contradictions within ideas. Yet, whereas Hegel's notion of the cunning of reason led to a faith in the ultimate triumph of freedom, Woolf's show-down
between civilisation and barbarism could go either way. Woolf used this
idea to explain the failure of the western democracies to respond to the
threat of fascism. Writing in 1939 just before the outbreak of war, Woolf
argued that while it was the fascist barbarians outside who seemed like the
greater threat at the moment, it was the internal barbarians that would
finally destroy a civilisation by undermining its values and cohesiveness:

> The crude barbarian and the dictator is [sic] only a temporary
> danger... he and his political system carry within them the seeds of
> their own disintegration... freedom is infinitely stronger than
> despotism... But a community of free men must trust in freedom...
> the danger to civilisation is... within the citadel.[20]

While praising Woolf's view of civilisation as a precursor to Bull and
Watson's work in *Expansion of International Society*, Wilson is ultimately
dismissive of Woolf's attempt to link civilisation to the international crisis
of the late 1930's, criticising what he sees as the Manichean division of the
world into civilisation and barbarism in *Barbarians at the Gates*.[21] While
Barbarians at the Gates does unfortunately create this impression, Woolf's
views of civilisation and barbarism are much less clearly distinguished in
other works. Certainly, in *Imperialism and Civilization* there is no clear
Manichean struggle, rather the forces that underpin civilisation in the West
become predatory and barbaric in the non-Western world.[22] While
Woolf's work on imperialism demonstrates how Western concepts turn
from being civilised to being predatory, his work on the evolving international order sees civilisation locked in a conflict between national and
international organisations and psychologies, and here there is certainly a

Manichean element. The national psychology is rooted in patriotism, and supports the establishment and power of nation-state based organs of government. Its result is a world of competing nation-states. The internationalist psychology is weaker, but it is the growing interdependence of global society that is creating international organs of government. Woolf draws two conclusions from this: first, that a strong international psychology that could provide support to international government is still lacking; and second that the national and international trends are contradictory, and that the national trend will lead to war and the undermining of civilisation.[23] This irreconcilable split between national and international logics, with the first drawing its strength from its control over mass psychology and the second from the global material realities, underlay Woolf's theory of international politics, and explains his growing pessimism after 1931. In a nutshell, the conflict between nationalism and internationalism was complicated by the former's control over mass psychology, and the latter's compatibility with the direction of global material trends.

Woolf first came to prominence as an international expert with the publication in 1916 of the Fabian-sponsored *International Government*. Written originally with the intent of discovering how future wars could be prevented, what began as a limited study on war prevention developed into a discussion of the possibilities of international government. The problem of war for Woolf was tied up with the general tendency in all human activities for the growth of complexity and interdependence. While in other areas this growing complexity has led to greater coordination between the institutions and machinery responsible for each activity, the international realm has remained tied to an older system of autonomous states developed when it was possible for states to be self-sufficient entities – what he would later label the nationalist political organisation. While diplomats do have their 'various methods of regulating the relationships of States – negotiation, mediation, arbitration, Conference – [they have] never coordinated them.'[24] Thus a coordinated international government, one that brought together independent and sovereign states in a free association under a legal machinery, was a necessary precondition for the lessening of the outbreak of war. Having said this, Woolf was at pains to point out that law alone was not enough, and that the shape of any international government had to take account of the non-rational beliefs of people, which at the current moment would make a tighter and more formally legal super-state an impossibility.[25] Woolf's advocacy of a free association of states as the more viable alternative at present places him, as Wilson suggests, amongst the earliest advocates of a league of nations. Also, by seeing the problem of war in terms of international coordination and relations Wilson is correct in seeing Woolf's analysis as predominantly 'third image', to use Kenneth Waltz's term, and therefore Woolf's approach is, like Norman Angell's *Great Illusion*, clearly a work of international theory.[26]

This free association of states that underpins the first part of *International Government* was only one of the forms of international order that Woolf sketched as alternatives to the international anarchy that led to the Great War. The second half of *International Government*, as well as his work on war aims during the Second World War, focused on the mass of technical, commercial, administrative and industrial developments that were creating a cosmopolitan order. Woolf's work on these developments strongly mirror's Mitrany's work on functional international government, which should not surprise us given Woolf's influence on Mitrany's early work.[27] Where they differed was in Woolf's concern that this emerging cosmopolitan government required some form of international federal political structure to co-ordinate it properly, otherwise it would not be strong enough to resist nationalist tendencies.[28] Wilson points out that there was a third intermediary form of international government in Woolf's writings, what Wilson calls international government through adjudication, which is located between the other two.[29] This is made up mainly of his work on the system of arbitration and conciliation under League auspices, and is discussed in more detail in chapter three. A fuller discussion of these three forms of international government in Woolf's thought can be found in Wilson. [30]

Woolf always distinguished between longer-term goals for civilisation and goals that were practical given the current political situation. During the two World Wars and the 1919 peace process, when the international situation was distinctly fluid, Woolf was willing to give free rein to his longer-term proposals, while as the League system coalesced he was content to settle for an international government based on forms of adjudication. As options narrowed in response to various international crises, especially between 1936 and 1939, Woolf stressed more immediate goals that clearly fell short of his preferred outcomes, but were consistent with his views of international government based on a great power concert. In the late 1930's this lowering of sights brought him into conflict with Philip Noel Baker, as discussed in chapter four. The cosmopolitan form of international government explored in the second part of *International Government* was his preferred longer-term goal, but as international events unfolded he was also willing to support a return to a great power concert in the short term. Woolf did not necessarily see any conflict between these different forms of international government, he was happy to advocate any one in different circumstances. What may have helped fuel Woolf's dispute with Noel Baker over the suggestion that the League system of adjudication be put aside temporarily in favour of a return to an Anglo-French led concert of powers was Noel Baker's sense that there was a clear tension between these two forms of international organisation. Certainly, Woolf did not see a tension at all.[31]

It is worth taking a closer look at Woolf's analysis of the political situation in the 1930s, since it reveals both the extent to which he reacted to specific conditions and the way that his international theory combined different aspects of international government.[32] His summary of the situation in 1930 simultaneously demonstrated his optimism about the future of international government and his worries about the structural weaknesses of internationalism more generally. Internationalism had received a boost from the horrors of the Great War. 'The glamour of nationalism had evaporated for many in the mud of Flanders or during a London air raid'.[33] Although embryonic, there now was an internationalist psychology, and the need to accomplish international tasks had resulted in the establishment of an efficient system of technical international government. There was also praise for the system of adjudication that was emerging to prevent the outbreak of war. Yet, Woolf was also aware of the weaknesses in this system, the most important being the need to develop a stronger and more robust international psychology: 'for the most part, international psychology is still weak, vacillating, and uninstructed.'[34] It would, he felt, require 'a century of unbroken peace' for 'the bonds of common interests between nations' to emerge from the successful exercise of international government.[35] Unfortunately, the world was unlikely to be left in peace that long. 'The danger to-day is that nationalism all over the world will start digging up the corpses which it recently made and buried so passionately.'[36] The continued dominance of the nationalist psychology left internationalism and international government dangerously exposed.

It was not long before Woolf was able to confirm his dire predictions. The vague internationalism found in the general population had proved too weak when faced with the nationalist policies of their statesmen, and the drift between 1930 and 1933 had been towards more nationalist governments unwilling to use the machinery of government to prevent war. This unwillingness to use the League and the failure of states to live up to their commitments under the Covenant had undermined popular faith in the League.[37] In 1933 Woolf still felt that the League could work given greater political will to use it, but the decision to make the League work now rested with the Great Powers. The only alternative was a drift towards another war.[38] Woolf now saw a general drift towards barbarism and war from 1914 onwards, with only a short period between 1918 and 1923 in which civilisation fought back. The current tide of barbarism he now traced back to 1925, which corresponded with the collapse of the Geneva protocol.[39] By the end of the Abyssinian crisis Woolf regarded the present manifestation of the League as moribund. Its failure in Manchuria in 1931 had all but destroyed it, but the failure of the League powers to deal with Italy's invasion of Abyssinia had proved fatal.[40] Looking at the quality of statesmanship in mid-1936, Woolf concluded that there was no will to resuscitate the League's system of collective security, and consequently the second best option was an alliance between Britain, France and Russia that would at least preserve a chance of peace and security.[41] By their inactivity the League powers had sent the message that the League would not try to prevent war between states, and as the outbreak of the war in Spain demonstrated, this meant that rearmament was now required in order to resist the attacks of aggressors.[42] The League might be dead, but Woolf believed that it could be resurrected. He saw little point in continuing to trust in the present machinery, but he felt that a new League could be built around an alliance of anti-fascist states – a peace front – that would combine guarantees to individual states with economic cooperation.[43] Thus, the clear failure to develop and use a more complex form of international machinery would force advocates of international government back onto a concert of powers. Yet, Woolf felt that the necessities of material development would once again make the building up of a more complex system of international government likely, and the destruction of the Second World War, like the Great War before it, would help fuel a revulsion against war that would once more weaken the nationalist claims and strengthen the internationalist.[44] While Woolf was trying to influence the shape of the post-war settlement after 1939, another branch of his international theory was proving far more influential on government policy and public opinion.

It is in the area of imperial and colonial policy that Woolf was the most influential in his lifetime. 'When the Labour Party came to power following its landslide election in 1945, it adopted a colonial policy that in broad outline Leonard Woolf had been advocating for more than a generation.' This has implications for the way that we view Woolf as an IR theorist, and for our reassessment of the relevance of inter-war IR writers in more general terms. 'Given that so much of what Woolf recommended in the 1920s became British government policy in the 1940s... the label "idealism," so often applied to Woolf's work on international politics, seems singularly inapt.'[45] Starting with his 1913 novel, *A Village in the*

Jungle, Woolf's anti-imperialist outlook was informed by his experiences as part of the colonial administration. Central to Woolf's view of the problem of colonialism was his belief that, because the societies of the colonies had been changed so fundamentally by their inclusion within European colonial empires, the hasty exit of the imperial powers from their colonies would bring disaster. The colonies, he argued, were now fully integrated into the international economy.[46] This meant that there was no going back to the pre-colonial forms of society, while the imperial powers had a duty to properly prepare their colonies for independence through a set of policies that accepted that the resources of the colony were a trust for its populations, and not the property of the imperial power. Although he was often at pains to point out that he opposed racism – indeed he was particularly opposed to white settler rule – his argument often assumed that western ways were superior, and that consequently much of the non-western 'races' were non-adult and required education.[47] While initially suspicious of elements of the League mandate system, he came to accept it for two main reasons. First, it represented a major change in western attitudes towards colonies by accepting that colonial territories were held in trust for their inhabitants. Second, it offered a template for the non-mandatory colonial territories.[48] Indeed, throughout the inter-war period Woolf advocated a radical plan for Africa, in which all the colonies would be brought under the mandate system, and that the colonies themselves would be combined in a continent-wide system of free trade and demilitarisation.[49] While this plan never came to anything, it was made Labour Party policy, and was included as part of Labour's alternative to the National Government's policy of appeasement.[50] While these proposals went further than governments were prepared to go at the time, the general tenor of Woolf's analysis did influence later attitudes to decolonisation.

Thus, despite lapses into a more literary style and an occasionally naïve faith in rationality, Woolf was a significant intellectual influence and faciletator in the period. His theories of international government and imperialism were important parts of the IR landscape of the inter-war period, while his roles within the Labour Party, and the intellectual landscape more generally, opened up debates about international politics that either shaped policy, or were integral parts of the criticism of the policy of various governments. While not as original as writers like David Mitrany, or even perhaps Norman Angell, his contribution to the intellectual climate that shaped IR in its early years is possibly without parallel. Yet, on balance, what effect did this intellectual world that Woolf did so much to create have on the Labour Party and the wider world?

The Role of Labour's Inter-War International Experts

The interaction between the Labour Party and key inter-war International Relations writers and intellectuals has until recently received no attention in the discipline of International Relations.[51] This is no deliberate oversight, but rather one of those accidents of a discipline's evolution that blinds it to some paths while opening it up to others. After 1945 the Anglo-American subject of International Relations turned its attentions to the problems of a very different world – one initially dominated by the logics of the Cold War – and the issues dealt with by the inter-war experts became of less interest to a modern International Relations audience, unless, that is, it could be defined within post-1945 terms. Yet, reassessing past international theories is useful in three ways: it helps us put the history of the discipline into its temporal context; it keeps alive a rich variety of international ideas that may prove useful again in the future; and it helps demolish Whig histories that are constructed by certain groups in order to control and discipline thought. The interaction between intellectual IR and the Labour Party also created its own interesting dynamics. Writers became more directly involved in the cut and thrust of democratic politics; while professional politicians were, at a time when many people did not even complete secondary education, exposed to a realm of ideas that might otherwise have been closed to them. What is interesting about this interaction within the inter-war Labour Party was how little friction this relationship caused. In fact, the major splits in the Party cut through, rather than between, the various groups; creating a number of interesting and enduring alliances between self-educated working class leaders from the unions, and middle class intellectuals. The association of Arthur Henderson with the members of the Advisory Committee – especially with Leonard Woolf, Philip Noel Baker and Hugh Dalton – in the 1920s is one example of this. The anti-appeasement group that brought together Ernest Bevin and Walter Citrine from the Trade Union movement, and Hugh Dalton, Philip Noel Baker and Leonard Woolf from amongst the University educated intellectual wing of the Party in the mid to late 1930s is another. This history tends to question the whole presumption underlying Morgenthau's analysis that it is possible to divide the practical subject of study – the statesmen – from those who do the study – the foreign policy expert.

Basically this concluding chapter deals with three issues that follow from the analysis in the preceding five chapters. First, there is the influence that the international writers had on the Labour Party, not to mention the question of how much their involvement with the Party affected their own writing. Here I return to an appraisal of the five experts that I

singled out earlier. Second, and following from this, is the extent that this
story can help us to flesh out an understanding of the history of International Relations theory during this period. The standard 'histories' tend
to revolve around the false dichotomies of realism and idealism. This
study has shown that what the writers at the time saw as important were
the question of the nature of international anarchy, the growth of interdependence, the creation of a system of pooled security based around
arbitration, sanctions and disarmament, the relation between capitalism
and war, imperialism, the effect of the ideological conflict with fascism,
and finally the prospect of functional cooperation within the broader
question of the form of international organisation. We cannot hope to
understand the writings of the international experts discussed in this book
without understanding the place of these concepts in their work and for
the society around them. Dividing the thought of the time into realist and
idealist camps does not help us at all in this respect. Finally, I would like to
finish this study by looking at the broader issue of social democratic
foreign policy, its relationship with liberal ideas of global governance, and
the narrower question of whether Labour's international policy during the
inter-war period can be described as liberal or socialist.

Consistently the work of the Advisory Committee on International
Questions – the channelling of expert advice from many of the major
international writers of the time to Labour's political leadership and Parliamentary members – was praised by senior Labour figures. While the
memoranda from the Advisory Committee were diverse, and often quite
technical in nature, they followed a general intellectual pattern that was in
tune with the aspirations and ideology of the leadership. The importance
of the Advisory Committee to the Party, not to mention the influence of
its individual members both inside and outside the Committee, is attested
to by the words of Labour's leaders, the presence of Advisory Committee
memoranda in so many collections of private papers, the number of
memoranda that became Party pamphlets or conference documents, and
finally the way that ideas in Advisory Committee memoranda would
become Party policy. Certainly, in government Ramsay MacDonald did
build firewalls between himself and the Advisory Committee, and even
went as far as to criticise findings in at least two memoranda. Yet, this in
itself is evidence of the high regard in which the Advisory Committee was
held. There were four foreign policy debates in which the roles of
Labour's international experts were key. These were: 1. moving the Party
from its denunciations of the peace and the League towards a pro-League
policy in the early 1920s; 2. informing the discussions about the form and
structure of the League from the mid-1920s to the early 1930s; 3. changing

Labour's views about collective defence and the threat of fascism after 1931; and 4. working to provide Labour with an effective set of war aims after 1939. The Advisory Committee's influence was strongest when Labour was out of office, and certainly during the first two Labour Governments Labour's international experts found their influence diminished both by the presence of an alternative source of advice in the shape of the civil service, and by Ramsay MacDonald's notorious secrecy while in office. Yet, as the arguments in the last four chapters have shown, Labour's policy even in government, by and large, was a product of its international experts.

Between 1918 and 1921, despite the frequent denunciations of the peace and the new League Covenant, it was the Advisory Committee that was the main source for policy documents that advocated working with the new structures. This story has been told in more detail by Henry Winkler, where Ramsay MacDonald and Arthur Henderson are presented as working with the rest of the Advisory Committee to change Labour into a pro-League Party, against the wishes of the majority of the membership.[52] While in chapter 2 I argue that Winkler has overplayed the strength and the depth of the opposition within the grassroots, I believe that he is broadly correct in his assessment. The often quite wild denunciations of the treaties that came out of the Advisory Committee prior to 1922 were tempered early on by memos that advocated working within the existing framework of the League. It is H.N. Brailsford who was clearly the most disappointed of the authors during this period, and he was also the last to be reconciled with a pro-League policy, waiting until Ramsay MacDonald's Geneva success in 1924. Others pushed for a League policy earlier. David Mitrany was certainly advocating engagement in 1920,[53] while denunciations had largely dried up by 1923 to be replaced by memoranda that advocated an overt League foreign policy.[54] The Advisory Committee and the writings of its membership created the intellectual background to the First Labour Government's engagement with France and Germany that led to the rapprochement of 1924 and the abortive Geneva Protocol. Despite its failure, the provisions and definitions of the Geneva protocol were used in later agreements, such as the Locarno Pact of 1925. I argue this point in chapter 3.

It is between 1922 and 1931 that Labour's international experts were at their most practical and their most visionary (see chapter 3). They were practical in that the relative peace of the period and the presence of two Labour Governments led to the development of plans for international order that built on existing structures and international realities. They were their most visionary in that these plans aimed towards the realisation of one of the major goals of their generation: the elimination of war as a tool of international statecraft. The framework for this was their own version of Clausewitz's 'wonderful trinity': arbitration, sanctions (or security) and disarmament. Both the memoranda of the Advisory Committee, and much of the other literary output of Labour's international experts, reflect this concern with constructing specific institutions and rules for a new international order that would be more consistent with the realities of an interdependent world. David Mitrany wrote on international sanctions,[55] Philip Noel Baker on disarmament and the Geneva Protocol,[56] William Arnold-Forster on arbitration[57] and Norman Angell on the important connection between all three.[58] To top this off it was Noel Baker and Leonard Woolf who wrote the international part of Labour's key policy document of 1928 *Labour and the Nation*.

Yet, despite the consensus amongst these experts over the importance of creating an arbitrations-sanctions-disarmament regime, there were worrying rumbles. Woolf had concerns over the conservative nature of law-based regimes and over the problem of finding a forum for non-legal disputes. Mitrany was worried that there was no will to carry out sanctions, especially military sanctions, that might be necessary to reassure the security concerns of France and the smaller powers. As well as this pacifist opposition in the Party, and the country as a whole, meant that in order to avoid a split in the Party, and to lose votes in the country, it was necessary for official publications and the public speeches of the leadership to avoid mentioning the issue of sanctions. This leads to two related criticisms of this project. The first is that it was fatally flawed in the short term in that there appeared to be no will amongst the British public, let alone the publics of the other great power democracies, to stand by their commitments once the gaps in the League were filled. The second is that, given this, the international experts also failed to convince the wider Party and public that sanctions, especially military sanctions, were going to be a necessary part of any working peace system based on the League machinery. Although many of them, often in a private capacity, wrote in support of the necessity of military sanctions and adequate security provisions,[59] the public face of the Party remained ominously silent on the issue of sanctions. While this bought the Labour Party internal peace and votes prior to 1931, it also contributed to the view that Labour was muddled on foreign policy issues. As I argue in chapter 4, the failure of the international experts to educate the wider Party and public on the need for sanctions is one of their most serious, although the mountain they would have had to climb certainly made their work on a League foreign policy in the first part of the decade appear like a relaxing promenade. There is a final related criticism, relevant to this period, that the whole attempt to close the gaps in the Covenant was itself based on a fundamental rationalist flaw to begin with. I will address this in more detail in the next section.

After Labour's defeat in 1931 Labour's international experts faced two challenges. The closest to them was the change in the configuration of the leadership of the Parliamentary Party. The 1931 election left the leadership of the PLP in the hands of a committed pacifist, George Lansbury. The disputes between the pro-pooled security majority in the National Executive and the pacifist leaders of the PLP were bruising, but ended in 1935 with the resignations of Ponsonby and Lansbury from their roles as leaders in the two Houses of Parliament. The second challenge was the rise of fascism. From 1934 onwards the policy of the Party was to support sanctions against aggression, and the Advisory Committee played its role by consistently producing memoranda that supported collective action against the dictators. The individual members of the Committee also wrote extensively on the threat of fascism. Before 1936 the memoranda called on the fulfilment of the commitments to sanctions, arbitration and disarmament, with the failure of the economic sanctions against Italy during the Abyssinia crisis there was widespread realisation that the League system was in crisis. This had been clear to many since Manchuria in 1931–2, but Abyssinia made it clear that the League sanctions regime, under the current conditions, was ineffectual. I have discussed this in more detail in chapter 4. During this period, and despite the opposition of its outgoing chairman C.R. Buxton, the Advisory Committee tended to align with the foreign policy triumvirate of Dalton, Bevin and Citrine. Increasingly the issue of disarmament took on a longer-term flavour, and the question of supporting the National Government's defence estimates and rearmament came up. By 1937 the Advisory Committee was arguing for an immediate international policy that turned from the League as the basis of British security policy towards a smaller alliance of anti-fascist states.[60] It was this memorandum that caused a temporary breach with Noel Baker, who remained committed to a full League policy well after the other members.[61] Opposition to fascism remained a central theme in the memoranda of the last half of the 1930s, and it was not for nothing that Woolf characterised the Advisory Committee as 'clearly… more anti-Hitler than the Party as a whole'.[62] Thus, the Advisory Committee and its members were broadly supportive of the pro-collective defence stance of the main Party leaders. They helped steer both the Party and the public towards collective action against the dictators, and finally towards an acceptance of the need to risk war. Although they were not the only voices attacking the appeasement of the National Government, through their Party memoranda and their more public writings they were part of the broad coalition campaigning for a radical change in British foreign policy. While the thought of the major members of the Advisory Committee did not follow exactly the same pattern, the broad trajectories of their ideas tended to be similar: support for collective action against fascist aggressors through the League gave way to support for an immediate (and armed) alliance of anti-fascist states against the Axis powers. After Munich all supported a tough stand against Germany, even at the cost of war.

Although the Advisory Committee was closed down from 1939 to 1944, its various members were still active within the Party in the war years. Particularly important was their role in the construction of Labour's war aims. While Noel Baker, Laski, and Dalton were involved in the drafting of Labour's war aims documents, Woolf, Angell and Mitrany kept up a stream of public domain discussions on the forging of the post-war order. Mitrany, who by this stage was no longer directly involved with Labour, honed his functional approach to international government during this time,[63] and while Labour figures generally (Woolf and Noel Baker, for example) were suspicious of the idea that functional organisations could bring peace without some kind of overarching 'political' organisation',[64] his influence on the discussions about the establishment of specialised agencies after the war was profound. A big question that crops up repeatedly in the war aims documentation is the issue of the power and future of the British-Soviet-American ('Big Three') alliance. There is a tension here. While many were of the opinion that the Big Three were the only states with the power to force through dramatic and much-needed changes to the international system, there were also worries about the alliance. These worries fall into two rough areas. The first is that the Big Three will break up, returning the world to a balance of power system that splits Europe into spheres of influence, and consequently ignoring the much-needed reforms to the international anarchy.[65] The second was that the Big Three would not devolve their power to a more responsible and inclusive international government structure, but continue to run the world as an oligopoly.[66] Both Brailsford and Woolf feared the coming of a new international anarchy pitting the Anglo-American sphere against a Soviet one, and in this sense they predicted the coming of the Cold War. Having said this, it was clear that only the Big Three, working in unison, would have the power to establish the overarching political organisation that was to replace the League. It is here that Mitrany's pessimism about the chances of creating a functioning state-based collective security system comes in. Criticisms of Mitrany's functional approach amongst Labour's international experts revolved around the argument that some kind of global political coordinating body was necessary to preserved the peace, and that functional organisations on their own were not enough. Yet, what if the international situation, and especially the relations between the Big Three, made the functioning of an effective political organisation problematic? In this sense Mitrany's functional approach, like Ramsay MacDonald's assessment of sanctions, was a recognition that there was not the will to establish a wider body. As a result, the functional organisations were the only serious alternatives to the return of an international anarchy.

While there were obviously more than just the Advisory Committee and its experts making inputs into Labour policy, the role of people such as Brailsford, Noel Baker, Angell, Mitrany and particularly Woolf were key at certain junctures in the Party's history. In histories of the Party it is usually the public faces of the Party that take the limelight. Henderson, Ramsay MacDonald, Dalton, Bevin and Attlee appear as the prime movers in the unfolding story. Yet, as this book has demonstrated, these high profile political players were in regular contact with the Party's international thinkers. The intellectual core of Labour's approach to international affairs could be found in the Advisory Committee on International Questions. At the same time, these experts were themselves grappling with the key foreign policy issues of the day.

The Idealist Muddle:
Towards a Better Understanding of Inter-War IR

What has hampered the discipline of International Relations from understanding the contributions of the various members of the Advisory Committee to international thought has been the false interpretation of them as part of some kind of flawed idealist paradigm. They have all been roundly dismissed without even being read. The fact that there never was such a paradigm, and that the problems faced by inter-war international writers led to very different kinds of splits between authors, comes out clearly from this study of just one part of the story of inter-war academic International Relations. Rather, there is a good case for arguing that there was a clear left-liberal (or liberal-socialist) paradigm that was predominant in Labour Party foreign policy circles, even if it was not without its pacifist and radical socialist opponents within the Party itself. There is always a danger, as Sylvest points out, that in placing people in paradigms 'ideal types turn to stereotypes.'[67] Yet, there is common ground here that also needs to be highlighted. Norman Angell, Leonard Woolf and Philip Noel Baker form the core of this paradigm. Although they often differed on particular points and specific issues – Noel Baker and Woolf, for example, split over the possible usefulness of the League in the late 1930s – they could all agree that: 1. The ultimate point of studying international relations was to abolish it as a separate sphere by introducing the norms of domestic politics into the international. While the state as an institution need not be abolished, the concept of national sovereignty was at the root of many of the problems of international coordination. National sovereignty was behind the unstable international anarchy, and while the principles of the international anarchy might have been applicable to an earlier less interdependent era, they were dangerous in the changed conditions of the modern world. 2. This meant that the main immediate need was for the establishment of the rule of law (although with provisions to prevent this law becoming the tool of supporters of the status quo) and the proper international political institutions to manage that law and give it force; 3. This could be established through international agreements, and that the impetus for these agreements would be international common interests in peace and prosperity. An exclusive nationalism was the major impediment to realising this, as well as vested (often capitalist) interests that profited from the state; 4. The success of these agreements could only be based on very precise and accurate information about the nature of the international system as a whole, as well as knowledge of the myriad of specific disputes and issues that dog international relations. David Mitrany and H.N. Brailsford were on the edges of this group largely because they could not sign up to all four of these points. Mitrany would be in accord with 1 and 4, but he would have seen 2 as a longer-term goal, and 3 as unobtainable and naïve. Brailsford would have agreed with 1 and 2 up to a point, but would have given a greater prominence to what he saw as the ultimate problem of the failings of capitalism. He would have agreed with 3, with the added protocol that this would be most likely amongst democratic socialist states, and he would have had little problem with 4. In this sense, the main subjects in this study are representatives of a paradigm and two factions on the edge of that paradigm. While it is useful to highlight the connections between these thinkers, we must also keep in mind that since paradigmatic boundaries enclose modes of thought, rather than agreements on specific policies, they are necessarily fluid.

Underlying this paradigm were a number of key assumptions that all five could certainly agree with: 1. There were no constant laws of history, rather changing conditions in the political environment, due to progress, required major changes in the way that human society was governed. These changes were not random, but rather tended to flow in the direction of greater interdependence and technological complexity. Having said this, it was possible for events to reverse this flow of history. Hegel's cunning of reason is absent here 2. Despite setbacks, the general tenor of human history was a progression to freer and more equitable systems of government. This was made possible by the role of human learning interacting on an otherwise selfish human nature. Again, rather than relying on a cunning of reason, this progress was the result of the actions of groups of individuals. 3. Armed with knowledge of a situation and a pragmatic rational outlook it was possible for people of good will to change the world for the better. These were assumptions common at the time to both liberalism and socialism, and are open to attack from later realists, but unlike the stereotypical idealism they are also capable of being defended from realist attack. The first assumption is itself a refutation of the strongly held realist notion that there are common laws of history that do not change. The left-liberals, rather, assumed that the natural order of history was flux, and that laws of historical behaviour changed in response to different institutional, economic or psychological realities. What worked well in one epoch might be a disastrous policy in another. The second is an attack on the old conservative idea, strongly present in classical realism, that human nature is the main influence on human action. Left-liberals assumed that an unconscious human nature interacted with a more conscious system of learning and education. It was the human ability to learn that provided human history with its long-term tendency to progression. Unlike the idealist straw man, left-liberals tended to assume, like realists, that human nature was pugnacious and violent. Where they differed from later realists was in their view that this violent nature was not the only influence on action. Finally, the third assumption did not necessarily compete with later realism. Even the most pessimistic realist such as Morgenthau carried the hope that a pragmatic and informed diplomacy would save the world from a third, and possibly grisly final, world war. These assumptions are unlikely to find favour with many current IR scholars, since they rest on claims about epistemology and history (specifically about the trans-cultural nature of knowledge and the idea of progress) that seem naïve to us now, but read through the beliefs of their time they stand up well against advocates of a return to realpolitik.

Yet, despite these intellectual weaknesses in the left-liberal approach, their grasp of the problems of international politics, as it unfolded in the inter-war period, was certainly far from unsophisticated. Their solutions to the problems of the twenty years' crisis were reasonable and well thought out by the standard of the times. A common modern anachronism is to regard any attempt to imagine a different future world order as in itself a utopian exercise divorced from a knowledge of the world as it really works. This approach ignores the particular circumstances of the inter-war period. Certainly, from the perspective of 1918 to 1931 not to be engaged in an analysis of how the world should change was a serious dereliction of duty in an international expert. The evidence of the Great War for many had proved that the order and rules associated with the old international anarchy was unsustainable. It was unsustainable for a number of reasons but key amongst these were: 1. that the growing interdependence of the international economy meant that major great power wars no longer had utility, and in fact undermined and threatened civilisation; 2. that the growth in modern technology had created arsenals that made war frighteningly destructive and ruinously expensive; and 3. that the state, upon which the international anarchy rested, could no longer be a self-sustaining entity, and thus needed to be superseded by new authorities that better suited the current state of human civilisation. For these reasons to blithely advocate the continuation of a system based on state sovereignty was a dangerously naïve position. To be realistic was to accept that the world had changed and to work at building institutions that were more in keeping with those changes than the old-fashioned sovereign state. Interestingly, this position is also held by E.H. Carr in his *Nationalism and After* and *Conditions of Peace*.[68]

If anything, what stands out about the schemes of the five writers discussed here is the timidity of their plans for the future order. Certainly, Woolf, Noel Baker and Angell, rather than imagining worlds beyond our current experience, stuck with writing about the development of institutions that already existed. Noel Baker talked about filling the gaps in the League Covenant in order to allow it to function as it was intended to. Woolf accepted the League as the most that the international community was willing to accept at the moment. As soon as the League started to falter he was willing to search for alternatives to a League-based foreign policy. Angell talked about the need for some kind of international authority to restrain states, but never totally abandoned the idea of the state. Even his later federalist war aims, based on Clarence Streit's plan for a federal union between the United States and the British Empire,[69] merely envisioned a confederal arrangement modelled on the already functioning British Empire and Commonwealth.[70] Brailsford's serious concerns about the incompatibility between capitalism and democracy led him to be suspicious of any organisation that did not directly deal with the problems caused by an unfair economic system. His grand schemes for international reforms – from his plan for Macedonia before the Great War, to his ideas for the democratisation of the League and the United Nations – were always qualified with statements along the lines that current powerful interests would never allow such a sensible reform. The most visionary was David Mitrany. His functional approach did envision a different system of global governance, although even here it was born out of a sense that other solutions, such as federalism or regional integration, were either impossible under current conditions, or so seriously weak as to fail to deal with the problems posed by the sovereign state.

This brings me back to the issue I raised at the end of the last chapter. What marks these writers off from the Kantian liberal tradition is their lack of utopian designs. Despite the fact that the conventional wisdom in IR is that they were discarded because they were too utopian, the only one of the five whose ideas were still discussed in IR classrooms after the 1960s was the only one to present a radical institutional departure from the sovereign state system: David Mitrany. This does go some way to explaining their disappearance from the IR mainstream after 1950. The vast bulk of the writing by these experts was designed to understand and to reform the world before the Great War, or between the two word wars. What place did Noel Baker's discussion of League of Nations disarmament have in the bipolar and ideologically charged competition of the Cold War? What relevance did Angell's view of the optical illusion of war have in a global climate in which ideological hatreds worth dying for underscored global competition? How would Woolf's analysis and criticism of colonialism shock in a world gearing up for the dissolution of empires and the cold-shouldering of minority white-settler interests? Could Leventhal's comment that Brailsford was largely forgotten after he stopped writing because his books were 'generally written in response to particular political events'[71] be equally applied to others of his generation? Could the realists have been right for the wrong reasons? These people were no longer relevant, but not because they ignored reality and built castles in the sky, but because they understood the facts of their time too well, and were consequently locked into the logic of a world that does not exist anymore.

There is some truth to this, but only some. Certainly much of their work does deal with particular pressing issues of the time, just as IR experts today give us their opinions on current events. Yet, at the same time they did address wider theoretical issues that were directly relevant to later realist discussions of the nature of international affairs, or issues that would resurface in IR after the end of East-West conflict. Specifically, many had a lot to say on 1. the nature and problems of realpolitik and international anarchy; 2. interdependence; 3. global democracy; and 4. the relationship between capitalism and peace/war.

While the major intellectual thrust of these writers was informed by what we would term interdependence theory today, they all carried within their approaches an understanding of what realpolitik and the international anarchy entailed. In the case of Woolf, Brailsford and Angell this meant detailed studies of how the international anarchy worked (or in Brailsford's case, how it led to disaster). In Noel Baker and Mitrany this understanding of realpolitik was more often implied, rather than clearly laid out and explained. Generally, they regarded realpolitik as the sub-standard set of principles that dominate when more complex systems of government are not applied or break down. This led them to be deeply critical of attempts to construct international organisations where sovereign states predominated, and the current status of the main political organs of the UN and aspects of the EU could be criticised using arguments from these five writers. In short, realists can be criticised for setting up the UN system for failure by basing modern international organisations on sovereign state membership. Equally, as writers who understood the profound changes that international interactions had undergone since the nineteenth century Woolf, Brailsford, Angell, Mitrany and Noel Baker also stand as ancestors of interdependence theory. Certainly much of the criticism that Woolf, Mitrany and Angell throw at the sovereign state system is based on their analysis of how social and economic relations have burst the bounds of the nation state. Noel Baker wrote on the consequences that mass armament played in an interdependent world. Equally, although some of them such as Mitrany were deeply suspicious of the European integration project, the ideas of these writers prefigured the intellectual underpinnings of the Treaties of Paris and Rome. The European project and the ideas of interdependence found in the liberal socialist paradigm are very closely related. A better acquaintance with these writers could help to bridge the divide between IR and EU studies. Yet, it was global, rather than regional, issues that interested these writers. All were particularly concerned with the extension of global democracy, an idea that is once more in vogue. Both Woolf and Brailsford wrote about the limits placed on the extension of democracy by global capitalist realities, while Mitrany's idea of functional democracy was an attempt to construct a concept of global democracy that conformed to the new patterns of economic interdependence and welfare capitalism. The involvement of Brailsford, Woolf and Angell in the capitalism and war debate of the 1930s is interesting as a corrective to some current thinking on the pacific nature of capitalism.[72] Brailsford's argument about the belligerency of capitalism, and Woolf and Angell's arguments about the deeper and more complex causes underlying war, can be used to show up some of the time-specific and naïve omissions in current claims about the pacific nature of capitalism. A full appraisal of the effects of capitalism on war would not be complete without the addition of their ideas and arguments.

Yet, while there is relevance to current debates, we must not also forget the weaknesses in this brand of liberal socialist thought. While these writers were more complex than many writing IR textbooks today realise, they still had major intellectual limitations, only some of which can be dismissed as products of the time. Certainly, by modern standards they were often rather philosophically simplistic. There is a naïve rationalism, which frequently informs their thought, and their common commitment to relevance and practical issues often meant that they were blind to the wider implications of many of their assumptions about the world. Woolf's blithe acceptance that certain non-western people's were 'non-adult', or Mitrany's distinction between culture and ideology are rhetorical devices that these authors left unexamined and unchallenged. Similarly, their use of history and historical example was often guilty of over-simplification and of imposing modern values on past events. All were progressives, and all consequently liked to present history as a unilinear progression.[73] They also made a number of errors of judgement during their time. Certainly, the negative aspects of the 1919 peace treaties were over-stated, and while none of them fell into the trap of explaining the rise of fascism as a consequence of the peace, they were nonetheless rather unappreciative of the pressures on the peacemakers, and a little to eager to accept the critical readings of the treaties and the process that created them. Yet, to be fair all did eventually grasp the opportunities offered by aspects of the Peace, such as the League. In terms of sanctions and the League of Nations perhaps they can be criticised for putting too much faith in the League's ability to impose sanctions. Perhaps any system of sanctions, however tightly defined, was going to be flawed as long as the League remained a conglomeration of sovereign states. The 1931–2 and 1935–6 crises demonstrated that states were quite willing and able to wriggle out of their commitments to collective security when they felt it was in their interests to do so. Many, like Noel Baker, had interpreted the League as a shell-state that laws and agreements could turn into an instrument of pacific internationalism. He and others certainly underestimated the effect that the League's initial structure would have. The exceptions here, perhaps, are David Mitrany and, in a rather different way, H.N. Brailsford. Mitrany's lean towards functional government from 1933 and Brailsford's doubts about the effectiveness of the League stand out here. Both realised, as did Carr in *Conditions of Peace*, that the stress on national sovereignty in the League, and the lack of a clear international authority, severely weakened the effectiveness of the League.

Having said all of this, and despite the setbacks to their visions of a better world, the liberal socialist paradigm did accomplish much over the last eighty years. We now take for granted many of the changes to the international anarchy that they proposed. Specifically, we do now have a system of arbitration and conciliation for some orders of disputes. Although this system is not without its critics on both the left and the right, it has made certain grades of dispute international legal issues. Trade disputes are handled through a comprehensive trades dispute settlement mechanism in the World Trade Organization, which includes the use of trade sanctions in the last resort; some organisations and regional blocs, such as the EU and NAFTA, have courts or panels with jurisdiction over matters formerly regarded as domestic politics; while international conferences make laws on the environment, diplomatic practice or the conduct of war that signatory states feel bound to uphold. The fact that these judicial mechanisms often come in for criticism reinforces Leonard Woolf's warning that legal mechanisms tend to support the status quo, and consequently can bring their own dangerous conservative biases. Still, in the world today so many of the disputes that were, in the past, settled by war are now the subject of peaceful arbitration, conciliation or negotiation. A second point where the liberal socialist paradigm seems to be firmly in line with the trends of the time, especially in liberal Western societies, is the reaction against the use of war as an instrument of policy in all but the most extreme of circumstances. Much of the trend towards this position was a result of the agitation and writings of inter-war IR experts, and the presence of two Nobel Peace Prize laureates amongst our five authors (three if you include Arthur Henderson) is a demonstration of this. Finally, turning to David Mitrany, the liberal socialist paradigm also produced the functionalist approach that both explained and informed much of the global and regional integration that has happened over the last half-century. While certainly not without his critics, Mitrany's functional approach has been a major part of liberal and socialist alternatives to power politics since 1945.

Socialists and Liberals:
The Problems of a Social Democratic Foreign Policy

As befits the ambiguity of the terms socialist and liberal themselves, there is no agreement on whether Labour's foreign policy during the inter-war period was primarily liberal or socialist. Michael Gordon's interpretation of Labour's foreign policy between 1914 and 1965 is that socialism is a constant, and that it was the question of how to react to 'things as they are today', in Attlee's words, that divided the Party. It was the view of the long-term irreconcilability of capitalism and socialism that was the common feature of Labour's international thought. Labour's conflicts in the 1920s, therefore, are interpreted as differences within a broad socialist consensus, and it was only in the 1930s that these conflicts cut 'directly to fundamentals.'[74] Most other analysts of the period stress the liberal nature of Labour foreign policy, influenced by the Liberal recruits to Labour studied by Catherine Cline.[75] While giving a nod to the socialist influence on Labour foreign policy, this is largely the line that Rhiannon Vickers takes: 'by far the most important influence on Labour's foreign policy were liberal views of international relations.'[76] Interestingly, Konni Zilliacus' 1949 retrospective *I Choose Peace* even took the line that much Labour foreign policy was neither liberal nor socialist, but an immature continuation of Tory principles.[77] Interestingly, the possible liberal character of Labour foreign policy during the inter-war period did not necessarily mean that it was not a radical foreign policy. The tradition of foreign policy dissent in Britain had reached a high level of maturity in the nineteenth century under the tutelage of doctrinal liberals and Liberal Party members.[78] British liberal criticism of foreign affairs far exceeded much socialist opinion in the rest of the world in terms of its radical intent, and the Liberal Party links of many of the trade union leaders that had helped to found the Labour Representation Committee meant that the connections between a radical liberal foreign policy and Labour pre-dated Labour's existence as a separate party. In addition, as mentioned in chapter one, despite the use of the term socialism to define Labour's ideological position (its opponents, and even some friends, in the inter-war period often referred to them as the socialists), the Party formed in 1900 and radically overhauled in 1918 was always a coalition of radical forces that included socialists, but was not exclusively so.

Thus, not only was there a strong connection between the Labour Party and liberalism, broadly defined, but British liberalism in foreign affairs had always been a radical force frequently far ahead of the Liberal Party's domestic agenda. It is not surprising, therefore, that the most radical members of the Labour Party in foreign affairs came from a Liberal, and sometimes even a Tory, background. The pacifist wing of the Party included the two Buxtons and Arthur Ponsonby, all former Liberals. On the radical socialist fringe Stafford Cripps came from a Conservative Party family. E.D. Morel, the radical thorn in the side of Ramsay MacDonald during Labour's first government, was a former Liberal. Amongst Labour's international writers and supporters of the Party's League policy most were former Liberals.[79] Generally, the former Liberals took a consistently more radical line in foreign affairs than those from the pre-1914 Labour Party. They were also just, if not more likely, to refer to their position on foreign affairs as socialist. It is here that the confusion between a liberal and socialist foreign policy starts. What separates Michael Gordon's claim that Labour consistently followed a socialist foreign policy from those who argue that it was primarily liberal are, first, the problem of defining liberal and socialist, and second, the question of emphasis. Gordon's contention that the socialist core of Labour's foreign policy is that capitalism causes war seems on the face of it anti-liberal, but the theoretical centre of this argument, as discussed in chapter four and the section on Brailsford in chapter two, was the work of J.A. Hobson, himself a Liberal defector to Labour. Hobson, like many British liberals, was not necessarily opposed to the idea of free markets or private enterprise, but he was opposed to the power relations and distortions in wealth distribution caused by the booty capitalism that underpinned contemporary economic activity. H.N. Brailsford gave Hobson's analysis a more radical spin, expanding the sphere of what could be regarded as nefarious capitalism, but the core remained Hobson's. Yes this was a socialist position, but it was also liberal. Opposition within Labour's intellectuals to Hobson's view of capitalism was equally as strong. Both Norman Angell, who eventually left the Party, and Leonard Woolf, who did not, felt that the causes of war were more psychological and institutional.[80] Interestingly, as we saw in chapter four, so did Hobson in the 1930s. They were less willing to blame capitalism for war, seeing many businessmen as equally concerned about the threat of war to prosperity, but could accept that some capitalists could be belligerent. This is where the question of emphasis comes in. Labour's foreign policy had many voices, and when we combine this with the ambiguities in British politics between radical liberalism and socialism it is not difficult to construct an argument that claims that Labour's foreign policy was either socialist or liberal.

Gordon, Vickers and many others have dealt with these tensions in relation to the Party Leadership, its record in government and the discussions in Conference. An analysis of the arguments within Labour's intellectual ranks helps complete this picture. Many of the same arguments that they record from speeches and conference also appear in the work of the international experts. Just as there was a core of the leadership following a consistent policy of disarmament-arbitration-sanctions, and later confrontation with the dictators, so there was a consistent core of intellectuals forming a liberal socialist paradigm that broadly supported the policies of this leadership. This book, by and large, has been the story of those intellectuals and the political environment that they inhabited.

What can this tell us about the broader question of social democratic foreign policy? While this study is only a small part of the history of social democracy's attempt to reshape the world, it is the story of an important and influential group of social democratic international experts. Social democrats have often had problems formulating an international policy that would differentiate themselves from their conservative rivals for political power. The tendency to concentrate on domestic reform and to let foreign policy be dictated by narrow national self-interest is never far away. While the world has changed since the inter-war period, social democracy could benefit from a better acquaintance with the work of the intellectuals that did so much to shape the policy of the Labour Party. The work of the members of the Advisory Committee was an attempt to create a distinct social democratic policy that was both workable and consistent with their internationalist ideals. Certain aspects of global politics have changed over the intervening six decades, but social democrats still face the same problem of coming to terms with an international environment that is not friendly to their ideals. Whether we see these inter-war writers as ultimately successful or not is secondary to what we can learn from their story about the perennial problem of constructing a social democratic foreign policy in a world still dominated by inter-state politics and by the problem of war.

NOTES AND REFERENCES

Chapter 1

1 David Long and Peter Wilson (eds), *Thinkers of the Twenty Years' Crisis. Interwar Idealism Reassessed* (Oxford: Clarendon, 1995); David Long, *Towards a New Liberal Internationalism: The International Theory of J.A. Hobson* (Cambridge: Cambridge University Press, 1996); Lucian M. Ashworth, *Creating International Studies. Angell, Mitrany and the Liberal Tradition* (Aldershot: Ashgate, 1999); Lucian M. Ashworth and David Long (eds) *New Perspectives in International Functionalism* (Basingstoke: Macmillan, 1999); Peter Wilson, *The International Theory of Leonard Woolf. A Study in Twentieth-Century Idealism* (New York: Palgrave Macmillan, 2003); Peter Wilson, 'The Myth of the First Great Debate', *Review of International Studies*, xxiv/5 (1998) pp.1–15; Lucian M. Ashworth 'Did the Realist Idealist Great Debate Really Happen? A Revisionist History of International Relations', *International Relations* xvi/1 (2002), pp.33–51; Brian Schmidt, *The Political Discourse of Anarchy: A Disciplinary History of International Relations* (Albany: State University of New York Press, 1998).

2 Craig N. Murphy, *International Organization and Industrial Change. Global Governance since 1850* (Cambridge: Polity, 1994). See also the recently published book by Andrew Williams, *Liberalism and War* (London: Routledge, 2006).

3 Ian Hall, 'Power Politics and Political Appeasement: Political Realism in British International Thought 1935–1955', *British Journal of Politics and International Relations* viii (2006), pp.174–192; Casper Sylvest, 'Continuity and Change in British Liberal Internationalism', *Review of International Studies*, xxxi (2005), pp.263–283.

4 David Carlton, *MacDonald Versus Henderson. The Foreign Policy of the Second Labour Government* (London: Macmillan, 1970); John F. Naylor, *Labour's International Policy. The Labour Party in the 1930's* (London: Weidenfeld and Nicolson, 1969); Michael R. Gordon, *Conflict and Consensus in Labour's Foreign Policy 1914–1965* (Stanford: Stanford University Press, 1969); Henry R. Winkler, *Paths Not Taken. British Labour and International Policy in the 1920's* (Chapel Hill: University of North Carolina Press, 1994); John Swift, *Labour in Crisis. Clement Attlee and the Labour Party in Opposition 1931–40* (Basingstoke: Palgrave, 2001); Henry R. Winkler, *British Labour Seeks a Foreign Policy, 1900–1940* (Somerset NJ: Transaction, 2004); R.M. Douglas, *The Labour Party, Nationalism and Internationalism, 1939–1951* (London: Routledge, 2004); Rhiannon Vickers, *The Labour Party and the*

World: Volume 1. The Evolution of Labour's Foreign Policy 1900–1951 (Manchester: Manchester University Press, 2003).

5 Casper Sylvest, 'Interwar Internationalism, the British Labour Party, and the Historiography of International Relations', *International Studies Quarterly* xlviii/2 (2004), pp.409–432.

6 Wilson, *Leonard Woolf*, p.viii.

7 Long, *Towards a New Liberal Internationalism;* Peter Lamb, *Harold Laski. Problems of Democracy, the Sovereign State and International Society* (New York: Palgrave Macmillan, 2004).

8 Archie Potts, *Zilliacus: A life for Peace and Socialism* (London: Merlin Press, 2002).

9 I say at least because an accurate list of committee members is not possible owing to the fluidity of membership. While the numbers of non-MPs that were members was controlled, all members of the Parliamentary Labour Party were entitled to join. As a result, there may have been other women on the Advisory Committee from time to time.

10 I have not yet been able to identify this member. Her name appears in a number of Advisory Committee lists.

11 Dorothy Frances Buxton, *The War for Coal and Iron* (London: Labour Party, 1921).

12 Catherine Ann Cline, *Recruits to Labour. The British Labour Party 1914–1931* (New York: Syracuse University Press, 1963), pp.71–2.

13 Sylvest uses the same reference to Butterfield and Whig histories: 'Interwar Internationalism'.

14 Ashworth, *Creating International Studies*, chapter 5; Ashworth, 'Did the Realist-Idealist Great Debate Really Happen?'. .

15 On this topic see also Wilson, 'Myth of the First Great Debate'; and Wilson, *International Theory of Leonard Woolf*, chapter 2.

16 Wilson, *International Theory of Leonard Woolf*, chapter 2.

17 James Ramsay MacDonald, *The Socialist Movement* (London: Williams and Norgate, 1911), p.ix.

18 Leonard Woolf, 'Introduction', in Leonard Woolf (ed.), *The Framework of a Lasting Peace* (London: George Allen & Unwin, 1917), pp.57–8. See also the discussion of Woolf's antipathy to the term utopian in Wilson, *International Theory of Leonard Woolf*, pp.31–2.

19 H.N. Brailsford, 'False Road to Security'' *New Leader*, 23 March 1923, p.4; and 'The Other France. A Realistic Study of the Outlook', *New Leader*, 15 February 1924, p.9.

20 H.N. Brailsford, *Olives of Endless Age. Being a Study of this Distracted World and its Need of Unity* (New York & London: Harper, 1928), chapter XIV.

21 H.N. Brailsford, *After the Peace* (London: Parsons, 1920), p.32.

22 Alfred Zimmern, 'I Have Joined the Labour Party' *New Leader*, 15 August 1924, pp.3–4.

23 J.A. Hobson, 'Is America Moving?', *Foreign Affairs*, July 1923, p.3.

24 C. Delisle Burns, 'British Foreign Policy – The Next Moves', *Foreign Affairs*, July 1924, p.9.

25 H.M. Swanwick, 'An Alternative Policy to the Draft Treaty of Mutual Assistance', *Foreign Affairs*, March 1924, p.171.

26 Letter from David Mitrany to William Gillies dated 15 May 1925, p.3. James Ramsay MacDonald Papers, Public Records Office, Kew, London. PRO 3069.

27 C. Delisle Burns, *International Politics* (London: Methuen, 1920). This text, written by a member of the Advisory Committee, was used by Philip Noel Baker when he taught IR at the London School of Economics.

28 See Hugh Dalton, *Towards the Peace of Nations. A Study in International Politics* (London: Routledge, 1928). The influence of Dalton's book can be gauged by how frequently it was quoted in memoranda and articles at the time.

29 David Mitrany, *The Problem of International Sanctions* (London: Humphrey Milford & OUP, 1925).

30 Philip Noel Baker, *Disarmament* (London: Hogarth, 1926); and *The Geneva Protocol* (London: Bell, 1925).

31 William Arnold-Forster, *Arbitrate! Arbitrate! Arbitrate! The Case for All-Inclusive Pacific Settlement of International Disputes* (London: Labour Party, 1927).

32 James T. Shotwell, War as an Instrument of National Policy and its Renunciation in the Pact of Paris (London: Constable, 1929).

33 F.E. Smith, 'Idealism in International Politics' in William Camp, *The Glittering Prizes. A Biographical Study of F.E. Smith First Earl of Birkenhead* (London: MacGibbon and Kee, 1960), pp.207–8.

34 Ibid. pp.208–10.

35 Ibid. pp.213.

36 Ibid. pp.216.

37 H. N. Brailsford, 'A Socialist Foreign Policy', in Christopher Addison *et al, Problems of a Socialist Government* (London: Victor Gollancz, 1933), pp.285–286.

38 Maurice Bourquin (ed.), *Collective Security. A Record of the Seventh and Eighth International Studies Conference. Paris 1934-London 1935* (Paris: International Institute of Intellectual Cooperation, 1936), pp.458–9.

39 E.H. Carr, *International Relations Between the Two World Wars (1919–1939)* (London: Macmillan, 1948), p.5. Originally written in 1937.

40 Salvador de Madariaga, *The World's Design* (London: Allen and Unwin, 1938), p.54, pp.82–5, p.125.

41 Leonard Woolf, *Barbarians at the Gate* (London: Victor Gollancz, 1939), p.61.

42 Leonard Woolf, *The International Post-War Settlement* (London: Fabian Society and Victor Gollancz, 1944), p.11.

43 See, for example, Leonard Woolf, 'The Future of the Small State', *The Political Quarterly* xiv/3 (1943), p.221.

44 A.L. Rowse, 'The End of an Epoch', in A.L. Rowse, *The End of an Epoch. Reflections on Contemporary History* (London: Macmillan, 1947), p.69.

45 Michael Foot, 'Introduction', in Konni Zilliacus, *The Mirror of the Past* (London: Victor Gollancz, 1944), pp.13–4. Interestingly, though Foot lumps Carr in with these conservatives, Carr was not an advocate of a return to pre-1914 diplomacy. See, for example, Carr's *Conditions of Peace* (London: MacMillan, 1942).

46 See also, the introduction to Carr's, *Conditions of Peace*. Here Carr again views the supporters of the League and collective security as conservatives protecting the order of the status quo powers.

47 H.N. Brailsford, for example, preferred to refer to his tradition of thought as socialist. See his contributions to Henry Brinton (ed.), *Does Capitalism Cause War?* (London: H & E.R. Brinton, 1935), p.18, p.37, pp.40–1.

48 A.L. Rowse, 'The Prospects of the Labour Party', in Rowse, *The End of an Epoch*, p.112.

49 E.H. Carr, *The Twenty Years' Crisis* (London: Macmillan, 1939), especially pp.278–282.

50 E.H. Carr, *Nationalism and After* (London: Macmillan, 1945), pp.47–74.

51 Ashworth, *Creating International Studies*, chapter 5; Wilson, *International Theory of Leonard Woolf*, chapter 2.

52 John H. Herz, *Political Realism and Political Idealism: A Study in Theories and Realities* (Chicago: University of Chicago Press, 1951); Herbert Butterfield, 'The Scientific Versus the Moralistic Approach in International Affairs' *International Affairs* xxvii/4 (1951), pp.411–22; Arnold Wolfers, 'The Pole of Power and the Pole of Indifference' in James N. Rosenau (ed.), *International Politics and Foreign Policy. A Reader in Research and Theory* (New York: Free Press, 1969), pp.176–9; Martin Griffiths, *Realism, Idealism and International Politics* (London: Routledge, 1992).

53 Socialist Union, *Socialism and Foreign Policy* (London: Book House, 1953), especially chapter 1.

54 Hedley Bull, 'The Theory of International Politics', 1919–1969' in Brian Porter (ed.), *The Aberystwyth Papers: International Politics 1919–1969* (London: Oxford University Press, 1972), 33–6.

55 Kenneth W. Thompson, 'Idealism and Realism: Beyond the Great Debate', *British Journal of International Studies* iii/2 (1977), pp.199–209.

56 Trevor Taylor, 'Utopianism', in Steve Smith (ed.), *International Relations: British and American Approaches* (Oxford: Basil Blackwell, 1985), pp.92–107; John Vasquez, *The Power of Power Politics: A Critique* (London: Francis Pinter, 1983), pp.13–19.

57 For Angell's rationalism and Mitrany's scepticism about the use of reason in politics see Ashworth, *Creating International Studies*. Mitrany was influenced here by Graham Wallas' views on reason and politics.

58 J. Ann Tickner, 'Hans Morgenthau's Principles of Political Realism: A Feminist Reformulation', *Millennium: Journal of International Studies* xvii/3 (1988), p.433.

59 A.J.R. Groom and William C. Olson, *International Relations Then and Now: Origins and Trends in Interpretation* (London: HarperCollins, 1991), pp.73–4.

60 Ibid. p.69.

61 Ibid. p.93.

62 Wilson also criticises Olsen and Groom's interpretation. See Wilson, *International Theory of Leonard Woolf*, pp.14–5.

63 Michael Banks, 'The Inter-Paradigm Debate' in Margot Light and A.J.R. Groom (eds), *International Relations. A Handbook of Current Theory* (Boulder: Lynne Rienner, 1985), p.10; James E. Dougherty and Robert L. Pfaltzgraff, *Contending Theories of International Relations. A Comprehensive Survey* (New York: Harper and Row, 1990), p.6–7; Steve Smith, 'Paradigm Dominance in International Relations: The Development of International Relations as a Social Science', *Millennium: Journal of International Studies* xvi/2 (1987), p.192; James Der Derian, 'Introduction: Critical Investigations', in James Der Derian (ed.), *International Theory. Critical Investigations* (Basingstoke: Macmillan, 1995), p.1.

64 Steve Smith, 'The Self-Images of a Discipline: A Genealogy of International Relations Theory', in Ken Booth and Steve Smith (eds), *International Relations Theory Today* (Oxford: Polity, 1995), p.14.

65 Wilson, *International Theory of Leonard Woolf*, p.20.

66 This was the main theme in his pre-war classic *The Great Illusion* (Norman Angell, *The Great Illusion. A Study of the Relation of MilitaryPower in Nations to their*

Economic and Social Advantage (Toronto: McClelland and Goodchild, 1911).) He returned to this theme regularly. See, for example, his summary of his ideas in Norman Angell, 'The International Anarchy', in Leonard Woolf (ed.), *The Intelligent Man's Way to Prevent War* (London: Victor Gollancz, 1933), pp.19–66.

67 Letter from David Mitrany to H.N. Brailsford, 14 September 1945; Letter from H.N. Brailsford to David Mitrany to H.N. Brailsford, 23 September 1945; Letter from David Mitrany to H.N. Brailsford, 25 September 1945. From the Mitrany Papers at the British Library of Political and Economic Sciences, London School of Economics.

68 H.N. Brailsford, *Property or Peace?* (London: Gollancz, 1934).

69 David Mitrany, *The Progress of International Government* (London: Allen & Unwin, 1933).

70 See, for example, Leonard Woolf, *Empire and Commerce in Africa. A Study in Economic Imperialism* (London: Labour Research Department and George Allen & Unwin, 1920), especially his final chapter on the future of Africa. See Wilson, *International Theory of Leonard Woolf,* pp.115–6.

71 See, for example his popular, *The League of Nations at Work* (London: Nisbet, 1927).

72 See Noel Baker, *Geneva Protocol.* For Noel Baker's work on the Labour Party's policy on war aims during the Second World War see chapter five.

73 See his *The Fruits of Victory* (New York: Garland 1972), especially pp.61–70 and pp.300–1. Originally published in 1921. See also his *Preface to Peace. A Guide for the Plain Man* (London: Hamish Hamilton, 1935).

74 See Norman Angell, *The Public Mind. Its Disorders: Its Explanation* (London: Noel Douglas, 1926).

75 See his contributions to Henry Brinton (ed.) *Does Capitalism Cause War?* (Maidstone: H & E.R. Brinton, 1935), pp.13–19, pp.37–41. This was an edited collection of an exchange of letters in *The New Statesman* between 9 Febuary and the 6 April 1935.

76 David Mitrany, *A Working Peace System. An Argument for the Functional Development of International Organisation* (London: Royal Institute for International Affairs/ Oxford University Press, 1943).

77 Hans J. Morgenthau, 'Introduction' in David Mitrany, *A Working Peace System* (Chicago: Quadrangle, 1966).

78 See the argument in Ashworth, *Creating International Studies,* 38–41 and chapter 4.

79 Noel Baker, *Geneva Protocol.*

80 Noel Baker, *League of Nations at Work,* pp.128–34.

81 See Wilson's discussion on this point in *International Theory of Leonard Woolf,* pp.73–4.

82 Leonard Woolf, 'Utopia and Reality', *Political Quarterly* xi/2 (1940), p.167.

83 See the discussion of his argument in *The Great Illusion* in Ashworth, *Creating International Studies,* pp.112–3.

84 See especially his *The Public Mind,* quoted above.

85 Leonard Woolf, *The War for Peace* (London: Routledge, 1940).

86 Ashworth, *Creating International Studies,* chapter 4.

87 See his analysis of British foreign policy in H. N. Brailsford, 'The Tory Policy of Peace', *The Political Quarterly* ix/3 (1938), pp.325–33.

88 *League of Nations at Work,* especially p.131.

89 Lorna Lloyd, 'Philip Noel Baker and Peace Through Law', in Long and Wilson, *Thinkers of the Twenty Years' Crisis*, pp.47–8.

90 Rowse, *End of an Epoch*, p.292.

91 For reasons internal to the debates within the Labour Party, and to the changes within Labour Party policy, I have slightly modified these periods in the following chapters.

92 For example, Brailsford wrote of 'the differences that divide Socialists from Sir Norman Angell'. In Brinton, *Does Capitalism Cause War*, p.13.

93 See, for example, my own *Creating International Studies*, p.125.

94 Zilliacus, *Mirror of the Past*, pp.281–2.

95 Hans J. Morgenthau 'Another "Great Debate": The National Interest of the United States", *The American Political Science Review* xlvi/4 (1952), p.961.

96 There is nothing new about this argument. I have been making this argument since my 1995 PhD thesis, while Peter Wilson, independently, has made the point in a number of places, and especially his 'The Myth of the First Great Debate' article quoted above.

97 A.J.P. Taylor, *The Troublemakers. Dissent Over Foreign Policy 1792–1939* (London: Panther, 1969). Originally published in 1957.

98 Ibid. p.181.

99 Ibid. p.181.

100 Ibid. p.170.

101 James Jupp, *The Radical Left in Britain. 1931–1941* (London: Frank Cass, 1982), p.18.

102 MacDonald, *The Socialist Movement*, p.235

103 Vickers, *Labour Party and the World*, p.58.

104 See Cline, *Recruits to Labour.*

105 H.N. Brailsford, 'A Parliament of the League of Nations' Advisory Committee on International Questions memo no. 44, January 1919. Labour Party Archives, Manchester.

106 Winkler, *Paths not Taken*, pp.34–5.

107 Ibid. pp.40–1.

108 Quoted in Konni Zilliacus, *I Choose Peace* (Harmondsworth: Penguin, 1949), p.341.

109 See the full text of the 1906 manifesto in F. W. S. Craig, *British General Election Manifestos 1900–1974* (Basingstoke: Macmillan, 1975), p.10. Admittedly the whole manifesto only contained twelve points, most of them only one sentence long, so the scant regard to foreign affairs is not as glaring as it might first appear. Compared to the place of foreign affairs in later manifestos, however, it is still a tiny proportion of the whole.

110 MacDonald, *Socialist Movement.*

111 Rhiannon Vickers discusses this myth, even quoting Ernest Bevin's condemnation of this myth to the 1958 Party Conference. Vickers, *Labour Party and the World*, pp.3–4.

112 For example, in their proposed resolution on the link between unemployment and indemnities, the Advisory Committee wrote: 'The causes of the industrial crisis through which this country is passing lie, for the most part, abroad.' Copy of 1921? resolution found in J.S. Middleton's papers, JSM/INT/52. See also 'How Mr Lloyd George has Killed the Coal Trade' 1921 Labour Party leaflet. Labour Party Archives, Manchester; and Buxton, *The War for Coal and Iron.*

113 An early example of this was G[eorge] Y[oung], 'Memorandum on the Reform of the Foreign Services' Advisory Committee on International Questions, no.10, July 1918. George Young, a former diplomat, followed this up with further memoranda on the democratisation of the foreign services in 1920 and 1921.

114 Undated and untitled memo, probably written for the first Advisory Committee meeting in 1918. Found at the beginning of the first box of Advisory Committee memoranda, Labour Party Archives, Manchester.

115 Vickers, *Labour Party and the World*, p.5.

116 Ibid. pp.6–8

117 Ibid. p.5.

118 See Angell, *The Public Mind*.

119 Labour Party, *Report of the Eighteenth Annual Conference* (London: Labour Party, 1918), p.141. The full 1918 Constitution is reprinted side-by-side the old 1914 Constitution in G.D.H. Cole, *A History of the Labour Party from 1914* (London: Routledge & Kegan Paul, 1948), pp.71–81. The international objective quoted here is the seventh of seven 'Party Objectives' laid out in article 3 of the 1918 Constitution.

120 David Powell, *British Politics, 1910–35. The Crisis of the Party System* (London: Routledge, 2004), p.106.

121 David Mitrany, 'The Making of the Functional Theory. A Memoir' in *The Functional Theory of Politics* (London: LSE and Martin Robertson, 1975), pp.7–8.

122 Supplement to the letter of invitation to serve on the Advisory Committee, from Arthur Henderson to Leonard Woolf, 26th March 1918. Leonard Woolf Papers. University of Sussex.

123 On 8 December 1920 the Advisory Committee on International Questions recommended that their memoranda 'be filed in the House of Commons' in order to facilitate closer cooperation between the Committee and the Parliamentary Party. Letter from the Advisory Committee to J.S. Middleton, Assistant Secretary to the Labour Party, dated 14 December 1920. Labour Party Archives, Manchester. JSM/INT/48. This had already been recommended to the Executive five months before: 'Letter to the Executive Committee', Advisory Committee on International Questions memo no.149a, July 1920. Labour Party Archives, Manchester.

124 Memoranda of the Advisory Committee on International Questions, Labour Party Archives, Manchester.

125 Ibid.

126 Minutes of the Meeting of the Advisory Committee on International Questions, 19 November 1920. Leonard Woolf Papers, University of Sussex.

127 An agenda for a meeting scheduled for 27th April 1922 recorded that 'Owing to the lack of attendance the meeting of the above committee, called for April 6, did not take place.' Leonard Woolf Papers.

128 Leonard Woolf, *Downhill all the Way. An Autobiography of the Years 1919–1939* (London: Hogarth, 1967), p.221.

129 Minutes of the meeting of the Advisory Committee on International Questions 22 June 1921. Held at the Royal Albion Hotel, Brighton. From the Leonard Woolf Papers.

130 In April 1921, for example the Committee drafted four leaflets that were used by the Executive: 'Labour's Policy for a True League of Nations', 'Why Labour Opposes Economic Imperialism', 'How Lloyd George has Killed the Coal

Trade' and 'Labour's Policy on the Peace Treaty'. Advisory Committee Memoranda, Labour Party Archives, Manchester.

131 John F. Naylor of Harvard University, notes on interview with Leonard Woolf, 24 July 1962. From the Leonard Woolf Papers.

132 Winkler, *Paths not Taken*, p.25.

133 Ibid. p.2.

134 Labour Party, *Report of the Twentieth Annual Conference* (London: Labour Party, 1920), p.39.

135 Letter from Hugh Dalton to Leonard Woolf, 29th April 1937. From the Leonard Woolf Papers.

136 Letter from J.S. Middleton to Leonard Woolf, 25 November 1943. Leonard Woolf Papers.

137 Norman Angell, *After All* (London: Hamish Hamilton, 1951), 238–44; Woolf, *Downhill all the Way*, 241–2.

138 Letter from James Ramsay MacDonald to Arthur Henderson, 30 March 1925. National Archives PRO 30/69 1170(II) 593–7; Letter from James Ramsay MacDonald's secretary to William Gillies, 9 April 1925. National Archives PRO 30/69 1170(II) p.469.

139 Note from J.S. Middleton to William Gillies, 17th December 1929. J. S. Middleton Papers, Labour Party Archives, Manchester. JSM/INT/78.

140 Angell, *After All*, p.239.

141 Mitrany, 'Making of the Functional Theory' pp.8–9.

142 Cline, *Recruits to Labour*, p.70.

143 Letter from William Gillies to Leonard Woolf, 13 September 1939. Leonard Woolf Papers.

144 See the correspondence between Morgan Phillips and H.R.G. Greaves on the future of the Advisory Committee in the box marked Advisory Committee on International Affairs minutes (1929–39; 1944–5), Labour Party Archives, Manchester.

145 Letter from Morgan Phillips to members of the Advisory Committee on Imperial Questions, no date but sent out in early 1950, in the box marked Advisory Committee on Imperial Questions Minutes (1924–49), Labour Party Archives, Manchester.

Chapter 2

1 Hugh Dalton, *Call Back Yesterday. Memoirs 1887–1931* (London: Frederick Muller, 1953), p.156.

2 Wilson, *International Theory of Leonard Woolf*, p.vi.

3 F.M. Leventhal, *The Last Dissenter: H.N. Brailsford and his World* (Oxford: Clarendon, 1985).

4 Ibid. p.1.

5 Michael Foot, 'The Knight Errant of Socialism', *Tribune,* 28 March 1958; Kingsley Martin, 'H. N. Brailsford', *New Statesman*, 29 March 1958, pp.403–4.

6 H.N. Brailsford, *Macedonia. Its Races and their Future* (London: Methuen, 1906), p.xi.

7 Ibid. pp.x–xi.

8 Ibid. pp.322–7.

9 Ibid. pp.332.

10 See Leventhal, *Last Dissenter*, p.4.

11 Brailsford acknowledged his great debt to Hobson's ideas in his 1947 L.T. Hobhouse Memorial Trust Lecture at the LSE. This was republished as, *The Life-Work of J.A. Hobson* (London: Oxford University Press, 1948).

12 J.A. Hobson, *Imperialism: A Study* (London: Nisbet, 1902). These ideas remained central to Hobson's view of international affairs. See J. A. Hobson, 'Thoughts on our Present Discontents', *Political Quarterly* ix/1 (1938), pp.47–57. For an in-depth study of Hobson's ideas see Long, *Towards a New Liberal Internationalism*.

13 H.N. Brailsford, *The War of Steel and Gold. A Study of the Armed Peace* (London: Bell, 1917), p.29. Originally published in 1914.

14 Ibid. pp.31–2.

15 The role of nationalism as an ideological facilitator is discussed in detail from p.182 onwards.

16 Ibid. pp.65–74.

17 Ibid. p.72.

18 Ibid. p.163.

19 See the discussion of *The Great Illusion* in chapter 4.

20 H.N. Brailsford, *A League of Nations* (London: Hedley, 1917), p.60.

21 Ibid. p.70.

22 Ibid. p.267.

23 Ibid. p.287.

24 Brailsford, 'A Parliament of the League of Nations', p.2. See also Brailsford, *League of Nations*, pp.312–3; and his appendix to the 1917 edition of *The War of Steel and Gold* entitled 'a Sketch of a Federal League', which advocated parliamentary representation in the League.

25 'Short Statement of War Aims', Advisory Committee on International Questions memo no. 6, 25 June 1918, p.1. Labour Party Archives, Manchester; Appendix 2 'Manifesto of the Committee of Action of the Berne International Labour and Socialist Conference', in Arthur Henderson, *The Peace Terms* (London: Labour Party, 1919), p.12.

26 H.N. Brailsford, *Our Settlement with Germany* (Harmondsworth: Penguin, 1944), pp.137–8.

27 Brailsford, 'A Parliament of the League of Nations', p.2.

28 *Last Dissenter*, p.163.

29 Brailsford, *After the Peace*, p.29.

30 Ibid. p.32.

31 Brailsford, *Olives of Endless Age*, p.48

32 See Leventhal, *Last Dissenter*, p.185.

33 H.N. Brailsford, 'Arbitrate or Disarm. A New View of Security', *New Leader*, 12 September 1924, pp.3–4.

34 *After the Peace*, p.160.

35 Brailsford, *Olives of Endless Age*, chapter X.

36 H.N. Brailsford in *New Statesman*, 7 September 1935.

37 H.N. Brailsford, *Towards a New League* (London: New Statesman and Nation, 1936), pp.3–4, pp.45–7.

38 Brailsford, 'Tory Policy of Peace', pp.325–33.

39 Leventhal, *Last Dissenter*, p.257.

40 *Olives of Endless Age*, especially the summary of his argument from p.48 onwards.

41 Brailsford, 'A Socialist Foreign Policy', p.278.

42 Ibid. pp.279–80.

43 Ibid. p.282.

44 Brailsford, *Towards a New League*, p.60.

45 Brailsford, 'A Socialist Foreign Policy', pp.282–3; Brailsford, *Towards a New League*, p.60.

46 Brailsford, *Towards a New League*, pp.61–4.

47 Dalton, *Towards the Peace of Nations*, p.17.

48 Brailsford, *Life-work of J. A. Hobson*, pp.26–7.

49 See Leventhal, *Last Dissenter*, p.223.

50 Mitrany, 'The Making of the Functional Theory', in David Mitrany, *The Functional Theory of Politics* (London: LSE & Martin Robertson, 1975), p.36.

51 Letter from H.N. Brailsford to David Mitrany, 14 September 1945, p.2. Mitrany Papers, British Library of Political and Economic Sciences, LSE, London.

52 Brailsford, *Our Settlement with Germany,* p.134–6.

53 Brailsford's comments on Daivd Mitrany's talk to the Fabian International Bureau's weekend conference on international security, 8–9 January 1944, pp.55–6. Mitrany Papers, British Library of Political and Economic Sciences, LSE, London.

54 *Our Settlement with Germany*, p.135.

55 *Olives of Endless Age*, p.32.

56 Undated and untitled memo, probably written for the first Advisory Committee meeting in 1918. Found at the beginning of the first box of Advisory Committee memoranda. Labour Party Archives, Manchester.

57 Margaret MacMillan, *Peacemakers. The Paris Conference of 1919 and its Attempt to End War* (London: John Murray, 2001), p.20.

58 Norman Angell, 'Peace Terms', Advisory Committee on International Questions memo no. 61, May 1919, 6. Labour Party Archives, Manchester.

59 George Young, 'Memorandum on the Reform of the Foreign Services'.

60 'Short Statement of War Aims'.

61 Halford J Mackinder. 'Geographical Pivot of History', *Geographical Journal* xxiii (1904), pp.421–37.

62 Halford J. Mackinder, *Democratic Ideals and Reality: A Study in the Politics of Reconstruction* (London: Constable, 1919).

63 Angell, *The Great Illusion*, pp.82–7.

64 *Great Illusion*, p.79.

65 Buxton, *The War for Coal and Iron*, pp.3–4, pp.6–9. Originally Advisory Committee on International Questions memo no. 196. See also the Labour Party leaflet, prepared by the Advisory Committee, entitled 'How Mr Lloyd George has Killed the Coal Trade', prepared in April 1921. Labour Party Archives, Manchester

66 For a left-of-centre contemporary analysis of the problem facing the coal Industry and the miners' union see Adolf Sturmthal, *The Tragedy of European Labour 1918-1939* (London: Victor Gollancz, 1944), pp.90–6.

67 War for Coal and Iron, pp.8–12.

68 David Mitrany, 'Memorandum on Labour Policy Concerning Commissions to be Set up Under the Peace Treaty', Advisory Committee on International Questions memo no. 125, January 1920. Labour Party Archives, Manchester.

69 Leonard Woolf, 'Punishment and Reparation at the End of the War', Advisory Committee on International Questions memo no. 37, November 1918. Labour Party Archives, Manchester.

70 J.A. Hobson, 'Economic War After the War', Advisory Committee on International Questions memo no. 24, undated, p.2. Labour Party Archives, Manchester.

71 'Draft Pamphlet on Foreign Policy', Advisory Committee on International Affairs memo no.228a, 1921, pp.1–2. Labour Party Archives, Manchester.

72 See, for example, H.N. Brailsford, 'Too Many Germans', *New Leader*, 20 October 1922, pp.5–6.

73 *War for Coal and Iron*, p.14.

74 E.D. Morel, 'No Peace Without Truth', *New Leader*, 19 September 1924, p.4.

75 The Labour Party, *Report of the Nineteenth Annual Conference 1919* (London: Labour Party, 1919), p.142.

76 See for example, the addendum to Norman Angell's *Peace Terms* memo.

77 'Short Statement on War Aims', p.2.

78 'Letter to the Executive Committee'.

79 Leonard Woolf, 'Proposals for the Immediate Establishment by the Allies of a League of Nations', Advisory Committee on International Questions memo no. 5, June 1918. Labour Party Archives, Manchester.

80 G. Lowes Dickinson, 'A League of Nations', Advisory Committee on International Questions memo no. 27, 22 October 1918. Labour Party Archives, Manchester.

81 Brailsford, 'A Parliament of the League of Nations', p.1.

82 Brailsford, 'A Parliament of the League of Nations' p.2.

83 E. D. Morel, 'Why the League Fails', *Foreign Affairs* v/4 (1923), p.70.

84 'Short Statement of War Aims', p.2. See also the flyer prepared by the Advisory Committee for the Labour Party: 'Why Labour Opposes Economic Imperialism', April 1921. Originally Advisory Committee on International Questions memo no 202. Labour Party Archives, Manchester.

85 'Short Statement of War Aims', p.2; 'Draft Pamphlet on Foreign Policy', p.15. See also Leonard Woolf, *Mandates and Empire* (London: League of Nations Union, 1920), pp.17–8; and Leonard Woolf, *Empire and Commerce in Africa,* p.358.

86 Leonard Woolf, 'Colonies', Advisory Committee on International Questions memo no. 23, September 1918, p.1. Labour Party Archives, Manchester.

87 Woolf, 'Colonies', 2; 'Short Statement of War Aims', p.2.

88 Woolf, 'Colonies', p.2.

89 Quoted in Woolf, 'Colonies', p.1.

90 'Draft Pamphlet on Foreign Policy', p.15.

91 For a discussion of the conflicts between the French delegation and the Anglo-American delegations in Paris on this issue see Macmillan, *Peacemakers*, pp.108–9.

92 'Draft Pamphlet on Foreign Policy', p.15. For this cautious enthusiasm see also Leonard Woolf, *Scope of the Mandates Under the League of Nations* (London: C.F. Roworth, 1921).

93 Woolf, 'Proposals for the Immediate Establishment'.

94 'Draft Pamphlet on Foreign Policy' pp.7–8; Leonard Woolf, 'The League of Nations and Disarmament', Advisory Committee on International Questions memo no. 25?, 1922, p.1. Labour Party Archives, Manchester.

95 'Labour and the League of Nations', Advisory Committee on International Questions memo no. 207a, May 1921, p.1. Labour Party Archives, Manchester.

96 Ibid. p.1.

97 Norman Angell, 'The Crux of our Foreign Policy', *New Leader*, 25 January 1924, p.9.

98 Morel, 'No Peace Without Truth', p.4.

99 E.D. Morel, *The Horror on the Rhine* (London: UDC 1921).

100 *Recruits to Labour*, p.79. For a fuller discussion of this 'black horror on the Rhine' moral panic see Robert C. Reinders, 'Racialism on the Left: E.D. Morel and the "Black Horror on the Rhine"', *International Review of Social History* xiii (1968), p.1.

101 H.N. Brailsford, 'Draft Memorandum on Disarmament', Advisory Committee on International Questions memo no. 198, April 1921, p.1. Labour Party Archives, Manchester.

102 Ibid. p.2.

103 Ibid. p.2.

104 Swanwick, 'An Alternative Policy to the Draft Treaty of Mutual Assistance', p.171.

105 'Labour Party Policy Concerning the Commissions', p.1.

106 Hobson, 'Economic War After the War'.

107 *War for Coal and Iron*, pp.1–3.

108 *War for Coal and Iron*, pp.2–3.

109 *War for Coal and Iron*, p.3, pp.4–5, pp.6–7.

110 MacMillan, *Peacemakers*, p.109.

111 Ibid. chapters 13–6.

112 Carr, *International Relations Between the Two World Wars*, p.9.

113 Chapter VII, 'The Control of Policy', *War of Steel and Gold*, pp.198–218.

114 See especially his seminal work, *Democracy and Diplomacy. A Plea for Popular Control of Foreign Policy* (London: Methuen, 1915).

115 Young, 'Reform of the Foreign Services'; *Labour Party, Control of Foreign Policy: Labour's Programme* (London: Labour Party, 1920?); George Young, 'The Reform of Diplomacy. A practical Programme', Advisory Committee on International Questions, May 1921. Labour Party Archives, Manchester.

116 'Open Diplomacy', Draft for insertion in pamphlet on Foreign Policy, Advisory Committee on International Questions memo no. 228(a), 1921. Labour Party Archives, Manchester.

117 Ponsonby, *Democracy and Diplomacy*, especially chapters 1–3.

118 *Control of Foreign Policy*, p.1.

119 See, for example, the first paragraph of *Control of Foreign Policy*, p.1.

120 *Control of Foreign Policy*, 2; Arthur Ponsonby, 'Popular or Parliamentary Control of Foreign Policy', Advisory Committee on International Questions memo no. 256, 1922, 1. Labour Party Archives, Manchester.

121 Young, 'Reform of the Foreign Services', p.10; 'Open Diplomacy', p.1; and *Control of Foreign Policy*, p.4.

122 Brailsford, *War of Steel and Gold*, pp.211–5; Ponsonby, *Democracy and Diplomacy*, chapter 8. In fact arguments for the creation of a Parliamentary foreign affairs committee even pre-dated these studies. See Philip Morrell, 'The Control of Foreign Affairs. The Need for a Parliamentary Committee', *The Contemporary Review*, November 1912, p.563, pp.659–67.

123 Young, 'Reform of the Foreign Services', p.11; *Control of Foreign Policy*, p.2.

124 'Open Diplomacy', p.1.

125 *Control of Foreign Policy*, pp.4–5.

126 Young, 'Reform of the Foreign Services', 11; *Control of Foreign Policy*, pp.2–3; and 'Open Diplomacy', p.1; Ponsonby, 'Popular or Parliamentary Control', p.1.

127 The full text of the original Ponsonby Rule can be found in *Hansard* H.C. Deb. (1924) 171, c.1999–2005. For a more bare-bones mention of this see *Vickers, Labour Party and the World*, p.86.

128 See Brailsford's discussion of the Levantine Consular Service in his *War of Steel and Gold*, pp.215–6.

129 Young, 'Reform of the Foreign Services', p.1.

130 Young, 'Reform of the Foreign Services' pp.2–5; Young, 'Reform of Diplomacy', pp.6–7.

131 Young, 'Reform of Diplomacy', pp.7–9.

132 Young, 'Reform of Diplomacy', p.9.

133 'Reform of Diplomacy', 4–5; *Control of Foreign Policy*, p.5.

134 *Control of Foreign Policy*, pp.5–6.

135 'Reform of Diplomacy', p.9.

136 'Reform of Diplomacy', pp.8–9.

137 'The Foreign Office and Labour Governments', Advisory Committee on International Questions memo no. 333d, 1925. Labour Party Archives, Manchester.

138 Letter from James Ramsay MacDonald to Arthur Henderson, 30 March 1925. Public Record Office PRO 30/69 1170(II) 593–7; Letter from James Ramsay MacDonald's secretary to William Gillies, 9 April 1925. Public Record Office PRO 30/69 1170(II) 469

139 Letter from James Ramsay MacDonald to Philip Noel Baker, 25 May 1925. Ramsay MacDonald Papers, Public Record Office PRO 30/69 1170(I) 43–4.

140 Quoted in Winkler, *Paths not Taken*, p.54.

141 George Lansbury, *My Life* (London: Constable, 1928), p.214.

142 George Lansbury, 'To the Electors of Bow and Bromley', electoral flyer for the 1935 General Election, 2–3. Paper no. 361, George Lansbury Papers, British Library of Political and Economic Science, London School of Economics and Political Science, London.

143 'I wish I had as much faith & hope in Christianity as you have!' Letter from Arthur Ponsonby to George Lansbury, 22 October 1933. George Lansbury Papers, British Library of Political and Economic Science, London School of Economics and Political Science. Emphasis in the original.

144 Cline, Recruits to Labour, p.93.

145 See Arthur Ponsonby, The Covenant of the League of Nations (London, 1920).

146 Arthur Ponsonby, 'Disarmament by Example' *The Contemporary Review*, December 1927, p.690.

147 Letter from Charles Roden Buxton to Arthur Greenwood, dated 27 July 1937, WG/PCE/120i; and letter from Charles Roden Buxton to William Gillies, dated 27 July 1937, William Gilllies Papers WG/PCE/122i. Labour Party Archives, Manchester.

148 See, for example, H.M. Swanwick *New Wars for Old* (London: Women's International League, 1934); and H.M. Swanwick *Collective Insecurity* (London: Jonathan Cape, 1937).

149 See, for example, William Gillies' report on the Party Annual conference in 1923, where an ILP member proposed a blanket opposition to the Estimates: 'British Labour's Foreign Policy', *Foreign Affairs* v/2 (1923), p.31.

150 Quoted in Chris Wrigley, *Arthur Henderson* (Cardiff: GPC Books, 1990), p.177.

151 Labour Party, *Report of the Thirty-Fifth Annual Conference* (London: Labour Party, 1935), p.174.

152 Eric Estorick, *Stafford Cripps: Prophetic Rebel* (New York: John Day, 1941), p.82.

153 Quoted in Vickers, *Labour Party and the World*, p.109.

154 John Gunther, *Inside Europe* (London: Hamish Hamilton, 1940), pp.358–9. Originally published in January 1936.

155 Estorick, *Stafford Cripps*.

156 Quentin Hogg, *The Left was Never Right* (London: Faber & Faber, 1945); Winston Churchill, *The Gathering Storm* (Boston: Houghton Mifflin, 1948), especially p.111, p.114, p.117, p.124. Despite his criticism of what he sees as the pacifist majority in the Labour Party, Churchill is very complimentary towards Attlee, Bevin and the Trades Union members of the Party, who he sees as bringing the Party around to a more robust foreign policy. The good working relationship between Churchill, Attlee and Bevin during the wartime coalition may go some way towards explaining Churchill's equivocal position towards Labour in comparison to Hogg's more robust attack.

157 Mary Agnes Hamilton, *Remembering My Good Friends* (London: Jonathan Cape, 1944), p.105.

158 Brigadier-General Sir J.E. Edmonds, quoted by John Terraine in J.F.C. Fuller, *The Decisive Battles of the Western World and their Influence on History. Volume Two 1792-1944* Edited by John Terraine (St Albans: Paladin, 1972), p.389. For a fuller discussion of the extent of Germany's defeat in 1918 see Garry Sheffield *Forgotten Victory. The First World War Myths and Realities* (London: Headline, 2001), chapter 9. Sheffield calls the final 1918 campaign 'the greatest military victory in British history.' (p.220).

159 Macmillan, *Peacemakers*, p.476.

160 The full text of the Armistice is reprinted in David Lloyd George, *War Memoirs* Volume II (London: Odhams, 1936), pp.2044–2053.

161 Ibid. p.490.

162 Hamilton, *Remembering my Good Friends*, p.106.

163 Cline, *Recruits to Labour*, p.99.

Chapter 3

1 Lloyd, 'Philip Noel-Baker and Peace Through Law', p.50.

2 A facsimile of this list has been produced by the imperial war museum: *The Black Book (Sonderfahndungsliste G.B.)* (London: Imperial War Museum, 1989). Interestingly Angell, Hobson, Woolf and Brailsford are also all on the list. E.H. Carr and David Mitrany are not.

3 David J. Whittaker, *Fighter For Peace. Philip Noel-Baker 1889-1982* (York: William Sessions, 1989). Lloyd, 'Philip Noel-Baker', pp.25–50.

4 Lloyd, 'Philip Noel-Baker', p.25.

5 See, for example, Noel Baker, *Geneva Protocol*, p.13; and Noel Baker, *Disarmament*, pp.48–50; also Philip Noel Baker, 'The Present Position with Regard to Disarmament', Advisory Committee on International Questions memo no. 345, July 1926, p.6. Labour Party Archives, Manchester.

6 Noel Baker, *Disarmament*, p.50.

7 *Geneva Protocol*, pp.13–6, pp.192–3; *Disarmament*, p.50, p.129.

8 Noel Baker, *Disarmament*, p.129.

9 *Geneva Protocol* chapter 7.

10 Leonard Woolf, 'Draft Report for the International Socialist Conference: The League of Nations and Disarmament', Advisory Committee on International Questions memo no. 251, 1922, p.3. Labour Party Archives, Manchester.

11 *Disamament*, pp.17–9.

12 *Ibid*, 19. See also Philip Noel Baker, 'Peace and the Official Mind' in Philip Noel Baker et al, *Challenges to Death* (London: Constable, 1934), p.72.

13 *Disarmament*, pp.4–5.

14 See the argument in Philip Noel Baker, *The Private Manufacture of Armaments* (London: Victor Gollancz, 1936). Also, Noel Baker, 'Peace and the Official Mind', pp.72–3.

15 'Peace and the Official Mind', p.72.

16 *Disarmament*, p.41.

17 Ibid. p.42, p.46.

18 Ibid. pp.48–50.

19 Noel Baker, *League of Nations at Work*, p.viii.

20 Noel Baker, *Geneva Protocol*, p.192.

21 *League of Nations at Work*, p.128.

22 See, for example, the discussion in *League of Nations at Work*.

23 'Peace and the Official Mind', pp.67–89.

24 *League of Nations at Work*, p.134.

25 Philip Noel-Baker, 'Copy of a Letter to Mr C.R. Buxton from Mr P. Noel-Baker', Advisory Committee on International Questions memo no. 480, May 1937. Labour Party Archives, Manchester.

26 A.L. Rowse, 'The Prospects of the Labour Party (1937)', in *The End of an Epoch*, p.113.

27 Lloyd, 'Philip Noel-Baker', p.48.

28 *Disarmament*, p.17.

29 Lloyd, 'Noel-Baker', p.50.

30 Philip Noel Baker, 'Notes on Mr Woolf's Paper on the International Situation', Advisory Committee on International Questions memo no. 464, March 1936. Labour Party Archives, Manchester.

31 Noel-Baker, *League of Nations at Work*, p.131.

32 Philip Noel Baker, 'The Four Pillars of a New World Order', in Clement Attlee et al, *Labour's Aims in War and Peace* (London: Lincolns-Prager, 1940), p.125.

33 Philip Noel Baker, 'Draft Declaration by the Labour Movement on Herr Hitler's Proposals for Peace', International Sub-Committee of the National Executive Committee memo, 9 October 1939, pp.1–2, pp.4–5; Philip Noel Baker, 'The Peace Aims of the Labour Party', International Sub-Committee of the National Executive Committee memo, 23 September 1939, p.1. Both held in the James Middleton collection of the Labour Party Archives, Manchester.

34 Philip Noel Baker, 'Notes on Mr Dalton's Outline Sketch of the Principles Upon Which a Declaration of Post-War International Policy Should be Based' International Department memo, November 1943?, p.5. William Gillies Papers, Labour Party Archives, Manchester.

35 *Selected Letters of Gertrude Bell* (Harmondsworth: Penguin, 1953), p.345.

36 For a discussion of this see Carlton, *MacDonald Versus Henderson*, p.23–4

37 Dalton, *Towards the Peace of Nations.*

38 Winkler, *Paths Not Taken*, p.1.

39 Rhiannon Vickers also criticises Winkler on this point: *The Labour Party and the World*, p.72–3.

40 Brailsford, 'Arbitrate or Disarm. A New View of Security', p.3. Although Brailsford, in the final analysis, doubted that disarmament and arbitration would work without first dealing with the issue of economic imperialism.

41 Carlton, MacDonald Versus Henderson, p.29; Winkler, *Paths Not Taken*, p.2. For MacDonald's view on the importance of habits of mind see his, *Protocol or Pact. The Alternative to War* (London: Labour Party, 1925), p.5.

42 See the discussion of this in Wrigley, *Arthur Henderson*, p.133.

43 Quoted in Winkler, *Paths Not Taken*, p.94.

44 See Wrigley, *Arthur Henderson*, pp.151–2.

45 Winkler, *Paths Not Taken*, p.90.

46 C. Delisle Burns, 'Notes on the League', Advisory Committee on International Questions memo no. 143, 8 June 1920. Labour Party Archives, Manchester

47 Carr, *International Relations Between the Two World Wars*, p.81.

48 Carlton, *MacDonald Versus Henderson*, p.59.

49 'Revision of the Treaty of Versailles', Advisory Committee on International Questions memo no. 254a, 1922; Woolf, 'League of Nations and Disarmament'. Both in the Labour Party Archives, Manchester.

50 Woolf, 'League of Nations and Disarmament', p.1, p.4.

51 'Draft Resolution for Labour Party Annual Conference', Advisory Committee on International Questions memo no. 245z, approved by the Executive on 31 May 1922. Labour Party Archives, Manchester

52 'The Need for a League Foreign Policy', Advisory Committee on International Questions memo no. 287, 9 July 1923, 4. Labour Party Archives, Manchester.

53 'Need for a League Policy', p.6.

54 'Need for a League Policy', p.6, p.9 and p.10.

55 'Need for a League Policy', Part II.

56 Labour Party, *Labour and the Nation*, First edition (London: Labour Party, 1928), p.41.

57 Dalton, Towards the Peace of Nations, p.90.

58 Both Noel Baker and Salvador de Madariaga, the two biggest names in the study of disarmament at the time, argued that disarmament was made necessary by the major changes that had occurred. Noel Baker, *Disarmament*; Salvador de Madariaga, *Disarmament* (London: Humphrey Milford/Oxford University Press, 1929), pp.25–6.

59 'To talk about articles 10 [guaranteeing member-state's territorial integrity and independence] and 16 as constituting a "collective security system", as many political scientists have done, is to ascribe powers to the League which it never possessed.' Ruth B. Henig, *The League of Nations* (Edinburgh: Oliver and Boyd, 1973), p.10.

60 Noel Baker, *League of Nations at Work*, p.131.

61 See, for example, Noel Baker *Geneva Protocol*, pp.13–9; Mitrany, *The Problem of International Sanctions*, p.2, and Norman Angell, *Arbitration, Sanctions, Disarmament* (London: National Council for the Prevention of War, nd).

62 Salvador de Madariaga called this a 'World-Community', and for him disarmament would not take place until cooperation replaced conflict in international affairs. De Madariaga, *Disarmament*, p.48, p.52.

63 Naylor, *Labour's International Policy*, p.3.

64 Arthur Ponsonby, *Now is the Time. An Appeal for Peace* (London: Leonard Parsons, 1925).

65 William Arnold-Forster, 'Commentary on the British Government's Observations to the League, on Arbitration and Security', Advisory Committee on International Questions memo no. 386, February 1928. Labour Party Archives, Manchester.

66 Leonard Woolf, *International Government* (London: George Allen & Unwin, 1916), pp.52–9.

67 For a discussion of Britain's reservations see Carlton, *MacDonald versus Henderson*, pp.76–8.

68 William Arnold-Forster, 'All Inclusive Arbitration', Advisory Committee on International Questions memo no. 346, August 1926, pp.7–8. Labour Party Archives, Manchester; Arnold-Forster, *Arbitrate! Arbitrate! Arbitrate!*, pp.9–10.

69 This was a major reason why Arnold-Forster regarded the Conservative opposition to the Protocol and optional clause 'as so much "eye-wash"'. William Arnold-Forster, 'The British Government and Arbitration', *Foreign Affairs* vii/5 (1925), pp.129–30.

70 William Arnold-Forster and Leonard Woolf, 'Proposed Recommendation to the Executive Regarding a Convention for Pacific Settlement', Advisory Committee on International Questions memo no. 355a, nd, p.1. Labour Party Archives, Manchester.

71 Arnold-Forster and Woolf, 'Convention for Pacific Settlement', pp.2–3.

72 See, for example, William Arnold-Forster, 'Note on the Franco-American and Anglo-American Arbitration Treaties', Advisory Committee on International Questions memo no. 387, February 1928. Labour Party Archives, Manchester.

73 Dalton, *Peace of Nations*, p.211.

74 Ponsonby, *Now is the Time*, pp.106–9.

75 See William Arnold-Forster, 'Sanctions (Commentary on Mr Buxton's Paper)', Advisory Committee on International Questions memo no. 365, May 1927, p.5n. Labour Party Archives, Manchester; Noel Baker, Geneva Protocol, chapter 7.

76 Charles Roden Buxton, 'Sanctions in the Covenant and the Protocol', Advisory Committee on International Questions memo no. 358, March 1927. Labour Party Archives, Manchester.

77 See especially her contribution to a debate on sanctions between herself and William Arnold-Forster, reprinted in: H.M. Swanwick and W. Arnold-Forster, *Sanctions of the League of Nations Covenant* (London: Council for Prevention of War, 1928), especially p.24 and p.27.

78 Ramsay MacDonald, *Protocol or Pact*, p.5.

79 Arnold-Forster, 'Sanctions', p.3–4; David Mitrany, 'A Labour Policy on Sanctions', Advisory Committee on International Questions memo no. 366, May 1927, p.2. Labour Party Archives, Manchester.

80 Noel Baker, *Geneva Protocol*, p.133.

81 Arnold-Forster, 'Sanctions', p.3.

82 Arnold-Forster, 'Sanctions', p.4; Mitrany, 'Labour Policy on Sanctions', p.2.

83 Mitrany, *Problem of International Sanctions*, p.2.

84 Dalton, *Peace of Nations*, p.235.

85 Mitrany, *Problem of International Sanctions*, p.27.

86 Arnold-Forster, 'Sanctions', p.8.

87 Mitrany, 'Labour Policy on Sanctions', p.2, p.7. See also Mitrany, *Problem of International Sanctions*, pp.12–3.

88 Dalton, *Peace of Nations*, p.145; Noel Baker, *Disarmament*, pp.16–23; de Madariaga, *Disarmament*, pp.2–12.

89 Norman Angell, *The Foundations of International Polity* (London: William Heineman, 1914), pp.163–93.

90 Noel Baker, *Disarmament*, p.7.

91 Angell, *After All*, p.252.

92 Noel Baker, *Disarmament*, pp.48–50; de Madariaga, *Disarmament*, p.36, p.48, p.52.

93 See, for example, Noel Baker, 'The Present Position with Regard to Disarmament', p.2. This optimism was not shared by C.R. Buxton ('The British Government is at the moment the greatest obstacle to disarmament'): C.R. Buxton, 'Report on Disarmament', Advisory Committee on International Affairs memo no. 347, 5 September 1926, pp.3–4. Labour Party Archives, Manchester.

94 See, for example, Noel Baker, *Disarmament*, p.24.

95 'Proposals for the Disarmament Conference', Advisory Committee on International Questions memo no. 424b, June 1931, p.3. Labour Party Archives, Manchester.

96 Noel Baker, *Disarmament*, p.129.

97 Norman Angell, 'Behind these Failures', *Foreign Affairs* xi/1 (1928), p.4.

98 Noel Baker, *Disarmament*, pp.39–41.

99 Ibid. p.41.

100 Dalton, *Peace of Nations*, p.291; 'Proposals for the Disarmament Conference', p.17.

101 See the discussion in Edward Warner, 'Douhet, Mitchell, Seversky: Theories of Air Warfare', in Edward Meade Earl (ed.), *Makers of Modern Strategy. Military Thought from Machiavelli to Hitler* (New York: Atheneum, 1967), pp.485–503. Originally published in 1941.

102 For an American pacifist view see Emily Greene Balch, 'The Relation of Civil Aviation to Disarmament', paper presented at the Women's International League for Peace and Freedom, Grenoble, 24 April 1932. Emily Greene Balch Papers, Wellesley College, Mass. Series III, reel 22. Like Henderson, Philip Noel Baker and Angell Balch was a Nobel Peace Prize laureate, winning her prize in 1946.

103 See, for example, Carlton, *MacDonald versus Henderson*, p.73.

104 Norman Angell, 'Pacifists and Cruisers: Two Views. I the Uses of Power', *New Leader*, 29 February 1924, p.3.

105 See Carr, *International Relations Between the Wars*, p.88.

106 See H.M. Swanwick, 'The Draft Treaty of Mutual Assistance', *Foreign Affairs* v/8 (1924), pp.153–4; and Swanwick, 'An Alternative to the Draft Treaty of Mutual Assistance', pp.170–1.

107 H.N. Brailsford, 'A New Start for the League. Arbitration and the Chains of Versailles', *New Leader*, 26 September 1924, pp.10–11.

108 Zimmern, 'I Have Joined the Labour Party', pp.3–4.

109 This is the argument in Noel Baker's *Geneva Protocol.*

110 Noel Baker, *Geneva Protocol*, p.18.

111 Ponsonby, *Now is the Time* pp.106–9

112 See Arnold-Forster, 'Sanctions', p.5; Noel Baker, *Geneva Protocol*, chapter 7.

113 Gordon, *Conflict and Consensus in Labour's Foreign*, pp.51–2; Ramsay MacDonald, *Protocol or Pact*, p.5.

114 Noel Baker, *Geneva Protocol.*

115 Letter from William Arnold-Forster to James Ramsay MacDonald, 13 August 1927. National Archives PRO 30/69/1170(1) 429.

116 J.A. Hobson, 'What Outlawry of War Signifies', *Foreign Affairs* vi/4 (1924), pp.79–80.

117 'Report of the Sub-Committee on the Security Pact', Advisory Committee on International Questions memo no. 339a, July 1925, p.1. Labour Party Archives, Manchester.

118 Charles Roden Buxton, 'Memorandum on the Pact of Locarno', Advisory Committee on International Questions memo no. 340, October 1925, p.1. Labour Party Archives, Manchester; 'Memorandum on the Pact of Locarno' Advisory Committee on International Questions memo no. 340, November 1925, 1. George Lansbury Papers, LSE. The latter was a final amended version of the former that was sent on to the Party Executive.

119 Letter from William Gillies to George Lansbury, 25 October 1933, p.1. George Lansbury Papers, LSE.

120 Buxton, 'Memorandum on the Pact of Locarno', 340, 2; 'Memorandum on the Pact of Locarno', 340a, p.2.

121 'Memorandum on the Pact of Locarno', 340a, 4. Words in italics were handwritten additions, presumably added by the Executive as a clarification.

122 Buxton, 'Memorandum on the Pact of Locarno', 340, p.2.

123 Norman Angell, 'Memorandum on the Reactionary Attitude of the Government in International Affairs', Advisory Committee on International Questions memo no. 341, November 1925, p.1. Labour Party Archives, Manchester.

124 Buxton, 'Memorandum on the Pact of Locarno', 340, p.3; 'Memorandum on the Pact of Locarno', 340a, p.3; Angell, 'Memorandum on the Reactionary Attitude', p.5.

125 Buxton, 'Memorandum on the Pact of Locarno', 340, p.3; 'Memorandum on the Pact of Locarno', 340a, p.3;

126 Leonard Woolf, 'Proposals for the "Outlawry of War"', Advisory Committee on International Questions memo no. 379a, December 1927, pp.1–3. Labour Party Archives, Manchester; 'Report on American Proposals for the Outlawry of War', Advisory Committee on International Questions memo no. 383a, February 1928, pp.2–3. Labour Party Archives, Manchester.

127 J.M. Kenworthy and George Young, 'Revised Memorandum on Outlawry of War', Advisory Committee on International Questions memo no. 379c, pp.1–2.

Labour Party Archives, Manchester; 'Report on American Proposals for the Outlawry of War', pp.3–4.

128 Wrigley, *Arthur Henderson*, 166; Carlton, *MacDonald versus Henderson*, p.73.

129 Carlton, *MacDonald versus Henderson*, p.73n.

130 *Labour and the Nation*, p.41.

131 Ibid. p.41.

132 Ibid. pp.41–2.

133 *Towards the Peace of Nations*, p.15.

134 Ibid. p.8.

135 Ibid. p.211, p.235.

136 Ibid. p.294, p.297.

137 See, for example, Carolyn J. Kitching, *Britain and the Problem of International Disarmament 1919–1934* (London: Routledge, 1999), pp.134–5, pp.176–7.

138 Editorial comment in Hugh Dalton, *The Political Diary of Hugh Dalton 1918–40, 1945–60* (London: Jonathan Cape, 1986), pp.54–5.

139 Carlton, *MacDonald versus Henderson*, p.75.

140 Carr, *International Relations Between the Two World Wars*, p.121.

141 Carlton, *MacDonald versus Henderson*, p.75.

142 Ibid. p.98–9.

143 Dalton, *Call Back Yesterday*, p.254.

144 Carlton, *MacDonald versus Henderson*.

145 See the discussion in Vickers, *Labour Party and the World*, p.96.

146 A full blow-by-blow account of the sequence of events leading up to the formation of the National Government is given in Humphry Berkeley, *The Myth that will not Die. The Formation of the National Government 1931* (London: Croom Helm, 1978). Berkeley argues that MacDonald was more a victim of circumstances; although it is Ernest Bevin, and to a lesser extent Oswald Moseley, who really understood the nature of the fiscal crisis. Snowden does not come out well at all.

147 Rowse, 'The Prospects of the Labour Party (1937)', in *The End of an Epoch*, p.103.

148 Angell, 'Memorandum on the Reactionary Attitude', p.1.

149 Noel Baker, *League of Nations at Work*, p.131, p.134.

150 Quoted in Donald S. Birn, 'The League of Nations Union and Collective Security', *Journal of Contemporary History* ix/3 (1974), pp.131–2.

Chapter 4

1 *War of Steel and Gold. A Study of the Armed Peace*, p.161.

2 Groom and Olson, *International Relations Then and Now*, chapters 4–5.

3 Albert Marrin, *Sir Norman Angell* (Boston: Twayne, 1979); J.B.D. Miller, *Norman Angell and the Futility of War* (New York: St Martin's, 1986); Ashworth, *Creating International Studies*. For a sympathetic look at Angell's classic *The Great Illusion* see Cornelia Navari, 'The Great Illusion Revisited: The International Theory of Norman Angell', *Review of International Studies* xv/4 (1989), pp.341–58.

4 Jaap de Wilde, 'Norman Angell: Ancestor of Interdependence Theory' in James N. Rosenau and Hylke Tromp (eds), *Interdependence and Conflict in World Politics* (Aldershot: Avebury, 1989); Jaap de Wilde, *Saved from Oblivion: Interdependence*

Theory in the First Half of the Twentieth Century (Aldershot: Dartmouth, 1991), pp.61–90.

5 Kenneth Younger, 'The Great Illusion', *The Listener*, 10 January 1963, pp.51–2.

6 Angell, 'Peace Terms', p.1.

7 Labour Party, *Report of the Nineteenth Annual Conference 1921* (London: Labour Party, 1921), p.200.

8 *The Fruits of Victory*.

9 Angell, *After All*, pp.231–2.

10 *The Public Mind. Its Disorders: Its Explanation.*

11 See, especially, Brinton , *Does Capitalism Cause War?*

12 *This Have and Have-Not Business. Political Fantasy and Economic Fact* (London: Hamish Hamilton, 1936).

13 Norman Angell, 'Japan, the League and Us', *Time and Tide*, November 1931, pp.1302–3; *This Have and Have Not Business*, pp.189–201.

14 See Norman Angell, *Peace with the Dictators? A Symposium and Some Conclusions* (London: Hamish Hamilton, 1938); and Norman Angell, 'The New John Bull' *Political Quarterly* vii/3 (1936), pp.311–29.

15 Norman Angell, 'Who are the Utopians? And Who the Realists?', *Headway*, January 1940, pp.4–5.

16 Norman Angell, *Why Do We Fight* (London: Hamish Hamilton, 1939); *Why Freedom Matters* (Harmondsworth: Penguin, 1940).

17 See, for example, Norman Angell, *The Steep Places. An Examination of Political Tendencies* (London: Hamish Hamilton, 1947).

18 Ashworth, *Creating International Studies*, chapter 3.

19 This argument is discussed in detail in Angell, *The Great Illusion.*

20 Angell, *Great Illusion*, pp.147–51, p.226, p.229; Norman Angell, *Peace Theories and the Balkan War* (London: Horace Marshall, 1912), pp.29–30, p.47; Norman Angell, *The Foundations of International Polity*, p.89.

21 Angell, Great Illusion, p.28; Angell, Foundations of International Polity, pp.153–4.

22 Angell, *Great Illusion*, pp.57–8, p.60. Emphasis in the original.

23 Angell, *Great Illusion*, pp.27–8, pp.48–9; Angell, *Foundations of International Polity*, pp.95–6.

24 Angell, *Peace Theories*, pp.16–7; p.21; pp.47–9.

25 Angell, *Fruits of Victory*, p.299.

26 Angell, *Fruits of Victory*, p.61. See also the argument in one of his later works: Norman Angell and Harold Wright, *Can Governments Cure Unemployment?* (London: Dent, 1931), p.1, pp.6–9, p.140.

27 Norman Angell, *If Britain is to Live* (London: Nisbet, 1923), p.96.

28 For Angell's full argument see his *The Public Mind.*

29 *If Britain is to Live*, p.29.

30 *If Britain is to Live*, pp.15–31; Norman Angell, 'The Press and the Public Mind. The Lessons of Palmerston's Power', *New Leader*, 11 July 1924, p.4.

31 Fruits of Victory, p.xxiii; *The Public Mind*, Part II.

32 This was the central argument of Angell's later work *Why Freedom Matters*, especially pp.52–6. See also *If Britain is to Live*, p.123; and *The British Revolution and American Democracy. An Interpretation of British Labour Programmes* (Toronto: McClelland Goodchild and Stewart, 1919), p.192.

33 See, for example, Norman Angell, 'Educational and Psychological Factors', in Woolf (ed.), *The Intelligent Man's Way to Prevent War*.
34 Angell, 'Pacifists and Cruisers: Two Views. I The Uses of Power', *New Leader*, 29 February 1924, p.3.
35 Angell, 'Japan, the League and Us', pp.1302–3.
36 Angell, *This Have and Have-Not Business*, pp.189–201.
37 Angell, 'New John Bull', 311–29; Angell, *Peace with the Dictators?*, chapter VIII.
38 Angell, 'Who Are the Utopians? And Who the Realists?', p.4.
39 See Norman Angell, *This Have and Have-Not Business*; also Norman Angell, *Must it be War?* (London: Labour Book Service, 1939), pp.225–9.
40 For the changes to the meaning of the word pacifist during this period, and Norman Angell's place in those changes, see Louis R. Bisceglia, 'Norman Angell and the Pacifist Muddle', *Bulletin of the Institute of Historical Research* xlv/3 (1972), pp.104–19.
41 Cecil, 'Foreword', pp.3–4.
42 Hobson's theory of under-consumption can be found in J. A. Hobson, *The Evolution of Modern Capitalism* (Londson: Scott, 1894). His classic work on the effect that this has on international affairs is his *Imperialism*.
43 Brailsford, *War of Steel and Gold*, chapter 5.
44 J.A. Hobson, 'Causes of War' unpublished and undated paper in the possession of David Long, pp.12–3. I am very grateful to David for sending me a copy of this paper.
45 Ibid. p.15.
46 Ibid. p.16.
47 Brailsford, *Life-Work of J. A. Hobson*, p.26.
48 Brailsford, 'Arbitrate or Disarm', p 4.
49 Dalton, *Towards the Peace of Nations*, p.15.
50 Angell, *After All*, p.253.
51 Brailsford, 'Tory Policy of Peace', pp.332–3.
52 "Vigilantes" *Inquest on Peace. An Analysis of the National Government's Foreign Policy* (London: Victor Gollancz, 1935), pp.286–92; "Vigilantes", *Why the League has Failed* (London: Victor Gollancz, 1938), pp.62–6; K. Zilliacus, *Why We are Losing the Peace* (London: Victor Gollancz, 1939), chapter IV. Zilliacus wrote under the name "Vigilantes" while he still worked for the League of Nations.
53 Brailsford, 'A Socialist Foreign Policy', pp.282–5.
54 Brailsford, *Property or Peace? Pp.*284–5.
55 Brailsford, *Towards a New League*, chapter IV.
56 Harold J. Laski, 'Economic Foundations of Peace', in Leonard Woolf (ed.), *The Intelligent Man's Way to Prevent War* (London: Victor Gollancz, 1933), pp.543–7.
57 Norman Angell, 'Get Effective Defence and You Get the League', *The New Outlook*, 10 June 1936, pp.15–7; Leonard Woolf, 'Labour's Foreign Policy', *Political Quarterly* iv/4 (1933), pp.504–24.
58 H.N. Brailsford in Brinton, *Does Capitalism Cause War?*, pp.13–19.
59 Leonard Woolf in Brinton, *Does Capitalism Cause War?*, pp.21–3.
60 Norman Angell in Brinton, *Does Capitalism Cause War?*, pp.24.
61 Ibid. pp.30–3.
62 Ibid. p.36.
63 H.N. Brailsford in Brinton, *Does Capitalism Cause War?*, pp.40–1.
64 H.J. Laski in Brinton, *Does Capitalism Cause War?*, pp.41–2.

65 Angell, *After All*, p.252.
66 Rowse, 'The Prospects of the Labour Party (1937)', p.104. Emphasis in the original.
67 Arthur Henderson, *Labour's Foreign Policy* (London: Labour Party, 1933), p.3.
68 See, for example, Woolf, 'Labour's Foreign Policy', pp.523–4.
69 Labour Party, *For Socialism and Peace. The Labour Party's Programme of Action 1934* (London: Labour Party, 1934), p.10.
70 Swift, *Labour in Crisis*, p.68.
71 *British Labour Policy on War. A Reminder* (London: British Anti War Movement, 1934). The pamphlet included a preface by John Strachey.
72 Labour Party, *Report of the Thirty-Fifth Annual Conference*, p.179.
73 Ibid. p.179.
74 Letter from Arthur Ponsonby to George Lansbury, 17 September 1935. George Lansbury Papers no. 208, BLPES.
75 Letter from Arthur Ponsonby to George Lansbury, 17 September 1935. George Lansbury Papers no. 207, BLPES.
76 Labour Party, *Report of the Thirty-Fifth Annual Conference*, pp.175–6.
77 Ibid. pp.178–9.
78 'Cato', *Guilty Men* (London: Victor Gollancz, 1941), p.34.
79 Swift, *Labour in Crisis*, p.58.
80 See the discussion in Swift, *Labour in Crisis*, pp.103–6; and Henry Pelling, *A Short History of the Labour Party* Fourth Edition (Basingstoke: Macmillan, 1972), p.82.
81 Gordon, *Conflict and Consensus in Labour's Foreign Policy*, p.76.
82 Vickers, *The Labour Party and the World*, p.127.
83 Labour Party, *Labour's Immediate Programme* (London: Labour Party, 1937), p.8.
84 See, for example, Leonard Woolf, 'The Ideal of the League Remains', *The Political Quarterly* vii/3 (1936), pp.330–45.
85 See Gordon, *Conflict and Consensus*, p.67.
86 Sturmthal, *The Tragedy of European Labour*, p.265.
87 Letter from George Lansbury to R.C. Allen, 11 May 1937, George Lansbury Papers no. 162, BLPES.
88 George Lansbury, 'Notes on George Lansbury's Interview with Hitler, 19.iv.37, George Lansbury Papers no. 157, BLPES.
89 Letter from George Lansbury to R.C. Allen, 11 May 1937, George Lansbury Papers no. 162, BLPES.
90 The exiled German Social Democratic Party denounced Lansbury's visit, contradicting the claim that Hitler wanted peace. Labour's International Department Duly noted the protest. 'Mr George Lansbury's Visit to Adolf Hitler. Protest of the German Social Democrats', International Department Memorandum, JD/INT/1/1, Labour Party Archives, Manchester.
91 Letter from Charles Roden Buxton to William Gillies, 27 July 1937, p.1. William Gillies Papers, WG/PCE/122i. Labour Party Archives, Manchester.
92 Sturmthal, *Tragedy of European Labour*, p.262.
93 'The Labour Party's Policy with Regard to the League and Sanctions', Advisory Committee on International Questions memo no. 431a, March 1933, pp.1–2. Labour Party Archives, Manchester.

94 'The Labour Party's Policy Regarding the League of Nations', Advisory Committee on International Questions memo no 433a, April 1933, p.1. Labour Party Archives, Manchester.
95 'Labour Party's Policy Regarding the League of Nations', p.3.
96 'Labour Party's Policy Regarding the League of Nations', pp.2–3.
97 'Labour Party's Policy Regarding the League of Nations', p.6.
98 Leonard Woolf, 'Meditation on Abyssinia', *The Political Quarterly* vii/1 (1936), p.17.
99 Carr, *International Relations Between the Two World Wars*, p.226.
100 Herbert Morrison, 'A New Start with the League of Nations', lecture delivered to the Geneva Institute of International Relations, Geneva, 21 August 1936. International Department, ID/INT/3/1i. Labour Party Archives, Manchester.
101 Leonard Woolf, 'Memorandum on the Attitude which the Party Should Adopt to Proposed Reforms of the League', Advisory Committee on International Questions memo no. 468, July 1936, p.6. Labour Party Archives, Manchester.
102 'Memorandum on an Immediate Policy for the Party in Relation to the International Situation and Proposals for a New Security Agreement', Advisory Committee on International Questions memo no. 479a, April 1937, 1. Labour Party Archives, Manchester; Ivor Thomas and Leonard Woolf, 'Memorandum on Factors in the International Situation to be Considered in Relation to any New Security Agreement', Advisory Committee on International Questions memo no. 473, December 1936, p.14. Labour Party Archives, Manchester.
103 'Memorandum on an Immediate Policy for the Party'. Also see the discussion in Thomas and Woolf, 'Memorandum on Factors in the International'.
104 See, for example, Leonard Woolf, 'The Resurrection of the League', *The Political Quarterly* viii/3 (1937), pp.337–52; Leonard Woolf, 'Arms and Peace', *The Political Quarterly* viii/1 (1937), pp.21–35; Woolf, 'Ideal of the League Remains', pp.330–45.
105 Susan Lawrence, 'Note on Policy', Advisory Committee on International Questions memo no. 469, July 1936, p.1. Labour Party Archives, Manchester.
106 Woolf, 'Memorandum on the Attitude which the Party Should Adopt', p.6.
107 C.R. Buxton, 'Comments on the "Memorandum on Factors in the International Situation" etc. (No. 473)', Advisory Committee on International Questions memo no. 475, January 1937, pp.1–3.
108 Ibid. p.2.
109 Ibid. pp.2–3.
110 An anonymous critic, 'Comment on the "Memorandum on Factors in the International Situation to be Considered in Relation to any New Security Agreement"', Advisory Committee on International Questions memo no. 478, April 1937. Labour Party Archives, Manchester.
111 Noel-Baker, 'Copy of a Letter to Mr C.R. Buxton'.
112 Rowse, 'The Prospects of the Labour Party (1937)', p.113.
113 Alan James, *Peacekeeping in International Politics* (London: Macmillian, 1990), p.80.
114 Labour Party, *Report of the 37th Annual Conference* (London: Labour Party, 1937).
115 Naylor, *Labour's International Policy*, p.1.
116 'The Labour Party's Policy and the Services Estimates', Advisory Committee on International Questions memo no. 441a, January 1934, p.1. Labour Party Archives, Manchester.

117 Buxton, 'Comments on the "Memorandum on Factors in the International Situation"'; and Brailsford, 'The Tory Policy of Peace', p.329.
118 Carr, Twenty Years' Crisis, p.282.
119 'The Labour Party's Policy and the Services Estimates', p.2.
120 'Memorandum on Minorities', Advisory Committee on International Questions memo no. 453, February 1935. Labour Party Archives, Manchester.
121 Woolf, 'Memorandum on the Attitude which the Party Should Adopt', p.6. See also the argument in his Barbarians at the Gate.
122 'The Flight from Collective Security', Advisory Committee on International Questions memo no. 486a, March 1938. Labour Party Archives, Manchester.
123 Angell, 'The New John Bull' pp.311–329.
124 Brailsford, 'Tory Policy of Peace', pp.325–33.
125 This was also Clement Attlee's position. See Swift, Labour in Crisis, p.112.
126 See, for example, 'The Labour Party's International Policy', Advisory Committee on International Affairs memo no. 502a, March 1939. Labour Party Archives, Manchester; and Bob Fraser's comments in 'Informal Discussion on the New International Situation and Labour Party Policy in Regard Thereto' unpublished memo 19 November 1938, p.4. Hugh Dalton Papers 4/1 pp.12–17, British Library of Political and Economic Sciences, LSE, London.
127 'Labour Party's International Policy', p.2.
128 'Labour Party's International Policy', pp.1–2.
129 'Revised Memorandum on Peaceful Change', Advisory Committee on International Affairs memo no 493a and 489a, May 1938, revised July 1939, p.1. Labour Party Archives, Manchester; 'Labour Party's International Policy', p.2.
130 'Revised Memorandum on Peaceful Change', p.2, p.5.
131 'International Policy and Peaceful Change', Advisory Committee on International Affairs memo no. 484b, February 1938, p.1. Labour Party Archives, Manchester; 'Revised Memorandum on Peaceful Change', p.5.
132 'Revised Memorandum on Peaceful Change', p.2; 'Labour Party's International Policy', pp.4–5.
133 'International Policy and Peaceful Change', p.2.
134 W. Arnold-Forster, 'Bilateral Pacts and Collective Security', Advisory Committee on International Questions memo no. 504a, June 1939, p.1. Labour Party Archives, Manchester.
135 See, for example, excerpt from a Speech by Hugh Dalton at Durham on Saturday, 29 October 1938, Hugh Dalton Papers, BLPES. Dalton 6/2 13.
136 'Informal Discussion on the New International Situation', p.1.
137 Angell, Must it be War?, p.233.
138 'Labour Policy After Munich', Labour Party Policy Committee memo no. 8, 8 October 1938, pp.5–8. Hugh Dalton Papers 4/3 pp.64–76. British Library of Political and Economic Sciences, LSE, London.
139 Ibid. p.9.
140 Ibid. p.13.
141 'Informal Discussion on the New International Situation', p.4.
142 Hugh Dalton, excerpt of a speech given in Leeds on 15th October 1938. Hugh Dalton Papers 6/2 12. British Library of Political and Economic Sciences, LSE, London.

143 Hugh Dalton, excerpt of a speech given in Durham on 29 October 1938. Hugh Dalton Papers 6/2 12. British Library of Political and Economic Sciences, LSE, London.

144 'Informal Discussion on the New International Situation', pp.1, 5.

145 'Revised Memorandum on Peaceful Change', p.3.

146 Arnold-Forster, 'Bilateral Pacts and Collective Security', p.3.

147 Ibid. p.2.

148 Comments by W.N. Ewer, in 'Comments Received from Some Members of the International Committee Upon Memorandum no. 504,' Advisory Committee on International Questions, June 1939. Labour Party Archives, Manchester.

149 Letter from Robert Cecil to Hugh Dalton, 28th November 1938, p.1. Hugh Dalton Papers 5/2 pp.20–2. British Library of Political and Economic Sciences, LSE, London.

150 Ibid, p.3.

151 'The Position of the Labour Party After Munich' Policy Sub-Committee general policy document no. 3, November? 1938. Hugh Dalton Papers 4/3 pp.41–59. British Library of Political and Economic Sciences, LSE, London.

152 'Notes on Policy Committee Discussion', attached to document in previous note. Hugh Dalton Papers 4/3 pp.60–3. British Library of Political and Economic Sciences, LSE, London

153 'Cato', *Guilty Men*, p.61. 'Cato' was the *nom de plume* for three journalists: Michael Foot, a future leader of the Labour Party, Frank Owen and Peter Howard.

154 See Rowse, 'The End of an Epoch', in *End of an Epoch*, pp.68–9; and 'Cato', *Guilty Men*, pp.61–4.

155 Woolf, *Barbarians at the Gate*, pp.208–13. The Hoare-Laval pact in December 1935 was a French and British plan to settle the dispute between Italy and Abyssinia by giving Italy extensive parts of Abyssinia. A popular outcry in Britain forced the British government to disavow it.

156 Quoted in Vickers, *Labour Party and the World*, p.137.

157 See, for example, Vernon Bartlett, 'The War Horizon', in Bertrand Russell *et al.*, *Dare We Look Ahead?* (New York: Macmillan, 1938), pp.34–6.

158 Vickers, *Labour Party and the World*, pp.139–40.

159 *The British Anti-War Movement pamphlet British Labour Policy on War. A Reminder*, cited above, is a good example of this.

160 See, for example, Angell, *Must it be War?*

Chapter 5

1 Morgenthau, 'Introduction', in Mitrany, *Working Peace System*, p.11.

2 David Mitrany, 'Marx v. the Peasant' in T.E. Gregory and Hugh Dalton (eds), *London Essays in Economics: In Honour of Edwin Cannan* (London: Routledge, 1927), pp.319–376.

3 Mitrany, *Problem of International Sanctions*.

4 Ashworth, *Creating International Studies*; Ashworth and Long, *New Perspectives on International Functionalism*; Per Hammarlund, *Liberal Internationalism and the Decline of the State. The Thought of Richard Cobden, David Mitrany and Kenichi Ohmae* (New York: Palgrave Macmillan, 2005). For a comprehensive biography and biblio-

graphy see also Dorothy Anderson, 'David Mitrany (1888–1975): An Appreciation of his Life and Work', *Review of International Studies* xxiv (1998), pp.577–92.

5 Mitrany, 'The Making of the Functional Theory', pp.16–17.

6 'The Making of the Functional Theory', pp.8–9

7 Letter from William Gillies to James Ramsay MacDonald. 19 May 1925. James Ramsay MacDonald Papers, National Archives, London. PRO3069/460. Gillies erroneously reports that Mitrany is a member of the Party.

8 For a discussion of the relationship between Mitrany's concept of function and those of Tawney, Laski and Cole see David Long, 'International Functionalism and the Politics of Forgetting', *International Journal* xlviii/2 (1993), pp.355–79.

9 Mitrany, *Progress of International Government*; David Mitrany, *The Effects of the War in South Eastern Europe* (New Haven: Yale University Press, 1936).

10 For Mitrany's findings from his German trip see his letter to William Gillies (forwarded to James Ramsay MacDonald and Arthur Henderson) dated 15 May 1925. James Ramsay MacDonald Papers, Public Record Office, London. PRO3069/470-79.

11 David Mitrany 'Memorandum on the Minorities Problem', Advisory Committee on International Questions memorandum no. 385, February 1928, p.1. Labour Party Archives, Manchester.

12 Ibid. p.2.

13 Ibid. pp.4–10.

14 Mitrany, 'The Making of the Functional Theory', p.14.

15 Leonard Woolf claimed that this tendency 'to develop a not altogether rational attachment to some foreign nation, nationality or race' was fundamentally a nineteenth century liberal trait. The assumption is that the twentieth century liberals and socialists were more global. Woolf, *Downhill All the Way*, p.246.

16 It is interesting to note that J.R.R. Tolkien, the author of *The Lord of the Rings*, once equated the evil land of Mordor in his book with the Balkans. Admittedly he was at the time explaining the distance between the Shire and Mordor, but still it demonstrates the extent to which it was common at the time to see the Balkans as a realm of ancient savageries.

17 David Mitrany, Address to the American Historical Association, Brown University, 1937. Quoted in 'The Making of the Functional Theory', p.14.

18 David Mitrany, *The Land and the Peasant in Rumania. The War and Agrarian Reform* (London: Humprey Milford & Oxford University Press, 1930), pp.xxv–xxxi.

19 *Land and the Peasant in Rumania*, xxix; Mitrany, 'Marx v. the Peasant', p.320.

20 See the discussion in 'Marx v. the Peasant'. This argument was later expanded into a book fourteen years later – David Mitrany, *Marx Against the Peasant. A Study in Social Dogmatism* (London: Weidenfeld and Nicolson, 1951) – and was the subject of a subsequent programme on British radio – David Mitrany, 'Marx, Stalin and the Peasants', *The Listener*, 20 March 1952, pp.455–6.

21 Mitrany, 'Marx v. the Peasant', pp.366–8.

22 Ibid. pp.369–70.

23 David Mitrany, 'Large Scale and Peasant Farming in Eastern Europe', paper presented at the Conference on European Agriculture, March 1942, p.2. Mitrany Papers, British Library of Political and Economic Sciences, LSE, London.

24 See Graham Wallas, *Social Judgement* (New York: Harcourt Brace, 1935), pp.20–4.

25 Graham Wallas, *Human Nature in Politics* (Boston and New York: Houghton Mifflin, 1916), chapter IV.

26 While there is no agreement on where Mitrany got his notion of function from, the fact that Hobhouse, one of his mentors, was using the term in 1911 suggests this as the most likely source. See my discussion of this in Ashworth, *Creating International Studies*, pp.39–41. For the view that he may have got it from Wells see: James Patrick Sewell, *Functionalism and World Politics. A Study Based on United Nations Programs Financing Economic Development* (Princeton: Princeton University Press, 1966), p.8n. For the argument that there is a link to Cole, Tawney and Laski see: Long, 'International Functionalism and the Politics of Forgetting', pp.355–79.

27 Harold Laski, *A Grammar of Politics* (London: George Allen & Unwin, 1925), chapter 11.

28 Mitrany, *Problem of International Sanctions*, pp.v–vi.

29 A reference to his wife, the writer and artist Ena Limebeer. Obviously the family originally owned this copy.

30 Mitrany, *Problem of International Sanctions*, pp.10–3.

31 Mitrany, *Problem of International Sanctions*, p.71.

32 David Mitrany, 'Political Lessons of the Schuman Plan', paper intended for publication in the *Political Quarterly*, but withdrawn due to a disagreement with Leonard Woolf, 1954. The Mitrany Papers. British Library of Political and Economic Sciences, LSE, London.

33 *Progress of International Government*, pp.129–30.

34 David Mitrany, 'Memorandum on Studies in *International Relations*', unpublished paper dated 1933–4; David Mitrany, 'A Realistic Interpretation of Security' Lecture to the Student's International Union, 16 July 1935, pp.4–6; David Mitrany, 'Ouline for a Paper on Pacifism', no date, p.1; all from the Mitrany Papers. British Library of Political and Economic Sciences, LSE, London. Mitrany, Progress of International Government, 42; Mitrany, *A Working Peace System*, p.10.

35 Mitrany, Progress of International Government, p.103; Mitrany, *Working Peace System*, p.10; David Mitrany, 'The Problem of Equality in Historical Perspective', in *A Working Peace System* (Chicago: Quadrangle, 1966), p.104.

36 *Progress of International Government*, p.17; 'Research in International Relations', unpublished paper dated 28 November 1931, p.4. The Mitrany Papers. British Library of Political and Economic Sciences, LSE, London.

37 David Mitrany, 'International Consequences of National Planning', *Yale Review* xxxvii/1 (1947), pp.25–6.

38 Mitrany, 'International Consequences of National Planning', p.24; David Mitrany, 'Interrelation of Politics and Economics in Modern War', *Annals of the American Academy of Political and Social Science* cxcii (1937), pp.84–5; David Mitrany, 'Pan-Europa – A Hope or a Danger?', *Political Quarterly* i/4 (1930), pp.463–5.

39 David Mitrany, 'The Prospects of Integration: Federal or Functional?' in A.J.R. Groom and Paul Taylor (eds), *Functionalism. Theory and Practice in International Relations* (New York: Crane Russak, 1975) pp.60–2; David Mitrany, 'The Functional Approach to World Organisation', *International Affairs* xxiv/3 (1948), pp.351–3; David Mitrany, 'Functional Federalism', in *Working Peace System* (1966), p.172; *Working Peace System* (1943), p.11. For a full discussion of Mitrany's criticism of federalism see Ashworth, *Creating International Studies*, pp.90–1.

40 See, for example, the argument in David Mitrany, *The Road to Security* (London: National Peace Council, 1944), especially pp.14–6.

41 See Mitrany, *Progress of International Government*, p.136.

42 Mitrany, *Effects of the War in South Eastern Europe*, pp.70–1 and chapter 5.

43 For Mitrany's view that state centralisation was a necessary precondition for the waging of modern war see his 'Interrelation of Politics and Economics in Modern War', pp.82–88.

44 For a fuller discussion of this question of loyalties see Ashworth, *Creating International Studies*, pp.95–9.

45 See, for example, Brent F. Nelsen and Alexander C-G. Stubb's note on p.99 of their edited collection *The European Union. Readings on the Theory and Practice of European Integration* (Boulder Co. & London: Lynne Rienner, 1994): 'Functionalism failed as a theory for several reasons, but one stands out: it contained no theory of politics.'

46 Letter from William Gillies to Leonard Woolf dated 13 September 1939, 1 D1a. Leonard Woolf Papers, University of Sussex.

47 Minutes of the Central Committee (Special Sub-Committee), no. 1, 6 August 1941, p.2. Hugh Dalton Papers 7/10 pp.9–10. British Library of Political and Economic Sciences, LSE, London; Letter from George Dallas to Leonard Woolf dated 20 September 1941. 1 D1a. Leonard Woolf Papers, University of Sussex.

48 Letter from Leonard Woolf to James Middleton 24 November 1943; reply from James Middleton to Leonard Woolf 25 November 1943; reply from Woolf to James Middleton 27 November 1943; 1 D1a. Leonard Woolf Papers, University of Sussex.

49 Letters from Philip Noel Baker to Leonard Woolf dated 28th December 1943 and 16th February 1944, 1 D1a. Leonard Woolf Papers, University of Sussex.

50 See, for example, the letter from Philip Noel Baker to Leonard Woolf dated 18 February 1944, 1 D1a. Leonard Woolf Papers, University of Sussex.

51 Vickers, *The Labour Party and the World*, pp.141–2.

52 See, for example, Hugh Dalton's speech in Cambridge on 6th May 1940 in which he saw Chamberlain's and Simon's resignations as the only possible way to restore confidence in Britain's war effort. Hugh Dalton Papers 6/2 37. British Library of Political and Economic Sciences, LSE, London.

53 Vickers, *Labour Party and the World*, p.143

54 Sturmthal, *The Tragedy of European Labour*, p.90.

55 Zilliacus, *I Choose Peace*, pp.66–7.

56 Churchill, *The Gathering Storm*, p.666.

57 See the short discussion in Vickers, *Labour Party and the World*, p.144.

58 A.L. Rowse, 'Apology by Way of Preface' in *The End of an Epoch*, p.12.

59 Dalton, *Political Diary*, pp.342–4.

60 Churchill, *Gathering Storm*, p.667.

61 See Fitzroy Maclean, *Eastern Approaches* (London: Pan, 1956), p.231.

62 See, for example, the discussion of American views in Stephen E. Ambrose, *Rise to Globalism. American Foreign Policy Since 1938* (Harmondsworth: Pelican, 1983), pp.45–52.

63 Vickers, *Labour Party and the World*, p.145.

64 Vickers, *Labour Party and the World*, pp.149–50.

65 Gordon, *Conflict and Consensus in Labour's Foreign Policy*, p.83.

66 Harold Laski, 'A Manifesto to the German People on British Labour's Peace Aims', International Sub-Committee of the National Executive Committee memo, September 1939 p.1; Harold Laski, 'British Labour Peace Aims', International Sub-Committee of the National Executive Committee memo, September 1939 p.1; Philip Noel Baker, 'Draft Declaration by the Labour Movement on Herr Hitler's Proposals for Peace', International Sub-Committee of the National Executive Committee memo, 9 October 1939, pp.1–2; Philip Noel Baker, 'The Peace Aims of the Labour Party', International Sub-Committee of the National Executive Committee memo, 23 September 1939, p.1. All four held in the James Middleton collection of the Labour Party Archives, Manchester.

67 Laski, 'Manifesto to the German People', p.1.

68 Laski, 'British Labour's Peace Aims' 6; Noel Baker, 'Draft Declaration by the Labour Movement', pp.2–3.

69 Hugh Dalton, *Hitler's War: Before and After* (Harmondsworth: Penguin, 1940), p.130.

70 Laski, 'British Labour's Peace Aims' 6; Noel Baker, 'Draft Declaration by the Labour Movement', pp.4–6.

71 Dalton, *Hitler's War*, chapter XII.

72 Noel Baker, 'Draft Declaration by the Labour Movement', p.3; Noel Baker, 'Peace Aims of the Labour Party', p.2. For Noel Baker's commentary on his proposals see his 'Note on the Draft "Peace Aims of the Labour Party"', International Sub-Committee of the National Executive Committee memo, 23 September 1939, pp.2–3. James Middleton collection of the Labour Party Archives, Manchester.

73 The Labour Party National Executive Committee, 'Appendix II. Labour, the War, and the Peace', in The Labour Party, *Report of the 39th Annual Conference 1940* (London: Labour Party, 1940), p.188.

74 Ibid. p.189.

75 See the texts of these broadcasts published as Philip Noel Baker, 'Messages to the German Workers' in Clement Attlee et al, *Labour's Aims in War and Peace* (London: Lincolns-Prager, nd), pp.43–7.

76 Ibid, 190. Laski's view that the capitalist nature of society is behind national sovereignty, and therefore war, was a major part of his analysis in his 'British Labour's Peace Aims', pp.2–4.

77 See Noel Baker, 'Note on the Draft', p.1: 'I have not used the word "Socialism" nor inserted some of the ideas of Professor Laski's drafts. This is not because I do not think that the lesson of present events is that Socialism is indispensable both here and abroad; but I have the feeling that to lay stress on Party principles and to use Party language in any document issued in the immediate future would create the impression that we were trying to use the national emergency for Party ends. I think it might also prejudice its reception in Germany, France and the United States.'

78 Harold Laski '1st Laski Draft', International Sub-Committee of the National Executive Committee memo, undated [probably September-October 1939], p.1. James Middleton collection of the Labour Party Archives, Manchester.

79 See, for example, the advocacy of a compromise peace with the anti-Hitler military cliques in J.F.C. Fuller's 1958 classic history *The Generalship of Alexander the Great* (Ware: Wordsworth, 1998), pp.312–4. Fuller argues that Alexander would have made better use of the German opposition, and that Churchill's

unconditional surrender stance helped prolong the war. Fuller, perhaps, misses the point that, if it was German militarism that the Allies were fighting, why would they want to make a compromise peace with the German military? He also overestimates the strength of the German opposition, even in the army. Most German generals, even the most virulently anti-Nazi like von Manstein, refused to oppose the Nazi government as long as Germany appeared to be winning the war. Their anti-fascist activities only surfaced after the disasters of Stalingrad, Kursk and North Africa.

80 Letter from Philip Noel Baker to Hugh Dalton, 17 November 1939. Hugh Dalton Papers 5/2 46. British Library of Political and Economic Sciences, LSE, London.

81 See the various comments on Laski in Dalton, *The Political Diary.*

82 'International Post-War Settlement', 3rd Draft, 7 March, 1944, p.2; 'Report of the National Executive Committee 1943–4', p.1. Both documents held in the William Gillies Papers, Labour Party Archives, Manchester.

83 'International Post-War Settlement,' 3rd Draft, p.3; 'Report of the National Executive Committee 1943–4', p.1.

84 Letter from Harold Laski to Hugh Dalton, dated 27 March 1944, p.1. Hugh Dalton Papers 7/10 69. British Library of Political and Economic Sciences, LSE, London.

85 'International Post-War Settlement,' 3rd Draft, p.6; 'Report of the National Executive Committee 1943–4', p.2.

86 'International Post-War Settlement,' 3rd Draft, p.7; 'Report of the National Executive Committee 1943–4', p.2.

87 'International Post-War Settlement,' 3rd Draft, p.7. This section was deleted from the final version.

88 'International Post-War Settlement,' 3rd Draft, pp.7–8; 'Report of the National Executive Committee 1943–4', p.2.

89 Letter from Philip Noel Baker to Hugh Dalton, 8th April 1944, pp.5–6. Hugh Dalton Papers 7/10 pp.72–5. British Library of Political and Economic Sciences, LSE, London.

90 'International Post-War Settlement,' 3rd Draft, pp.8–9; 'Report of the National Executive Committee 1943–4', p.2. The word 'definitely' was omitted from the NEC report.

91 Dalton, *Hitler's War*, pp.156–7.

92 'International Post-War Settlement,' 3rd Draft, p.9; 'Report of the National Executive Committee 1943–4', p.2.

93 'International Post-War Settlement,' 3rd Draft, p.9.

94 Philip Noel Baker, 'Notes on Mr Dalton's Outline Sketch of the Principles Upon Which a Declaration of Post-War International Policy Should be Based' International Department memo, November 1943?, pp.4–5. William Gillies Papers, Labour Party Archives, Manchester. This document was a response to Dalton's earlier sketch, rather than to the 1944 drafts, but it adequately demonstrates Noel Baker's unhappiness with certain aspects of the minorities question.

95 Ibid. p.4.

96 Brailsford, *Our Settlement with Germany*, p.97.

97 Allan G.B. Fisher and David Mitrany, 'Some Notes on the Transfer of Populations', *The Political Quarterly* xiv/4 (1943), pp.363–71.

98 Woolf, *The International Post-War Settlement*, pp.13–4.

99 Woolf, *The International Post-War Settlement*, p.16.
100 Letter from James Walker to Hugh Dalton, dated 17 April 1944, 2. Hugh Dalton Papers, 7/10 80. British Library of Political and Economic Science, LSE, London.
101 Letter from Hugh Dalton to Mary E. Sutherland, dated 18 April 1944. Hugh Dalton Papers, 7/10 79. British Library of Political and Economic Science, LSE, London.
102 Letter from Hugh Dalton to Harold Laski, dated 12th April 1944. Hugh Dalton Papers, 7/10 41. British Library of Political and Economic Science, LSE, London.
103 Dalton, *Hitler's War*, pp.145–6.
104 Brailsford, *Our Settlement with Germany*, pp.76–9.
105 Mitrany, *Road to Security*, p.19.
106 Labour Party, *Report of the 43rd Annual Conference* (London: Labour Party, 1944), p.139.
107 David Mitrany, 'Nationality and Nationalism' in Mitrany, *Functional Theory of Politics*, pp.139–43. This was a previously unpublished paper.
108 Laski, 'British Labour's Peace Aims', p.2.
109 Ibid. pp.2–3.
110 Laski, 'C. The Further Future', document attached, along with the rest of the final draft of the international statement, to the letter from Hugh Dalton to William Gillies, dated 12 April 1944. William Gillies Papers, Labour Party Archive, Manchester.
111 Woolf, *International Post-War Settlement*, p.3.
112 Dalton, *Hitler's War*, pp.156–7.
113 See Noel Baker, 'Draft Declaration by the Labour Movement', 3; and Noel Baker, 'Notes on Mr Dalton's Outline Sketch', 6. See also Dalton, *Hitler's War*, p.25.
114 The Labour Party National Executive Committee, 'Appendix II. Labour, the War, and the Peace', in Labour Party, *39th Annual Conference*, p.189.
115 Dalton, *Hitler's War*, chapter XV.
116 Labour Party, *43rd Conference 1944*, p.133.
117 'Memorandum Submitted by the Moseley Divisional Labour Party' Advisory Committee on International Questions memo no. 6 (new series), 14 February 1945, p.1. Labour Party Archives, Manchester.
118 'Moseley Divisional Labour Party', p.1.
119 Ivor Thomas, 'The Form of the International Authority', Advisory Committee on International Questions memo no. 1 (new series), September 1944, p.1. Labour Party Archives, Manchester.
120 Woolf, *International Post-War Settlement*, p.7.
121 See, for example, Woolf, *International Post-War Settlement*, pp.6–8.
122 Untitled paper, dated 20th October 1939, p.1. J.S. Middleton Papers, Labour Party Archives, Manchester.
123 *39th Annual Conference 1940*, p.190.
124 *43rd Annual Conference 1944*, p.132.
125 Dalton, *Hitler's War*, p.25.
126 Woolf, *International Post-War Settlement*, p.9.
127 Noel Baker, 'Draft Declaration by the Labour Movement', p.4.

128 'The Dumbarton Oaks Proposals', Advisory Committee on International Questions memo no. 2b, November 1944, p.7. Labour Party Archives, Manchester.

129 Laski, 'British Labour's Peace Aims', p.6; Noel Baker, 'Draft Declaration by the Labour Movement', p.5; 39th Annual Conference 1940, p.189.

130 Dalton, *Hitler's War*, chapter XV.

131 'Notes on Mr Dalton's Outline Sketch', p.5.

132 Ibid. p.5.

133 Thomas, 'Form of the International Authority', p.1; Dalton, *Hitler's War*, p.157.

134 Noel Baker, 'Draft for Section on International Political Organisation', p.2. Attached to letter from Philip Noel Baker to Harold Laski dated 8th April 1944, William Gillies Papers, Labour Party Archives, Manchester. Hugh Dalton cut this section out of the final draft.

135 Noel Baker, 'Notes on Mr Dalton's Outline Sketch', p.5; 'Draft for Section on International Political Organisation', p.2.

136 Noel Baker, 'Notes on Mr Dalton's Outline Sketch', p.5; 'Draft for Section on International Political Organisation', p.2.

137 'Dumbarton Oaks Proposals', pp.7–8.

138 Noel Baker, 'Notes on Mr Dalton's Outline Sketch', p.5.

139 'Draft for Section on International Political Organisation', p.3.

140 Laski, 'British Labour's Peace Aims', p.4.

141 Noel Baker, 'Draft Declaration by the Labour Movement', p.2.

142 'Dumbarton Oaks Proposals', p.6.

143 Thomas, 'Form of the International Authority', p.1.

144 See, for example, Woolf, *International Post-War Settlement*, p.11.

145 'Dumbarton Oaks Proposals', p.6.

146 Noel Baker, 'Draft for Section on International Political Organisation', p.3; 'Report of the National Executive Committee 1943–4'.

147 Thomas, 'Form of the International Authority', p.1.

148 Noel Baker, 'Peace Aims of the Labour Party', p.3.

149 See Noel Baker, 'Draft for Section on International Political Organisation', pp.2–3.

150 Dalton, 'International Post-War Settlement' 3rd Draft, p.13.

151 'Moseley Divisional Labour Party', p.1.

152 Harold Laski, 'The Structure of International Government', Report of the Fabian International Bureau Weekend Conference, 8–9 January 1944, p.61, p.63. Mitrany Papers, British Library of Political and Economic Sciences, LSE, London.

153 See Noel Baker, 'Note on the Draft', p.4. Noel Baker, 'Peace Aims of the Labour Party', p.4.

154 Dalton, 'International Post-War Settlement' 3rd Draft, p.11; 'Report of the National Executive Committee 1943–4', p.3.

155 'International Post-War Settlement' 3rd Draft, 12; 'Report of the National Executive Committee 1943–4', p.3.

156 Noel Baker, 'Draft for Section on International Political Organisation', pp.2–3.

157 Mitrany, *The Road to Security*, pp.16–19.

158 'Democracy and Democratic Leadership', in *End of an Epoch*, p.101.

159 Letter from Philip Noel Baker to Hugh Dalton, 8th April 1944, p.2.

160 'Report of the National Executive Committee 1943–4', p.3.

161 W. Arnold-Forster, 'International Controls', in Julian Huxley et al, *When Hostilities Cease. Papers on Relief and Reconstruction Prepared for the Fabian Society* (London: Victor Gollancz, 1943), pp.48–9.

162 'Comments on the Memorandum by an Official', attached to Leonard Woolf, 'International Broadcasting', Advisory Committee on International Questions memo no. 3 (new series), November 1944, p.1. Labour Party Archives, Manchester.

163 Woolf, 'International Broadcasting', p.1.

164 Ibid. p.1.

165 Ibid. pp.2–3.

166 'Comments on the Memorandum by an Official', p.1–2.

167 Ibid. p.2.

168 Noel Baker, 'Note on the Draft', p.4.

169 Brailsford, *Our Settlement with Germany*, pp.137–8.

170 'International Post-War Settlement' 3rd Draft, p.10.

171 'Report of the National Executive Committee 1943–4', p.2.

172 *43rd Annual Conference 1944*, p.131.

173 Ibid. p.132–3

174 Vickers, *Labour Party and the World*, p.147

175 Noel Baker, 'Notes on Mr Dalton's Outline Sketch', p.3.

176 'Dumbarton Oaks Proposals', p.6.

177 Leonard Woolf, 'The United Nations', *The Political Quarterly* xvi/1 (1945), pp.18–19.

178 'Moseley Divisional Labour Party', p.1.

179 H.N. Brailsford in the debate following William Arnold-Forster's paper 'Post-War Balance of Power' Report of the Fabian International Bureau Weekend Conference, 8–9 January 1944, p.14. Mitrany Papers, British Library of Political and Economic Sciences, LSE, London.

180 Brailsford, *Our Settlement with Germany*, p.135.

181 See John Kent, 'British Postwar Planning for Europe 1942–45', in Antonio Varsori and Elena Calandri (eds), *The Failure of Peace in Europe, 1943–48* (Basingstoke: Palgrave, 2002), pp.40–7.

182 Leonard Woolf, 'How to Make Peace', *The Political Quarterly* xii/4 (1941), p.374.

183 Woolf, *International Post-War Settlement*, p.12–3.

184 For Woolf's discussion of this 'realist' proposal for spheres of influence see Woolf, 'Future of Small States', p.221–2.

185 See Ambrose, *Rise to Globalism*, p.44–5.

186 For a discussion of Bevan's campaign see Vickers, *Labour Party and the World*, p.145. For Zilliacus' position see his *I Choose Peace*, pp.71–2.

187 'Dumbarton Oaks Proposals', p.7.

188 *43rd Annual Conference*, p.140.

189 'Dumbarton Oaks Proposals', pp.4–5

190 Vickers, *Labour Party and the World*, p.150.

191 Ibid. p.152.

192 'Report of the National Executive Committee 1943–4', p.1.

193 Philip Noel Baker, 'Foreword' to Socialist Union, *Socialism and Foreign Policy* (London: Book House, 1953), pp.6–7.

194 See, for example, H.N. Brailsford's comment in the Report of the Fabian International Bureau Weekend Conference, 8–9 January 1944, p.55. Mitrany Papers, British Library of Political and Economic Sciences, LSE, London.

Chapter 6

1 Letter from Philip Noel Baker to Leonard Woolf, 16 February 1944, p.2. The Leonard Woolf Papers. University of Sussex.

2 Wilson, *International Theory of Leonard Woolf.*

3 Ibid. p.2.

4 Ibid. pp.115–6.

5 Ibid. p.3.

6 Leonard Woolf, *Quack, Quack!* (London: Hogarth, 1935).

7 Woolf, *Empire and Commerce in Africa.*

8 Wilson, *International Theory of Leonard Woolf*, p.73.

9 See, for example, Mary Parker Follett *The New State* (London: Longmans, 1918), and L.T. Hobhouse, *Liberalism* (New York: Oxford University Press, 1964). The latter was originally published in 1911. Peter Wilson does not agree with my interpretation of Woolf as a new liberal, seeing him instead as a thorough Fabian socialist.

10 See, for example, the discussion in Woolf, *Barbarians at the Gate*, pp.155–8.

11 Letter from Harold Laski to Leonard Woolf 2 July 1936, thanking Woolf for a kind review of his book. Monk's House Papers, University of Sussex.

12 Wilson, *International Theory of Leonard Woolf*, p.74.

13 See Arnold J. Toynbee, *A Study of History. Abridgement of Volumes I–VI by D.C. Somervell* (New York & London: Oxford University Press, 1947), especially parts III and IV.

14 Leonard Woolf, *Imperialism and Civilization* (London: Hogarth, 1928), p.7.

15 Woolf, *Barbarians at the Gate*, pp.41–3.

16 *Imperialism and Civilization*, pp.9–10.

17 See, for example, the argument in Woolf, *The International Post-War Settlement*, p.10.

18 *Barbarians at the Gate*, pp.155–8.

19 This pervades the argument of *Barbarians at the Gate*, especially p.141. Peter Wilson has pointed out to me that this might owe far more to Woolf's classical education than to British Hegelianism.

20 Woolf, *Barbarians at the Gate*, pp.218–9.

21 Wilson, *International Theory of Leonard Woolf*, p.68, p.85,

22 Woolf, *Imperialism and Civilisation*, pp.9–10.

23 Leonard Woolf, 'From Serajevo [sic] to Geneva', *The Political Quarterly* i (1930), pp.186–206.

24 Woolf, *International Government*, p.100.

25 Woolf, *International Government*, pp.105–25.

26 Wilson, *International Theory of Leonard Woolf*, p.24, p.30.

27 On this issue see Wilson, *International Theory of Leonard Woolf.*

28 See, for example, Woolf, *International Post-War Settlement*, p.7.

29 Wilson, *International Theory of Leonard Woolf*, pp.33–4.

30 Ibid. chapter 3.

31 Wilson also makes this point that Woolf saw no tension between his views of international government. *International Theory of Leonard Woolf*, p.34.

32 For a fuller account of this see ibid.

33 Woolf, 'From Serajevo to Geneva', p.189.

34 Ibid. p.197.

35 Ibid. p.196.

36 Ibid. p.197.

37 Leonard Woolf, 'From Geneva to the Next War' *The Political Quarterly* iv (1933), pp.30–43.

38 Woolf, 'Labour's Foreign Policy', p.508; Leonard Woolf, 'Introduction', in Leonard Woolf (ed.), *The Intelligent Man's Way to Prevent War* (London: Victor Gollancz, 1933), pp.7–18.

39 Woolf, 'Introduction', p.7.

40 Woolf, 'Meditation on Abyssinia', pp.16–32.

41 Woolf, 'Memorandum on the Attitude which the Party Should Adopt to Proposed Reforms of the League'; Leonard Woolf, 'Ideal of the League Remains', pp.330–45.

42 Woolf, 'Arms and Peace', pp.21–35.

43 Woolf, 'The Resurrection of the League', pp.337–352.

44 See the discussions in Woolf, 'How to Make Peace', pp.367–79; Leonard Woolf, 'Introduction', in Julian Huxley *et al.*, *When Hostilities Cease* (London: Victor Gollancz, 1943), pp.11–17; Woolf, *The International Post-war Settlement*; and Leonard Woolf, 'The United Nations', pp.12–20.

45 Wilson, *International Theory of Leonard Woolf*, pp.115–6. Wilson has two chapters (5 and 6) on Woolf's analysis of Imperialism. Many of the issues mentioned below are explored in more depth in these two chapters.

46 Woolf, *Empire and Commerce in Africa*, pp.357–8; Woolf, *Imperialism and Civilization*, pp.119–20.

47 See, for example, *Imperialism and Civilization*, chapter 6.

48 Woolf, *Mandates and Empire*, especially, pp.5–7 and pp.17–18; Woolf, *Scope of the Mandates under the League*, pp.1–3.

49 Leonard Woolf, 'Colonies', pp.1–2; Woolf, *Empire and Commerce in Africa*, pp.362–8.

50 Labour Party, *The Empire in Africa: Labour's Policy* (London: Labour Party, 1921) especially p.10; Labour Party, *The Demand for Colonial Territories and Equality of Economic Opportunity* (London: Labour Party, 1936), especially pp.45–51. See also the following Advisory Committee memos: 'The Labour Party's International Policy', pp.4–5; 'Revised Memorandum on Peaceful Change', p.2 and p.5; and 'International Policy and Peaceful Change', p.1. Many of the above were obviously written, or partially written, by Woolf.

51 See Sylvest, 'Interwar Internationalism', pp.409–432.

52 Winkler, *Paths Not Taken*.

53 David Mitrany, 'Memorandum on Labour Policy Concerning Commissions to be Set up Under the Peace Treaty'.

54 See especially 'The Need for a League Foreign Policy', p.4.

55 Mitrany, 'A Labour Policy on Sanctions'; Mitrany, *The Problem of International Sanctions*.

56 Noel Baker, 'The Present Position with Regard to Disarmament'; Noel Baker, *Disarmament*; and *Geneva Protocol*.

57 Arnold-Forster, 'All Inclusive Arbitration'; Arnold-Forster, *Arbitrate!*

58 Angell, *Arbitration, Sanctions, Disarmament*.

59 See Dalton, *The Peace of Nations*, p.211; Arnold-Forster, 'Sanctions (Commentary on Mr Buxton's Paper)'. Also see the comment of Arthur Henderson quoted in Angell, *After All*, p.252.

60 'Memorandum on an Immediate Policy for the Party in Relation to the International Situation and Proposals for a New Security Agreement'; Thomas and Woolf, 'Memorandum on Factors in the International Situation to be Considered in Relation to any New Security Agreement'.

61 Noel-Baker, 'Copy of a Letter to Mr C.R. Buxton from Mr P. Noel-Baker'.

62 Transcript of John F. Naylor's interview with Leonard Woolf, 24 July 1962, Leonard Woolf Papers, ID6, University of Sussex Library, Falmer, UK.

63 See especially Mitrany, *Progress of International Government*, p.42; David Mitrany, *Working Peace System*; and Mitrany, *Road to Security*.

64 See, for example, Woolf, *The International Post-War Settlement*, p.7; Philip Noel Baker, 'Notes on Mr Dalton's Outline Sketch of the Principles Upon Which a Declaration of Post-War International Policy Should be Based' International Department memo, November 1943?, pp.4–5. William Gillies Papers, Labour Party Archives, Manchester.

65 H.N. Brailsford in the debate following William Arnold-Forster's paper 'Post-War Balance of Power' Report of the Fabian International Bureau Weekend Conference, 8–9 January 1944, p.14. Mitrany Papers, British Library of Political and Economic Sciences, London; Brailsford, Our Settlement with Germany, p.135; Woolf, *The International Post-War Settlement*, pp.12–3.

66 'The Dumbarton Oaks Proposals'; Woolf, 'The United Nations', pp.18–19.

67 Sylvest, 'Interwar Internationalism', p.428.

68 See especially Chapter 10 of *Conditions of Peace*.

69 Clarence Kirshman Streit, *Union Now with Britain* (London: Jonathan Cape, 1941).

70 See Norman Angell, 'War Aims – III. Past Policy and the Future', *The Spectator*, 10 November 1939, pp.640–1.

71 Leventhal, *Last Dissenter*, 1.

72 For a recent version of this see J.W. Smith, *Cooperative Capitalism: A Blueprint for Global Peace and Prosperity* (Sun City AZ: Institute for Economic Democracy, 2005).

73 For a fuller discussion of these weaknesses as they apply to Angell and Mitrany see Ashworth, *Creating International Studies*, pp.133–48.

74 Gordon, *Conflict and Consensus in Labour's Foreign Policy*, especially chapters 1–2.

75 Cline, *Recruits to Labour*.

76 Vickers, *The Labour Party and the World*, p.5.

77 Zilliacus, *I Choose Peace*, especially chapters V and X.

78 See A.J.P. Taylor's masterful, if not always complimentary, commentary *The Troublemakers*.

79 For a full list of these former Liberals see, Cline, *Recruits to Labour*.

80 Although in Woolf the division between capitalism and psychological causes of war did not exist, because he saw capitalism as psychological. For a summary of Woolf's position here see Wilson *International Theory of Leonard Woolf*.

BIBLIOGRAPHY

Private Papers

David Mitrany Papers, British Library of Political and Economic Sciences, London School of Economics, London, UK.

Emily Greene Balch Papers, Wellesley College Library, Massachusetts, USA.

George Lansbury Papers, British Library of Political and Economic Sciences, London School of Economics, London, UK.

Hugh Dalton Papers, British Library of Political and Economic Sciences, London School of Economics, London, UK.

James Ramsay MacDonald Papers, National Archives, Kew, London, UK.

Leonard Woolf Papers, University of Sussex, Falmer, Sussex, UK.

Labour Party Archives, Labour History Archive and Study Centre, Manchester, UK.

Papers of Party Office Holders

J.S. Middleton Papers
William Gillies Papers

Conference Reports

Report of the Eighteenth Annual Conference (London: Labour Party, 1918).

Report of the Nineteenth Annual Conference (London: Labour Party, 1919).

Report of the Twentieth Annual Conference (London: Labour Party, 1920).

Report of the Nineteenth Annual Conference (London: Labour Party, 1921).

Report of the Thirty-Fifth Annual Conference (London: Labour Party, 1935).

Report of the Thirty-Seventh Annual Conference (London: Labour Party, 1937).

Report of the Thirty-Ninth Annual Conference (London: Labour Party, 1940).

Report of the Forty-Third Annual Conference (London: Labour Party, 1944).

Committee Minutes

Advisory Committee on Imperial Questions Minutes.

Advisory Committee on International Questions Minutes.

Advisory Committee on International Questions Memoranda.

Anon, first untitled and undated memo, no number, 1918?

———. 'Short Statement of War Aims', no.6, 25 June 1918

———. 'Letter to the Executive Committee', no.149a, July 1920.

———. 'Draft Pamphlet on Foreign Policy', no.228a, 1921.

———. 'Labour and the League of Nations', no.207a, May 1921.

———. 'Open Diplomacy', Draft for insertion in pamphlet on Foreign Policy, no. 228(a), 1921.

———. 'Draft Resolution for Labour Party Annual Conference', no.245z, approved by the Executive on 31 May 1922.

———. 'Revision of the Treaty of Versailles', no.254a, 1922.

———. 'The Need for a League Foreign Policy', no.287, 9 July 1923.

———. 'The Foreign Office and Labour Governments', no. 333d, 1925.

———. 'Report of the Sub-Committee on the Security Pact', no.339a, July 1925.

———. 'Report on American Proposals for the Outlawry of War', no.383a, February 1928

———. 'Proposals for the Disarmament Conference', no.424b, June 1931.

———. 'The Labour Party's Policy with Regard to the League and Sanctions', no.431a, March 1933.

———. 'The Labour Party's Policy Regarding the League of Nations', no 433a, April 1933.

———. 'The Labour Party's Policy and the Services Estimates', no.441a, January 1934.

———. 'Memorandum on Minorities', no.453, February 1935.

———. 'Comment on the "Memorandum on Factors in the International Situation to be Considered in Relation to any New Security Agreement"', no.478, April 1937.

———. 'International Policy and Peaceful Change', no.484b, February 1938.

———. 'The Flight from Collective Security', no.486a, March 1938.

———. 'The Labour Party's International Policy', no.502a, March 1939.

———. 'Revised Memorandum on Peaceful Change', no.493a and 489a, May 1938, revised July 1939.

———. 'The Dumbarton Oaks Proposals', no.2b (new series), November 1944.

Angell, Norman, 'Peace Terms', no.61, May 1919.

———. 'Memorandum on the Reactionary Attitude of the Government in International Affairs', no.341, November 1925.

Arnold-Forster, William, 'All Inclusive Arbitration', no.346, August 1926.

——. 'Sanctions (Commentary on Mr Buxton's Paper)', no.365, May 1927.

——. 'Commentary on the British Government's Observations to the League, on Arbitration and Security', no.386, February 1928.

——. 'Note on the Franco-American and Anglo-American Arbitration Treaties', no.387, February 1928.

——.William, and Leonard Woolf, 'Proposed Recommendation to the Executive Regarding a Convention for Pacific Settlement', no.355a, nd.

——. 'Bilateral Pacts and Collective Security', no.504a, June 1939.

Brailsford, H.N., 'A Parliament of the League of Nations' no.44, January 1919.

——. 'Draft Memorandum on Disarmament', no.198, April 1921.

Buxton, Charles Roden, 'Memorandum on the Pact of Locarno', no.340, October 1925

——. 'Report on Disarmament', no.347, 5 September 1926.

——. 'Sanctions in the Covenant and the Protocol' no.358, March 1927.

——. 'Comments on the "Memorandum on Factors in the International Situation" etc. (no.473)', no.475, January 1937.

Delisle Burns, C., 'Notes on the League', no.143, 8 June 1920.

Ewer, W.N., 'Comments Received from Some Members of the International Committee Upon Memorandum no.504,' June 1939.

Hobson, J.A., 'Economic War After the War', no.24, undated.

Kenworthy, J.M., and George Young, 'Revised Memorandum on Outlawry of War', no.379c, nd.

Lawrence, Susan, 'Note on Policy', no.469, July 1936.

Lowes Dickinson, G., 'A League of Nations', no.27, 22 October 1918.

Mitrany, David, 'Memorandum on Labour Policy Concerning Commissions to be Set up Under the Peace Treaty', no.125, January 1920.

——. 'A Labour Policy on Sanctions', no.366, May 1927.

——. 'Memorandum on the Minorities Problem', no.385, February 1928.

Moseley Divisional Labour Party, 'Memorandum Submitted by the Moseley Divisional Labour Party' no.6 (new series), 14 February 1945.

Noel Baker, Philip, 'The Present Position with Regard to Disarmament', no.345, July 1926.

——. 'Notes on Mr Woolf's Paper on the International Situation', no.464, March 1936.

——. 'Copy of a Letter to Mr C.R. Buxton from Mr P. Noel-Baker', no.480, May 1937.

Ponsonby, Arthur, 'Popular or Parliamentary Control of Foreign Policy', no.256, 1922.

Thomas, Ivor, and Leonard Woolf, 'Memorandum on Factors in the International Situation to be Considered in Relation to any New Security Agreement', no.473, December 1936.

——. 'The Form of the International Authority', no.1 (new series), September 1944.

Woolf, Leonard, 'Proposals for the Immediate Establishment by the Allies of a League of Nations', no.5, June 1918.

——. 'Colonies', no.23, September 1918

——. 'Punishment and Reparation at the End of the War', no.37, November 1918.

——. 'Draft Report for the International Socialist Conference: The League of Nations and Disarmament', no.251, 1922.

——. 'The League of Nations and Disarmament', no.25, 1922.

——. 'Proposals for the "Outlawry of War"', no.379a, December 1927.

——. 'Memorandum on the Attitude which the Party Should Adopt to Proposed Reforms of the League', no.468, July 1936.

——. 'Memorandum on an Immediate Policy for the Party in Relation to the International Situation and Proposals for a New Security Agreement', no.479a, April 1937.

——. 'International Broadcasting', no.3 (new series), November 1944.

Young, George, 'Memorandum on the Reform of the Foreign Services', no.10, July 1918.

——. 'The Reform of Diplomacy. A Practical Programme', no number, May 1921.

International Sub-Committee of the National Executive Committee Memos

Laski, Harold J., 'A Manifesto to the German People on British Labour's Peace Aims', September 1939.

——. 'British Labour Peace Aims', September 1939.

——. 'First Laski Draft', undated [probably September-October 1939]

Noel Baker, Philip, 'The Peace Aims of the Labour Party', 23 September 1939.

——. 'Note on the Draft "Peace Aims of the Labour Party"', 23 September 1939.

——. 'Draft Declaration by the Labour Movement on Herr Hitler's Proposals for Peace', 9 October 1939.

Secondary Sources Published or Written Before 1949
Books

Angell, Norman, *The Great Illusion. A Study of the Relation of Military Power in Nations to their Economic and Social Advantage* (Toronto: McClelland and Goodchild, 1911).

———. *Peace Theories and the Balkan War* (London: Horace Marshall, 1912).

———. *The Foundations of International Polity* (London: William Heineman, 1914).

———. *The British Revolution and American Democracy. An Interpretation of British Labour Programmes* (Toronto: McClelland Goodchild and Stewart, 1919).

———. *The Fruits of Victory* (New York: Garland 1972). Orig. pub. in 1921.

———. *If Britain is to Live* (London: Nisbet, 1923).

———. *The Public Mind. Its Disorders: Its Explanation* (London: Noel Douglas, 1926).

———. *Preface to Peace. A Guide for the Plain Man* (London: Hamish Hamilton, 1935).

———. *This Have and Have-Not Business. Political Fantasy and Economic Fact* (London: Hamish Hamilton, 1936).

———. *Peace with the Dictators? A Symposium and Some Conclusions* (London: Hamish Hamilton, 1938).

———. *Must it be War?* (London: Labour Book Service, 1939).

———. *Why Do We Fight* (London: Hamish Hamilton, 1939).

———. *Why Freedom Matters* (Harmondsworth: Penguin, 1940).

———. *The Steep Places. An Examination of Political Tendencies* (London: Hamish Hamilton, 1947).

Angell, Norman, and Harold Wright, *Can Governments Cure Unemployment?* (London: Dent, 1931).

Attlee, Clement et al., *Labour's Aims in War and Peace* (London: Lincolns-Prager, 1940).

Bell, Gertrude, *Selected Letters of Gertrude Bell* (Harmondsworth: Penguin, 1953).

Bourquin, Maurice (ed.), *Collective Security. A Record of the Seventh and Eighth International Studies Conference. Paris 1934-London 1935* (Paris: International Institute of Intellectual Cooperation, 1936).

Brailsford, H.N., *Macedonia. Its Races and their Future* (London: Methuen, 1906).

———. *The War of Steel and Gold. A Study of the Armed Peace* (London: Bell, 1917).

———. *A League of Nations* (London: Hedley, 1917).

———. *After the Peace* (London: Parsons, 1920).

———. *Olives of Endless Age. Being a Study of this Distracted World and its Need of Unity* (New York & London: Harper, 1928).

———. *Property or Peace?* (London: Gollancz, 1934).

———. *Our Settlement with Germany* (Harmondsworth: Penguin, 1944).

———. *The Life-Work of J.A. Hobson* (London: Oxford University Press, 1948).

Brinton, Henry (ed.), *Does Capitalism Cause War?* (London: H & E.R. Brinton, 1935).

Carr, E.H., *The Twenty Years' Crisis* (London: Macmillan, 1939).

———. *Conditions of Peace* (London: MacMillan, 1942).

———. *Nationalism and After* (London: Macmillan, 1945).

———. *International Relations Between the Two World Wars (1919–1939)* (London: Macmillan, 1948).

'Cato', *Guilty Men* (London: Victor Gollancz, 1941).

Churchill, Winston, *The Gathering Storm* (Boston: Houghton Mifflin, 1948).

Cole, G.D.H., *A History of the Labour Party from 1914* (London: Routledge & Kegan Paul, 1948).

Dalton, Hugh, *Towards the Peace of Nations. A Study in International Politics* (London: Routledge, 1928).

———. *Hitler's War: Before and After* (Harmondsworth: Penguin, 1940).

Delisle Burns, C., *International Politics* (London: Methuen, 1920).

Estorick, Eric, *Stafford Cripps: Prophetic Rebel* (New York: John Day, 1941).

Follett, Mary Parker, *The New State* (London: Longmans, 1918).

Gestapo, the, *The Black Book* (Sonderfahndungsliste G.B.) (London: Imperial War Museum, 1989).

Gunther, John, *Inside Europe* (London: Hamish Hamilton, 1940).

Hamilton, Mary Agnes, *Remembering My Good Friends* (London: Jonathan Cape, 1944).

Hobhouse, L.T., *Liberalism* (New York: Oxford University Press, 1964). Originally published in 1911.

Hobson, J.A., *The Evolution of Modern Capitalism* (Londson: Scott, 1894).

———. *Imperialism: A Study* (London: Nisbet, 1902).

Hogg, Quentin, *The Left was Never Right* (London: Faber & Faber, 1945).

Lansbury, George, *My Life* (London: Constable, 1928).

Laski, Harold J., *A Grammar of Politics* (London: George Allen & Unwin, 1925).

Lloyd George, David, *War Memoirs Volume II* (London: Odhams, 1936).

MacDonald, James Ramsay, *The Socialist Movement* (London: Williams and Norgate, 1911).

Mackinder, Halford J., *Democratic Ideals and Reality: A Study in the Politics of Reconstruction* (London: Constable, 1919).

Madariaga, Salvador de, *Disarmament* (London: Humphrey Milford/Oxford University Press, 1929).

———. *The World's Design* (London: Allen and Unwin, 1938).

Mitrany, David, *The Problem of International Sanctions* (London: Humphrey Milford & OUP, 1925).

———. *The Land and the Peasant in Rumania. The War and Agrarian Reform* (London: Humprey Milford & Oxford University Press, 1930).

———. *The Progress of International Government* (London: Allen & Unwin, 1933).

———. *The Effects of the War in South Eastern Europe* (New Haven: Yale University Press, 1936).

———. *A Working Peace System. An Argument for the Functional Development of International Organisation* (London: Royal Institute for International Affairs/Oxford University Press, 1943).

Noel Baker, Philip, *The Geneva Protocol* (London: Bell, 1925).

———. *Disarmament* (London: Hogarth, 1926).

———. *The League of Nations at Work* (London: Nisbet, 1927).

———. *The Private Manufacture of Armaments* (London: Victor Gollancz, 1936).

Ponsonby, Arthur, *Democracy and Diplomacy. A Plea for Popular Control of Foreign Policy* (London: Methuen, 1915).

———. *The Covenant of the League of Nations* (London, 1920).

———. *Now is the Time. An Appeal for Peace* (London: Leonard Parsons, 1925).

Rowse, A.L., *The End of an Epoch. Reflections on Contemporary History* (London: Macmillan, 1947).

Shotwell, James T., *War as an Instrument of National Policy and its Renunciation in the Pact of Paris* (London: Constable, 1929).

Streit, Clarence Kirshman, *Union Now with Britain* (London: Jonathan Cape, 1941).

Sturmthal, Adolf, *The Tragedy of European Labour 1918–1939* (London: Victor Gollancz, 1944).

Swanwick, H.M., *Collective Insecurity* (London: Jonathan Cape, 1937).

Toynbee, Arnold J., *A Study of History. Abridgement of Volumes I–VI by D.C. Somervell* (New York & London: Oxford University Press, 1947).

Wallas, Graham, *Human Nature in Politics* (Boston and New York: Houghton Mifflin, 1916).

———. *Social Judgement* (New York: Harcourt Brace, 1935).

Woolf, Leonard, *International Government* (London: George Allen & Unwin, 1916).

——. *Empire and Commerce in Africa. A Study in Economic Imperialism* (London: Labour Research Department and George Allen & Unwin, 1920).

——. *Imperialism and Civilization* (London: Hogarth, 1928).

——. (ed.), *The Intelligent Man's Way to Prevent War* (London: Victor Gollancz, 1933).

——. *Quack, Quack!* (London: Hogarth, 1935).

——. *Barbarians at the Gate* (London: Victor Gollancz, 1939).

——. *The War for Peace* (London: Routledge, 1940).

Zilliacus, Konni, *Inquest on Peace. An Analysis of the National Government's Foreign Policy* (London: Victor Gollancz, 1935).

——. *Why the League has Failed* (London: Victor Gollancz, 1938).

——. *Why We are Losing the Peace* (London: Victor Gollancz, 1939).

——. *The Mirror of the Past* (London: Victor Gollancz, 1944).

——. *I Choose Peace* (Harmondsworth: Penguin, 1949).

Chapters in Books

Angell, Norman, 'The International Anarchy', in Leonard Woolf (ed.), *The Intelligent Man's Way to Prevent War* (London: Victor Gollancz, 1933).

——. 'Educational and Psychological Factors', in Leonard Woolf (ed.), *The Intelligent Man's Way to Prevent War* (London: Victor Gollancz, 1933).

Arnold-Forster, William, 'International Controls', in Julian Huxley et al., *When Hostilities Cease. Papers on Relief and Reconstruction Prepared for the Fabian Society* (London: Victor Gollancz, 1943).

Bartlett, Vernon, 'The War Horizon', in Bertrand Russell et al., *Dare We Look Ahead?* (New York: Macmillan, 1938)

Brailsford, H.N., 'A Socialist Foreign Policy', in Christopher Addison et al., *Problems of a Socialist Government* (London: Victor Gollancz, 1933).

Foot, Michael, 'Introduction', in Konni Zilliacus, *The Mirror of the Past* (London: Victor Gollancz, 1944).

Laski, Harold J., 'Economic Foundations of Peace', in Leonard Woolf (ed.), *The Intelligent Man's Way to Prevent War* (London: Victor Gollancz, 1933).

Mitrany, David, 'Marx v. the Peasant' in T. E. Gregory and Hugh Dalton (eds), *London Essays in Economics: In Honour of Edwin Cannan* (London: Routledge, 1927).

——. 'Nationality and Nationalism' in Mitrany, David, *The Functional Theory of Politics* (London: LSE and Martin Robertson, 1975). An unpublished paper from the 1930s.

Noel Baker, Philip, 'Peace and the Official Mind' in Philip Noel Baker et al., *Challenges to Death* (London: Constable, 1934).

——. 'The Four Pillars of a New World Order', in Clement Attlee et al., *Labour's Aims in War and Peace* (London: Lincolns-Prager, 1940).

Smith, F.E., 'Idealism in International Politics' reprinted in William Camp, *The Glittering Prizes. A Biographical Study of F. E. Smith First Earl of Birkenhead* (London: MacGibbon and Kee, 1960).

Warner, Edward, 'Douhet, Mitchell, Seversky: Theories of Air Warfare', in Edward Meade Earl (ed.), *Makers of Modern Strategy. Military Thought from Machiavelli to Hitler* (New York: Atheneum, 1967). Originally published in 1941.

Woolf, Leonard, 'Introduction', in Leonard Woolf (ed.), *The Framework of a Lasting Peace* (London: George Allen & Unwin, 1917).

——. 'Introduction', in Leonard Woolf (ed.), *The Intelligent Man's Way to Prevent War* (London: Victor Gollancz, 1933).

——. 'Introduction', in Julian Huxley et al., *When Hostilities Cease* (London: Victor Gollancz, 1943).

Articles in Academic Journals

Angell, Norman, 'The New John Bull' *Political Quarterly* vii/3 (1936), pp.311–29.

Brailsford, H.N., 'The Tory Policy of Peace', *The Political Quarterly* ix/3 (1938), pp.325–33.

Fisher, Allan G.B., and David Mitrany, 'Some Notes on the Transfer of Populations', *The Political Quarterly* xiv/4 (1943), pp.363–71.

Hobson, J.A., 'Thoughts on our Present Discontents', *Political Quarterly* ix/1 (1938), pp.47–57.

Mackinder, Halford J., 'Geographical Pivot of History', *Geographical Journal* xxii (1904), pp.421–37.

Mitrany, David, 'Pan-Europa – A Hope or a Danger?', *Political Quarterly* i/4 (1930), pp.457–378.

——. 'Interrelation of Politics and Economics in Modern War', *Annals of the American Academy of Political and Social Science* clxxxii (1937), pp.82–8.

——. 'International Consequences of National Planning', *Yale Review* xxxvii/1 (1947), pp.18-31.

——. 'The Functional Approach to World Organisation', *International Affairs* xxiv/3 (1948),pp.350–363.

Morrell, Philip, 'The Control of Foreign Affairs. The Need for a Parliamentary Committee', *The Contemporary Review* dlxiii (1912), pp.659–67.

Ponsonby, Arthur, 'Disarmament by Example' *The Contemporary Review* cxxxii (1927), pp.690.

Woolf, Leonard, 'From Serajevo to Geneva', *The Political Quarterly* i (1930), pp.186–206.

——. 'From Geneva to the Next War' *The Political Quarterly* iv/1 (1933), pp.30–43.

——. 'Labour's Foreign Policy', *Political Quarterly* iiii/4 (1933), pp.504–24.

——. 'Meditation on Abyssinia', *The Political Quarterly* vii/1, pp.16–32.

——. 'The Ideal of the League Remains', *The Political Quarterly* vii/3 (1936), pp.330–45.

——. 'Arms and Peace', *The Political Quarterly* viii/1 (1937), pp.21–35.

——. 'The Resurrection of the League', *The Political Quarterly* viii/3 (1937), pp.337–52.

——. 'Utopia and Reality', *Political Quarterly* xi/2 (1940), pp.167–182

——. 'How to Make Peace', *The Political Quarterly* xii/4 (1941), pp.367–79.

——. 'The Future of the Small State' *The Political Quarterly* xiv/3 (1943), pp.209–224.

——. 'The United Nations', *The Political Quarterly* xvi/1 (1945), pp.12–20

Pamphlets

Angell, Norman, *Arbitration, Sanctions, Disarmament* (London: National Council for the Prevention of War, nd).

Arnold-Forster, *William, Arbitrate! Arbitrate! Arbitrate! The Case for All-Inclusive Pacific Settlement of International Disputes* (London: Labour Party, 1927).

Brailsford, H.N., *Towards a New League* (London: New Statesman and Nation, 1936).

British Anti War Movement, *British Labour Policy on War. A Reminder* (London: British Anti War Movement, 1934).

Buxton, Dorothy Frances, *The War for Coal and Iron* (London: Labour Party, 1921).

Henderson, Arthur, *The Peace Terms* (London: Labour Party, 1919).

——.*Labour's Foreign Policy* (London: Labour Party, 1933).

Labour Party, *Control of Foreign Policy: Labour's Programme* (London: Labour Party, 1920?).

——.*The Empire in Africa: Labour's Policy* (London: Labour Party, 1921).

——.*Labour and the Nation*. First edition (London: Labour Party, 1928).

——.*For Socialism and Peace. The Labour Party's Programme of Action 1934* (London: Labour Party, 1934).

——.*The Demand for Colonial Territories and Equality of Economic Opportunity* (London: Labour Party, 1936).

——.*Labour's Immediate Programme* (London: Labour Party, 1937).

MacDonald, James Ramsay, *Protocol or Pact. The Alternative to War* (London: Labour Party, nd [1925]).

Mitrany, David, *The Road to Security* (London: National Peace Council, 1944).

Morel, E.D., *The Horror on the Rhine* (London: UDC 1921).

Swanwick, H.M., *New Wars for Old* (London: Women's International League, 1934).

Swanwick, H.M., and William Arnold Forster, *Sanctions of the League of Nations Covenant* (London: Council for Prevention of War, 1928).

Woolf, Leonard, *Mandates and Empire* (London: League of Nations Union, 1920).

——. *Scope of the Mandates Under the League of Nations* (London: C. F. Roworth, 1921).

——.*The International Post-War Settlement* (London: Fabian Society and Victor Gollancz, 1944).

Newspapers and Periodicals

Angell, Norman, 'The Crux of our Foreign Policy', *New Leader*, 25 January 1924, p.9.

——. 'Pacifists and Cruisers: Two Views. I the Uses of Power', *New Leader*, 29 February 1924, p.3.

——. 'The Press and the Public Mind. The Lessons of Palmerston's Power', *New Leader*, 11 July 1924, p.4.

——. 'Behind these Failures', *Foreign Affairs*, October 1928, p.4.

——. 'Japan, the League and Us', *Time and Tide*, November 1931, pp. 1302–3.

——. 'Get Effective Defence and You Get the League', *The New Outlook*, 10 June 1936, pp.15–7.

——. 'War Aims – III. Past Policy and the Future', *The Spectator*, 10 November 1939, pp.640–1.

——. 'Who are the Utopians? And Who the Realists?', *Headway*, January 1940, pp.4–5.

Arnold-Forster, William, 'The British Government and Arbitration', *Foreign Affairs*, November 1925, pp.129–30.

Brailsford, H.N., 'Too Many Germans', *New Leader*, 20 October 1922, pp.5–6.

——. 'False Road to Security", *New Leader*, 23 March 1923, p.4.

——. 'The Other France. A Realistic Study of the Outlook', *New Leader*, 15 February 1924, p.9.

——. 'Arbitrate or Disarm. A New View of Security', *New Leader*, 12 September 1924, p.3–4.

——. 'A New Start for the League. Arbitration and the Chains of Versailles', *New Leader*, 26 September 1924, pp.10–11.

Delisle Burns, C., 'British Foreign Policy – The Next Moves', *Foreign Affairs*, July 1924, p.9.

Gillies, William, 'British Labour's Foreign Policy', *Foreign Affairs*, August 1923, p.31.

Hobson, J.A., 'Is America Moving?', *Foreign Affairs*, July 1923, p.3.

———. 'What Outlawry of War Signifies', *Foreign Affairs*, October 1924, pp.79–80.

Morel, E.D., 'Why the League Fails', *Foreign Affairs*, October 1923, p.70.

———. 'No Peace Without Truth', *New Leader*, 19 September 1924, p.4.

Swanwick, H.M., 'The Draft Treaty of Mutual Assistance', *Foreign Affairs*, February 1924, pp.153–4

———.'An Alternative Policy to the Draft Treaty of Mutual Assistance', *Foreign Affairs*, March 1924, p.171.

Zimmern, Alfred, 'I Have Joined the Labour Party' *New Leader*, 15 August 1924, pp.3–4.

Unpublished Papers not in Specific Archives

Hobson, J.A., 'Causes of War', paper presented at the South Park Ethical Society, nd. Paper in the possession of David Long.

Post-1950 Secondary Sources

Books

Ambrose, Stephen E., *Rise to Globalism. American Foreign Policy Since 1938* (Harmondsworth: Pelican, 1983).

Angell, Norman, *After All* (London: Hamish Hamilton, 1951).

Ashworth, Lucian M., *Creating International Studies. Angell, Mitrany and the Liberal Tradition* (Aldershot: Ashgate, 1999).

Ashworth, Lucian M., and David Long (eds), *New Perspectives in International Functionalism* (Basingstoke: Macmillan, 1999).

Berkeley, Humphry, *The Myth that will not Die. The Formation of the National Government 1931* (London: Croom Helm, 1978).

Carlton, David, *MacDonald Versus Henderson. The Foreign Policy of the Second Labour Government* (London: Macmillan, 1970).

Cline, Catherine Ann, , *Recruits to Labour. The British Labour Party 1914–1931* (New York: Syracuse University Press, 1963).

Craig, F.W.S., *British General Election Manifestos 1900–1974* (Basingstoke: Macmillan, 1975).

Dalton, Hugh, *Call Back Yesterday. Memoirs 1887–1931* (London: Frederick Muller, 1953).

———. *The Political Diary of Hugh Dalton 1918–40, 1945–60* (London: Jonathan Cape, 1986).

Dougherty, James E., and Robert L. Pfaltzgraff, *Contending Theories of International Relations. A Comprehensive Survey* (New York: Harper and Row, 1990).

Douglas, R.M., *The Labour Party, Nationalism and Internationalism, 1939–1951* (London: Routledge, 2004).

Fuller, J.F.C., *The Decisive Battles of the Western World and their Influence on History. Volume Two 1792–1944.* Edited by John Terraine (St Albans: Paladin, 1972).

———. *The Generalship of Alexander the Great* (Ware: Wordsworth, 1998).

Gordon, Michael R., *Conflict and Consensus in Labour's Foreign Policy 1914–1965* (Stanford: Stanford University Press, 1969).

Groom, A.J.R., and William C. Olson, *International Relations Then and Now: Origins and Trends in Interpretation* (London: HarperCollins, 1991).

Griffiths, Martin, *Idealism and International Politics* (London: Routledge, 1992).

Hamarlund, Per, *Liberal Internationalism and the Decline of the State. The Thought of Richard Cobden, David Mitrany and Kenichi Ohmae* (New York: Palgrave Macmillan, 2005).

Herz, John H., *Political Realism and Political Idealism: A Study in Theories and Realities* (Chicago: University of Chicago Press, 1951).

Henig, Ruth B., *The League of Nations* (Edinburgh: Oliver and Boyd, 1973).

James, Alan, *Peacekeeping in International Politics* (London: Macmillian, 1990).

Jupp, James, *The Radical Left in Britain. 1931–1941* (London: Frank Cass, 1982).

Kitching, Carolyn J., *Britain and the Problem of International Disarmament 1919–1934* (London: Routledge, 1999).

Lamb, Peter, *Harold Laski: Problems of Democracy, the Sovereign State and International Society* (New York: Palgrave Macmillan, 2004).

Leventhal, F.M., *The Last Dissenter: H.N. Brailsford and his World* (Oxford: Clarendon, 1985).

Long, David, *Towards a New Liberal Internationalism: The International Theory of J.A. Hobson* (Cambridge: Cambridge University Press, 1996).

Long, David and Peter Wilson (eds), *Thinkers of the Twenty Years' Crisis. Interwar Idealism Reassessed* (Oxford: Clarendon, 1995).

Maclean, Fitzroy, *Eastern Approaches* (London: Pan, 1956).

MacMillan, Margaret, *Peacemakers. The Paris Conference of 1919 and its Attempt to End War* (London: John Murray, 2001).

Marrin, Albert, *Sir Norman Angell* (Boston: Twayne, 1979).

Miller, J.B.D., *Norman Angell and the Futility of War* (New York: St Martin's, 1986).

Mitrany, David, *Marx Against the Peasant. A Study in Social Dogmatism* (London: Weidenfeld and Nicolson, 1951).

——. *The Functional Theory of Politics* (London: LSE and Martin Robertson, 1975).

Murphy, Craig N., *International Organization and Industrial Change. Global Governance Since 1850* (Cambridge: Polity, 1994).

Naylor, John F., *Labour's International Policy. The Labour Party in the 1930's* (London: Weidenfeld and Nicolson, 1969).

Nelsen, Brent F., and C-G. Stubb (eds), *The European Union. Readings on the Theory and Practice of European Integration* (Boulder Co. & London: Lynne Rienner, 1994).

Pelling, Henry, *A Short History of the Labour Party Fourth Edition* (Basingstoke: Macmillan, 1972).

Potts, Archie, *Zilliacus: A life for Peace and Socialism* (London: Merlin Press, 2002).

Powell, David, *British Politics, 1910–35. The Crisis of the Party System* (London: Routledge, 2004).

Schmidt, Brian, *The Political Discourse of Anarchy: A Disciplinary History of International Relations* (Albany: State University of New York Press, 1998).

Sewell, James Patrick, *Functionalism and World Politics. A Study Based on United Nations Programs Financing Economic Development* (Princeton: Princeton University Press, 1966).

Sheffield, Garry, *Forgotten Victory. The First World War Myths and Realities* (London: Headline, 2001).

Socialist Union, *Socialism and Foreign Policy* (London: Book House, 1953).

Swift, John, *Labour in Crisis. Clement Attlee and the Labour Party in Opposition 1931–40* (Basingstoke: Palgrave, 2001).

Taylor, A.J.P., *The Troublemakers. Dissent Over Foreign Policy 1792–1939* (London: Panther, 1969).

Vasquez, John, *The Power of Power Politics: A Critique* (London: Francis Pinter, 1983).

Vickers, Rhiannon, *The Labour Party and the World: Volume 1. The Evolution of Labour's Foreign Policy 1900–1951* (Manchester: Manchester University Press, 2003).

Whittaker, David J., *Fighter for Peace. Philip Noel Baker 1889–1982* (York: William Sessions, 1989).

Wilde, Jaap de, *Saved from Oblivion: Interdependence Theory in the First Half of the Twentieth Century* (Aldershot: Dartmouth, 1991).

Williams, Andrew, *Liberalism and the War: The Victors and the Vanquished* (London: Routledge, 2006)

Wilson, Peter, *The International Theory of Leonard Woolf. A Study in Twentieth Century Idealism* (New York: Palgrave, 2003).

Winkler, Henry R., *Paths Not Taken. British Labour and International Policy in the 1920's* (Chapel Hill: University of North Carolina Press, 1994).

Winkler, Henry R., *British Labour Seeks a Foreign Policy 1900–1940* (Somerset NJ: Transaction, 2004).

Woolf, Leonard, *Downhill all the Way. An Autobiography of the Years 1919– 1939* (London: Hogarth, 1967).

Wrigley, Chris, *Arthur Henderson* (Cardiff: GPC Books, 1990).

Chapters in Books

Banks, Michael, 'The Inter-Paradigm Debate' in Margot Light and A.J.R. Groom (eds), *International Relations. A Handbook of Current Theory* (Boulder: Lynne Rienner, 1985).

Bull, Hedley, 'The Theory of International Politics', 1919–1969' in Brian Porter (ed.), *The Aberystwyth Papers: International Politics 1919–1969* (London: Oxford University Press, 1972).

Der Derian, James, 'Introduction: Critical Investigations', in James Der Derian (ed.), *International Theory. Critical Investigations* (Basingstoke: Macmillan, 1995).

Kent, John, 'British Postwar Planning for Europe 1942–45', in Antonio Varsori and Elena Calandri (eds), *The Failure of Peace in Europe, 1943–48* (Basingstoke: Palgrave, 2002).

Lloyd, Lorna, 'Philip Noel Baker and Peace Through Law', in David Long and Peter Wilson (eds), *Thinkers of the Twenty Years' Crisis. Interwar Idealism Reassessed* (Oxford: Clarendon, 1995).

Mitrany, David, 'The Problem of Equality in Historical Perspective', in David Mitrany, *A Working Peace System* (Chicago: Quadrangle, 1966).

——. 'Functional Federalism', in David Mitrany, *A Working Peace System* (Chicago: Quadrangle, 1966).

——. 'The Prospects of Integration: Federal or Functional?' in A.J.R. Groom and Paul Taylor (eds), *Functionalism. Theory and Practice in International Relations* (New York: Crane Russak, 1975).

——. 'The Making of the Functional Theory', in David Mitrany, *The Functional Theory of Politics* (London: LSE & Martin Robertson, 1975).

Morgenthau, Hans J., 'Introduction' in David Mitrany, *A Working Peace System* (Chicago: Quadrangle, 1966).

Smith, Steve, 'The Self-Images of a Discipline: A Genealogy of International Relations Theory', in Ken Booth and Steve Smith (eds), *International Relations Theory Today* (Oxford: Polity, 1995).

Taylor, Trevor, 'Utopianism', in Steve Smith (ed.), *International Relations: British and American Approaches* (Oxford: Basil Blackwell, 1985).

Wilder, de, Jaap, 'Norman Angell: Ancestor of Interdependence Theory' in James N. Rosenau and Hylke Tromp (eds), *Interdependence and Conflict in World Politics* (Aldershot: Avebury, 1989).

Wolfers, Arnold, 'The Pole of Power and the Pole of Indifference' in James N. Rosenau (ed.), *International Politics and Foreign Policy. A Reader in Research and Theory* (New York: Free Press, 1969).

Articles

Anderson, Dorothy, 'David Mitrany (1888–1975): An Appreciation of his Life and Work', *Review of International Studies* xxiv (1998), pp.577–92.

Ashworth, Lucian M., 'Did the Realist-Idealist Debate Really Happen? A Revisionist History of International Relations' *International Relations* xvi/1 (2002), pp.33–51.

Birn, Donald S. 'The League of Nations Union and Collective Security', *Journal of Contemporary History* ix/3 (1974), pp.131–159

Bisceglia, Louis R., 'Norman Angell and the Pacifist Muddle', *Bulletin of the Institute of Historical Research* xxxxv/3 (1972), pp.104–19.

Butterfield, Herbert, 'The Scientific Versus the Moralistic Approach in International Affairs' *International Affairs* xxvii/4 (1951), pp.411–22.

Hall, Ian, 'Power Politics and Political Appeasement: Political Realism in British International Thought 1935–1955' *British Journal of Politics and International Relations* viii (2006), pp.174–92.

Long, David, 'International Functionalism and the Politics of Forgetting', *International Journal* xxxxviii/2 (1993), pp.355–79.

Morgenthau, Hans J. 'Another "Great Debate": The National Interest of the United States', *The American Political Science Review* xxxxvi/4 (1952), pp. 221–256.

Navari, Cornelia, 'The Great Illusion Revisited: The International Theory of Norman Angell', *Review of International Studies* xv/4 (1989), pp.341–58.

Reinders, Robert C., 'Racialism on the Left: E.D. Morel and the "Black Horror on the Rhine"', *International Review of Social History* xiii (1968), pp. 606–627.

Smith, Steve, 'Paradigm Dominance in International Relations: The Development of International Relations as a Social Science', *Millennium: Journal of International Studies* xvi/2 (1987), pp.189–206.

Sylvest, Casper, 'Interwar Internationalism, the British Labour Party, and the Historiography of International Relations', *International Studies Quarterly* xxxxviii/2 (2004), pp.409–32.

———. 'Continuity and Change in British Liberal Internationalism' *Review of International Studies* xxxi (2005), pp.263–83.

Thompson, Kenneth W., 'Idealism and Realism: Beyond the Great Debate', *British Journal of International Studies* iii/2 (1977), pp.199–209.

Tickner, J. Ann, 'Hans Morgenthau's Principles of Political Realism: A Feminist Reformulation', *Millennium: Journal of International Studies* xvii/3 (1988), pp.429–440.

Wilson, Peter, 'The Myth of the First Great Debate', *Review of International Studies* xxiv/5 (1998) pp.1–15.

Newspaper and Periodical Articles

Foot, Michael, 'The Knight Errant of Socialism', *Tribune,* 28 March 1958.

Martin, Kingsley, 'H.N. Brailsford', *New Statesman,* 29 March 1958, pp. 403–4.

Mitrany, David, 'Marx, Stalin and the Peasants', *The Listener,* 20 March 1952, pp.455–6.

Younger, Kenneth, 'The Great Illusion', *The Listener,* 10 January 1963, pp. 51–2.

INDEX